The Souterrains of Ireland

The Souterrains of Ireland

MARK CLINTON

Wordwell

First published in 2001
Wordwell Ltd
PO Box 69, Bray, Co. Wicklow
Copyright © the author

ISBN 1 869857 49 6

British Library Cataloguing-in-Publication Data.
A catalogue record for this book is available from the British Library.

This publication has received support from the Heritage Council under the 2001 Publications Grant Scheme.

Cover design: Rachel Dunne and Nick Maxwell

Typeset in Ireland by Wordwell Ltd.

Printed by Brookfield Printing Co.

Contents

List of figures

List of plates

Acknowledgements

This book would not have been written were it not for the initial prompting, ongoing encouragement and nagging persistence of Professor Etienne Rynne, to whom I shall remain eternally grateful. My sincere thanks are also due to Professor Charles Thomas, who became Etienne's chief fellow-conspirator and the source of much additional information on the souterrains of Cornwall and Brittany.

Credit must also go to Dr Matthew Stout for spending endless hours with me in dark confined spaces throughout County Meath, and for making the dots look presentable on the accompanying figures; to Professor Barry Raftery and Dr Patrick F. Wallace for good advice and general guidance; to Eamonn P. Kelly, Mary Cahill, Raghnall Ó Floinn, Nessa O'Connor and Dr Andrew Halpin of the NMI for suffering endless harassment; to P. David Sweetman for full access to the files of *Dúchas*/OPW; to Victor M. Buckley for valuable discussion on the souterrains of Antrim and Down, and for much additional material; to Erin Gibbons for the very welcome opportunity to excavate the souterrain at Ballynavenooragh, Co. Kerry; to Dr Geraldine Stout of *Dúchas* for access to the material on counties Dublin and Westmeath; to Paul Gosling (and *Dúchas*) for access to the County Galway survey material, and for his long (standing?) comradeship in the world of souterrains; to Michael Moore of *Dúchas* for access to the material on counties Kildare, Waterford and Roscommon; to J. P. (Max) McCarthy and Ursula Egan for additional data on the souterrains of County Cork; to Nick F. Brannon for full access to the files of the DOE (NI) and to Claire Foley, Carol White and Terry McNamara for making the work in Belfast such a cohesive operation; to Professor Michael Herity for getting the publication ball rolling with the souterrain at Loughcrew, Co. Meath; to Siobhán O'Rafferty and the Royal Irish Academy for access to and use of the Ordnance Survey material; to Professor George Eogan for providing preliminary notes on the souterrain cluster at Knowth, Co. Meath; to John Sheehan for an advance copy of the Iveragh Survey; to Ian McNeil Cooke for information on the fogous of Cornwall; to Isabella Mulhall and Denis Buckle for translating a multitude of French articles and papers; and to Mark Sinclair for translating the Danish texts.

A special word of thanks to Carine O'Grady for typing the work in such an efficient, cheery and speedy manner; to Norah B. Kelly (assisted by Hazel Ruane) for epic technological restoration work; to Dermot Quirk and Sarah Johnson for confirming that the text was a rough approximation of the English language; to Conor Newman, Dr Finbar McCormick, Fionnbarr Moore, Ed Bourke, Avril Purcell, and my old comrades Barry, Ned, Pat and Matt for sending reinforcements when they were needed.

Last (but never least) I wish to thank Alison Kelly for epic photocopying and for being an encouraging and patient sounding-board; Bernard Clinton, Bernard D. Clinton (and Alison) for providing the transport; Kathleen Clinton for keeping the supply lines open; and my girls, Ruth and Emily, for suffering countless instances of 'Ssshh'!

Dedicated to the memory of Professor Ruaidhrí de Valera (a true professor in every sense of the word), who, more than a quarter of a century ago, launched me on the souterrain trail with the never-forgotten words of advice: 'Beware the Badger!'

1

Introduction

'**G**one to ground' and 'gone to earth' are popular expressions active in the public imagination. Indeed, it could be argued that it was by observing the natural habits of burrowing animals such as foxes or badgers that the early inhabitants of this island became familiar with the idea of seeking refuge underground. From the Bronze Age onwards in Ireland the idea of burrowing into the earth became a reality with the advent of copper-mining (J.S. Jackson 1968, 92). It was not until the latter half of the first millennium AD, however, that the indigenous population of Ireland undertook the digging or tunnelling of subterranean places of retreat for themselves. These are known as souterrains.

What exactly is a souterrain? The word itself is French in origin: *sous* meaning 'under' and *terrain* meaning 'ground'. In short, therefore, a souterrain is an underground structure. Colloquially these structures will invariably be referred to throughout the island as 'caves', conforming to the Irish designations *uaimh* or *óin*. Souterrains are generally marked 'cave' on Ordnance Survey maps. These underground structures can be either simple or complex in form, ranging from a short length of undifferentiated passage/chamber to a labyrinthine arrangement of passages and chambers. The original entrance would often have been disguised so as to avoid detection by hostile forces. Rare examples also included a hidden exit which served as an escape route for the people hiding in the souterrain.

Souterrains were realised in two basic forms — either tunnelled or drystone-built in prepared trenches. Occasionally the two techniques were combined. A small number were constructed of timber.

Tunnelled souterrains

These were excavated out of either the natural till or bedrock. Given that the excavations were never of inordinate depth, there are examples of souterrains featuring rock-cut walls and an earth-cut roof. Earth-cut souterrains have only

Fig. 1—Distribution of earth-cut souterrains.

been discovered in significant numbers in the extreme south of the island, their greatest concentration lying south of the River Lee in County Cork (see Fig. 1). In its simplest form an earth-cut souterrain would have been tunnelled down from the ground surface, with the resultant debris being removed through the aperture which would ultimately form the entrance feature (see Fig. 2b). A more sophisticated method involved the digging of a shaft to the desired level of the souterrain floor. From this shaft, or shafts, the chambers and their interconnecting passages would have been tunnelled, the resultant debris being conveniently removed through the open-topped shaft(s). Upon completion of the souterrain and the creation of an entrance passage, the shaft(s) would have been sealed off with either drystone walling or upright slabs. The shaft(s) would then have been backfilled to the ground-surface level (see Fig. 2a).

Rock-cut souterrains were realised in exactly the same way as the earth-cut souterrains (Pl. 4). Interestingly, the most extensive known example of a rock-cut souterrain in Ireland, at Rathmore, Co. Antrim (Chart 1940, 43), was created in the most basic fashion, the debris from the eight exposed chambers and interconnecting passages having been removed through the entrance feature. Construction shafts in rock-cut souterrains are, like earth-cut souterrains,

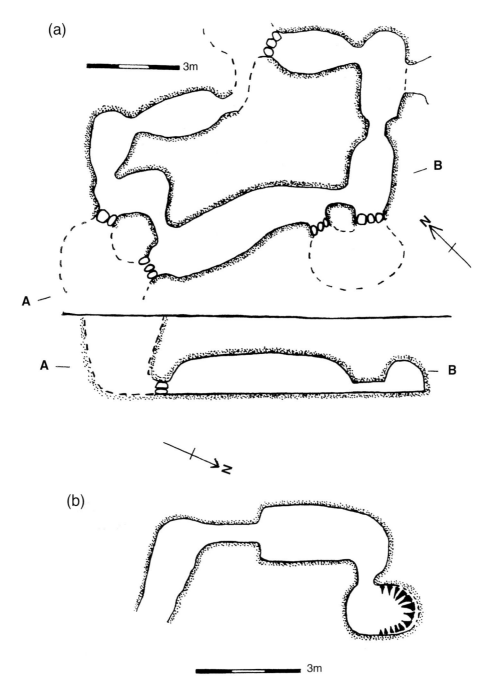

Fig. 2—(a) Lisheen, Co. Cork (after Fahy): earth-cut souterrain featuring construction shafts.
(b) Tullig, Co. Kerry (after Cooke): earth-cut souterrain of simple type.

Fig. 3—Distribution of construction shafts.

concentrated in the extreme south of the island (see Fig. 3). There are, however, two known examples in the extreme north — at Ballintemple, Co. Londonderry (May and Cooper 1939, 82), and Norrira, Co. Donegal (Colhoun 1946, 84).

There would appear to be a dichotomy in the distribution patterns of the earth-cut and the rock-cut souterrains. While the earth-cut souterrains are predominantly confined to the extreme south of the island (see Fig. 1), the rock-cut souterrains are focused on two very distinct areas — the extreme south and the extreme north (see Fig. 4). Besides the tantalising suggestion of a connection represented by the occurrence of the two known construction shafts in the north, there is no other available evidence which might indicate a direct association between the two groups of rock-cut souterrains.

Some souterrains combined either the rock-cut or the earth-cut method with elements of drystone building. The former combination is found mostly in the north-east, while the latter is almost exclusive to the south and south-west (see Fig. 5). At the crudest level, a rock cleft could be provided with a lintelled roof, as for example at Poulnabrone (Westropp 1899, 377) and Teergonean (E. Rynne, pers. comm.), Co. Clare, or Dooey, Co. Donegal (Lacy 1983, 234). Similarly, a rock- or earth-cut trench could be provided with a flagstone roof. This practice

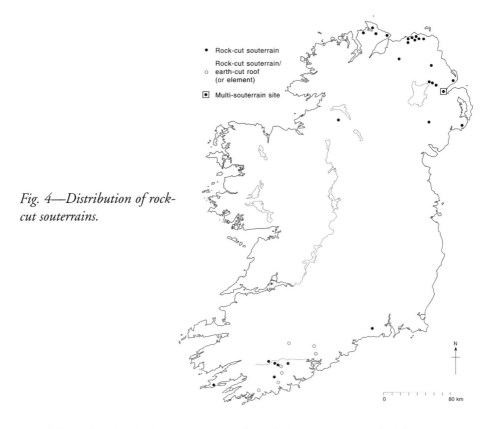

- Rock-cut souterrain
- Rock-cut souterrain/ earth-cut roof (or element)
- Multi-souterrain site

Fig. 4—Distribution of rock-cut souterrains.

N

0   80 km

was followed in both the extreme north and the extreme south. The souterrain at Donegore, Co. Antrim (Lawlor 1915–16, 41), was mostly rock-cut but also featured a section of lintelled roofing. The souterrain at Ballyknock North, Co. Cork (Barry 1890–1, 516), was entirely earth-cut except for the roof, which consisted of stone lintels. In contrast, souterrains of mixed construction in the east and west were predominantly drystone-built structures, displaying an element of opportunism in the incorporation of sections of the exposed bedrock (see Pl. 1). In fact in these latter areas, to date, only the souterrains at Belpere, Co. Meath, and Lavally 2, Co. Galway (Gosling *et al.*, forthcoming, no. 5887), featured an entirely rock-cut passage. The partly rock-cut souterrain at Lisnawully, Co. Louth (Tempest 1912–15, 21), featured an unusual ground-plan for the region. It is possible, therefore, that it too made greater use of the bedrock than was normal. Unfortunately the souterrain has been closed for many years.

The entrances to a number of the rock-cut, or mostly rock-cut, souterrains in the north-east of Ireland were sited in the face of either a rocky eminence or the steep-sided slope of a river bank. At Clogher Anderson, Co. Antrim (Fagan 1838a), the entrance to the rock-cut souterrain was 4.26m above the base of a 'cliff' and 1.52m below its summit. Rough steps cut in the rock facilitated an

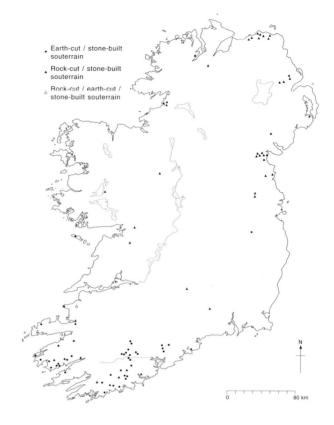

Fig. 5—Distribution of souterrains of mixed construction.

Earth-cut / stone-built souterrain

Rock-cut / stone-built souterrain

Rock-cut / earth-cut / stone-built souterrain

N

0   80 km

approach from the base of the eminence. Similarly, the reported rock-cut souterrain at Templepatrick, Co. Antrim, featured an entrance that was located 'in the face of the rock' (O'Laverty 1884, 238). The entrance to the rock-cut souterrain at Pollee, Co. Antrim, was 'cut into the face' of the western bank of the Artoges River (McAuley 1991). The entrance to the mostly rock-cut souterrain at Ballymartin, Co. Antrim (Lawlor 1916–18, 81; 1918–19, 1), was cut into the face of an 'almost perpendicular basalt cliff', 2.19m above the bed of the Ballymartin River and 3.96m below the summit of the bank. A more remarkable series of these horizontally entered souterrains occurred at Cave Hill in Ballyaghagan, Co. Antrim (Reynolds and Turner 1902, 73; Chart 1940, 53), where no fewer than five rock-cut souterrains have been recorded in the 'almost perpendicular' cliff face. Save for extremely hazardous and badly weathered ledges, these refuges are practically inaccessible (the highest being approximately 40m above the level of the most convenient pathway). Whether these hypogea were man-made creations or the enhanced adaptations of natural caves has not been satisfactorily determined. It is significant, however, that sherds of 'souterrain ware', the indigenous domestic pottery of the latter half of the first millennium AD in the north-east region, have been discovered in the accumulated spillage located below the souterrains. Similarly, the souterrain at Aghanaglack, Co. Fermanagh, was described as a 'natural cave' which had been 'improved by human agency' (Chart 1940, 159). Indeed, the possibility must be considered that at least some of the horizontally entered rock-cut souterrains and the 'adapted' natural caves represent early manifestations of the monument in the north-east region.

If one were to argue that souterrains were primarily created for use as refuges then rock-cut souterrains would have been the more secure of the tunnelled forms. They would have been almost impossible to detect and difficult to dig out. The earth-cut souterrains would have been vulnerable to roof collapse and, once detected, very easy to breach. By their very nature neither form was conducive to the creation of elaborate impedimental devices, and they therefore relied on severe constrictions in their interlinking arteries to achieve any degree of internal security. Alternatively, it could be argued that an ignorance of developed impedimental devices prevented their deployment in the tunnelled souterrains. It may be stated that elaborate impedimental devices are severely lacking in the extreme south. The question arises, therefore, as to whether the tunnelled souterrains are the earliest examples of the monument in Ireland. Ironically, the most persuasive evidence in support of such a proposition comes from the east, where tunnelled souterrains are practically unknown. At Commons (Duleek), Co. Meath (Clinton, forthcoming a), an earth-cut souterrain of the simplest form was uncovered within the precincts of an early church site (see Pl. 22). This souterrain was totally atypical of the souterrains in the Meath group. Indeed, with the exception of Belpere, even where the natural bedrock was not only exposed but was deeply cut into no significant attempts were made to incorporate the rock into the fabric of any of the souterrains in the greater Meath group. Again, at Killashee, Co. Kildare (R. Moore 1918–21), a mostly earth-cut souterrain was discovered immediately adjacent to the early church site. Significantly, the fact that souterrains associated with early church sites can take on a distinctive identity has been established in County Cork, where 'the largest recorded tunnelled souterrains in the county' (McCarthy 1983, 100) were discovered in the vicinity of church sites. Lucas (1971–3, 172) has also drawn attention to the frequency of the association of souterrains with early ecclesiastical sites. Could it be possible, therefore, that the tunnelled souterrains, or at least the examples located in the east and in the extreme south, were introduced as an imported concept by churchmen returning from sojourns abroad?

Drystone-built souterrains

The overwhelming majority of the known souterrains in Ireland are drystone-built structures. Their construction involved the digging of a series of trenches, the number depending on the complexity of the individual souterrain. Drystone walls were raised against the sides of the trenches. The raw material consisted of either gathered field stones or quarried rock, or a combination of both. In the case of larger chambers, particularly beehive/oval chambers, rocks with a pronounced back-projection would have been favoured. These, when held in place by the downward pressure of the external backfill, would have enabled the builders gradually to lessen the width of the enclosed space by utilising the corbelling technique (Leask 1955, 17). The inclined passage or chamber walls would finally have been capped with a flagstone roof (see Pl. 6).

The excavation of the two eastern chambers in the souterrain at Spittle Quarter, Co. Down (Brannon 1990, 41), provided evidence of another, hitherto unknown technique employed by the souterrain-builders. The trench dug to accommodate the larger of the two chambers had been left with overhanging edges, and the upper courses of the drystone walls could be wedged tightly into the 'arch' thus formed. This technique would have prevented the walls from collapsing during the construction of the chamber. The final addition of the roofing lintels and the eventual pressure from the backfill would have further strengthened the overall structure. Where corbelling was absent, or less pronounced, longer lintels would have been required. In the case of a circular beehive chamber, the walls would have been gradually inclined to the point where they were ready to receive a substantial capstone (or occasionally two or more lesser capstones) (see Pl. 14). The entire construction would then have been covered over with backfill to ground-surface level (see Fig. 6).

Some drystone-built souterrains were constructed in the banks of ringforts, but the practice was not universal. Most such examples, based on the available evidence, appear to be concentrated in a small number of distinct areas. In County Antrim examples have been recorded at such sites as Browndod (O'Laverty 1884, 193), in the inner rampart of a multivallate ringfort; Ballyhill Lower (B. Williams 1986, 9); Shane's Castle (Warhurst 1971, 58); and Dreen (Lawlor 1918–19, 8). A second cluster is found in County Waterford, at such sites as Ballygunnermore (P. Power 1887–8; 1906, 18), Ballysallagh (Fahy 1954) and Scartlea (Moore 1989b). Isolated examples are known from elsewhere: Coarha Beg, Co. Kerry (Mitchell 1989, 42), Kiltale, Co. Meath (Rynne 1974, 267), and Cloghboley 2, Co. Sligo (McGuinness 1991), may be cited. A variation on the theme was where the inner bank of a ringfort was utilised to accommodate the projecting roof of a chamber. A notable example occurred at

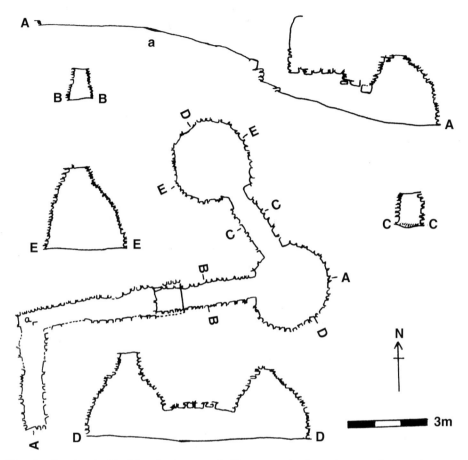

Fig. 6—Bective 1, Co. Meath: drystone-built souterrain featuring trapdoor and circular beehive chambers.

Dromkeen East, Co. Kerry (Twohig 1974, 8), where an impressive example of a beehive chamber featured a maximum height of 3m. In order to accommodate this height the builders had sited the chamber under the line of the bank. This pattern was repeated at Ishlaun, Co. Roscommon (Conroy 1995a), where the roof of the circular chamber was again accommodated by the bank. An analogous practice was the construction of intramural chambers in the wall of a cashel. The souterrain passage at Kimego West (Leacanabuaile), Co. Kerry (S.P. Ó Riordáin and Foy 1941, 85), culminated in a chamber which had been built in the cashel wall. A lintelled entrance in the wall of the cashel at Clogher, Co. Sligo (O'Rorke 1890, 383; Mount 1994), provided entry to a passage, 0.6m in width. Having turned to follow the line of the wall, the passage culminated in a 'short' chamber. The intramural chamber at Kilcashel, Co. Mayo (Hurley 1984), featured two entrances. Access to the chamber was controlled by two constrictions *c.* 1.5m in length. Again, at Altagore, Co. Antrim (O'Laverty 1887, 524), an opening in the cashel wall provided entry to an intramural chamber.

It is interesting to note that the aforementioned cashels at Clogher and Kilcashel were also credited with fully subterranean souterrains. This feature was also recorded at Ballynavenooragh, Co. Kerry (Gibbons, forthcoming). It has been suggested that in the case of platform ringforts the souterrain may on occasion have been raised as a free-standing structure which would have been buried as the platform was raised to the required level, for example at Deer Park Farms, Co. Antrim (Lynn 1989, 197).

Wooden souterrains

In the early 1980s a farm improvement scheme in County Fermanagh caused the excavation of a univallate ringfort, leading to the discovery of a remarkable structure. Owing to the level of the water-table the lower reaches of a wood-built souterrain were uncovered in a long and narrow earth-cut trench (B.B. Williams 1985, 75) (see Fig. 7). The souterrain consisted of two conjoined chambers with an escape passage extending to the exterior of the ringfort. The walls of the chambers consisted of upright oak timbers, which survived to heights of between 0.2m and 0.6m. The chambers were divided by a wooden partition, with two timber uprights indicating the former existence of a doorway (*ibid.*, 77). There was no surviving evidence for the roof, but it must have consisted of planks or split logs. The discovery of this wooden structure at Coolcran confirmed the earlier indications that timber was sometimes used in the construction of souterrains. The excavations at Ballycatteen, Co. Cork (S.P. Ó Ríordáin and Hartnett 1943–4, 1), had revealed the presence of (at least) three souterrains in the interior of the ringfort. A series of rock-cut post-holes in the floors of all three chambers in Souterrain B indicated the former presence of a wooden roof in an otherwise drystone-built structure (*ibid.*, 16). The absence of roofing lintels in the other two souterrains led the excavators to suggest that all three souterrains had featured wooden roofs (*ibid.*, 15). At Letterkeen, Co. Mayo (S.P. Ó Ríordáin and MacDermott 1951–2, 89), it was also established that the earth-cut souterrain had originally featured a wooden roof, indicated by the presence of substantial post-holes in the floor. At Raheennamadra, Co. Limerick (Stenberger 1966, 37), the excavation of a ringfort revealed the presence of a souterrain. This consisted of two conjoined chambers with an escape passage leading to the exterior of the ringfort (strikingly similar, in fact, to the ground-plan of the souterrain at Coolcran). Again, the presence of post-holes in the floor of the souterrain indicated the former presence of a wooden roof in an otherwise

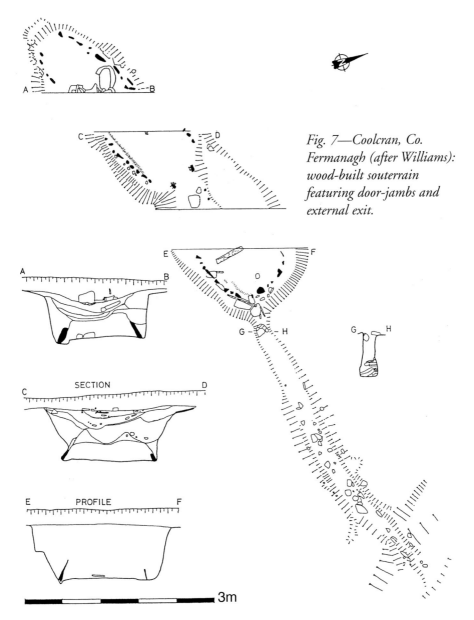

Fig. 7—Coolcran, Co. Fermanagh (after Williams): wood-built souterrain featuring door-jambs and external exit.

3m

drystone-built structure (*ibid.*, 42).

It will have been noticed that all of these wood-built souterrains were discovered as a result of excavations. This, of course, is not surprising. A wood-built souterrain could only be expected to leave a depression or hollow as evidence of its former existence — that is, if the depression had not been backfilled at some point in time. There was no indication of the souterrain at Coolcran, for example, prior to excavation. Furthermore, in an unenclosed context the chances of a 'suggestive' depression being identified as evidence for a souterrain are extremely small. Many ringforts have been recorded as containing suggestive depressions. It should be stressed, however, that one must always allow for stone-looting (many roofing lintels have ended up in kitchen floors!). At Donaghmore, Co. Louth, it was suggested that the roofing material for Souterrain B was obtained by looting the lintels from Souterrain A (E. Rynne, pers. comm.). Nevertheless, it is not impossible that a number of these depressions in ringforts may represent the vestigial remains of wood-built souterrains.

Discovery

It should never be automatically assumed that a report of a 'cave' will lead to the discovery of a souterrain. Indeed, even a number of 'souterrains' in the archaeological record have been incorrectly identified. Corn-drying kilns (Gailey 1970, 52) are very similar in ground-plan and overall design to the simple 'passage leading to small beehive chamber' type of souterrain. Thus, for example, it will be seen that, upon re-examination, the reported souterrains at Ballinlough Little, Co. Meath (Rotheram 1893–6, 307), Mullagh, Co. Cavan (Lucas 1971–3, 172), and Boolareagh, Co. Tipperary (Rynne 1962–5, 188), may well be corn-drying kilns. There have been more exotic misinterpretations. The alleged souterrain listed under Balsaw, Co. Meath (M. Moore 1987, 50), would appear from detailed local accounts to have been a cist-burial, while the 'souterrain' in the churchyard at Clongill, Co. Meath (D. O'Sullivan 1955), turned out to be a nineteenth-century family burial-vault.

While taking the inevitable tales of 'underground passages' running between the local castle and the Protestant church, or from the Hill of Tara to the Hill of Slane, with the proverbial pinch of salt, it is worth noting that if one is informed that the 'other end' of a souterrain is located in a field or rath in the next townland, or indeed in the next parish, one is occasionally on the trail of another souterrain. Inevitably, a 'cave' will on occasion turn out to be just that, a natural cave. This was the case with the alleged souterrain at Carrickshedoge, Co. Wexford (Mahr 1937, 386; S.P. Ó Ríordáin 1938–40, 178).

The vast majority of known souterrains have come to light as the result of accidental discoveries. Inevitably most of these discoveries have been made in agricultural contexts. There have, however, been exceptions to this rule. The souterrain at Athboy, Co. Meath (Rynne 1967a), was uncovered during the construction of McCann's hardware shop. The discovery of a souterrain at Fennor, Co. Meath (Rynne 1965c, 229), was the result of the construction of a new bungalow. Following the official archaeological inspection and survey of the site, the builders of the bungalow adjusted the planned layout of the house. This, however, led to the discovery of either an additional section of the original souterrain or possibly a second structure. Rather than alter their plans again, the builders simply incorporated the souterrain into the overall design. As a result the souterrain may now be accessed through a trapdoor in the bedroom floor!

The introduction of deeper ploughing technology in recent times has led to the discovery of hitherto-unsuspected subterranean structures. The beehive type of chamber with its elevated roof (see Fig. 6) has been particularly vulnerable to modern mechanically driven ploughs. The lifting of the capstone of the beehive chamber at Leggagh, Co. Meath, in 1996 is typical of this type of discovery. It is usually the disturbance of a lintel in the roof of a passage that leads to the discovery of the souterrain. A typical example of this occurred at Killally, Co. Louth, in 1997 (Clinton and Stout 1997, 129). One of the more colourful discoveries was made in 1930 at Dunisky, Co. Cork (Gogan 1930). A boy out ferreting observed that the animal had disappeared down what initially appeared to be a rabbit-hole. His father, while exploring this discovery, dropped a crowbar down the cavity. Rather than lose this valued implement it was decided to widen the opening enough for the boy to enter. Unfortunately the boy got stuck and had to be chiselled out. Word of these exploits reached the ears of the local authorities, and the Free State CID duly arrived upon the scene. An arms-dump was immediately suspected and explosives were deemed necessary to broaden the cavity. After several explosions a rock-cut souterrain was added to the archaeological record. Half a century later the present writer was questioned by the gardaí about an alleged arms-dump in a cemetery at Killegland, Co. Meath. It was only after the cemetery had been surrounded by armed gardaí and soldiers and a quick excavation carried out that his story of a recently discovered (and immediately resealed) drystone-built souterrain was accepted (*The Meath Chronicle*, 31 July 1982). The authorities were right to be suspicious; Evans (1958, 118), for example, described one souterrain in Co. Antrim that was 'littered with the remains of home-made bombs'.

Historical accounts

Souterrains have the distinction of being among a select number of archaeological monuments that make an appearance in the ancient literature. Their presence in such sources as the annals, the Lives of the saints, the ancient law-tracts, etc., has been well documented by Lucas (1971–3). The majority of these texts, or at least the extant copies, date from the last few centuries of the first millennium AD to the earliest centuries of the second millennium AD. It is clear from the references and the entries that the writers were comfortably familiar with souterrains (usually referred to as an *uamh* — a cave) and that their intrinsic nature did not warrant any special explanation. The ancient law-tracts tell us that the price for building a souterrain was two cows (*'agus da ba ar uamairecht*) (Atkinson 1901, 94) — incidentally the same price as that for a cashel. Among the better-known references to 'caves' that appeared in the annals were the entries regarding Knowth and Dowth in County Meath (where the prehistoric tombs are now known to have been incorporated into proven souterrain complexes) being raided by the foreigners in AD 863 (Mac Airt and Mac Niocaill 1983, 319) and the 'caves' of Ciarraige Luachra being plundered by the Vikings of Dublin in 873 (Mac Airt 1951, 134). There are also accounts of people being discovered hiding in 'caves', for example in the *Dindsenchas* (Stokes 1894, 448) or the *Vitae sanctorum Hiberniae* (Plummer 1910, 246), or being smothered in these 'caves', for example in the *Annals of Loch Cé* (Hennessy 1871, 57) or the *Cogadh Gaedhel re Gallaibh* (Todd 1867, 23).

The growth of research

In more recent times, the existence of souterrains in Ireland had become known as early as the eighteenth century. Writers such as Thomas Molyneux (1725), Walter Harris and Charles Smith (1744), William Beauford (1789) and Francis Grose (1791) made reference to these 'artificial caves' (*ibid.,* vi). Molyneux (1725, 209) made it clear that these caves were not a natural phenomenon but had in fact been 'contrived'. He described an average drystone-built souterrain with a lintelled roof and, remarkably, included a sketch-plan (unfortunately the site was not identified). Harris and Smith (1744, 195) assembled the available data on souterrains in County Down. This could be regarded as the first regional study. The writers felt it important to stress that the artificial caves included in their study had either been personally inspected by themselves or had been recorded on 'indisputable authority'. Their scrupulousness was commendable, given the fact that to this day the number of archaeological writers who have actually spent any significant amount of time physically examining souterrains is disappointing.

The term 'souterrain' first made its appearance in the early nineteenth century. Thomas Wood (1821, 261) described the underground structures associated with some raths as an *uamh talmhan* or a 'souterrain'. He also made a distinction between drystone-built and earth-cut souterrains in the south of Ireland. The latter he described as consisting of 'two to three chambers, each resembling a baker's oven' (*ibid.,* 266). He further described these chambers as being connected by severely restricted apertures. A sketch-plan of a drystone-built souterrain (unfortunately not identified) indicated the presence of an escape passage (*ibid.*, 267).

The Ordnance Survey of Ireland was established in order to obtain detailed maps upon which valuation of the land could be based. In tandem with the cartography, detailed notes were taken on the natural resources and the historical and archaeological aspects of each parish. Thus the talents and endeavours of such scholars as John O'Donovan, Eugene O'Curry and George Petrie, and the surveying skills of soldiers such as C.W. Ligar and John Stokes, were brought to bear on the archaeology of Ireland. Not only were many individual souterrains (marked as 'caves') indicated on the maps (which began to be published in the 1830s), but both accurate descriptions and plans were included in the accompanying documentation. The flair and detail displayed in these plans was not to be matched until well into the last century. On the broader scale, archaeologists were now equipped with highly detailed maps of each and every townland, which was to help in locating and pinpointing individual sites.

In 1895 W.G. Wood-Martin published *Pagan Ireland*, which has been described as 'the first extensive work of synthesis on Irish prehistoric archaeology' (Herity and Eogan 1977, 12). It contained a succinct description of an average souterrain: 'These passages are built of uncemented stones, and are covered with flagstones, the extremities of which rest on the parallel walls; and whilst some are too low to stand erect in, and the explorer has to proceed on hands and knees, others are upwards of six feet in height, and of corresponding breadth' (Wood-Martin 1895, 204). By the turn of the century souterrains were firmly lodged in the archaeological psyche and it is not surprising that Thomas J. Westropp, in his seminal paper 'The ancient forts of Ireland: being a contribution towards our knowledge of their types, affinities and structural features' (1896–1901), should have suggested that 'the subject of souterrains … is of sufficient independent importance to form the subject of a separate essay' (*ibid.*, 666). In the interim he presented a very comprehensive account of the knowledge available to date.

As souterrains became better known as a monument type in their own right to antiquarians, and latterly to archaeologists, so too did many of their characteristic features, and on a broader front their general associations and overall distribution. Needless to say, theories as to their basic function and dating fluctuated and abounded as time and knowledge progressed.

Perceived function

The intrinsic nature of these subterranean structures was quickly ascertained by the early writers. They were artificial caves built of unmortared stones and roofed with long slabs of rock. They consisted of combinations of passages and chambers. But what were they for? The perceived function or purpose of the artificial caves never really extended far beyond a core of three preferred explanations. While Molyneux (1725, 209) suggested that they were 'contrived for the convenient disposal of their stores, their arms, provisions, (etc.)' only, the majority of the early writers opted for a dual purpose: storage and refuge. Writers such as Harris and Smith (1744, 195), Beauford (1789, 84), Wood (1821, 263), Wakeman (1858, 38), Wood-Martin (1895, 205) and Knox (1917–18, 33) fall into this category. In the north-east of Ireland a third school of thought gained momentum. The discovery of significant amounts of pottery and charcoal deposits in a number of souterrains led to the belief that the artificial caves were subterranean dwelling-places. Indeed, so many sherds of a crude domestic-type pottery were discovered in these subterranean monuments that it became known as 'Souterrain Ware' (Ryan 1973, 619). Air-vents were interpreted as chimneys, the charcoal deposits as fireplaces, and the pottery as the remains of domestic debris. Lawlor (1915–16, 45; 1916–18, 85; 1918–20, 214), one of the great pioneers of souterrain studies, was firmly convinced that they were the dwelling-places of 'a race of cave-dwellers' (1915–16, 46). This view was not universally held. Early writers such as Molyneux had stated that the artificial caves 'could never be designed to accommodate men' (1725, 209). He was not alone in his opinion. Wood called them 'incommodious' and thus 'they could not have been designed for habitation' (1821, 267). John Cooke (1906–7, 8) defined them as 'places of temporary retreat or refuge, or for storage, and little else'.

Most modern writers have remained firmly in either the refuge or storage camps (or, more typically, a combination of both), but the habitation aspect did persist. Seán P. Ó Ríordáin (1953, 32) and Ruaidhrí de Valera (1979, 70) perpetuated the theory in an attempt to address the presence of the pottery and the charcoal deposits in the souterrains. It was not until 1979 that the possibility that even the occasional souterrain had been intended as a dwelling-place was firmly rejected. Richard Warner (1979, 133) flatly stated that 'the view that souterrains were dwellings ... can obviously be dismissed out of hand'. A comprehensive reading of the archaeological literature will support that view. It will be seen that the vast majority of pottery remains were discovered in the vicinity of the entrance feature. It is quite clear that the pottery in fact belonged to the associated surface house/settlement and had simply filtered down or had been dumped into the 'mouth' of the souterrain. It will also be observed that charcoal deposits, when not discovered in the entrance feature of a souterrain, are frequently found beneath an air-vent. This is the root of the fireplace and chimney assumption. It should also be stressed that many other deposits of ash or cinders were the result of latter-day usage of souterrains (invariably of a dubious nature — smugglers, rapparees and arms-storers, for example).

The storage versus refuge argument persists to this day. The tide ebbs and flows as to which is the correct interpretation. As noted above, the majority of writers have straddled both concepts. Writers such as Macalister (1949, 272, 274), the de Paors (1958, 87), Evans (1966, 29) and Lucas (1971–3, 169) represent this school of thought. Indeed, Lucas maintained that 'all the features and peculiarities which they present are consonant with either view' (*loc. cit.*). Other writers have opted for an exclusive interpretation. Charles Thomas (1972, 77) stated that 'very few seem to be either suitable or likely places of refuge'. Richard Warner would strenuously advocate the direct opposite. He has dismissed the notion that souterrains in Ireland were constructed for 'normal storage' (1979, 131). Subsequent writers (Edwards 1990, 30; Mallory and McNeill 1991, 196, for example) have tended to follow Warner's lead.

The present writer will suggest that while the majority of souterrains were primarily built as refuges they would also have served as ad hoc storage facilities and, furthermore, that a number of the simpler souterrains were primarily intended as stores but with the potential for use as hiding-places.

Recognition of association

In the early days of research souterrains were generally, and understandably, looked upon as being an integral feature of an enclosed settlement. Molyneux (1725, 209) noted that they were to be found in 'many of the larger forts'. Wood (1821, 266) pointed out that some of the 'Belgic forts in the south of Ireland' contained souterrains. Wood-Martin (1895, 204) observed that 'in the interior of many earthen forts and stone cashels there are often chambers and subterraneous passages'. Indeed, so prevalent was the association in the minds of most writers that souterrains were frequently referred to as 'rath-caves' (for example Ferguson 1870–9b., 129). Not all writers automatically subscribed to this view. T.J. Westropp (1896–1901, 668), while accepting that many souterrains were associated with enclosures, maintained that 'in many instances there is no evidence to connect them with forts'. It was H.C. Lawlor, however, who first objected to the use of the term 'rath-cave'. He stated that for every souterrain discovered in an enclosure 'probably forty or fifty … survive today totally unconnected with a rath' (1916–18, 101). Gradually it became acceptable for writers to support the existence of both enclosed and unenclosed souterrain sites (for example Jope 1966, 115), the caveat of course being that there must be a considerable number of sites where an enclosure was destroyed at some point, leaving a superficially unenclosed souterrain site.

Westropp (1920, 117) introduced promontory forts into the equation. S.P. Ó

Ríordáin accepted the association between souterrains and ringforts, cashels and promontory forts, and quite rightly observed that no souterrain had ever been found in association with a hillfort (1953, 30). He further allowed for the probable existence of unenclosed souterrain sites (1942, 16). In the fifth revised edition of Ó Ríordáin's *Antiquities of the Irish countryside*, Ruaidhrí de Valera (1979, 65) rowed back on this latter acceptance, maintaining that although there was evidence for unenclosed souterrains it was not conclusive.

It was only in recent years that studies on individual counties began to make an impact on the ongoing debate. In 1978 Victor M. Buckley presented his studies on the souterrains of counties Antrim and Down. His research revealed that the pattern of association could vary radically from county to county. While the majority of the souterrains in County Down were associated with an enclosure, the reverse was true in the neighbouring county of Antrim (Buckley 1978, 40, 41). In the extreme south of the island J.P. McCarthy was working on the souterrains of County Cork. The results of his research were to prove equally enlightening. Just over half of the souterrains in the county were found to be associated with ringforts (McCarthy 1977, 44). Two other county surveys were conducted during the late 1970s; while neither has, as yet, been formally completed, the results were compatible with the findings in County Antrim. In both County Louth (Paul Gosling, pers. comm.) and County Meath (Clinton, unpublished) a significant majority of souterrains were found to be associated with open settlement sites.

An association between souterrains and church sites has long been mooted. Harris and Smith (1744, 195) placed the souterrain at Slanes, Co. Down, 'close to Slanes Church Yard, in a plain field'. Ó Ríordáin (1965, 31) and de Valera (1979, 70) suggested that souterrains could have been used as 'safes' for valuables being held at church sites. It was A.T. Lucas (1971–3, 172) who first produced a sample list of early ecclesiastical sites known to possess a souterrain. Leo Swan (1983, 274) listed the souterrain as a recognised feature of an ecclesiastical site. Ann Hamlin (1976, 173) tempered this association with the statistic that only approximately 8% of the early church sites in the north of Ireland possessed a proven souterrain. One inescapable fact is that not one souterrain has, to date, been scientifically proven to be integral to a church site. Indeed, the present writer devoted two years in the mid-1970s to the assembling of an almost endless inventory of souterrains, most of which could only be advanced as being 'potentially' associated with church sites. Several problems present themselves. If a church and a souterrain are located in an enclosure, are they contemporary? Alternatively, did the enclosure and the souterrain pre-date the church (i.e. was it formerly a secular site that was subsequently donated to the church)? If a souterrain is located immediately outside the perimeter of an ecclesiastical enclosure, as, for example, at Dulane, Co. Meath (Rynne and Prendergast 1962, 37), was it associated with an adjacent unenclosed secular site that either pre-dated or post-dated the church site, or indeed was contemporary with it, or simply shared a suitable location with it? Only future extensive scientific excavation can resolve these questions.

Observations on distribution

In the initial phase of study it was inevitable that individual writers would only tend to be familiar with limited localised areas of the island. Early attempts at discussing the distribution of souterrains thus involved a certain amount of speculation and generalisation. Beauford suggested that they were to be found in 'several parts of Ireland' (1789, 84). Wood was aware of significant numbers in 'the south of Ireland' (1821, 266). The realisation that the monument was not ubiquitous was first approached by Lawlor in the early part of the last century. He noted that 'none, or at any rate very few, are found between the rivers Boyne and the Slaney, and, taking a line roughly from this area north-west right across Ireland to Leitrim and Mayo I believe that whole district is practically without them' (Lawlor 1918–20, 216). He was also aware of the fact that certain counties were heavily endowed with the monument. He declared that 'the counties of Antrim, Down, Cork and Kerry, probably contain as many souterrains as all the rest of Ireland' (1916–18, 94).

It was not until 1973 that the first distribution map of souterrains in Ireland was produced (see Fig. 8). Etienne Rynne, who had conducted extensive fieldwork on souterrains in many parts of the island, provided the map as an illustration to accompany A.T. Lucas's distinguished paper on 'the evidence on souterrains available in the literary sources' (1971–3, 165). Subsequent research work has not invalidated this map. The heavy concentrations suggested by Rynne (and previously by Lawlor) in counties such as Antrim, Cork and Kerry have been confirmed. North Louth was added to that list by Rynne. The only other published distribution map of souterrains in Ireland made its appearance as recently as 1997 in F.H.A. Aalen, K. Whelan and M. Stout's *Atlas of the Irish rural landscape*. This map was based on the Topographical Files of the National Monuments Services of both the Republic and Northern Ireland. The preliminary nature of this map should be stressed, however, as not all sites indicated on the map have been validated through fieldwork. A random selection of counties will illustrate the point. There are twenty souterrain sites indicated in County Offaly on the map (Aalen *et al.* 1997, 49). The published *Archaeological inventory of County Offaly* (O'Brien and Sweetman 1997, 49) lists only two

Fig. 8—Distribution of souterrains in Ireland (after Rynne).

'definite' and three 'possible' souterrain sites (the present writer would question the validity of two of the 'possible' sites — they are based on accounts of a subterranean feature running between a castle and a church and between a castle and a motte respectively). Similarly, the map indicates four souterrains in County Laois, while the published *Archaeological inventory of County Laois* (Sweetman *et al.* 1995, 35) lists two 'possible' sites. Again, the map indicates 40 souterrain sites in County Cavan, while the published *Archaeological inventory of County Cavan* (O'Donovan 1995, 149) lists only four 'definite' sites and 43 'possible' sites. A definitive distribution map of souterrains in Ireland will only be attainable when all the counties have been thoroughly researched.

In the interim it may be said that the distribution pattern is a very uneven one. While areas such as Antrim, north Louth and Cork/Kerry possess an inordinate number of sites, other areas, such as County Carlow, with its one possible site, are practically devoid of souterrains. While natural features such as mountains, peatbogs and lowlands subject to regular flooding are obvious reasons for many of the 'gaps' in the overall distribution pattern, other 'voids' are not so easily explained. The practical absence of the monument in the area of the early historic kingdom of Leinster is one such example (Clinton 1998, 117; 2000a, 275). Other gaps are more localised. For example, it may be observed that there is a stark contrast between the numbers of souterrains in the northern (dense) and the southern (sparse) parts of County Louth. The land in both areas is of a good quality. It is well documented that there was a strict political divide between the two areas during the relevant centuries. North Louth constituted the minor kingdom of Conaille-Muirthemne, while most of southern Louth was in the hands of the Fir Arda Ciannachta (a subkingdom of Brega). The fact that there are morphological differences between the two groups of souterrains is also significant. In fact, most of the souterrains in south Louth, with their beehive chambers, are typical of the greater Meath type. It may ultimately transpire that this contemporary political division had a crucial impact on the distribution pattern of the souterrains in County Louth.

Evolving chronology

Past research into the dating of souterrains can be neatly divided into two periods, which could be termed 'pre-Cush' and 'post-Cush'. Until the publication of the excavations at Cush, Co. Limerick (S.P. Ó Ríordáin 1938–40), antiquarians and latterly archaeologists had been almost unanimous in their assignment of souterrains to the latter half of the first millennium AD, based on two criteria. Many early writers were of the opinion that these monuments had been built as bolt-holes against raids by the Norse/Vikings. Harris and Smith (1744, 197) suggested that since many souterrains were to be found in coastal areas they must have been 'made as places to retreat to on the sudden, to secure their persons and most portable and valuable effects, for a short time, from the inroads and piracies of the Danes'. The other key element was the fact that many souterrains contained reused ogham stones in their structure (usually as roofing lintels). Ferguson (1870–9b, 130), for example, stated that, owing to the presence of these stones, 'the age of the rath-caves would be assigned to some time after the Christian era'. Lawlor (1915–16, 31) went so far as to chide 'more or less learned archaeologists talking glibly of the stone age, bronze age and the iron age' in the dating of souterrains. He was firmly of the opinion that owing to the presence of the reused ogham stones souterrains could not be dated any earlier than the fifth–seventh centuries AD. (*ibid.*, 46). He later refined his dating on the basis of structural types. The 'crude' (Lawlor 1916–18, 93) or 'rough built' (*ibid.*, 89) souterrains of County Antrim he assigned to the fourth–seventh or eighth centuries AD (*ibid.*, 93), while the more finely built souterrains of County Down were allowed to advance into the ninth century AD.

All was to change with the publication of a group of enclosed souterrains at Cush, Co. Limerick. Ó Ríordáin (1938–40, 176) dated the occupation of the settlement to the Late Bronze Age and Early Iron Age. On this basis he stated that 'the custom of building ringforts and souterrains dates back at least to the beginning of Late Bronze Age times' (*ibid.*, 178). The key to his dating analysis was the perceived relationship between the souterrain in Ringfort 5 and a series of five cist-burials. Burial No. 1 was 'set in an irregular pocket' in 'reddish filling' (*ibid.*, 110). The cordoned urn was sitting mouth-upwards and overflowing with cremated bones. This same reddish stratum of sand and clay partly filled and covered the souterrain. Thus Ó Ríordáin (*ibid.*, 113) concluded that the souterrain must have pre-dated the burial. A careful reading of the detailed report, which is somewhat ambiguous in parts, would suggest that it seems more likely that the unroofed souterrain had been backfilled at some point in antiquity and that deposits originally associated with the immediately adjacent cist-burial phase of occupation at the site were utilised in this operation. It should also be noted that in order to justify the dating of the souterrain and the enclosure to the Late Bronze Age Ó Ríordáin was forced to conclude that the attendant rotary quernstones must also belong to the said period (*ibid.*, 163), a view now unsustainable by the general archaeological record. In passing it might be noted that the Late Bronze Age date assigned to the cordoned cinerary urn by Ó Ríordáin (*ibid.*, 176) has been amended by later research to the Middle Bronze Age (Kavanagh 1976, 334).

The impact of the Cush excavations on the dating of souterrains is immediately apparent in the 1949 revision of *The archaeology of Ireland* by R.A.S. Macalister. He admits that had the question 'when were the souterrains built?' been posed in the very recent past the unhesitating answer would have been '… say round about AD 800–900' (Macalister 1949, 276). In the wake of the Cush excavation he felt obliged to amend this to the Late Bronze Age, while still maintaining that 'perhaps the majority' (*ibid.*, 278) of souterrains belonged to the ninth century AD or thereabouts. This general perception was to be sustained for almost 40 years. Consequently J. Raftery (1951, 174) held that souterrains of the 'gallery' type were in existence by the Late Bronze Age, while Evans (1966, 29) maintained that some souterrains must be pre-Christian and others medieval. In 1942, and again in 1953, Ó Ríordáin reiterated the 1940 dating scheme in his *Antiquities of the Irish countryside* (first and third editions) (1942, 17; 1953, 33). By the time of the 1979 revision of this book, however, the idea of a Late Bronze Age origin for souterrains was being quietly challenged. De Valera simply omitted any reference to the Cush site while, apparently rather reluctantly, suggesting that souterrains were probably established by the Early Iron Age (1979, 72). The two watershed papers on souterrains by Richard Warner, published in 1979 and 1980, effectively ended this lately held view of a prehistoric origin for souterrains in Ireland. Warner argued convincingly that the entire assemblage of domestic artefacts at Cush could only be realistically dated to the latter half of the first millennium AD (1979, 126; 1980, 84).

The fact that the overwhelming majority of souterrains have failed to yield any 'casual finds' of any description has not helped in their dating. Neither have very many been scientifically excavated. If an object is found on the floor of a souterrain then the likelihood is that the souterrain was, if not in use, at least still open and thus accessible. While the object would not pinpoint the date of construction of the monument, it would at least help to define its general period of use. The available evidence would seem to indicate that once souterrains ceased to be of any practical use they were either deliberately or casually sealed off; for example, one of the souterrains at Ballybarrack, Co. Louth, was used for a time as a rubbish-tip (E.P. Kelly, pers. comm.). The fact that practically every object that has so far been discovered on the floor of a souterrain can be dated to the latter half of the first millennium AD or the earliest centuries of the second millennium AD must be indicative of the general floruit of the monument.

A sample of these finds will illustrate the point. At Balrenny, Co. Meath (Eogan and Bradley 1977, 96), a bronze ringed pin uncovered on the floor of the souterrain chamber is of a type that can be dated to the ninth–tenth centuries AD (Fanning 1969, 10). At Crossdrum Lower, Co. Meath (Rotheram 1915, 171), a bronze ringed pin found on the floor of the (?) chamber is of a type that can be dated to the late tenth–twelfth centuries AD (Fanning 1983, 329; 1988, 168). An iron sickle was discovered in the wall of the outer chamber in the souterrain at Beaufort, Co. Kerry (Connolly 1992, 20). The writer suggested that the sickle could be dated to the period between AD 500 and 1200.

Reference has already been made to 'Souterrain Ware', — the class of pottery discovered at many souterrain sites in the north-east of Ireland. It should be stressed that this pottery is also found at other types of settlements dating from the early historic period in the north-east, and that the term 'Souterrain Ware' is therefore somewhat misleading. The chronological range of 'Souterrain Ware' stretches, in the main, from the sixth/seventh century AD to the second half of the twelfth century AD (Ryan 1973, 626, 627).

From as early as the middle of the nineteenth century antiquarians began to record the presence of re-employed ogham stones in souterrains. Writers such as R.R. Brash, S. Ferguson, C. Graves and, somewhat later, the archaeologist R.A.S. Macalister were pioneers in this field of research. Ogham stones appear to have flourished in the fifth century and the first half of the sixth century AD. Their use would appear to have declined in the second half of the sixth century and for all practical purposes to have died out in the early seventh century AD (McManus 1991, 97). The importance of ogham stones in relation to souterrains lies in their relatively close dating.

It has proved possible to date many of the ogham stones incorporated into the souterrains on the palaeographic evidence. It should be stressed that many individual souterrains contain ogham stones of different dates. In these instances it is clear that the souterrain-builders purloined the stones in one swoop and that this operation occurred at some point after the date of manufacture of the most recent of the stones. Thus, for example, it may be proposed that the souterrain at Monataggart, Co. Cork, which contains ogham stones ranging in date from the early fifth century AD to the early seventh century AD (F. Moore 1998, 28, 29) was constructed at some time after the early seventh century. There are also souterrains, however, that only incorporate one ogham stone. At Burnfort, Co. Cork, for example, the sole ogham stone is of early fifth-century date (*ibid.,* 28). It is technically possible, therefore, that this souterrain could have been built at any point after the early fifth century AD. Thus the key question to be addressed is whether the removal of ogham stones and their subsequent incorporation into souterrains occurred in or about one period (in the mid-seventh century AD or later?) or whether it was a case of gradual removal (from the mid-fifth century AD onwards?) as individual stones may have been deemed, for unknown (and localised) reasons, 'redundant'.

While the 'casual' finds noted above are important they do not date closely the precise period of construction of the souterrains in question. Fortunately other evidence is available, albeit, to date, to a very limited extent. Seasonal changes in the wood growth of trees produce distinctive annual rings. Dendrochronology involves the study of these rings. There is only one dendrochronological date available from a souterrain in Ireland — from a wood-built souterrain at Coolcran, Co. Fermanagh (B. Williams 1985, 69). Thus the souterrain could be accurately dated to AD 822 ± 9.

Radiocarbon dating is a second scientific method which can be used to determine the age of a souterrain. The earliest calibrated radiocarbon dates from a souterrain in Ireland came from Liscahane, Co. Cork (D. Power *et al.* 1997, 281), and centred on the sixth century AD. The latest date determined so far was 930 ± 80 BP (Mitchell 1989, 10) and was obtained from occupational debris in a souterrain at Cool West on Valentia Island, Co. Kerry. The calibrated date is AD 1305–1529 (Stuiver and Braziunas 1993).

In conclusion, therefore, it may be firmly stated that the available evidence — be it the 'casual' finds, the associated pottery, the reused ogham stones or the scientific dating data — firmly places the souterrains of Ireland in the latter half of the first millennium and the earliest centuries of the second millennium AD.

The recognition of structural aspects

There has been a slow trickle of information over the years regarding the structural aspects of souterrains in Ireland. The fact that the majority of souterrains consist of a distinguishable combination of passages and chambers was recognised as early as 1725, when Thomas Molyneux described these as 'long galleries' and 'closets' (1725, 209). He also noted the universal absence of the use of mortar (*loc. cit.*). Walter Harris and Charles Smith were the first to observe the presence of cupboards or cubby-holes in a souterrain at Cargagh, Co. Down; these they described as 'niches' (1744, 195). They also noted the presence of corbelling in the upper reaches of the souterrain at Slanes, Co. Down (*loc. cit.*). Thomas Wood (1821, 263) described the incorporation of escape passages into a number of souterrains. He also noted the presence in the south of Ireland of a number of earth-cut souterrains (*ibid.,* 266). This type of souterrain was also referred to by Samuel Ferguson, who observed that 'when the nature of the ground admits it, they are often excavated in the natural earth' (1870–9b, 131), and by W.G. Wood-Martin, who wrote that 'a few were burrowed out in the drift' (1895, 206). The latter also recognised the presence of air-vents in some of the stone-built souterrains (*ibid.,* 205).

The sheer scale, thoroughness and professionalism of the fieldwork carried out in the preparation of the Ordnance Survey maps and in the compiling of the ancillary documentation could not but further our understanding of the complex nature of many souterrains. Credit must be given to such workers as J. Stokes, C.W. Ligar, T. Fagan and John O'Donovan for being among the first to recognise many individual features. Stokes (1838), for example, recorded the cubby-hole ('a squared cavity') in the souterrain at Moneynick, Co. Antrim, and the cupboard ('square keep') in the souterrain at Rallagh, Co. Londonderry (Stokes 1835). Fagan (1838b) identified an air-vent ('a sort of funnel or airhole') in the roof of the souterrain at Ballyhome, Co. Antrim, and a well in the floor of

of entrance features. He succeeded in identifying three types: (1) a simple opening in the roof; (2) a stepped entrance; and (3) a sloping ramp (Macalister 1949, 270). He also dealt with trapdoors (*ibid.*, 271), air-vents (*loc. cit.*) and escape passages (*ibid.*, 272). To Macalister the most intriguing structural feature that had been brought to his attention was 'a rectangular porthole cut through a wide slab which otherwise closed the end of the passage' (*ibid.*, 275). He had been brought to see it in a souterrain at Dromavally, Co. Kerry (O'Connell 1939, 46; Clinton 1997, 6), and added that he had 'never seen one elsewhere in a souterrain' (*loc. cit.*). Only one other example of a porthole-slab had previously been published — in the souterrain at Cloghane, Co. Kerry (Deane 1893–6, 105) — and only four others were to come to light prior to detailed survey work in the 1980s. These were located at Kimego West (Leacanabuaile) (S.P. Ó Ríordáin and Foy 1941, 90), Coolnaharragle Lower (Ó Ciobháin 1944), Carhoo East (Waddell 1970a, 15) and Kealduff Upper (Ryan 1976, 5), all in County Kerry.

It was not until 1942 that the first modern comprehensive paper on souterrains appeared. An entire chapter in Seán P. Ó Ríordáin's *Antiquities of the Irish countryside* was devoted to the monument. All known (to date) structural aspects of souterrains in Ireland were touched upon. For the first time the general reader was provided with detailed descriptions of such features as 'opes' (construction shafts which are a feature of many tunnelled souterrains) (Ó Ríordáin 1942, 14), drains (*loc. cit.*), air-vents (and the hidden nature of their external extremities), and trapdoors (which he described as being characteristic of souterrains in County Down and County Galway) (*loc. cit.*). This publication was generally regarded as containing the best-realised account of souterrains in Ireland for almost the next 40 years (it underwent a subtle yet substantial revision by Ruaidhrí de Valera in 1979). To all intents and purposes it was, however, superseded by the appearance in 1979 of Richard Warner's paper 'The Irish souterrains and their background' (augmented in 1980 by a 'companion' paper, 'Irish souterrains: later Iron Age refuges', by the same writer). Warner dealt in a very incisive fashion with many of the known structural aspects of souterrains in Ireland. Any limitations in these papers were as a result of the lack of a comprehensive database pertaining to the actual numbers of any given feature, and their distributions. Warner's work became the authoritative touchstone for all subsequent writers, such as Edwards (1990).

Foreign origins, outside influences?

Souterrains are not unique to Ireland. Indeed, the idea of a secure underground refuge-cum-storage space could almost be regarded as universal. The concept also spans the ages. There are descriptions by Tacitus, the Roman historian, of the practice in Germania 'of hollowing out caves underground and heaping masses of refuse on the top' (Mattingly 1948, 114). In these the indigenous population could 'escape the winter's cold and store their produce' (*loc. cit.*). Variations on the theme can be found elsewhere, for example in the American Midwest of the late nineteenth century, where the female inhabitants of a settlement would retire to a small 'underground fort or cellar' (Warner 1979, 133) when in danger of attack by the Native Americans. The practice of building subterranean structures was also, apparently, pursued in nineteenth-century New Zealand, where their presence was usually disguised by driving cattle about above the structure until the surface was one uniform mass of 'puddle' (Kinahan 1883–4a, 11).

Closer to home, and of more potential relevance, are the souterrains of Brittany, Cornwall and Scotland. It should be stressed at the outset, however, that there is no proven evidence for the importation of the souterrain concept from abroad and it is therefore quite possible that they were an independent indigenous development.

The souterrains in Brittany are practically all tunnelled. They usually take the form of a cluster of chambers connected by simple constrictions. All of the souterrains were, essentially, associated with habitation sites (Giot 1973, 49). They are notable for the wealth of ceramic remains which they contain. Unfortunately this bounty of material goods has detracted from a more in-depth study of the structures themselves. The souterrains in Brittany have been dated, on the basis of the pottery, to *c.* 600–100 BC (Giot 1971, 213; 1973, 57). There is thus a considerable gap in time between their epoch and the postulated era of souterrains in Ireland (the late first millennium–early second millennium AD). The most tantalising aspect of the Breton souterrains is their tunnelled nature. Tunnelled souterrains in Ireland, as has been noted above, are predominantly located in the extreme south of the island, the very area in which one might expect influences from western France. There is also the persisting problem of actually dating the tunnelled souterrains in the south of Ireland. It is not impossible that they are earlier than the main body of (predominantly) drystone-built souterrains. Were it to transpire that the souterrain 'idea' was imported, then it would seem to be a very active possibility that the concept arrived in the south of Ireland as a result of later first-millennium AD contacts with western France.

The souterrains in Cornwall are equally problematic in relation to Ireland. Unlike their Breton counterparts these are drystone-built structures (with extremely rare tunnelled appendages). In capacity they would compare to the largest of the examples in Ireland. Furthermore, there are a number of structural parallels. The impressive beehive chamber at Carn Euny (P. Christie 1978, 309) is almost as big as the largest known beehive chamber in Ireland (Clinton 1993, 120). Again, however, it is the probable divergence in dating that precludes a direct association. The souterrains or fogous, as they are known in Cornwall, have been dated to between the fifth century BC and the second century AD (Christie 1978, 309; I. Cooke 1993, 60). It is not impossible, however, that the concept of a subterranean refuge-cum-storage space could have travelled from Cornwall to Ireland (Thomas 1972, 76).

Scotland presents us with further dilemmas. Not only are the souterrains of that land divided into quite disparate groups (Wainwright 1953a, 219) but as a body they would appear to be earlier in date than their counterparts in Ireland. This raises the fundamental question of how the souterrain 'idea' arrived in Scotland in the first place. There are no known souterrains in either Wales or England (excluding Cornwall). It is totally perplexing that these areas should be excluded, given that the merits of a secure refuge-cum-cool storeroom would have been recognised in these intervening lands. The souterrains of Scotland are predominantly drystone-built structures. The most impressive examples occur in southern Pictland (Wainwright 1955, 91). These have been linked to isolated surface dwellings (Thomas 1971, 44; Barclay 1978–80, 206) after the fashion of the unenclosed souterrain sites in Ireland. They contain such notable features as long curving chambers, usually paved, and narrow entrance passageways.

None of the other souterrain groups in Scotland achieved the overall dimensions of the southern Pictland group. Those in Sutherland basically consisted of undifferentiated passage/chambers. Souterrains in the Orkneys and Shetland invariably featured chambers whose roofs were supported by upright pillars.

There are two basic problems that would appear to preclude a direct association between the souterrains of Scotland and Ireland. There is a striking absence of the monument in the south-west of Scotland (Thomas 1971, 45) — the very area where, for both historical and geographical reasons, one would expect potential associations. Secondly, there is a diversity in dating. Thomas (1972, 76) has argued that it is difficult to prove that the souterrains of Scotland were in use prior to the late pre-Roman Iron Age. The bulk of the sites in southern Pictland would appear to date from between the first and third centuries AD (Wainwright 1963, 24). It should be noted, however, that there are a number of ambiguities in the resolution of Scottish souterrains. Sadly, it has not been an area of intensive study. Nevertheless it should be noted that there are known examples of subterranean features of souterrain-like appearance in Kincardineshire with a dating range between the third century BC and the sixth century AD (Watkins 1978–80a, 122). Furthermore, there are a number of enigmatic sites in southern Pictland, for example Ardross 1 (Wainwright 1953a,

228), that do not conform structurally to the surrounding group. It is not impossible that some of these souterrains may turn out to be later in date. It should also be remembered that there are a number of rock-cut souterrains in the extreme north of Ireland. Should any of these prove to be earlier in date than the main souterrain body then there still remains the possibility that some inspiration for the souterrains in the north of Ireland arrived independently from Scotland.

Pl. 1—Killally (Souterrain 1), Co. Louth: souterrain of mixed construction.

Pl. 2—Clogher, Co. Sligo: stepped entrance feature, possibly restored in the nineteenth century.

Pl. 3—Ballynavenooragh, Co. Kerry: associated house (on built platform) with air-vent opening.

Pl. 4—Dunisky, Co. Cork: rock-cut souterrain.

Pl. 5—Dunisky, Co. Cork: construction shaft.

Pl. 6—Ballynavenooragh, Co. Kerry: roof of souterrain after excavation.

Pl. 7—Smerwick, Co. Kerry: porthole-slab.

Pl. 8—Guilford, Co. Westmeath: cubby-hole.

Pl. 9—Newrath Big 2, Co. Meath: unrestricted-type passage.

Pl. 10—Caherfurvaus, Co. Galway: elevated trapdoor.

*Pl. 11—Oldbridge 1, Co.
Meath: restricted-type passage.*

*Pl. 12—Newrath Big 2, Co.
Meath: murder-hole.*

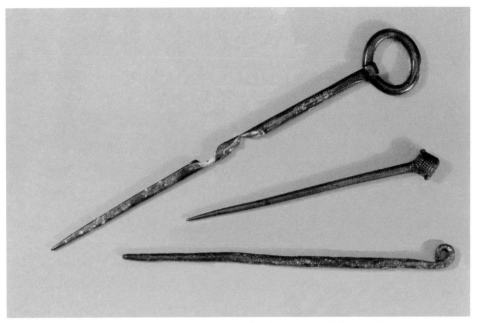

Pl. 13—Dowth, Co. Meath: associated finds. (Courtesy of the NMI.)

Pl. 14—Loughcrew, Co. Meath: roof of beehive chamber (with air-vent).

Pl. 15 —Carrowntemple, Co. Sligo: souterrain site potentially associated with church enclosure.

Pl. 16 —Guilford, Co. Westmeath: cobbled floor of chamber.

Pl. 17—Newrath Big 1, Co.
Meath: stepped feature.

Pl. 18—Dunisky, Co. Cork:
rock-cut bench in chamber.

Pl. 19—Stonefield, Co. Meath: hillock featuring open settlement with associated souterrain.

Pl. 20—Ballynahow, Co. Kerry: horizontal slab and jambstone in restriction.

Pl. 21—Donaghmore, Co. Louth: air-vent in end chamber.

Pl. 22—Commons, Co. Meath: earth/gravel-cut souterrain.

Pl. 23—Newrath Big 2, Co. Meath: cupboard.

Pl. 24—Glencolmcille, Co. Donegal: cross-slab in souterrain roof.

2

Distribution

It should always be remembered that souterrains are ultimately appendages to settlement sites. The souterrain-builder would have sought out the most suitable site for the structure (essentially a well-drained and elevated location). However, the siting of the settlements themselves would have finally determined the general environment and location of the associated souterrains.

There were widespread areas which would have been unsuitable for extensive settlement in early historic Ireland. Much of the coastal zone, especially along the western seaboard, is dominated by inhospitable mountains. Significant areas of the midlands were covered by bogland. Indeed, it would appear that over one third of the island was unsuitable for settlement (Stout 1997, 39).

The palynological evidence indicates that there was a major expansion in agriculture from about the second or third century AD (B. Raftery 1994, 124; Stout 1997, 46). This occurred in tandem with, or was facilitated by, the introduction of new agricultural technology (Mitchell 1976, 166). An increase in population and settlement inevitably followed. There is a marked increase in the number of references in the annals to woodland clearance and wasteland reclamation from about AD 800 or slightly earlier (Ó Corráin 1972, 49). Stout (1997, 24) has advanced persuasive evidence that the majority of Ireland's ringforts and crannogs were probably constructed and occupied between the beginning of the seventh century AD and the end of the ninth century AD.

Souterrains have been discovered in every part of the island. Current estimates would suggest a minimum figure of 3000–3500. The distribution pattern, however, is most uneven (see Fig. 10). While such areas as west Cork, north Antrim, south Galway and north Louth contain almost overwhelming numbers of souterrains, other areas, such as counties Carlow and Limerick, for example, are almost devoid of the monument. Occupying the middle ground are large tracts of land where souterrains occur consistently but not densely. The greater Meath area (comprising counties Meath, Westmeath, south Louth, north Dublin, south Longford and north Offaly) or north County Galway, to take two examples, would fall into this category. Some gaps in the overall distribution

Heavy concentration
Even distribution
Negligible distribution

Fig. 10—Distribution of souterrains in Ireland.

N

0   80 km

pattern of the souterrains are easily explained by expanses of mountains, bogs and generally low-lying terrain (more prone to flooding). It must always be remembered that souterrains, unlike most other ancient monuments, were totally reliant on a favourable water-table.

The north-central region, comprising counties Cavan and Fermanagh and areas of counties Longford, Tyrone, Monaghan and Armagh, is not over-endowed with souterrains. B.B. Williams (1985, 79) has implied that the apparent absence of souterrains in County Fermanagh might be explained by the suggestion that many took the form of wooden structures after the fashion of the souterrain at Coolcran (*ibid.*, 69). Such structures, once collapsed, would indeed be difficult to recognise unless they were manifested by suggestive depressions within the confines of an enclosure. Indeed, even those wooden souterrains which were sited in an enclosure might not be immediately apparent, as was the

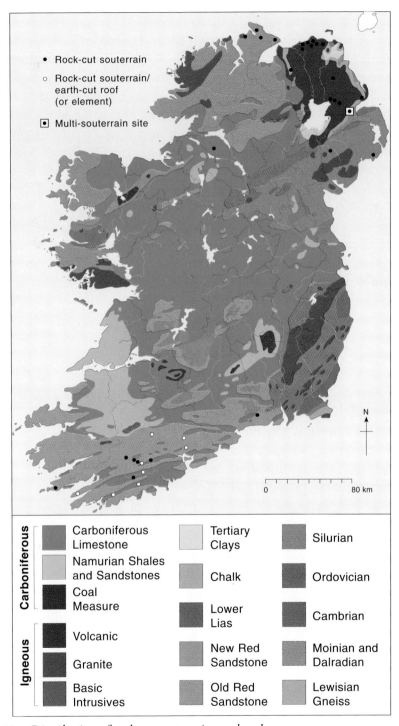

- • Rock-cut souterrain
- ○ Rock-cut souterrain/
  earth-cut roof
  (or element)
- ⊡ Multi-souterrain site

0   80 km

Carboniferous
- Carboniferous Limestone
- Namurian Shales and Sandstones
- Coal Measure

Igneous
- Volcanic
- Granite
- Basic Intrusives

- Tertiary Clays
- Chalk
- Lower Lias
- New Red Sandstone
- Old Red Sandstone

- Silurian
- Ordovician
- Cambrian
- Moinian and Dalradian
- Lewisian Gneiss

Fig. 11—Distribution of rock-cut souterrains and geology.

case at Coolcran. Interestingly, in County Cavan (O'Donovan 1995, 149) 34 of the 43 possible souterrains were represented by depressions located within the confines of a ringfort. The possibility that at least some of these suggested souterrains may have been wooden structures was illustrated by an account of the reported discovery of a 'timber-lined tunnel' at Gortnakillew (*ibid.*, 151). The county was otherwise credited with only four souterrains. Given the number of lakes and proved or suspected crannog sites in the Cavan/Fermanagh region, could it be that the indigenous population was more conversant with, and thus utilised, timber building techniques? The area might thus have the hidden potential for many future discoveries.

The vast majority (approximately 95%) of souterrains in Ireland were either completely or predominantly drystone-built. Drystone-built souterrains can be found in all parts of the island. In contrast, tunnelled souterrains are restricted in their distribution. Rock-cut souterrains occur in two clusters, in the extreme north and in the extreme south of the island (see Fig. 4). Neither group was confined to an area that was underlain by only one particular type of rock. The southern group were cut in both Carboniferous limestone and old red sandstone. Similarly, in the north the western souterrains in the group had been cut in Moinian and Dalradian rock, while their eastern counterparts were cut in volcanic rock (basalt) (see Fig. 11). Earth-cut souterrains are even more restricted in their distribution, being practically confined to the extreme south of the island (see Fig. 1). Again, they were not restricted to areas with one specific soil type. They extend from the grey-brown podzolic soil zone (towards their eastern limits) to the peats and peaty gleys soil zone (towards their western limits). A small number occur in an area of shallow brown earths (see Fig. 12). In other words, the souterrains were tunnelled in areas of both poor wet soil and good-quality dry soil. Economically speaking there would have been pronounced differences in the agricultural potential of these zones. It is interesting, therefore, to see that neither the physical attributes nor the quality of the soil appeared to determine the siting of these souterrains.

Buckley (1986, 108) has argued that certain souterrain concentrations in Ulster and Oriel reflected the heartlands of political groups. He advanced five examples to illustrate the point. The north Antrim/east Londonderry group he equated with the territory of the Dál Riata and subject kingdoms of the Ulaid, such as the Fir Chráibe (who were settled to the west of the River Bann); the mid-Antrim group with the Dál nAraide; the south Down group with the Dál Fiatach; the north Donegal group with the Cenél nEógain; and the north Louth group with the Conaille-Muirthemne (*ibid.*, 109).

Warner (1986, 111) flatly contradicted these correlations. He quite rightly observed that the north Donegal group stretched through the lands of different

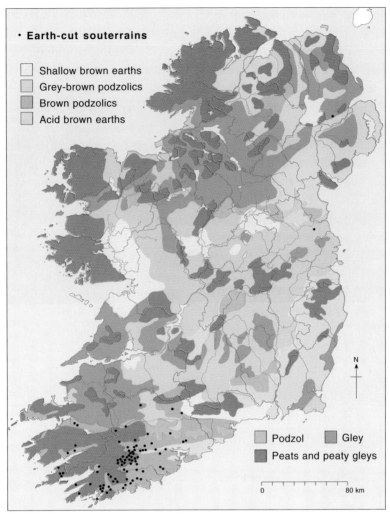

· Earth-cut souterrains

☐ Shallow brown earths
☐ Grey-brown podzolics
☐ Brown podzolics
☐ Acid brown earths

N

☐ Podzol   ☐ Gley
☐ Peats and peaty gleys

0   80 km

Fig. 12—Distribution of earth-cut souterrains and soils.

tribes, including the Cenél Lugdech, Cenél Nenda and Fir Maige Itha, and original territory belonging to the Cenél nEógain (Byrne 1973, 258, 120, 114). Similarly there are problems with the north Antrim group. As Warner (1986, 112) observed, this concentration transcends the borders of such disparate tribes as the Dál Riata, the Eilne and the Fir Chráibe (Byrne 1973, 107, 109, 115). Thus, as indicated by Warner, the north Antrim group of souterrains simultaneously spanned 'three tribes, three ethnic groups, and two political divisions' (*loc. cit.*).

The eastward extension of the Cenél nEógain from their homelands on the Inishowen Peninsula had begun as early as the sixth century. They had subdued all territories to the west of the River Bann by the ninth century (Byrne 1973,

95). The presence of souterrains on the Inishowen Peninsula indicates that the creation of these monuments was not unknown to the Cenél nEógain. Judging by the large number of souterrains sited east of the Bann it would appear likely that the Dál Riata were also familiar with these structures. Taking the Fir Chráibe into the equation, one can see how it is impossible to determine exactly who was responsible for the construction of the souterrains that lie to the immediate west of the River Bann.

Buckley's equation of the mid-Antrim concentration with the Dál nAraide is more convincing. Warner accepted this point but noted that their subsepts to the north and east of the heartland were 'far less in favour' (1986, 112) of souterrains. This is not altogether a true picture of the situation; there are sufficient numbers of souterrains in these areas and there is no escaping the fact that the concentration in the heartland is dense.

The Uí Thuirtri originated in the east Tyrone/south-east Londonderry area, a region not at all well endowed with souterrains. They started pushing across the River Bann, north of Lough Neagh, by the late eighth century. They had ousted the Eilne from their lands between the rivers Bann and Bush by the tenth century (Byrne 1973, 125). Similarly the Dál nAraide, 'cousins' of the Eilne, were under increasing pressure from the Dál Fiatach, who were eating into the southern limits of their territory (*ibid.*, 126). The Dál Fiatach, based in north Down/south Antrim, would not appear to have indulged in significant souterrain construction. The balance of probability, therefore, would suggest that the souterrains of mid-Antrim were either built by or for the Dál nAraide and their 'cousins' the Eilne as they came under increasing pressure from the south and west.

The 'ownership' of the south Down group of souterrains is also problematic. Warner (1986, 112) rightly noted that Buckley's equation with the Dál Fiatach did not tally with the full extent of their territory. Byrne (1973, 119) has explained how the Dál Fiatach had expanded to the shores of Lough Neagh by the end of the eighth century. There is a marked absence of souterrains in north Down. While there would be a stronger argument in favour of crediting the south Down souterrains to a collateral branch of the Dál Fiatach — the Leth Cathail — there is a slight spillage of sites into the neighbouring lands of Uí Echach Cobo and the unrelated Monaig (Byrne 1973, 119, 107, 121).

The final example advanced by Buckley was the suggested linkage between the north Louth group of souterrains and the Conaille-Muirthemne. It has been established that this minor kingdom was extant from the late seventh century (Byrne 1973, 118) to the early or mid-twelfth century (L. Murray 1940, 450, 453). Indeed, its position in the Ulaid orbit was apparently consolidated by an agreement made in the mid- to late eighth century (Byrne 1973, 118). There can be little doubt that the souterrains in north Louth were constructed by or for the Conaille-Muirthemne, although admittedly there is a spillage of sites into the neighbouring lands of the unrelated Mugdorna Maigen (Ó Corráin 1972, 15; Byrne 1973, 117).

It is the opinion of the present writer that souterrain concentrations cannot be accepted as indicators of political areas. It might be suggested, however, that independent 'schools' of souterrain-builders were, initially, focused on individual minor kingdoms. It was almost inevitable that a successful innovation would eventually transcend the borders into the neighbouring territories. These, after all, would have been the people most likely to encounter the souterrains, and appreciate their effectiveness, on the inevitable forays.

Warner (1986, 112) stated that the north Louth souterrain group extended into south Louth, i.e. Brega. This assertion may be rejected on morphological grounds. The majority of the souterrains in south Louth, in the lands of the Fir Arda Ciannachta (P. Walsh 1940, 519), conform both structurally and in their distributional pattern to the greater Meath group. It is interesting to note that souterrains in the intervening lands of mid-Louth, occupied by the unrelated Fir Rois (Mac Iomhair 1961–4, 144; Byrne 1973, 117), display morphological elements of both the north and south Louth groups.

It is worth reiterating at this point that souterrain concentrations do not always permeate a recognised political unit in its entirety. The absence of souterrains in the northern lands of the Dál Fiatach has already been noted. It may also be stated that there is a marked fall-off in the number of souterrains in the southern part of County Meath, i.e. southern Brega. One wonders whether that was in any way related to the fact that the rulers of southern Brega were based at a crannog (Lagore) (Byrne 1968, 397) while the rulers of northern Brega were located at (the souterrain-rich) Knowth. Again, the kingdom of Osraige, which flourished from the seventh to the twelfth century (Ó Corráin 1972, 6, 169), had souterrains in its southern part only; these were undoubtedly an overspill from the neighbouring territory of the Déise, who were based in County Waterford.

The existence of different 'schools' of souterrain-builders may be detected in the limited distribution of certain structural aspects. Trapdoors, for example (see Chapter 6.4), were confined to the west and the north-east. A more extreme example can be seen in the distribution of porthole-slabs (see Chapter 6.12), which were restricted exclusively to the territory of the Corcu Duibne on the Dingle and Iveragh peninsulas in west Kerry (Clinton 1997, 5).

The debate regarding the possible relationship between souterrain concentrations and recognised political areas must be considered against the evidence from the historical kingdom of Leinster. It has already been suggested

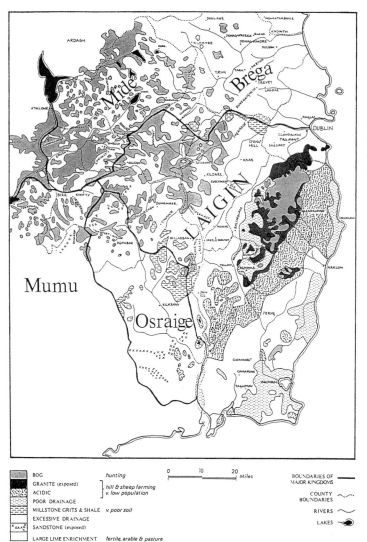

Fig. 13—Early historic Leinster: soils and settlement (after Smyth).

by the present writer (Clinton 1998, 117; 2000a, 275) that there was a pronounced lack of souterrains in this area. A more comprehensive picture may now be presented. Smyth (1982, 21) has delineated the extent of the kingdom between the eighth and twelfth centuries. In modern terms it occupied the following areas: south County Dublin, County Kildare (excluding the barony of Carbury), County Laois (excluding the western baronies of Clarmallagh, Clandonagh and Upper Woods), County Offaly (excluding the western baronies of Garrycastle, Kilcoursey, Ballygowan, Ballyboy, Eglish, Ballybritt and Clonlisk), County Wicklow, County Carlow, County Wexford, and a narrow sliver of the eastern part of the barony of Gowran in County Kilkenny (see Fig. 13).

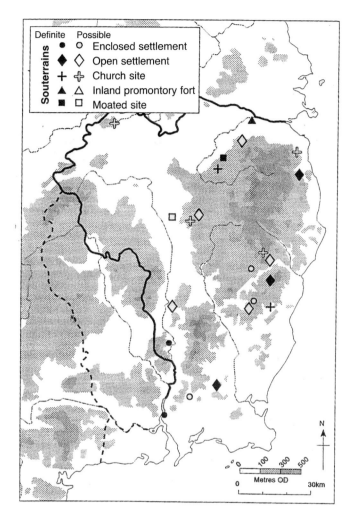

Definite Possible

Souterrains

● ○ Enclosed settlement
◆ ◇ Open settlement
+ ⊹ Church site
▲ △ Inland promontory fort
■ □ Moated site

Fig. 14—Souterrains of early historic Leinster.

N

Metres OD

0   30km

A comprehensive search through the Topographical Files of the NMI and the OPW, and the published archaeological literature, has revealed that these areas are practically devoid of souterrains. In fact it may be stated that the historic kingdom of Leinster, to date, has produced no more than nine definite and approximately a dozen possible souterrain sites (see Fig. 14). These are striking statistics when one considers that minor kingdoms such as those of the Conaille-Muirthemne (in north County Louth) and the Corcu Duibne (in west Kerry) were in possession of approximately 200–300 souterrains apiece.

The evidence from Leinster has profound implications for other gaps in the souterrain distribution pattern. As the entire indigenous topographical spectrum was represented in the kingdom the practical absence of the monument cannot be attributed to any geographical or environmental factors. Interestingly, the density of ringforts in Leinster is amongst the lowest on the island (Stout 1997,

59). A correlation between the low density of ringforts and the practical non-existence of souterrains in Leinster is not, however, a model that can automatically be applied elsewhere. For example, there is a high density of ringforts in the east Limerick area (*ibid.*, 83) while souterrains are practically absent. By contrast, a median ringfort density in north Louth (*ibid.*, 66) coincides with a very high souterrain density. The actual occurrence of souterrains in Leinster, albeit in minimal numbers, proves that the indigenous population was not only familiar with the monument but also capable of building them.

The context or potential association of the known souterrains in Leinster is noteworthy. The souterrains at Killashee, Co. Kildare (Beauford 1789, 84; Browne 1922, 14), and Kilnahue, Co. Wexford (M. Moore 1996a, 44), are in the immediate vicinity of church sites. Four possible souterrains — Timolin, Co. Kildare (Fitzgerald 1903–5, 166); Oldcroghan, Co. Offaly (O'Brien and Sweetman 1997, 49); Rathmichael, Co. Dublin (Clinton 1998, 123); and Killaduff, Co. Wicklow (Topographical Files, NMI) — are also located at church sites. The souterrain at Lucan and Pettycanon, Co. Dublin (Clinton 1998, 119), is sited in an inland promontory fort. There are also souterrains apparently associated with open settlements — Carrig (M. Moore 1996a, 44) and Kellystown (A.B. Ó Ríordáin 1969, 49), Co. Wexford, and Kilmacanoge South (Rynne 1967b), Co. Wicklow. Possible souterrains associated with open settlements were recorded at Bustyhill, Co. Dublin (Clinton 1998, 122), Kiltillahan, Co. Wexford (M. Moore 1996a, 44), Killaduff 2, Co. Wicklow (Topographical Files, NMI), and, superficially, 'Bagnalstown', Co. Carlow (Brindley and Kilfeather 1993, 97). The souterrain at Tipper South, Co. Kildare (Topographical Files, OPW), was located in a rectangular enclosure. Interestingly, so was the possible souterrain at Clogorrow, Co. Kildare (Darby 1899–1902, 191; Fitzgerald 1899–1902, 133). These two enclosures would appear to be medieval moated sites, a Norman introduction (Barry 1988, 529). It is known that at Baltrasna, Co. Meath (Feeley 1990–1, 151), a souterrain was discovered in a ploughed-out moated site. In these instances it would appear to be a case of continuity of settlement rather than a direct association. In the entire kingdom of Leinster, to date, only the souterrains at Ballyduff, Co. Kilkenny (Topographical Files, OPW), and Fisherstown, Co. Wexford (Michael Moore, pers. comm.), and the possible souterrains at Cushenstown, Co. Wexford (Lewis 1837, vol. I, 264; M. Moore 1996a, 44), and Ballycumber South, Co. Wicklow (Grogan and Kilfeather 1997, 71), appear to have been located in ringforts. Considering that there are in excess of 400 ringforts in County Wexford alone (Bennett 1989, 50), these are emphatic statistics.

The structural aspects of the Leinster souterrains are also enlightening.

Morphologically, the souterrain at Lucan and Pettycanon in south County Dublin conforms in all aspects to the greater Meath group. Similarly, the souterrain at Tipper Upper, Co. Kildare, with its two sub-beehive chambers, would appear to owe its ultimate inspiration to the same group. The souterrain at Fisherstown on the banks of the River Barrow in County Wexford was of the Waterford type. The mostly earth-cut souterrain at Killashee, Co. Kildare, is unique in the kingdom and may be of an earlier date. The souterrain at Ballyduff, Co. Kilkenny, is in the immediate area of the strategic Pass of Gowran. Significantly, there are at least three souterrain sites on the Osraige side of the pass. The available data on the remaining structures in Leinster would seem to indicate that they were of a very insubstantial nature. Therefore, while Lucan and Pettycanon and Tipper Upper may be regarded as overspills from the Meath 'school', Ballyduff as an overspill from the southern Osraige 'school', and Fisherstown as an overspill from the Deíse 'school' of souterrain-building, the remaining examples, significantly located in the interior of the kingdom, may represent local attempts to construct their own variations of the monument.

It is impossible to say, on the basis of the available evidence, why the inhabitants of Leinster chose not to build souterrains on any significant scale. Indeed, given the fact that they were apparently familiar with the monument, it may well have been a matter of choice. There are a number of vague possibilities or factors which may have influenced their decision. The kingdom of Leinster did enjoy a substantial natural line of defence along its borders. This extended from the steep valley of the River Liffey to the Bog of Allen in the midlands, to the Slieve Bloom Mountains, to the Castlecomer plateau, to the River Barrow. Comings and goings tended to be restricted to strategic points such as the river crossing near Leixlip (Ryan 1949, 68), the headlands of the River Boyne near Cloncurry (Smyth 1982, 10), or the Pass of Gowran (Hogan 1910, 328; Smyth 1982, 11). It is possible, therefore, that the kingdom may have escaped much of the external petty raiding endemic elsewhere. Internally the territory was largely subdivided topographically by such natural features as the Wicklow Mountains, the Blackstairs Mountains and the Castlecomer plateau. Politically there was also a north/south divide. In the north of the kingdom the Uí Dúnlainge long reigned supreme. It has been recognised that their three major subdivisions — the Uí Dúnchada, the Uí Fáeláin and the Uí Muirdaig — rotated the northern kingship with remarkable regularity between the mid-eighth and the mid-eleventh centuries (Ó Corráin 1972, 26; Smyth 1982, 79). Similarly, in southern Leinster the Uí Chennsalaig, in association with the related tribes of Uí Dega and Uí Dróna, held sway from the ninth to the twelfth century (Smyth 1982, 60). These secure hegemonies, relatively safe behind their naturally enhanced borders, may have slightly reduced the frequency of the internecine wranglings that continuously plagued other regions. This is not to say that Leinster was a haven of peace and tranquility. No dynasty in early historic Ireland held onto its position without sporadic, if not persistent, internal and external quarrelling. Indeed, it has been written that the Leinster annalists recorded 'a relentless inter-tribal slaughter' (Smyth 1982, 5) during the latter part of the early historic period. Several major hostile incursions by large forces are also well documented (Ó Corráin 1972, 119, 126, 137, etc.). Therefore it might all be a question of 'degree'; that is to say, how intensive or persistent did petty raiding have to become before the afflicted would consider it expedient to incur the unwanted expense of building souterrains? Is it possible that the nature or intensity of raiding in Leinster never crossed that fragile threshold?

For now, all that can be said with any certainty is that, judging by the evidence from Leinster, the uneven distribution pattern of souterrains in Ireland would not appear to have been simply determined by either topographical or technological considerations alone.

3

Association

S outerrains are found in a specific number of different contexts — open settlements, enclosed sites, church sites, promontory forts and medieval sites. For many years an association with ringforts and cashels has been recognised, even to the point that when there was no sign of an enclosure it was presumed to have been ploughed out. In the few instances where it was conceded that there was no associated enclosure it was believed that these were 'isolated' souterrains (S.P. Ó Ríordáin 1953, 31), the theory being that these souterrains were sited apart from a settlement in order to avoid detection. While it is possible that such isolated souterrains might have existed, this has not yet been proven. Difficulties of association arise when a souterrain is discovered in the immediate vicinity of a ringfort, or, as at Coyne, Co. Westmeath (Glasscock 1969–75, 230), where a souterrain is found immediately adjacent to two enclosed sites; in these cases it is impossible to determine, without excavation, whether the souterrain and the enclosure(s) were related or even contemporary features.

Open settlements

In general it may be accepted that the discovery of an apparently unassociated souterrain is a firm indication of an otherwise superficially undetectable unenclosed settlement. Indeed, at Cargin Demesne, Co. Roscommon (M. Moore 1996b), an unenclosed souterrain site was found with an associated field system. The absence of an enclosure has been conclusively proven by trial-trenching at such sites as Harryville, Co. Antrim (Jope 1950), Randalstown, Co. Meath (Campbell 1987, 31; pers. comm.), and Farrandreg, Co. Louth (D. Murphy 1998, 279).

Regional variations in association are beginning to emerge. In County Meath (Clinton, unpublished) a minimum of 65% to a maximum of 75% of souterrains would appear to be associated with unenclosed settlements, whereas in south County Galway (Gosling et al., forthcoming) only 13% of the souterrains were associated with unenclosed settlements. Preliminary research in County Antrim (Buckley 1978, 40) suggested that only 25% of the souterrains were associated with an enclosure. This pattern was inverted in County Down (*ibid.*, 41), where 75% of the souterrains were associated with enclosures. In County Louth (P. Gosling, pers. comm.) the available evidence suggested that 30% of the souterrains were associated with enclosures. In County Cork (McCarthy 1977, 44) out of a total of 458 souterrains 286 were associated with ringforts while 141 were associated with open settlement. Again, on the Dingle Peninsula, Co. Kerry (Cuppage 1986, 231), out of a total of 250 souterrains 145 were associated with ringforts while 50 were associated with open settlement (an additional 25 souterrains associated with clochauns should also be included in the unenclosed category). Similarly, on the Iveragh Peninsula, Co. Kerry (A. O'Sullivan and Sheehan 1996, 223), out of a total of 211 souterrains 66 were associated with open settlement and an additional 21 were associated with unenclosed hut sites. Preliminary research on the island as a whole would seem to suggest that up to 60% of souterrains may have been associated with open settlement (Buckley 1988–9, 64).

In the greater Meath area, souterrain-related open settlement sites are frequently located on prominent natural hillocks (see Pl. 19). Owing to a lack of excavation the precise nature and full extent of these open settlements have yet to be fully established.

Enclosed sites

It has hitherto been argued that the vast majority of souterrains in Ireland were associated with ringforts (de Valera 1979, 65). Where there is no evidence for an enclosure it has been implied that this was the result of destruction. In some instances this argument may be valid. The souterrain at Rathiddy, Co. Louth (Rynne 1962, 129), for example, was initially reported as an unenclosed feature. Aerial photography subsequently revealed that the souterrain in fact lay within the confines of an enclosure (Buckley and Sweetman 1991, 139). The present writer would argue, however, that given the number of souterrains associated with open settlement in the east (approximately 70%), a note of caution should be exercised. There are already a number of sites where open settlement would appear to have succeeded enclosed settlement. At Togherstown (Souterrain 2), Co. Westmeath (Macalister and Praeger 1929–31, 75), the souterrain was shown to have traversed the inner fosse. At Knowth, Co. Meath (Eogan 1991, 120), extensive excavation has demonstrated that all nine souterrains post-dated the enclosed phase of settlement at the site. This phenomenon is not confined to the east. At Ballywee, Co. Antrim (Lynn 1975, 4), excavation revealed that the northern element of an apparent conjoined ringfort configuration was in reality too insubstantial in nature to qualify as an enclosure *per se*. Again, at Letterkeen, Co. Mayo (S.P. Ó Ríordáin and MacDermott 1951–2, 100), it was clearly established that the souterrain post-dated the initial settlement phase at the site. The point is that, especially in areas where open settlement was strongly represented, it must be considered as an active possibility that many superficially enclosed souterrains may ultimately turn out to constitute a two-phase settlement site. In short, unless a souterrain is stratigraphically proven to be a primary or integral feature in a ringfort, there is no valid reason why it should be automatically assumed to have been contemporary with the enclosure.

Souterrains at enclosed sites may either occur within the interior of the enclosure or be incorporated into the bank (in a ringfort) or wall (in a cashel) of the enclosure. Their precise siting would be determined by the location of the associated house(s). There may be as many as three souterrains in an enclosure, as for example at Ballybarrack, Co. Louth (Kelly 1977) (see Fig. 15). Three

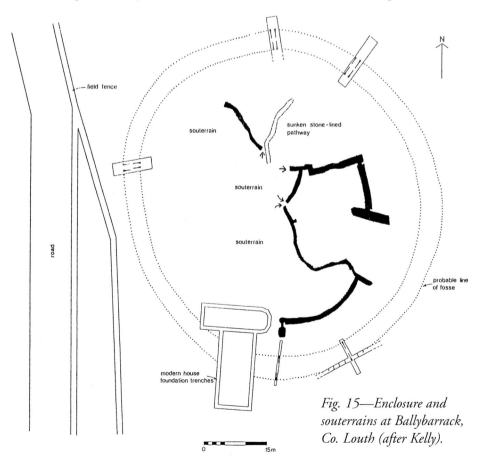

Fig. 15—Enclosure and souterrains at Ballybarrack, Co. Louth (after Kelly).

souterrains were also discovered in the multivallate ringfort at Ballycatteen, Co. Cork (S.P. Ó Ríordáin and Hartnett 1943–4, 13). As only a little over a quarter of the interior of the enclosure was excavated it is possible that there could have been more.

Church sites

It has long been recognised that souterrains occur within the environs of early church sites. It must be stressed at the outset that no souterrain has yet been scientifically linked to an early church site. Indeed, current excavations in the monastic settlement on Great Skellig Island, off the coast of County Kerry, have discovered that the reported souterrain (de Paor 1955, 186; Edwards 1990, 120) is in fact a water-cistern (E. Bourke, pers. comm.). Nonetheless, there are a number of convincing potential examples. Lucas (1971–3, 172) listed a number of sites, for example Straid (Glencolmcille), Co. Donegal, Kane, Co. Louth (see Fig. 16), Fore, Co. Westmeath, and Killala, Co. Mayo. S.P. Ó Ríordáin (1953, 31) suggested that a souterrain at a church site may have been intended to fulfil the same functions as a round tower — that is, to provide a secure storage area for church valuables or church-protected property in times of danger. Indeed, theft was increasingly becoming a problem for the church in the late first millennium/early second millennium (Doherty 1980, 84).

At Templebryan North, Co. Cork (Killanin and Duignan 1967, 167), a large enclosure contained the remains of a 'primitive' church in addition to a well ('Tobernakilla'), a pillar-stone (3.35m in height) with an incised cross on its western face (terminals expanding in the pattée style) and a faint ogham inscription on the adjoining angle, and two souterrains. Significantly, while one of the souterrains was earth-cut (Twohig 1976, 31), the other was drystone-built (McCarthy 1977, 315). Thus there are many issues to be resolved at the site. Was the earth-cut souterrain an early integrated feature of the church site? Did the earth-cut souterrain pre-date the drystone souterrain? Did they fulfil different functions, perhaps at different times?

The monastic site at Monasterboice, Co. Louth (Gosling 1981, 74; D. Murphy 1993, 16), would appear to have featured four concentric enclosures. To date four souterrains have been detected within the confines of these enclosures. The most potentially interesting (known) souterrain at the site was described by Leask as being 'mainly rock-cut, lintelled over, and most irregular in plan' (in Keenan 1945–8, 52). Souterrains in the east were not generally mainly rock-cut. As previously discussed (see Chapter 1), there are some indications that potentially early examples of souterrains occurred within the environs of church

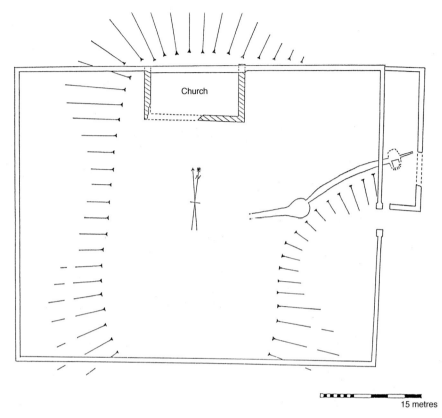

Fig. 16—Church site and souterrains at Kane, Co. Louth (after Clinton and Gosling).

sites. This is not to say that all souterrains occurring in the context of a church site were primitive in form, nor indeed early in date. An enclosure at Carrowntemple, Co. Sligo (Wallace and Timoney 1987, 43) (Pl. 15), contained the ruins of a medieval church, a graveyard, a souterrain and, most interestingly, fourteen decorated graveslabs. These were of ninth-century date, at the earliest (P.F. Wallace, pers. comm.). The most significant aspect of the slabs in relation to the souterrain is the fact that both were made of sandstone. As limestone is the prevailing bedrock type in the locality there is a distinct possibility that the graveslabs and the souterrain were a contemporaneous development at the site. An early monastic site, attributed to St Broccaidh, at Meelick, Co. Mayo (Killanin and Duignan 1967, 433), contains a graveslab which it has been claimed cannot be older than the late tenth or early eleventh century (Crawford 1922, 179). The site also contains a round tower. A souterrain was discovered within the curving perimeter of the enclosure (J. Raftery 1967), approximately 50m from the tower. Sadly no attempt was made to establish the chronological relationship between the tower and the souterrain. The remains of a 'rudely built' church at Templemaley (Ballyhee Townland), Co. Clare, were assigned to *c.* 1080 on the basis of the type of window employed in the building (Westropp 1900–2, 146). A souterrain was discovered quite close to the west end of the church. This was a drystone-built structure with a wide passage (Westropp 1917, 3). The 'roomy' type of passage is usually found in the more complex, and probably later, class of souterrain.

Shancough, Co. Sligo, was the site of an early church foundation associated with St Patrick. The *Tripartite Life of Patrick* (Stokes 1887, 95), a mid-tenth-century text probably compiled in the eleventh century (*ibid.*, lxiii), related an episode involving 'four glass chalices' (*ceitri cailig glainid*) resting on a stone altar 'under the ground' (*fotalmain*). O'Rorke (1890, 274) suggested that the underground dimension of the story implied the presence of a souterrain. He further stated that the souterrain 'may still be seen under the walls of the old church'. A more recent report states that the souterrain is visible to the east of the church, with its main passage extending towards the building (Mount 1993c). At Cartronhugh, Co. Sligo (Topographical Files, OPW), an opening to a souterrain was visible in the floor of a rectangular structure. This 'building', described as a possible church, was sited along the projected line of an enclosure.

An irregular oval enclosure (*c.* 72m by *c.* 52m) of a type commonly found around early church sites and monasteries was excavated at Killederdadrum (Lackenavorna Townland), Co. Tipperary (Manning 1984, 237). Besides the suggestive name of the site, the enclosure contained post-medieval burials, and there are known references to a medieval parish in the locality. The existence of three circular houses was established within the confines of the enclosure. House 1, towards the western extremity of the site, had a diameter of 8.8m, and its door faced east. The south-western side of its foundation trench was cut by a deep oblong trench (*ibid.*, 261), which was interpreted as the remains of a looted souterrain. The sides of the trench were vertical. It was 3m in maximum width, flat-bottomed, and 4.4m in exposed length (it was not fully excavated). Its northern (i.e. house) end sloped down steeply to a depth of 1m. The projected line of the bank of the enclosure, however, might suggest that the souterrain was originally afforded a greater height. The bottom course of the 'northern' wall of the souterrain remained *in situ*. The souterrain was judged to have post-dated the house. There was no evidence, however, to suggest that the souterrain was associated with any other structure. It might be suggested, therefore, that the souterrain could have been a later addition to the house. The excavation of a circular house at Loher, Co. Kerry (see below), established just such a sequence of events. A sherd of E-ware pottery discovered at Killederdadrum was assigned to the main period of occupation (*ibid.*, 261). Thus a date of around the sixth or seventh century AD or later could be proposed for the main period of occupation. It should be noted that Edwards (1990, 121) has called the early ecclesiastical credentials of this site into question.

The early monastic site at Kiltiernan East, Co. Galway (Westropp 1919, 178), encapsulates many of the problems relating to the projected association of a souterrain and a church site. The circular enclosure was delineated by a stone-built wall and encompassed up to four acres (Killanin and Duignan 1967, 317). The church, which lay towards the centre of the enclosure, was described as being 'early' on the basis of its flat-headed doorway (Harbison 1970, 96). The interior of the enclosure was subdivided into fifteen or sixteen sub-enclosures by radial and other walls (Waddell and Clyne 1995, 149). A souterrain was sited to the west of the church. This was in a poor state of repair. It was represented by a hollow, *c.* 9m by 4m, with elements of the drystone walling and lintelled roof still evident. It had obviously suffered further interference since the early part of the century, when 'many' of the roofing lintels were still *in situ* (Westropp 1919, 178). The remains of up to ten house sites were detectable at ground level. House 1, for example, had an internal length of *c.* 7m and an internal width of *c.* 3.96m (Waddell and Clyne 1995, 164). House 2 was a more substantial structure, with an internal length of 15.9m and an internal width of 4.27m (*ibid.,* 168). Excavation of four of the houses and the nave of the church yielded no precise dating evidence. The finds did, however, suggest that the site was occupied as early as the ninth century. Unfortunately the immediate environs of the souterrain were not excavated. Thus the exact relationship between the souterrain and the monastic site remains undefined. Furthermore, other key questions remain unresolved. Did the souterrain (site?) pre-date the church or were they contemporary features? Indeed, could the souterrain have belonged to some post-primary use of the site? A related question was raised by Hamlin (1976, 173). In the case of a souterrain that lies immediately beyond the confines of a church enclosure, did that souterrain belong to the monastic community or to an 'extramural' settlement? Indeed, was the physical proximity of the souterrain to the church site purely fortuitous?

On a broader scale, it is worth noting that souterrains would not appear to have been a universal feature of early ecclesiastical sites in the early historic period. Hamlin (1976, 170), in her exhaustive study of the sites in the north of Ireland, could only find convincing evidence for the presence, or former presence, of a souterrain at 23 of the sites — a mere one-twelfth of the total number in the inventory (*ibid.,* 173).

In short, there are a growing number of persuasive indications in support of an intrinsic association between souterrains and ecclesiastical sites; however, the body of evidence, to date, remains almost purely circumstantial (Clinton forthcoming a).

Promontory forts

There are about 250 known coastal promontory forts in Ireland (B. Raftery 1994, 48). These are found all around the coastline, wherever suitable sites were available. The largest concentrations are in the south and west; for example, there are approximately 28 in County Clare (Gleeson 1991, 59) and approximately 58 in County Cork (Westropp 1920, 128).

Souterrains have been recorded at a small number of sites, for example at Duneendermotmore and Duncermna, Co. Cork (Westropp 1920, 117). However, as 'remarkably few' (Edwards 1990, 41) promontory forts have been excavated, the exact relationship between the souterrains and the forts has not been determined. This was also the case at Dunbeg, Co. Kerry (Du Noyer 1858, 4; Barry 1981, 295). Here the souterrain actually extended out from the inner rampart of the fort, running beneath the entrance causeway (Barry 1981, 309). The excavator proposed that its location and relationship with the rampart suggested that it had a primarily defensive function (*ibid.*, 311). There are no parallels for such a location. Generally the souterrain would have been positioned within the inner confines of the ramparts. Examples of this arrangement may be seen at such sites as Dunluce, Co. Antrim (Hamlin 1982, 28), Townparks, Co. Donegal (Lacy 1983, 227), Carrowhubbock North, Co. Sligo (Topographical Files, OPW), and Minard West, Co. Kerry (Cuppage 1986, 96). It is not impossible, therefore, that the souterrain at Dunbeg was a late addition to the site. Indeed, given the closely set arrangement of four banks and five fosses, and the limited space available within the inner rampart, the causeway would have been as good a place as any in which to insert a souterrain. It was conceded that the souterrain proved impossible to date (Barry 1981, 311).

The dating of promontory forts has not been satisfactorily resolved. The significance of the early first-millennium BC radiocarbon date obtained at Dunbeg (*ibid.*, 324) has been questioned by Raftery (1994, 48). The other dates from the site indicated an eighth/ninth- or tenth/eleventh-century AD presence (*loc. cit.*). O'Kelly (1952, 32) suggested that some promontory forts may date from the Iron Age; Edwards (1990, 41) allowed the possibility of a slightly earlier origin. The late survival of other sites has been noted by Westropp (1920, 114).

Many writers, for example Edwards (1990, 43) and Barry (1981, 323), have commented on the lack of occupation debris at promontory forts. Indeed, some sites have failed to produce any signs of occupation at all, for example Doonagappul on Clare Island, Co. Mayo (Casey 1993, 53) — the implication being that promontory forts may not have been occupied *per se* but rather acted as places of temporary retreat. All the indications are that souterrains were associated with settlement sites. Therefore it may ultimately transpire that souterrains located in promontory forts are secondary features associated with subsequent settlement.

Medieval sites

Rotheram (1893–6, 310) noted the presence of souterrains in the 'large moats' at Newtown (Killallon) and at Moat, Co. Meath. These two 'large moats' are in fact mottes (Graham 1980, 51). Orpen (1907, 241) also recorded both sites. He observed that the entrance passage to the souterrain at Moat was quite low down on the side of the mound and that this was unusual as souterrains normally descend. A field inspection of the site revealed that the so-called entrance passage was in fact an inner passage and that the end chamber had apparently been destroyed by the builders of the motte. There was also evidence of internal alterations and it would appear that the souterrain was put to some use by the Norman settlers. Souterrains under mottes would have been associated with an earlier settlement, either an open settlement on a hillock or a ringfort. Similarly, souterrains superficially contained by a moated site, as, for example, at Baltrasna, Co. Meath (Feeley 1990–1, 151), or Castleskreen, Co. Down (Jope 1966, 169), would also have belonged to earlier settlements. The passage grave mound at Knowth, and also possibly at Dowth, Co. Meath, with their souterrain-associated settlements, were also used as motte sites by the Norman settlers (Byrne 1968, 399; Graham 1980, 51). These sites, therefore, are evidence of continuity of settlement. There is no suggestion of a primary relationship between the medieval structures and the souterrains.

Associated houses

It has been suggested that in instances where a souterrain opens directly from an associated house, the house will be of rectangular form (Edwards 1990, 31). Whilst this argument would appear to hold true in the north and east, it is as yet unproven in the west and is more complex in the south.

At Craig Hill, Co. Antrim (Waterman 1956b, 87) (see Fig. 17), the souterrain opened directly from the back wall of a rectangular house (overall dimensions 3.66m by 5.49m). The carefully constructed entrance of the souterrain was integrated into the surviving basal courses of the back wall of the house. Furthermore, the construction trench for the souterrain undercut the rear of the house. It was thus quite apparent that the souterrain and the house were contemporary features. Close parallels were recorded at Ballywee, Co. Antrim

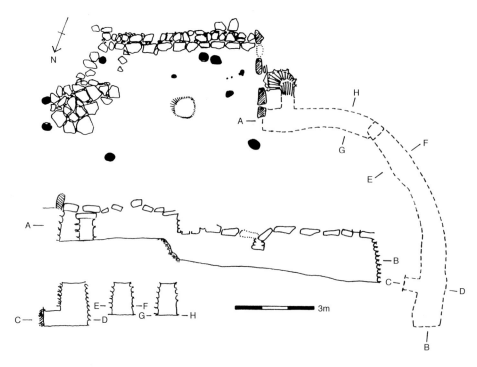

Fig. 17—Craig Hill, Co. Antrim (after Waterman): rectangular house and drystone-built souterrain featuring chamber of expanded-terminal type, rock-ramp impediment and cubby-hole.

(Lynn 1975, 4), where the souterrain opened directly from a rectangular house (overall dimensions 8m by 16m), and at Antiville, Co. Antrim (Waterman 1971, 65), where the souterrain opened directly from the south-west corner of a rectangular house (overall dimensions 5.18m by 3.66m). Another probable example was recorded at Rathmullan, Co. Down (Lynn 1981–2, 65). Here the first two phases of occupation were associated with circular wooden houses, while Phases 3 and 4 were associated with rectangular buildings featuring drystone footings. The souterrain was judged to be a feature of Phase 3 of the settlement. A potential example of an indirect association between a rectangular house and a souterrain was recorded at Shane's Castle, Co. Antrim (Warhurst 1971, 58), where traces of one timber and two stone and clay buildings were uncovered within the interior of the ringfort. All were rectangular in form. It was not possible, however, to conclusively link any of these structures to the souterrain.

At Drumaroad, Co. Down (Waterman 1956a, 73), it would appear that both phases of settlement possessed a square house. In the first phase the evidence was only suggestive, but in Phase 2 it was conclusive. The internal dimensions of the latter house were in the region of 5.49m by 5.18m, judging by the paved floor. At a distance of 1.52m from the house a souterrain trench was discovered. The excavator assigned this feature to Phase 1 but no definite evidence was provided to support this assertion. He also concluded that the construction of the souterrain had never been completed, based on the complete absence of any stonework or the remains of a wooden structure. The present writer would argue that it is equally possible that the trench was originally simply roofed with logs and may have represented a primitive variation on the souterrain theme. The maximum depth of 1m would only have facilitated such a crude basic form.

A ringfort at Drumgolat, Co. Monaghan (McCormick 1978, 326), contained a raised rectangular area, 0.3m above the overall level of the interior of the ringfort and measuring 7m by 8m. The entrance to a souterrain lay 1m inside the northern perimeter of this suspected house site. The souterrain extended 'out' of the house. Again, at Lisduff, Co. Longford (McCabe 1975), an 'unusually' large enclosure, delineated by a substantial bank with a wide and shallow external fosse, contained a rectangular house site, represented by a broad, low, earthen bank. Immediately outside its northern corner an opening (modern?/ancient?) into a souterrain could be observed.

A possible exception to the prevailing pattern in the north was uncovered in an excavation at Downpatrick, Co. Down (Brannon 1988a, 295; 1988b, 6). Here a suspected timber-built souterrain was discovered in close proximity to the remains of a round timber house. Prodigiously, the fill in the souterrain contained two Hiberno-Norse coins and a fragment of gold foil decorated in an early twelfth-century Urnes style. These finds provided an early twelfth-century date for the termination of use and backfilling of the souterrain. It has been argued (see below) that round houses would have been generally obsolete by the twelfth century and thus the association at Downpatrick must be questionable.

At Knowth, Co. Meath (Eogan 1986, 24; 1991, 120), the remains of at least thirteen rectangular houses were discovered in an open settlement complex that also featured the remains of nine souterrains.

The evidence from the south is more diverse. At Darrara, Co. Cork (J. O'Sullivan 1990, 225; O'Sullivan *et al.* 1998, 31), three earth-cut souterrains were revealed during the course of an excavation. Two of the souterrains, it would appear, had direct access from a round house.

At both Kimego West (Leacanabuaile), Co. Kerry (S.P. Ó Ríordáin and Foy 1941, 85) and Ballynavenooragh, Co. Kerry (Gibbons, forthcoming), the souterrains extended from the floors of circular stone-built houses (Pl. 6). Both houses were enclosed by cashels. At Raheennamadra, Co. Limerick (Stenberger 1966, 37) (see Fig. 18), the souterrain intersected the line of a circular house but their exact relationship remained a little unclear. Similarly, at Lisleagh 2, Co.

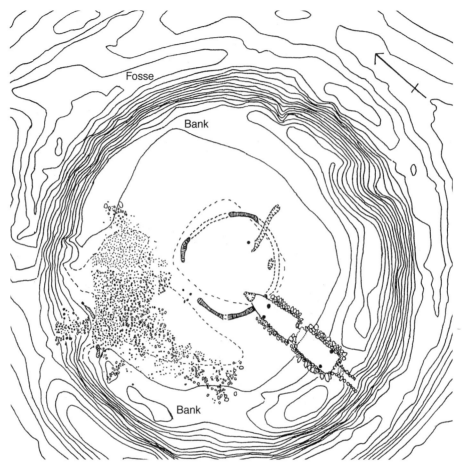

Fig. 18—Raheennamadra, Co. Limerick (after Stenberger): ringfort, circular house and souterrain (featuring wooden roof and external exit).

Cork (Monk 1995, 105), the souterrain intersected the line of one of the four circular houses discovered during the course of the excavation. A possible association between a circular house and a mostly earth-cut souterrain was recorded at Underhill, Co. Cork (O'Kelly and Shee 1968, 40). The foundation course of a curving wall was uncovered in the area immediately above the souterrain. Judging by the line of the wall, however, it would not appear that the souterrain opened directly from the house. At Oldcourt, Co. Cork (Ó Cuileanáin and Murphy 1961–2, 79), the souterrain was not directly connected to either of the two houses discovered in the course of the excavation. Both houses were oval in form and were not contemporary. There was, however, no evidence for the former presence of any rectangular structures. The excavation of a cashel at Loher, Co. Kerry (O'Flaherty 1986, 26; A. O'Sullivan and Sheehan 1996, 191), provided an invaluable insight into the sequence of structural developments at one settlement in the south-west region within the relevant period. No fewer than five identifiable structures were uncovered. The two earliest structures in the cashel were round houses constructed of driven stakes. One of these houses was followed by a round stone-built house with an internal diameter of 6.6m. The walls were preserved to a height of (on average) 1.3m. Excavation revealed that a souterrain had subsequently been incorporated into the body of this house. Its entrance, in the western half of the interior of the house, measured 1.1m by 1.3m. The final phase of building at the site was marked by the construction of a rectangular house with internal dimensions of 7.55m by 6.3m and a (surviving) height of 1.2m. It overlay the second of the original wooden circular houses. The rectangular house was also shown to have post-dated the adjoining stone-built circular house (the one containing the souterrain). It is worth noting that the circular house with the souterrain at Kimego West (Leacanabuaile), Co. Kerry (see above), also pre-dated the building of an adjoining rectangular house.

At Farrandau (Knockdrum), Co. Cork (Somerville 1931, 1), a souterrain of mixed construction had direct access from the south-west corner of a square house. The overall dimensions of the house were 5.18m by 5.18m. Interestingly, this was very similar in size to the house noted at Drumaroad, Co. Down (see above). The floor of the house at Farrandau was also paved. The evidence from Cush, Co. Limerick (S.P. Ó Ríordáin 1938–40, 83), was both inconclusive and varied. The house in Ringfort 1 (*ibid.,* 89), for example, was possibly circular, while the house in Ringfort 3 (*ibid.,* 97) was possibly rectangular. Both ringforts contained souterrains but their relationships to the houses remained unclear. This was also the case in relation to the souterrain in Ringfort 5 (*ibid.,* 104), where the remains of several houses were uncovered. The earliest structure was possibly circular in form. Two later structures were also circular while another was rectangular.

The evidence from the west of Ireland is not insubstantial, but it has, to date, been somewhat localised. At Cahercommaun, Co. Clare, a 'roughly round hut' (Hencken 1938, 20), 6m in internal diameter, was linked to Souterrain A. The fact that the souterrain was apparently associated with the wall of the enclosure indicated that it was a primary feature of the settlement. Evidence for at least two round houses was uncovered at Letterkeen, Co. Mayo (S.P. Ó Ríordáin and MacDermott 1951–2, 100), but the souterrain could not be firmly linked to either. Indeed, the excavators suggested that it may even have been later in date (*ibid.,* 104). At Ballyjennings, Co. Mayo (Lavelle *et al.* 1994, 41), a cashel contained three independent house sites. House 1 was circular in form with a diameter of 10.5m. The perimeter wall survived to a height of 0.6m. This house contained the entrance to a souterrain. The remaining two house sites were square and rectangular respectively. Neither contained a souterrain.

The platform ringfort at Ballymartin, Co. Mayo (*ibid.*, 22), featured two house sites, described as 'subrectangular'. House 1 (diameter 3.1m north–south, 2.8m east–west; surviving height 0.3m) contained a souterrain. The evidence from other sites in County Mayo is less definite but is nonetheless significant. The cashels at Askillaun (O'Hara 1991, 117) and Doonty (*ibid.*, 126) both contained collapsed souterrains. They also contained circular house sites. The diameter of the house in the former site was 4.5m. Unfortunately it was not specified whether there was any direct association between the houses and the souterrains. The same ambiguity exists in relation to the ringforts at Cloonfinish (*ibid.*, 135), Cullin (*ibid.*, 137), Doonmaynor 1 (*ibid.*, 137) and Doonmaynor 2 (*ibid.*, 138). All four sites contained souterrains and the remains of round houses. The diameter of the house at Cullin was 11.2m.

An unenclosed circular house site was discovered at Killoran South, Co. Sligo (O'Conor 1993g). The diameter varied between 6.9m (north–south) and 6.1m (east–west). Its perimeter was defined by an earthen bank, 3–3.4m wide, revetted on its northern and western (internal) sides by a series of rocks. An opening to a (blocked-up) souterrain was visible in the south-eastern sector of the house.

A cashel at Cuilsheeghary More, Co. Sligo (Mount 1993a), contained a circular/oval house site with a given internal diameter of 6.6m. The perimeter of the house was defined by a wall of medium-sized slabs (0.9–1m in thickness), rising to a height of 0.5m. The house site enclosed the north-western end of an L-shaped souterrain. There was no visible entrance into the souterrain. The possibility of a 'hatch' entrance, however, cannot be excluded.

A small rectangular house was recorded in a cashel at Treanmore, Co. Sligo (Mount 1993b). To the east of the house the looted remains of a souterrain were discernible. The internal dimensions of the house were 2.5m by 1.2m and 0.5m in (surviving) height. The walls were 1.2m thick.

To summarise, therefore, the early indications are that a significant number of souterrains located in the south and west of Ireland may ultimately be found to be associated with round houses.

Lynn (1978) has argued convincingly for a transition from round to rectangular houses in the early historic period, the changeover probably being complete by the end of the tenth century (*ibid.*, 37). Rectangular houses associated with souterrains, such as those at Ballywee or Craig Hill, Co. Antrim, or the multiple examples at Knowth, Co. Meath, would thus date from towards the end of the period, or later. Conversely, round houses associated with souterrains, such as those at Kimego West and Loher, Co. Kerry, or Ballyjennings, Co. Mayo, and Killoran South, Co. Sligo, may date from an earlier phase. Thus it is not impossible that many souterrains in the south and west slightly pre-dated those in the north and east.

4

Function

Over the past 50 years the debate on the purpose or function of souterrains has been primarily focused on two theories. While some writers have argued that they were created as refuges, others have suggested that they were used for storage. There were also those, for example S.P. Ó Ríordáin (1953, 31) and de Valera (1979, 71), who advanced the idea that certain types of souterrains may have fulfilled either function.

Evans (1966, 29), having considered the refuge theory, opted for storage. He suggested that their primary purpose was to serve as a cellar where dairy products could be stored at an even temperature.

Souterrains containing a single chamber were advanced as storerooms by Macalister (1949, 272), although he accepted the more complex and impedimental structures as refuges. The 'simple' souterrains were also proposed as underground stores by M. de Paor and L. de Paor (1958, 87), who regarded the more complex examples as refuges that could be used as stores 'in more peaceful times' (*loc. cit.*). The storage theory was accepted by Thomas, who wrote that 'very few seem to be either suitable or likely places of refuge' (1972, 77). The evidence in favour of both schools of thought was put very succinctly by Lucas when he wrote that 'all the features and peculiarities which they present are consonant with either view' (1971–3, 172).

In recent years the refuge interpretation has been in vogue. Warner (1979, 131; 1980, 92) has argued that the prime motivation for the construction of a souterrain was the desire to create a secure place of refuge.

Before addressing the two main theories, other past suggestions regarding the function of souterrains should be considered.

Earlier proposals in the archaeological literature that souterrains were used as dwelling-places may be discounted. At the best of times souterrains are dark and damp places that would not be conducive to healthy living conditions. Investigation of reports of domestic pottery in souterrains will invariably reveal that the finds came from the area of a formerly open entrance feature. Accounts of a fireplace or a chimney usually indicate the presence of an air-vent, a cubby-hole or even an entrance shaft. Charcoal infiltration from the associated surface settlement often gave rise to stories of fireplaces. Latter-day use of souterrains as hide-outs for rapparees or robbers often resulted in the remains of 'modern' fires being left in the souterrain.

Souterrains have, in the main, managed to remain free from allegations of 'a ritual dimension'. There are, however, two exceptions. There is no denying that the hybrid souterrain/natural cave in the townland of Glenballythomas at Rathcroghan, Co. Roscommon, is a rather enigmatic creation. This 'cave' was regarded in the literature as a gate to hell (Lucas 1971–3, 188) or the Otherworld (Waddell 1998, 352). The presence of two ogham stones in the roof of the souterrain, one bearing the name 'Maeve' (*loc. cit.*), only serves to add to the mystique.

It has also been suggested that a cave on one of the two islands in Lough Derg, Co. Donegal, was a souterrain (MacRitchie 1900, 167; Lucas 1971–3, 189). This 'cave' was referred to in the *Annals of Ulster* as *uaim Purgodoire Patraig* (MacCarthy 1895, 416). It too may once have been regarded as a 'mouth of hell' (Lucas 1971–3, 190) or 'purgatory' (MacRitchie 1900, 166) but was apparently subsequently 'exorcised'.

These two sites are exceptional; there are no further examples of souterrains being regarded as anything other than purely utilitarian structures. There are other known hybrid souterrain/natural caves, for example at Ballyegan, Co. Kerry (Byrne 1991, 5), but none has been introduced into the realms of mythology. There is also the case of the partially unroofed, and perpetually flooded, souterrain at Kiltarnaght, Co. Mayo (Knox 1917–18, 39; Topographical Files, NMI), which has latterly served as a holy well. This is a good example of how a mundane monument can subsequently take on a ritual dimension.

The nature of the entrance feature is a good indication of the primary function of a given souterrain. Both ramp entrances and stepped entrances (Pl. 2) would suggest ease of access, and in these instances storage considerations may have been the main concern. Conversely, a pit-drop or a shaft entrance would suggest security. Similarly, an unrestricted passage would indicate ease of mobility, while a restricted passage, or especially a constriction, would imply defence. The range of impedimental devices, such as trapdoors, porthole-slabs, protruding jambstones, head obstructions, etc., would also strongly indicate the defensive nature of a sizeable number of souterrains in Ireland, and thus their construction primarily as refuges.

It has been suggested that much of the cattle-raiding in early historic Ireland took place at night (Lucas 1989, 167; McCormick 1995, 34). It would seem likely, therefore, that raiding parties with other movable assets in mind, such as

Fig. 19—
Donaghmore, Co.
Louth (after
Rynne),
Souterrain A:
reconstruction of
wattle gate/door
at entrance to
souterrain.

slaves, would also avail of the cover of darkness. Given that the disguised entrance to a souterrain would be hard to find at the best of times, the added benefit of a dark night would make discovery almost impossible. Therefore even the simplest of souterrains, with no internal impediments, once provided with a disguisable entrance, would have functioned as a very effective refuge.

Warner's (1979, 131; 1980, 92) total dismissal of a 'normal' storage function for any souterrain in Ireland is impossible to justify. The presence of a secure fireproof structure, enhanced by a cool even temperature, at the heart of a settlement would have been impossible to ignore, whatever the primary motivation for its construction. It is highly likely, given their structural form, that at least some of the less complex souterrains could have been built specifically as storage places. The entrance to the souterrain at Ballynavenooragh, Co. Kerry (Clinton, forthcoming b), was sited in the floor of a circular house. The opening was actually partly set in an alcove in the stone wall of the house. Structurally, this alcove would have been impossible to disguise. Moreover, the sloping ramp that facilitated entry to the chamber incorporated a pair of steps and what might be described as an 'armrest', both obviously designed to create an easy access. The chamber itself was roomy and featured an air-vent. There were no impedimental devices of any description. Thus there can be little doubt that this souterrain was intended to serve as a cool storage place.

The vestigial remains of wooden doors have been discovered at the entrances to a number of souterrains, for example Souterrain A at Donaghmore, Co. Louth

(Rynne 1965a) (see Fig. 19). The former presence of these doors may cast some light on the function of the souterrains in question. The flimsy nature of the doors — either wattle or light wooden affairs — would tend to suggest storage rather than refuge. They could only have been intended to keep out scavenging animals, either domestic or wild. They would have afforded little protection against even a lightly armed raider.

There have been a number of references to the presence of 'guardrooms' or 'guardchambers' in souterrains. These are small side chambers usually located close to the entrance feature. Examples may be seen in the souterrains at Aghnahoo, Co. Tyrone (McKenna 1930, 196), and Ardtole, Co. Down (Bigger and Fennell 1898–9, 146) (see Fig. 20). It is more than likely, given their location, that these chambers served as convenient storerooms.

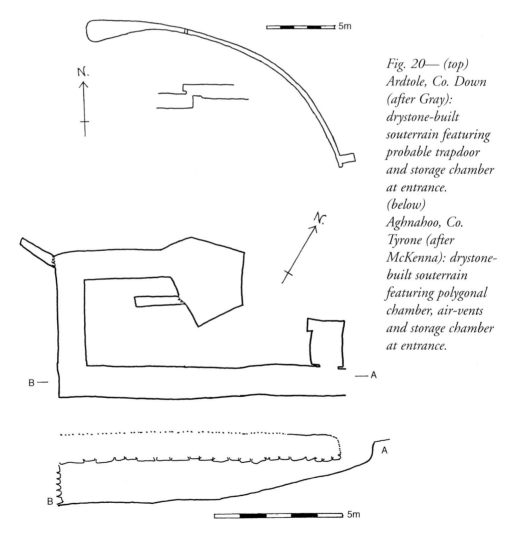

Fig. 20— (top) Ardtole, Co. Down (after Gray): drystone-built souterrain featuring probable trapdoor and storage chamber at entrance. (below) Aghnahoo, Co. Tyrone (after McKenna): drystone-built souterrain featuring polygonal chamber, air-vents and storage chamber at entrance.

Warner (1980, 92) has used the absence of any contemporary narratives describing souterrains as normal storage places as evidence for a non-storage function. It might be suggested, however, that the sheer mundanity of the practice would not have encouraged any such references to be made in the first place.

At sites such as Bawntaaffe (Rynne 1957–60a, 96) and Ballybarrack (Kelly 1977), Co. Louth, a number of souterrains were discovered in very close proximity to each other (in an enclosure at the latter site). Rynne (1957–60a, 102) suggested that the individual souterrains may have served different purposes, the more complex structures serving as refuges while the simple undifferentiated passage/chamber examples provided a cool storage facility. There is evidence to suggest that even some of those souterrains that were obviously built as refuges may have provided a storage dimension. At Crossdrum Lower, Co. Meath (Rotheram 1897, 427), for example, there was a subchamber located close to the entrance. This lay 'outside' the inner sanctum of the souterrain, as delineated by a trapdoor device, and would thus have been very convenient for regular access.

The known artefacts from souterrains do not help in determining the function of the monument. Personal objects, such as ringed pins or beads, could just as easily have been lost when taking refuge as when fetching some stored goods. The more precious objects, such as the silver penannular brooch from Cahercommaun, Co. Clare (Hencken 1938, 23), the bronze-coated iron bell from Oldcourt, Co. Cork (Ó Cuileanáin and Murphy 1961–2, 88), or the glass vessel from Mullaroe, Co. Sligo (Harden 1956, 154; Bourke 1994, 168, 205), were probably hidden at a time of danger, but the finding of this type of 'luxury' item is the exception rather than the rule.

The presence of wooden vessels in the souterrains at Ballyaghagan, Co. Antrim (Evans 1950, 13), and Balrenny, Co. Meath (Eogan and Bradley 1977, 102; Edwards 1990, 30), might suggest storage, but then again they could have contained supplies which had been brought into the souterrains at a time of danger. The only objects of a potential defensive nature found were a number of iron knives, but these could just as easily have been used for domestic purposes.

S.P. Ó Ríordáin (1953, 31) suggested that souterrains located at church sites may have fulfilled the same functions as round towers. Besides securing the church valuables and personnel, the souterrain might also have contained property deposited by lay neighbours in order to avail of church protection.

One of the most enduring arguments against the storage interpretation is the general lack of finds from souterrains. It is probable that only goods held in containers, or alternatively food produce that could be hung from simple stakes hammered between the stones in the walls, would have been stored. Given the absence of pottery from most parts of the island during the relevant period, it is almost certain that wooden and leather vessels were in general use. These would not have survived except in exceptional circumstances. Neither would any of the foodstuffs. Should any items of value have been stored in souterrains then either the rightful owner or an interloper would have subsequently removed them (unless the object was well hidden and perhaps even yet awaits discovery).

A number of potent arguments have also been raised against the refuge theory. It has been pointed out that souterrains could effectively have become death-traps if the aggressors decided to dig or smoke the occupants out. Alternatively, it has been suggested that the occupants could have been smothered or starved to death if the aggressors chose to seal them inside the souterrain. The general lack of human remains in souterrains has also been used to reject the refuge interpretation. As Mallory and McNeill (1991, 196) observed, however, if the desired booty was the occupants themselves then there would be no danger of being smothered within or, alternatively, of being slain if dug out. Slavery was rampant in the relevant period (Ó Corráin 1972, 47; Holm 1986, 321) and there was no gain in mindless slaughter. Therefore the souterrain could be looked upon as a more than worthwhile ploy with which to attempt to evade capture. Given the small size of the average raiding party, the time at their disposal, and the active possibility that the raid was taking place at night, it is not difficult to see the attraction of a secure subterranean bolt-hole.

William Beauford (1789, 84), in describing the souterrain at Killashee, Co. Kildare, wrote: 'These caves, with others of a similar nature found in several parts of Ireland, were the granaries or magazines of the ancient inhabitants, in which they deposited their corn and provisions, and into which they also retreated in time of danger'. It is the opinion of the present writer that the converse is probably closer to the truth — in other words, that the majority of souterrains in Ireland were built with refuge in mind but on a day-to-day basis functioned as convenient cold storage places.

5

Associated finds and chronology

Precise dating of the vast majority of individual souterrains in Ireland has not proved possible. This is simply the result of both the small number of sites that have been scientifically excavated and the paucity of finds relating to the construction phases of souterrains. Indeed, souterrains are somewhat notorious for their lack of finds in general. However, while it remains unclear when exactly the monument first made its appearance in Ireland, there are very firm indications as to its period of general use.

The early material

Davies (1939) suggested that souterrains might have been derived from the megalithic tradition and built by men who had forgotten how to manipulate large rocks. Even before the publication of the definitive report, the excavations at Cush, Co. Limerick, had prompted the advancement of a Middle Bronze Age date for at least one of the souterrains at the site (Mahr 1937, 280). The actual report shifted the period of construction of the souterrain slightly towards the point of transition between the Middle Bronze Age and the Late Bronze Age (S.P. Ó Ríordáin 1938–40, 177). A re-reading of the excavation report would suggest that the interpretation of the stratigraphy at the site was flawed. The roof of the key souterrain had been removed and the conjoined chambers filled in at some point in antiquity. This apparent backfilling of the souterrain would have involved the utilisation of convenient deposits, including the Bronze Age stratum associated with an immediately adjacent cordoned urn burial (*ibid.*, 113).

There are a number of recorded examples of the discovery of redeposited bronze or copper axeheads in souterrains in Ireland. Two bronze axes were recovered from a probable souterrain at Paddock (Aghadown), Co. Cork (P. Power 1926, 57; Mahr 1937, 386; McCarthy 1978a, 71; D. Power 1992, 225).

Four copper axes were found in a 'cave' at Carrickshedoge, Co. Wexford (Bremer 1926, 88; Mahr 1937, 386). A bronze socketed axehead was allegedly discovered in a souterrain at Ballybowler South, Co. Kerry (Waddell 1970a, 16). 'Military weapons of copper or bronze' (Lewis 1837, vol. II, 322) were also reputedly recovered from the souterrain at Lucan and Pettycanon, Co. Dublin (Clinton 1998, 123). Two of these reports have proved to be misleading. The 'cave' at Carrickshedoge turned out on inspection to be a natural cave (S.P. Ó Ríordáin 1938–40, 178). The axehead from Ballybowler South had in fact been discovered in a surface mound of stones lying close to the souterrain opening (Cuppage 1986, 114). The alleged finds from Lucan and Pettycanon have never been scientifically examined and have proved impossible to trace (Clinton 1998, 129). It is almost certain that the two bronze axes from Paddock had been discovered elsewhere and were subsequently redeposited in the souterrain, possibly by the owners of the latter structure.

It has been suggested that two fragments of bronze leaf-shaped swords may have been found in a souterrain at Cooldorragh (Doon), Co. Offaly (Eogan 1965, 78). The original report, however, is not convincing regarding the place of discovery (Topographical Files, NMI).

Decorated slabs of prehistoric age

There are at least six examples of decorated stones featuring Bronze Age concentric motifs from souterrains in Ireland (an alleged seventh example was noted at Drumlohan, Co. Waterford (Kirwan 1987, 36)).

From a dating perspective the most relevant discovery was made in one of the three souterrains in the enclosed complex at Ballybarrack, Co. Louth (E.P. Kelly, pers. comm.). Here, a slab decorated with Early Bronze Age concentric motifs was used as an obstructive jamb in Souterrain 2. Significantly, another of the souterrains in the enclosure contained an ogham stone which had been deployed as a strategically placed roofing lintel.

At Gortdromagh, Co. Cork (D. Power 1992, 234), a displaced roofing slab, in a mostly rock-cut souterrain, featured eight cup-marks. Again, the souterrains at Glenmakee (Lacy 1983, 234) and at Creggan (Ryan 1972), both in County Donegal, contained roofing lintels which featured cup-marks, 28 in the case of Creggan. At Cooslughoga, Co. Mayo, Wilde (1867, 111; Westropp 1896–1901, 669) illustrated a flagstone wall in the middle chamber of the souterrain with two of its component stones featuring what appear to be cup-marks. These he described as artificial depressions, while drawing rather fanciful analogies with the 'cave' at Newgrange, Co. Meath. Similarly, at Emper, Co. Westmeath (Weir

1938, 146), a slab in the wall of an inner passage featured a cup-mark and a double-circle motif. Rynne (1964b, 123) has suggested that this stone may have been looted from the stone cist cemetery recorded by Weir in the field immediately adjoining the perimeter of the associated ringfort. This suggestion seems perfectly valid. Waddell (1970b, 134) has confirmed the existence of a flat cemetery of Bronze Age date at Emper, and the (rare) occurrence of capstones with a decorated underside has been documented (Herity and Eogan 1977, 134).

The employment of these decorated stones by the souterrain-builders was probably simply opportunistic. It would not appear likely, because of their pagan characteristics, that they were incorporated for any potential talismanic qualities, but this, of course, is not impossible. Another suggestion would be that they may have held some aesthetic appeal for the souterrain-builders. One deciding factor in the debate on whether these stones held any 'significance' or not would be the future discovery in a souterrain of a similarly decorated stone with the motifs located on the 'upper' (i.e. buried) face of the slab. In the interim they remain an interesting group of curios with no dating implications for their host monuments.

The Iron Age

Probably the most enigmatic find in a souterrain, to date, came from Souterrain B at Cahercommaun, Co. Clare (Hencken 1938, 23), where a human skull, practically complete except for the lower jaw, was uncovered towards the inner terminal of the souterrain. It rested on a small slab of limestone, which in turn lay on the exposed bedrock that constituted the floor of the souterrain. The skull lay on its left side, facing south. It had been placed in a carefully arranged setting of small flat stones. Immediately beneath the skull was a large iron hook. The remains of two iron knives lay beneath the small basal slab. The assemblage was embedded in, but not covered by, a stratum of ashes mixed with animal bones which overlay the entire floor of the souterrain and varied in depth from 0.65m to an average of 0.25m.

Movius, in his analysis of the human remains from Cahercommaun (Hencken 1938, 77), advanced the theory that the skull represented a foundation burial. Hencken (*ibid.*, 23) suggested that the presence of the hook indicated that the skull was originally displayed. Rynne (1992, 205) interpreted the skull and iron hook as evidence of a ritual burial, indicative of some form of head cult, and suggested that it could indicate a pagan Celtic date for the site.

The fact that the same souterrain also produced a silver brooch of ninth-century AD date (Hencken 1938, 23) must be regarded as significant. It was also uncovered in the stratum of mixed ash and animal bone (0.05m above the bedrock floor). The average original height of the souterrain was 1m. It is difficult to believe that a deposit averaging 0.25m in depth would have been tolerated by the ninth-century users of the souterrain. It is more likely to have been related to the eventual abandonment of the souterrain. The balance of probability, therefore, would suggest that the skull and iron hook at Cahercommaun represented a late survival of an ancient cult practice.

On a broader scale, no objects of an Iron Age date have ever been discovered in a souterrain in Ireland (Barry Raftery, pers. comm.).

The use of inscribed pillars and stones

Ogham inscriptions, engraved on pillars or stones, at their most basic bore the name of an individual. The individual's name could be augmented with that of the parent and on occasion with that of the tribe.

Judging by both the linguistic evidence and the data available from the early law-tracts, it would appear that the genesis of ogham-inscribed standing stones can be dated to the period encompassing the introduction of Christianity into Ireland, that is to say the late fourth and early fifth centuries AD. Some of the actual standing stones themselves may of course have been erected in an earlier epoch. Macalister (1945–9, vol. I, 158) suggested that the imposing monolith at Ballintermon, Co. Kerry, was 'a bronze-age monument adapted for the purposes of the ogham carver'. Again, the rather crude standing stone at Barnaveddoge, Co. Louth (Macalister 1916–17, 88), which also bears an ogham inscription, would appear to have affinities with a small localised cluster of otherwise uninscribed standing stones. These were tentatively proposed by McIvor (1955, 225; Mac Iomhair 1961–4, 144) as boundary stones erected to denote the southern frontier of the Fir Rois. Indeed, it is now widely accepted that ogham stones in general either served as memorial stones or, on occasion, as territorial markers.

De Valera (1979, 146) suggested that the practice of raising these commemorative stones may have begun in the Irish colonies in Wales. Hencken (1932, 226) more cautiously proposed that the originators would have been among those people in Ireland familiar with the Latin alphabet. Nevertheless, as the vast majority of the known examples of ogham stones occur in the south, and particularly in the south-west, of Ireland, that region would seem likely to be their ultimate place of origin.

As indicated above, ogham stones have also been recorded in Wales.

Hencken (1932, 208) referred to over 30 examples. This figure has lately been amended to 40 (McManus 1991, 44). Examples have also been recorded in Cornwall (5), Devon (2) and the Isle of Man (5) (*loc. cit.*). While in Ireland the ogham inscription invariably occurred alone, in Britain it was common to have an accompanying epitaph executed in Roman letters. On just under half of the known examples the inscription in Latin was longer (McManus 1991, 62). Thomas (1994, 68) has recently proposed a typology for the British oghams. He placed the longer accompanying Latin inscriptions at the end of the sequence of development. De Valera questioned the authenticity of 'a few' (1979, 145) ogham stones located in western Scotland. At least three of these may be accepted as genuine examples — Dunadd (Piggott 1982, 168), Poltalloch and Gigha Island (F. Moore, pers. comm.), all three sites in Argyll. In the east of Scotland, i.e. Pictland, a 'couple of dozen' (Jackson 1955, 138) ogham inscriptions have been recorded. These are of a most peculiar nature, however, and would not appear to belong to the mainstream tradition. They have been dated to the mid-eighth or possibly even the ninth century AD (*ibid.,* 139). Finally, the so-called 'Scholastic Oghams' (McManus 1991, 129) appear to be ultimately divorced from the orthodox tradition. According to McManus, their 'inspiration is different and the orthographical conventions they observe are recent' (*ibid.,* 44). Indeed, this late version of the script survived in use until relatively recent times (F. Moore, 1995).

From as early as the mid-nineteenth century archaeologists have noted the presence of reused ogham stones in souterrains. It was almost inevitable that these elongated free-standing stones would have attracted the attention of the souterrain-builders. They would have been perceived as eminently suitable raw material for a lintelled roof. Not surprisingly, most examples of souterrains incorporating reused ogham stones have been discovered in the south of Ireland, where the inscribed stones occur in their greatest numbers (see Fig. 21 and Appendix 1). There have been some notable discoveries. In 1889, at Ballyknock North, Co. Cork (Barry 1890–1, 516), no fewer than fifteen ogham stones were discovered in an otherwise earth-cut souterrain. Similarly, a lintel-built chamber at Knockshanawee, also in County Cork (Lee 1911, 59), yielded six ogham stones. At Drumlohan, Co. Waterford (W. Williams 1868–9, 35), ten examples were uncovered in the roof and walls, while at Coolmagort (near Dunloe), Co. Kerry (Graves 1883–4, 312), the roof of the souterrain featured six ogham-inscribed lintels while a seventh ogham stone acted as a supporting pillar.

The prime importance of ogham stones in relation to souterrains is their relatively precise dating. No modern writer has ever credibly placed them outside a fourth–eighth-century AD time-span. Indeed, as the ogham stones were probably mostly Christian commemorative stones, their appearance in Ireland

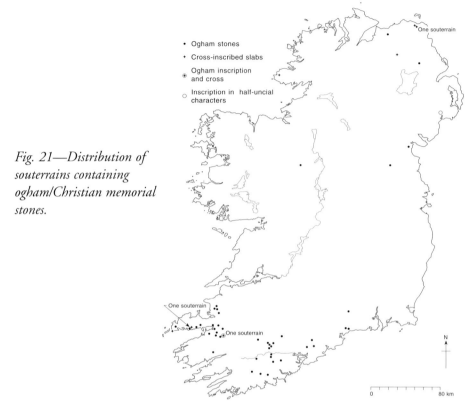

- • Ogham stones
- ✦ Cross-inscribed slabs
- ⊕ Ogham inscription and cross
- ○ Inscription in half-uncial characters

One souterrain

One souterrain

One souterrain

One souterrain

N

0   80 km

Fig. 21—Distribution of souterrains containing ogham/Christian memorial stones.

cannot have pre-dated the late fourth century at the earliest. Mac Niocaill (1972, 22) has stated that Christianity had arrived in the south of the island by at least the early fifth century. The fact that ogham stones also occurred in Wales proved to be extremely beneficial. The prime importance of these ogham stones lay in the bilingual ogham/Latin inscriptions. These constituted an otherwise unavailable body of evidence in the form of their palaeography which would appear to place them in a mid-fifth- to mid-sixth-century time-frame (Jackson 1950, 205). As there are no known souterrains in Wales it may be suggested that the widespread adaptation of the latter monument in Ireland post-dated the era of the Welsh colonies. These settlements are generally accepted to have disappeared by the end of the seventh century (Richards 1960, 144).

It has long been maintained that the reuse of ogham stones as building material in souterrains indicates a period when they were no longer regarded as sacrosanct. The decline in the use of ogham on memorial stones would appear to have begun in the latter half of the sixth century and to have been completed by the early seventh century (McManus 1991, 97). From the eighth century onward it was replaced by conventional script (*ibid.,* 128). The key issue to be addressed is whether or not all of the ogham stones had to be perceived as 'redundant' before any were taken by the souterrain-builders. Indeed, one need look no further than cross-inscribed slabs (see below) to better understand the relevance of the question.

Recent research by McManus has produced an outline relative chronology of ogham inscriptions (1991, 92). This work has been of invaluable assistance in the dating of many of the ogham stones incorporated into souterrains (see, for example, F. Moore 1998). What has emerged is that many of the souterrains can now be seen to contain ogham stones of varying dates. A number of examples will illustrate the point. The souterrain at Monataggart, Co. Cork (Ferguson 1870–9c, 292; see Appendix 1), contained four ogham stones, ranging in date from the early fifth century to the late sixth or early seventh century (F. Moore 1998, 28, 29). The souterrain at Tinnahally, Co. Kerry (Brash 1870–9c, 186; see Appendix 1), contained two ogham stones, dating from the middle to the second half of the sixth century and from the later sixth century respectively (F. Moore 1998, 29). Again, the souterrain at Rockfield, Co. Kerry (Brash 1870–9a; see Appendix 1), contained four ogham stones, ranging in date from the early or mid-fifth century to the middle or second half of the sixth century (F. Moore 1998, 28, 29). It can thus be stated with certainty that the souterrain at Monataggart was constructed at some point after the early seventh century. Similarly, Tinnahally and Rockfield cannot have been constructed earlier than the later sixth century. It is nevertheless impossible to say just exactly when they were made as they could conceivably have been built centuries later.

There are also many examples of souterrains containing only one ogham stone (see Table 2, Appendix 1). In a number of cases these stones are of an early date. For example, the souterrain at Burnfort, Co. Cork (Oldham 1840–4, 516; see Appendix 1), contained an ogham stone of early fifth-century date (F. Moore 1998, 28). Similarly, the souterrain at Corkaboy, Co. Kerry (Ferguson 1887, 111; see Appendix 1), contained an ogham stone belonging to the first half of the sixth century (F. Moore 1998, 28). While it might be suggested that souterrains containing several ogham stones, particularly of wide-ranging dates, had profited from the looting of a neighbouring cluster (a commemorative cemetery?), the occurrence of a single ogham stone might suggest the purloining of a former boundary stone or territorial charter stone. Should a territory change hands, or experience an altered border, it seems perfectly plausible that the new incumbents would be more than anxious to remove the visible manifestation of a former claimant. Thus it is not impossible that the souterrain at Burnfort, for example, could have been built at any time after, say, the mid-fifth century. The two most convincing arguments against this projected early looting of ogham stones, and in turn the construction of souterrains, are (a) the absence of the monument in Wales and the implied watershed of the end of the seventh century

(Richards 1960, 144), and (b) the fact that the earlier stones in the suggested clusters in the vicinity of, for example, Monataggart or Rockfield were left undisturbed for almost 200 and almost 150 years respectively. The most striking evidence in favour of an early date for the looting of at least some of the stones comes from Liscahane, Co. Cork (Ó Donnabháin 1982). The drystone-built souterrain at the site contained two ogham stones which had been employed as roofing lintels. The inscriptions can be dated to the sixth or seventh century (Fionnbarr Moore, pers. comm.). What is most important about this site is that it proved possible to take charcoal samples from the construction trench of the souterrain. The resulting dates were found to centre on the sixth century (D. Power *et al.* 1997, 281). Thus it may be advanced that the ogham stones were looted at that time. It is very possible, therefore, that the looting of ogham stones for the construction of souterrains spanned several centuries.

The apparently strategic placement of a number of ogham-inscribed stones in souterrains warrants attention. At Ballybarrack (Souterrain 3), Co. Louth (E.P. Kelly, pers. comm.), an ogham stone capped the entrance to an inner passage; at Spiddal, Co. Meath (Eogan 1990, 55), an ogham stone occurred immediately after the double stepped feature in Passage 1; at Rathkenny, Co. Kerry (McManus 1991, 68), one of the ogham stones was set over the entrance to the passage leading to the northern chamber, while a second was originally set above the entrance to the passage leading to the southern chamber. Many other ogham stones may similarly have been placed in a strategic setting, but unfortunately a significant proportion of the total number were carelessly removed from the host souterrains by over-enthusiastic antiquarians in the last century.

The ogham-inscribed stone found in the souterrain at Gearha South, Co. Kerry, has been described as a free-standing, non-functional pillar (McManus 1991, 70; A. O'Sullivan and Sheehan 1996, 232). This would certainly suggest a possible ulterior motive for its presence. It should be noted, however, that the souterrain had been completely destroyed prior to its investigation (O'Kelly and Kavanagh 1954a, 50), and that the pillar may originally have been topped with small wedging stones (inserted between the relevant roofing lintel and the top of the pillar) after the fashion of the pillar/roofing lintel arrangement featured at Carhoovauler, Co. Cork (McCarthy 1977, 181). Nonetheless, a free-standing, non-functional symbolic presence for the ogham pillar cannot be automatically excluded.

The occurrence of the two ogham stones in the drystone section of the souterrain/natural cave complex at Glenballythomas (Rathcroghan), Co. Roscommon, is of particular interest in the light of the Gearha South debate. Lucas (1971–3, 188) has recorded the importance of this 'cave' in the historical literature, while Herity (1987, 138) has advanced the possibility that the subterranean feature may have been enclosed by a monument of a ritual nature. The inscription on one of the stones refers to Maeve ('vraicci MAQI MEDVVI' — 'of Fraic son of Medf') (Waddell 1998, 352), which makes it all the more intriguing. Indeed, the evidence from the northern 'half' of the island in general is of particular interest. It raises an important question. Why are the only known ogham stones in County Londonderry (at Dunalis) and in County Antrim (at Carncome) located in souterrains? It was hardly due to a lack of local building material as no less than 409 other souterrains (Cleere 1990, 22) were constructed in County Antrim alone, without the inclusion of ogham stones. Furthermore, it should be noted that one of the two known stones in County Louth (at Ballybrack) and three of the five known ogham stones in County Meath (at Spiddal) also came from souterrains. Even in the extreme south it is quite surprising to discover that 55 of the 88 known ogham stones in County Cork (see Appendix 1) were uncovered in souterrains. It must be considered as a distinct possibility, therefore, that the souterrain-builders actively sought out ogham stones rather than simply 'stumbling' upon them.

There are known examples of ogham memorial stones of related individuals being uncovered in the one souterrain, for example at Knockshanawee, Co. Cork (two brothers), and, potentially, at Rockfield, Co. Kerry (father and son?) (McManus 1991, 53, 54). The relationship between these people and the souterrain-builders would be of particular interest, especially in areas of relative stability and thus continuity. If the majority of souterrains were to be accepted as primarily functioning as refuges, then they would only have been fully employed in times of extreme danger — in human terms, in times of anxiety. In this context, could it be possible that some of these memorial stones were regarded as a type of 'charm', and that it was for perceived quasi-talismanic properties as opposed to an alleged redundancy that at least some examples found themselves redeployed in souterrains? Obviously such an altered perception could only have occurred after their primary *raison d'être* was on the wane. Alternatively, if a given area was overrun by an intrusive, non-related grouping, the ogham stones might have been regarded, and subsequently used, in a more functional fashion. Thus the relationship or non-relationship between those individuals commemorated on the ogham stones and the souterrain-builders could conceivably have had some effect on the timing of the looting of the stones.

A limited number of cross-inscribed slabs and Christian memorial stones have also been discovered in souterrains. These slabs or stones can be divided into three categories:

    (i) cross-inscribed slabs;

    (ii) personal memorial slabs (featuring inscriptions written in the half-uncial character);

(iii) stones featuring ogham inscriptions accompanied by an incised cross.

Cross-inscribed slabs

There are eight recorded examples. These were discovered in souterrains at Drumeeny, Co. Antrim (two slabs) (Langtry 1870–1, 573; BNFC 1874, 212; O'Laverty 1879–82, 108; 1887, 422; Hamlin 1976, 437); at Straid, Glencolumcille, Co. Donegal (four slabs) (Price 1941, 87; Herity 1971, 20; Lacy 1983, 289; Herity *et al.* 1997, 103); at Aghacarrible, Co. Kerry (Graves 1864–74, 425; Ferguson 1887, 27; Macalister 1897, 21; 1896–1901, 280; 1945–9, I, 135; R. Orpen 1908–12, 14; Cuppage 1986, 104); and at Coumeenoole North, Co. Kerry (Macalister 1896–1901, 279; Cuppage 1986, 90).

The inscribed cross in the souterrain at Drumeeny, Co. Antrim, was described as a 'large Latin cross, formed by double incised lines', and as 'very regular, and extremely well executed' (Langtry 1870–1, 573). The sandstone slab upon which it was engraved was employed as a roofing lintel. Significantly, it was placed directly over the entrance to the second oblong chamber. A second flagstone, featuring a simpler equal-armed cross, had been removed from the souterrain to a nearby house. Its original position in the souterrain was not recorded.

In the roof of the eastern passage in the souterrain at Straid (Glencolumcille), Co. Donegal, a lintel features the (apparent) stem of an engraved cross, after the fashion of the design featured on the stones at Gannew and Curreen, Co. Donegal (Lacy 1983, 266), and at Cashel, also Co. Donegal (Herity 1971, 20). All that is now on display is a circular central depression surrounded by a circle, with the attached stem-line extending beyond the limits of the upper wall of the passage (see Pl. 24).

Three new cross-slabs have recently been discovered in the same souterrain (Herity *et al.* 1997, 81). Two were incorporated into the roof, while the third was utilised as a roof-support (whether the latter repair was carried out in antiquity or represents an imaginative 'modern' redeployment from a surface context is unclear). The two slabs incorporated into the roof feature a Latin cross and a cross-in-circle motif respectively, while the pillar-stone displays a simple linear Latin cross (*ibid.*, 103). A side slab in the wall of the 'eastern' chamber in the souterrain at Aghacarrible, Co. Kerry, featured two incised crosses. Both were encircled except for their stem-lines, which extended beyond the circles and terminated in bifurcated endings.

No specific data were available on the alleged cross-inscribed slab from the souterrain at Coumeenoole North, Co. Kerry.

Six groups of cross-forms have been identified by Lionard (1960–1, 97).

While there is a recognisable chronology, it was stressed that this is compromised by the fact that 'old forms inclined to linger' (*loc. cit.*). O'Kelly (1957–9, 80) suggested a developmental process ranging from a simple incised cross-in-circle motif to elaborate forms, for example the design on the cross at Church Island, Co. Kerry (O'Kelly and Kavanagh 1954b, 101).

The simple linear cross motif, as displayed on the examples from Drumeeny, was introduced into Ireland in the sixth century (Lionard 1960–1, 156). Recumbent stones, however, only made their appearance in the eighth century. Lionard suggested that plain outline crosses were used on recumbent slabs from the early eighth century but that their dating was as 'diverse as the crosses themselves' (*ibid.*, 108). He highlighted the ninth century as the century of the ringed crosses, adding that before it had passed expansional crosses had begun to supersede them (*ibid.*, 156).

The exposed element of the original cross at Straid, Co. Donegal, would conform to Lionard's description of crosses in circles that had 'handles', after the fashion of a flabellum, added to them (*ibid.*, 137).

Memorial inscriptions (half-uncial character)
There appears to be only one proven example of a stone featuring an inscription executed in the Latin or 'Celtic' languages (in half-uncial character) from a souterrain in Ireland. This occurred on a slab built 'into the end' (O'Laverty 1878, 91) of the souterrain at Naghan (Seaforde), Co. Down (Ferguson 1870–9b, 131; O'Laverty 1879–82; Macalister 1945–9, II, 121; Jope 1966, 116; Hamlin 1976, 687). Jope (1966, 116) suggested that the inscription was of a tenth-century date.

A second possible example was discovered in a souterrain at Clashygowan, Co. Donegal (Raftery 1956a). However, the inscription, which occurred on a small slab found in one of the two oblong chambers, would appear to have been of eighteenth- or nineteenth-century date.

Ogham inscriptions (accompanied by an incised cross)
Of the 41 known ogham stones featuring one or more crosses, only one stone was definitely uncovered in a souterrain. This was at the renowned site of Coolmagort (Dunloe), Co. Kerry (C. Graves 1885–6, 605; S.P. Ó Ríordáin 1965, 32; A. O'Sullivan and Sheehan 1996, 227). There is a strong possibility that a further example was uncovered at Whitefield, Co. Kerry (Macalister 1945–9, I, 208). The stone in question was one of four, of which two were definitely and two probably discovered in the one souterrain.

The cross at Coolmagort was small and simple and was inscribed in a circle. The cross at Whitefield, although larger, was also simple and was not encircled.

The position of the cross(es) on the majority of the ogham stones was such that it/they did not interfere with the actual inscriptions. Thus it is impossible to decide upon their relative order of appearance on the stone, or whether in fact they were contemporary features or not. However, in some instances, for example at Ballynahunt, Co. Kerry (Macalister 1945–9, I, 164), where the cross was executed on the original butt of the stone and was thus inverted with respect to the inscription, it could be shown that the incised cross was of a later date. Inversely, it is quite evident that the ogham inscription on the stone discovered at Church Island, Co. Kerry (O'Kelly and Kavanagh 1954b, 104), post-dated the accompanying exquisitely executed Maltese cross design as the inscription defaced the cross.

The position of the inscribed cross at Coolmagort is interesting. It is on the face of the pillar that is uppermost, i.e. the buried upper face of the 'lintel'. This would seem to imply that its presence was of little interest to the souterrain-builders (unless it was facing upwards/outwards to ward off harm).

Macalister (1945–9, I, 208) suggested that the cross at Whitefield was a later addition. Similarly, the cross at Coolmagort, because of its dimensions and execution, gives the impression of being an 'afterthought'. Neither form can be closely dated (Lionard 1960–1, 97, 155).

Material from the early historic period

The vast majority of the datable finds discovered in souterrains in Ireland belong to the latter half of the first millennium and the earliest centuries of the second millennium AD. The assemblage of objects in question may be arranged into a number of categories.

Coins

A hoard of eight coins was discovered during a rescue excavation conducted by Paul Gosling at Marshes Upper (Souterrain 2), Co. Louth (*Evening Press*, 10 December 1980). The coins were subsequently published by Michael Kenny (1987, 507), who identified them as seven Anglo-Saxon pennies of Aethelraed II and one Hiberno-Norse penny of Sitric III. He stated that the hoard had been deposited between 995 and 1000 (*ibid.*, 509). The excavations at Knowth, Co. Meath, revealed the presence of two coins on the floor of Souterrain 2 (Eogan 1977, 73) — a silver penny of Aethelstan and a silver penny of Eadred (Dolley 1969, 16). It was determined that these two Anglo-Saxon pennies had been lost about the middle of the tenth century (*ibid.*, 19; Gerriets 1985, 134). The surviving coins from a hoard discovered in the entrance area of a souterrain at

Castlefreke, Co. Cork, were also of mid-tenth-century date (Pagan 1974, 62). Interestingly, two of the surviving coins bore the name Aethelstan (McCarthy 1977, 484). Two silver Hiberno-Norse coins of eleventh/twelfth-century date were found in a backfilled souterrain at Downpatrick, Co. Down (Brannon 1988a, 295; 1988b, 6). It was suggested that the coins had been lost *c.* 1100. No further details were provided.

Personal objects

Ringed pins and stick-pins, forms of dress-pin or fastener, have been recorded at a variety of sites of later first/early second-millennium date in Ireland, including ringforts, crannogs and Viking settlements. The excavations at Dublin were instrumental in establishing a typological sequence for the later forms of the ringed pins (Fanning 1994, 57) and for the stick-pins (O'Rahilly 1998, 32).

Ringed pins have been found in a number of souterrains in Ireland. While some were simply found lying on the floor of a passage or chamber, and might thus be described as 'casual finds', there are a number of examples that came to light as a result of scientific excavation.

At Crossdrum Lower, Co. Meath (Rotheram 1915, 171), a bronze ringed pin was discovered (apparently) on the floor of the chamber. It featured a kidney-shaped ring and a polyhedral-shaped head. The outer facets of the head were decorated with a brambled motif. This type of pin has been dated to the late tenth–twelfth century (Fanning 1983, 329; 1988, 168; 1994, 54). Antiquarian exploration of the combined passage grave/souterrain complex at Dowth, Co. Meath (Frith 1974, 247; Deane 1887–91, 161; Coffey 1912, 48), led to the discovery of three pins (or elements of pins) (Pl. 13). One of these was an almost complete bronze ringed pin, found in the southern beehive chamber. It was plain-ringed and loop-headed. This type of pin enjoyed a long tenure and has been dated to between the late fourth/fifth and tenth centuries (Fanning 1969, 9; 1994, 52). A copper pin with a looped head was found in the integrated northern chamber of the passage grave. The ring was missing, and the problem thus arises as to whether it was of the spiral, plain or knob type. There is also the possibility that it was originally part of a penannular or pseudo-penannular brooch (Fanning 1994, 9). The third pin, also discovered in the southern chamber of the souterrain, was a bronze stick-pin (Armstrong 1921–2, 85) which featured three small protuberances at the extremities of its brambled, lozenge-shaped head. While stick-pins can be assigned an eleventh–thirteenth-century date range (Fanning 1983, 329; 1994, 56), there are some suggestions that pins with a brambled motif on the head might have emerged in the late tenth century (Raghnall Ó Floinn, pers. comm.).

An excavation at Ballyarra, Co. Cork (Fahy 1953, 55), uncovered an unroofed souterrain. The structure, judging by the nature of the fill, had come to be used as a dump by the inhabitants of the associated unenclosed settlement. Two elements of pins were discovered in backfill in the chamber — a bronze pin with a perforated baluster head, and an iron pin with a looped head. Perforated baluster-headed pins have been shown to have featured a spiral or (less commonly) a plain ring (Fanning 1994, 52, 54). While the former combination would place the pin between the late fourth/fifth and tenth centuries, the latter combination would indicate an early eighth–tenth-century date (*loc. cit.*). There are similar dating problems with the iron pin: as has been noted above, the simple looped type was combined with a number of different types of ring.

An earth-cut souterrain, originally featuring a wooden roof, was uncovered in a ringfort at Letterkeen, Co. Mayo (S.P. Ó Ríordáin and MacDermott 1951–2, 89). The upcast from the digging of the souterrain had covered over some earlier strata. A bronze ringed pin with a perforated baluster-shaped head and a spiral ring lay beneath these deposits (on the original ground-surface level) (*ibid.,* 105). This type of ringed pin has been shown to be one of the earliest forms known in Ireland (Fanning 1994, 52). It had gone out of fashion by the time of the Viking incursions (*ibid.,*13), and thus can be placed in a late fourth/early fifth–ninth-century time-frame (*ibid.,* 52–3).

The backfill covering a drystone-built souterrain at Craig Hill, Co. Antrim (Waterman 1956b, 87), contained a bronze ringed pin. It was of the looped-head/plain ring type and thus can be dated to the late fourth/early fifth–tenth-century period (Fanning 1969, 9; 1994, 52). An iron variation of this type was uncovered in Souterrain 2 at Knowth, Co. Meath (George Eogan, pers. comm.), which also produced a bronze ringed pin. It was polyhedral-headed and featured a plain ring. The head was decorated on the front and back with a cruciform design, and on the top and the upper facets with ring-and-dot motifs. This pin was discovered in primary fill on the floor of the souterrain. Its type has been dated to the eighth–tenth centuries (Fanning 1994, 54). A further example of this type of pin was uncovered on the floor of the souterrain at Balrenny, Co. Meath (Eogan and Bradley 1977, 102), and a fragment of a bronze pin was found in the fill of Souterrain A at Cahercommaun, Co. Clare (Hencken 1938, 72).

The stick-pin from Dowth has already been referred to above. Further examples are known from Knowth, Co. Meath, and from a number of sites in County Louth. The pin from Knowth came from the fill in the passage of Souterrain 4. It was bronze and had a biconical head (G. Eogan, pers. comm.). A pin at Donaghmore, Co. Louth, was discovered in black fill on the passage floor, close to the unroofed entrance of Souterrain A (Rynne 1965a). It had an undecorated bulbous head. At Farrandreg, Co. Louth, a copper-alloy stick-pin with a curving shaft was recovered from backfill in a delintelled chamber (D.

Murphy 1998, 267). While the writer categorised the pin as being of the Class 3 non-functional kidney-ringed type (*ibid.*, 275), it might be suggested that it is in fact closer to the Class 9 club-headed type (O'Rahilly 1998, 28), dating from the eleventh–thirteenth centuries (Fanning 1983, 329; 1994, 56). A bronze stick-pin with a flattened and notched head was found in fill used to block the entrance to Souterrain 4B at Marshes Upper, Co. Louth (Gowen 1992, 94). A date in the twelfth or thirteenth century was suggested for the pin (*ibid.*, 110). The base of a stick-pin also came from fill in Souterrain 3A at the same location (*ibid.*, 94). Curiously, there is at least a century between the dates assigned to the stick-pins from the Dublin excavations (O'Rahilly 1998, 32) and the stick-pins from the Waterford excavations (Scully 1997, 439), the latter group being the later in date.

Another form of dress-fastener was the pseudo-penannular ring-brooch (Fanning 1994, 5). These have been described as 'distant cousins of the ringed pins' (*loc. cit.*) and ultimately owe their origins to the pseudo-penannular brooches. At Cush, Co. Limerick, two bronze 'ring-headed pins' (S.P. Ó Ríordáin 1938–40, 149) were discovered in the fill of the unroofed Souterrain 8. One was described as featuring a setting for a stud of some material and (at the lower side of the ring) an attached animal-head projection (*loc. cit.*). This would appear to be a pseudo-penannular ring-brooch as opposed to a ringed pin. The second 'ring-headed pin' was very corroded; the proffered description is unfortunately lacking in detail. Judging by the illustration (*ibid.*, 147), the ring would appear to have featured buffer-terminals but this is not certain. It is possible, therefore, that it too may have been a pseudo-penannular ring-brooch, but it is not impossible that it could have been a loop-headed/plain ring type of ringed pin. Pseudo-penannular ring-brooches were in vogue during the second half of the eighth and the early ninth centuries (Fanning 1994, 5). Stenberger (1966, 44) recorded the discovery of a 'ring pin' at Raheennamadra, Co. Limerick, on top of the eastern wall of the northern chamber of the unroofed souterrain (the roof was probably made of wood). The ring was described as 'penannular with wide, flat, undecorated terminals' (*loc. cit.*). It would appear to be a penannular ring-brooch as opposed to a ringed pin. These were in fashion in the eighth and early ninth centuries (Fanning 1994, 5; Edwards 1990, 142).

A magnificent silver penannular brooch was discovered in Souterrain B at Cahercommaun, Co. Clare (Hencken 1938, 27), in the layer of ashes that covered the floor of the souterrain. It was suggested that the brooch had been manufactured about the year 800 (*ibid.*, 30).

Excavations conducted by Paul Gosling at Marshes Upper (Souterrain 2), Co. Louth, produced what was described as being probably a ringed pin or possibly a small brooch (Kelly 1986, 189). The object was heavily corroded and featured an incomplete loop (*ibid.,* 197) which had been realised by hammering flat the end of a length of bronze wire and rolling it over (*ibid.,* 180). The object was a mere 4.44cm in length. The find was made in primary fill on the floor of the souterrain and was assigned an eighth–tenth-century date. The object has since been re-evaluated and is now accepted as a ring-brooch of ninth–tenth-century date (E.P. Kelly, pers. comm.).

A fragment of a bone pin was discovered in Souterrain 1 at Killally, Co. Louth (Clinton and Stout 1997, 132–3). It featured a very roughly faceted polyhedral head with a circular disc on top. Only a fragment of the shank had survived. A 'rude' bone pin was recorded in the souterrain at Ardbraccan, Co. Meath (Duignan 1944b). Two bone pins with plain heads were found at the entrance to Souterrain B at Cahercommaun, Co. Clare (Hencken 1938, 73). A similar example was found in the fill of Souterrain A (*ibid.,* 72).

The discovery of beads in souterrains is decidedly rare. Only eight examples are known to date. Souterrain 4 at Cush, Co. Limerick (S.P. Ó Ríordáin 1938–40, 146), produced a light blue glass bead with white lines crossing at three points. These lines enclosed rosette motifs of a more delicate execution. Half of a perforated blue glass bead, featuring light blue circles surrounded by white on a dark blue base, was uncovered in the lower reaches of Souterrain 2 at Knowth, Co. Meath (G. Eogan, pers. comm.). A cylindrical antler bead was discovered in the fill covering the steps at the entrance to Souterrain B at Cahercommaun, Co. Clare (Hencken 1938, 73). A souterrain at Tonregee, Co. Donegal, produced a perforated bead fashioned from a horse's tooth (Topographical Files, NMI). Half a bone barrel-bead with an hourglass perforation was found in the thin basal stratum that constituted the floor level of the souterrain at Killanully, Co. Cork (Mount 1995, 132). A polished stone bead came from the upcast material from Souterrain 3 at Raheens (Ringfort No. 2), Co. Cork (Lennon 1994, 61), while a small black circular bead was recovered from backfill in a delintelled section of the souterrain at Farrandreg, Co. Louth (D. Murphy 1998, 273). An amber bead was amongst the souterrain-related finds from an excavation at Haggardstown, Co. Louth (McLoughlin 2000, 214). Edwards (1990, 93) has written that insufficient work has been done to date on the precise dating of beads of this period. They can, however, be assigned to the latter centuries of the first millennium AD.

Fragments of lignite and jet bracelets have been recovered from souterrains. A portion of a lignite bracelet was found at Dowth, Co. Meath (Frith 1974, 248). It featured a D-shaped section, a profile characteristic of many examples from the early historic period (Edwards 1990, 96). A possible additional example came from Haggardstown, Co. Louth (McLoughlin 2000, 214). A fragment of a jet bracelet was recovered from the souterrain at Coggrey, Co. Antrim (Lawlor

1916–18, 101). A fragment of a lignite bracelet was recorded in the souterrain at Ardbraccan, Co. Meath (Duignan 1944b). Neither of the latter objects is available for study. Fragments of one and of two jet bracelets were uncovered in Souterrain 6 and Souterrain 7 respectively at Knowth, Co. Meath (G. Eogan, pers. comm.). Roughly one quarter of a jet bracelet (slit longitudinally) came from the blocking fill in Souterrain 4A at Marshes Upper, Co. Louth (Gowen 1992, 102). Edwards (1990, 96) has also commented on the inadequacy of research on the dating of these objects.

Both men and women of the period would have been, presumably, quite hirsute, and combs would have been of no little personal importance. Interestingly, very few combs have been recovered from souterrains. A fragment of a bone comb was uncovered in the fill of Souterrain B at Cahercommaun, Co. Clare (Hencken 1938, 73). It was later categorised as a Class B comb by Dunlevy (1988, 377) and assigned a third–ninth/early tenth-century date (*ibid.,* 356). Souterrain 6 at Knowth, Co. Meath, produced a comb (G. Eogan, pers. comm.). It was categorised as a Class G type and can thus be assigned an eleventh–thirteenth-century date (Dunlevy 1988, 369). Both Souterrain 1 and Souterrain 2 at Knowth also produced small fragments of combs (G. Eogan, pers. comm.). A Class DI comb was recovered from the souterrain at Spiddal, Co. Meath (Eogan 1990, 48). Combs of this class are dated to the fifth–tenth centuries (Dunlevy 1988, 359). Several fragments of a Class F2 comb came from a primary silt stratum on the entrance ramp to Souterrain 4B at Marshes Upper, Co. Louth (Gowen 1992, 99). The endplate of a comb (almost identical to that of the previous find) was found on the floor of Souterrain 3B at the same location (*ibid.,* 98). It was therefore also accepted as a Class F2 comb. This class has been assigned a late ninth–twelfth-century date (Dunlevy 1988, 365).

Weaponry

Objects which might be categorised under this heading are noticeably scarce.

There are no known examples of a sword of early historic date from a souterrain in Ireland. This is somewhat surprising, given that the standard native Irish swords of the period were appreciably short — the longest known example being 66.6cm in total length (Rynne 1981, 93). Swords of this size would have been serviceable inside the larger souterrains. The only tenuous link with a sword was provided by a rune-inscribed copper-alloy strap-end that was discovered in the (back?)fill above the souterrain at Greenmount, Co. Louth (Lefroy 1871, 478). This bears an inscription which reads 'Domnall Sealshead owns this sword', and thus may be accepted as part of a sword fitting. It was assigned a date of *c.* 1100 (Ó Floinn 1992).

Spearheads have also proved to be elusive. Lawlor (1915–16, 33) recorded the discovery of a 'fine javelin head' made of iron in the souterrain at Knockdhu, Co. Antrim. He further described it as being socketed. At Graigue, Co. Galway, a corroded iron spearhead was recovered from disturbed topsoil near the entrance to the souterrain but 'outside the walls of the gallery' (Fitzpatrick 1990). It was assigned a ninth–tenth-century date (*ibid.*) and is probably of sub-Viking type (E. Rynne, pers. comm.).

Examples of axeheads are equally wanting. Lane-Fox (1867, 138) noted that an iron axe in his possession had come from a souterrain; unfortunately he failed to identify the souterrain in question. An iron axehead was uncovered in the fill covering the souterrain passage at Drakestown, Co. Meath (Topographical Files, NMI). It was of Viking type and dated from the ninth/tenth century. It was suggested that Souterrain C at Ballycatteen, Co. Cork, had been 'deliberately filled in' (S.P. Ó Ríordáin and Hartnett 1943–4, 38) at some (late?) point in antiquity. An axehead discovered in the fill 'almost on floor level' (*ibid.,* 41) is of a type that can be dated to the eleventh–sixteenth centuries (Andy Halpin, pers. comm.).

Knives would have served many different purposes, mostly of a domestic or general kind. In the confined spaces of a souterrain it is possible that they took on a defensive role. There was a variety of iron knife types in the early historic period (Edwards 1990, 88). Unfortunately such objects had a long tradition with little alteration in form (Fanning 1976, 156). Owing to their composition (iron) and size, knives have not always survived in a recognisable form. Indeed, there are numerous references in the archaeological literature to highly corroded but possible examples. Nonetheless, there are recorded discoveries of knives in souterrains. Both souterrains at Spiddal, Co. Meath (Eogan 1990, 41), produced knives — a fragment of a one-edged iron knife from Souterrain 2 (*ibid.,* 52), and a socketed knife with curved blade (with a portion of the wooden handle attached) from Souterrain 1 (*ibid.,* 50). Iron knives were recovered from Souterrains A and B at Cahercommaun, Co. Clare (Hencken 1938, 72, 73). A knife with a curved back and a straight cutting edge was found in association with the skull in Souterrain B (*ibid.,* 46). The other knives, although some had been considerably reduced by wear and sharpening, were of simple straight-backed form (*ibid.,* 44, 45). Knives were also found in Souterrains 1, 2 and 4 at Knowth, Co. Meath (G. Eogan, pers. comm.). A tanged iron knife, with the cutting edge apparently on the concave edge of the blade, was uncovered in backfill in Souterrain 3A at Marshes Upper, Co. Louth (Gowen 1992, 96).

Domestic and industrial objects
One of the most striking aspects of life in early historic Ireland was the widespread absence of pottery — the main exception to the rule being in the north-east, where significant remains of a type of domestic pottery have been

found. Many of the earliest discoveries of this pottery occurred in souterrains and hence it became known as Souterrain Ware. It should be stressed, however, that this pottery is also found at other types of settlement of the period (Ryan 1973, 619) and that the term 'Souterrain Ware' is therefore rather misleading. Ryan (1973, 626, 627) has stated that the chronological range of the pottery stretches from the sixth–seventh century (with possible earlier origins) to the second half of the twelfth century (if not later). Edwards (1990, 74, 75) modified this slightly to a seventh/eighth–thirteenth-century time-scale.

A re-reading of the early archaeological literature indicates that considerable amounts of the pottery found in souterrains came from the immediate area of the entrance feature, for example at Knockdhu, Co. Antrim (Lawlor 1915–16, 33), or Drumena, Co. Down (Berry 1926–7, 50). In other cases it can be seen that the souterrains were unroofed or breached in antiquity and that the subsequent infilling of the structure would have resulted in a more extensive spread of surface occupational material. In other words, the pottery was a feature of the associated settlements and had either simply fallen into or been dumped into the souterrains at the point of redundancy.

Limited quantities of imported pottery are also known from the early historic period. There are, to date, no known examples of these wares from a souterrain. Almost 30 sites in Ireland have now produced sherds of E-ware (Edwards 1990, 70). This pottery, possibly of northern or western French origin, survived in use until the seventh or possibly the eighth century. The date of its introduction has not yet been established. It is worth noting that there are some indications that at sites where both souterrains and sherds of E-ware were present, for example Rathmullan, Co. Down (Lynn 1981–2, 65), or Killederdadrum, Co. Tipperary (Manning 1984, 237), the souterrains post-dated the use of the pottery (Lynn 1981–2, 148; Manning 1984, 261). An apparent exception to this pattern occurred at Site 3 at Marshes Upper, Co. Louth, where the two souterrains and an enclosing ditch (containing three sherds of E-ware in the fill) were judged to be contemporary features (Gowen 1992, 58). The problem with this analysis is that the course of Souterrain B, which originated within the enclosure but mostly extended beyond it, would seem to have been deferred to by the ditch. In fact it was established that the ditch stopped short on both flanks of the souterrain (*ibid.*, 71). The possibility that the entrance to the enclosure occurred at this point may be excluded as a causeway, accepted as the entrance by Gowen, was uncovered along the north-eastern flank of the enclosure. The alternative suggestion must be that at least one of the souterrains pre-dated the enclosure (and consequently the E-ware pottery).

Surface occupation material in the entrance to the souterrain at Sheepland Mor, Co. Down (Rees-Jones 1971, 78), contained two sherds of glazed pottery of thirteenth–fourteenth-century date. Their presence would seem to indicate that the souterrain was still open if not in use at this time. Indeed, the question of when exactly souterrains in Ireland became obsolete has not yet been satisfactorily resolved. Elsewhere in the north a number of souterrains remained intact long enough to be blocked with material which contained thirteenth-century English pottery (Mallory and McNeill 1991, 231). The souterrain at Killyglen, Co. Antrim (Waterman 1968, 69), produced a few fragments of 'dark hand-made cooking pottery' of the type found elsewhere in association with English-style glazed wares of thirteenth-century date. There was conclusive evidence at Cloughorr, Co. Antrim (Harper 1972, 60), and convincing evidence at Ballyhornan (Souterrain 2), Co. Down (Lynn 1979, 88), for the deliberate violation and subsequent infilling of the entrances to the souterrains in the medieval period. The introduced material at both sites produced sherds of everted-rim coarseware. This type of pottery, which was a local response to Norman domestic ware, made its appearance in the late twelfth or early thirteenth century (Edwards 1990, 75). Similarly, in the east a thirteenth-century (Caroline Sandes, pers. comm.) potsherd was discovered deep in the hard compact layer which filled the unroofed beehive chamber at Stephenstown, Co. Dublin (Clinton 1998, 120). Again, at Boolies Little, Co. Meath (Sweetman 1982–3, 52), a sherd of medieval pottery, of late thirteenth/early fourteenth-century date, was found in the fill of the delintelled passage. A souterrain at Ballybarrack, Co. Louth (Kelly 1977), had been delintelled and used as a dump in the medieval period, and considerable quantities of pottery of thirteenth–fourteenth-century date were recovered (E.P. Kelly, pers. comm.). At Marshes Upper, Co. Louth (Gowen 1992, 110), it was suggested, again on pottery evidence, that two of the souterrains at the site may have been deliberately blocked, possibly as late as the twelfth century. At Randalstown, Co. Meath (Campbell 1987, 31), it was suggested that the souterrain had been 'largely destroyed probably in the medieval period'. Excavations at Ballycatteen, Co. Cork (S.P. Ó Ríordáin and Hartnett 1943–4, 1), revealed that the souterrains had been 'deliberately filled in' (*ibid.,* 13). Interestingly, the evidence from the pottery would suggest that at least one of the souterrains (Souterrain A) had been filled in at a remarkably late stage (*ibid.,* 38). Sherds of what appears to be fifteenth-century North Devon Ware (Caroline Sandes, pers. comm.) were recovered from the fill, one sherd from close to the floor level of the souterrain.

Quernstones, or more often fragments of quernstones, have been found in souterrains, occasionally as components of the structure. Generally they have either been deposited or simply fallen into the open entrance of the souterrain. At Dunderrow, Co. Cork, the entrance to a constriction had been blocked with a quernstone (O'Mahony 1908–9, 87). Fragments of a quernstone were discovered on the floor of the souterrain at Garranes, Co. Cork (Gillman 1896b, 420). Quernstones were also recovered from the souterrains at Murtyclogh, Co. Clare (T.L. Cooke 1849–51, 297), and Cross, Co. Down (Lawlor 1915–16, 45).

Twenty-six rotary quernstones (complete stones and fragments) were uncovered in Ringfort 10 at Cush, Co. Limerick (S.P. Ó Ríordáin 1938–40, 162). Of these the majority were found in the fill of the unroofed souterrain. Three querns also came from the fill in Souterrain 9 and an unspecified number from the fill in Souterrain 5 (*loc. cit.*). A fragment of a lower stone of a quern was found in the fill of an unroofed souterrain at Lackenavorna (Killederdadrum), Co. Tipperary (Manning 1984, 247). Similarly, one half of a lower stone of a rotary quern and a small fragment of the top stone of a quern came from backfill in Souterrain 4A at Marshes Upper, Co. Louth (Gowen 1992, 102, 103). A rotary quernstone, of 'large diameter' (S.P. Ó Ríordáin 1938–40, 176), had been incorporated into the roof of the western section of Souterrain 4 at Cush, Co. Limerick. Similarly, at Kill, Co. Kerry, a fragment of a disc quernstone had been used in the roofing of the entrance passage (Mary Cahill, pers. comm.).

S.P. Ó Ríordáin (1938–40, 163) observed that none of the querns excavated at Cush was of the beehive type. This was to be expected given that their distribution is confined to the northern two-thirds of the island (Caulfield 1977, 107; B. Raftery 1994, 124) and that none, to date, has been found at a settlement site (Caulfield 1977, 124). Hence it is not surprising that no beehive-type querns have been found in the context of a souterrain site. Neither have there been any specific references to the discovery of a pot-type quern either in or incorporated into a souterrain. Significantly, the latter type of quernstone was not introduced until medieval times (Caulfield 1969, 61). While the available information on the known quernstones from souterrains often lacks detail, the indications are that they were always of the disc-type quern. Unfortunately this type of quern enjoyed a lengthy period of currency, extending from about the first or second century AD (*ibid.*, 61), or slightly earlier (Caulfield 1977, 126), almost up to modern times (Caulfield 1969, 61). While the period of use of the Disc C subtype (the classification is based on the handle feature in the upper stone) can be narrowed, in the main, to the second millennium (*ibid.*, 62), this is of no benefit as no querns of this type have yet been identified in a souterrain.

A major technological advance in milling took place in Ireland in the seventh century with the introduction of the horizontal water-mill (Lucas 1953, 3; Baillie 1975, 26; 1982, 192), which would have reduced the drudgery and increased the production of flour. A millstone was originally incorporated into the wall of the outer chamber in the souterrain at Ballintermon, Co. Kerry (Kelly 1982–3b, 11). Similarly a millstone (possibly unfinished?) had been incorporated into the passage wall of Souterrain 2 at Spiddal, Co. Meath (Eogan

1990, 52). A possible example was recorded in the roof of a chamber in a souterrain at Donaghmore, Co. Louth (Tempest 1912–15, 26). These souterrains were therefore constructed at some point after the early seventh century.

A pruning-hook was retrieved from the floor of a souterrain at Killegland, Co. Meath (Clinton, forthcoming a). It had an overall length of 11cm with a cutting edge of 5cm. The socketed part, which featured an original C-section, contained a square-headed rivet which was still in position. This object may be compared to the two pruning-hooks found at Clontuskert Priory, Co. Galway (Fanning 1976, 138), the 'socketed cutting hook' from Church Island, Co. Kerry (O'Kelly 1957–9, 111), or the 'pruning knife' from Rigsdale, Co. Cork (Sweetman 1981, 202). The latter site is of key importance in the dating of these pruning-hooks. Rigsdale was a medieval moated site which proved possible to date closely. The date advanced was the end of the thirteenth century into the very early fourteenth century (*ibid.,* 205). O'Kelly (1957–9, 111) noted that the Church Island 'hook' had belonged to either a secondary occupation of the island or to some later period. The general material from Clontuskert, despite the lack of stratigraphy at the site (Fanning 1976, 161), would also support a medieval date for the pruning-hooks.

A stone ingot mould of ninth/tenth-century Viking type was discovered in 1947 in a souterrain at Cloan, Co. Cork (Mary Cahill, pers. comm.).

The presence of quernstones and millstones at souterrain sites has already been discussed. Other agricultural implements discovered in this context include a sickle, a ploughshare and a possible ard stone. The iron sickle, found in the wall of the outer chamber of the souterrain at Beaufort, Co. Kerry (Connolly 1992, 20), consisted of a tang (120mm long) and a curved blade (140mm long and 13–19mm wide). It was accepted as an early deposition by the writer and was assigned an early historic date (*ibid.,* 34). The possibility that it might belong to a slightly later period has also been raised (Raghnall Ó Floinn, pers. comm.). An iron ploughshare was uncovered in the basal fill of the unroofed entrance passage of a souterrain at Ballyegan, Co. Kerry (Byrne 1991, 5). It was 172mm in length, 115mm in maximum width, and 65mm in maximum thickness. It was similar to a ploughshare excavated at Wood Quay in Dublin (Brady 1987, 236) which was dated to the tenth century. A possible ard stone came from blocking fill in Souterrain 4A at Marshes Upper, Co. Louth (Gowen 1992, 102). Shaped like a stone axehead, it was 210mm long, 56mm wide and 35mm thick. It might also be noted that the ploughshare (or part of an ard — Edwards 1990, 62) from Kimego West (Leacanabuaile), Co. Kerry (S.P. Ó Ríordáin and Foy 1941, 92; Duignan 1944a, 136), came from the habitation layer in House A — the house directly associated with the souterrain (Ó Ríordáin and Foy 1941, 90).

Other domestic or industrial artefacts with a typical early historic period background have also been recovered from souterrains. A whetstone came from the fill of the unroofed souterrain at Killanully, Co. Cork (Mount 1995, 140); a second came from the entrance area of the souterrain at Farrandreg, Co. Louth (D. Murphy 1998, 267). Two hones were recovered at Marshes Upper, Co. Louth (Gowen 1992, 102), from primary silt in Souterrain 4A and blocking material in Souterrain 3B respectively. Six whetstones were recovered from deep in the fill of the unroofed souterrains at Ballycatteen, Co. Cork (Ó Ríordáin and Hartnett 1943–4, 31). Souterrains A and B at Cahercommaun, Co. Clare (Hencken 1938, 72, 73), each produced a whetstone. The latter souterrain also produced two hemispherical bone spindle-whorls (*ibid.*, 73). A fragment of a bone spindle-whorl came from blocking material in Souterrain 4B at Marshes Upper, Co. Louth (Gowen 1992, 99). Two bone needles were uncovered in primary fill on the floor of the innermost (expanded-terminal) chamber at Farrandreg, Co. Louth (D. Murphy 1998, 271). An iron fish-hook was found in Souterrain 5 at Knowth, Co. Meath (George Eogan, pers. comm.), and an iron chisel in Souterrain 1 at Spiddal, Co. Meath (Eogan 1990, 50). None of these objects, however, aid close dating of their host souterrains.

Miscellaneous objects
The fill of Souterrain A at Cahercommaun, Co. Clare (Hencken 1938, 20), contained a bone top or gaming-piece (*ibid.*, 64): the object could be spun and thus may well have functioned as a top. A carved bone disc found on the floor of a souterrain at Drumcliffe, Co. Sligo (Allen-French 1883–4), is a thirteenth-century (or later) gaming-piece (P.F. Wallace, pers. comm.). Bone dice and gaming-pieces are known from sites of early historic date (Edwards 1990, 86).

Two glazed tiles were discovered on the floor of a rock-cut souterrain at Dunderrow, Co. Cork (O'Mahony 1908–9, 85), both impressed with the identical image of a cock (*ibid.*, 87). The descriptions of the tiles would place them firmly in the medieval period. A corner fragment of a line-impressed glazed tile (featuring a floral motif) was found in the fill of the unroofed Souterrain 4A at Marshes Upper, Co. Louth (Gowen 1992, 105; Eames and Fanning 1988, 72). It was assigned a fourteenth–fifteenth-century date (Gowen 1992, 106).

A small glass vessel was recovered from a souterrain at Mullaroe, Co. Sligo (Topographical Files 1943, NMI). A mere 5cm in height, it is lime green in colour with a pearl banding about the neck. While this vessel, which is probably of Continental origin, has been variously assigned to the ninth century (Harden 1956, 154) and 'towards the end of the early medieval period' (Edwards 1990, 92), the Frankish parallels noted by Bourke (1994, 168) argue convincingly for an early seventh-century date. Owing to its fragile nature it cannot have been long in circulation prior to its deposition in the souterrain.

A flagstone-covered pit in a souterrain at Oldcourt, Co. Cork, contained a moss-wrapped bronze-coated iron hand-bell (Ó Cuileanáin and Murphy 1961–2, 83) of a known early Irish type. It conforms to all specifications of Bourke's Class 1 group (1980, 52), the only slight discrepancy being in its height of 12.5cm (excluding the handle); complete bells of the Class 1 type normally range in height from 14cm to 31cm. Consequently its rectangular mouth (measuring 8cm by 5.5cm) also diverged from the norm. Bourke (1980, 59, 61) assigned Class 1 hand-bells to the period 700–900 (with possible earlier origins and an enduring reputation).

An openwork cast-bronze mount was found in blocking material at the entrance to Souterrain 4C at Marshes Upper, Co. Louth (Gowen 1992, 94). It was 65mm long, 30mm wide and 3mm thick, and consisted of 'four perforated circular elements joined by C-shaped curves' (*loc. cit.*). A corroded oval element, featuring a possible zoomorphic design, crowned the object. Its other extremity terminated in a horizontal bar. Although there are no parallels for this object in Ireland it may have been a belt-hook of Continental origin (*ibid.*, 96).

A composite bronze escutcheon from a bowl was uncovered at the outer edge of the entrance passage to Souterrain 1 at Spiddal, Co. Meath (Eogan 1990, 48, 49). The escutcheon-plate was subcircular and would originally have featured three thistle-headed appendages (one was missing) riveted to each side and the base (Newman 1989–90, 47). The fact that the escutcheon would have been riveted to the bowl indicated a mid-eighth-century date (Newman 1990, 58). A small iron escutcheon or hook found in silt deposits beneath paving-stones in the chamber of Souterrain 4B at Marshes Upper, Co. Louth (Gowen 1992, 96), featured a centrally placed rivet.

A small bronze (bronzed tin?) patera was found by T.N. Deane in a souterrain at Monasterboice, Co. Louth (Topographical Files, NMI). It is probable, but not definite, that this was the mainly rock-cut souterrain that lies immediately north-west of the graveyard (Pentland 1898, 265; Keenan 1945–8, 52; Gosling 1981, 78). The patera is circular with a diameter of 4.5cm. It takes the form of a very shallow, flat-bottomed dish with a raised (flattened) rim, and is no more than 2–3mm deep. It survives in two fragments. The slight indications of a handle might suggest that it was originally part of a larger object. It has no parallels in the Irish archaeological record.

A fragment of gold foil decorated in the Urnes style was recovered from the backfill in an unroofed souterrain at Downpatrick, Co. Down (Brannon 1988b, 6). No further details were provided. The Irish Urnes style flourished in the late eleventh/early twelfth century (Graham-Campbell 1987, 150).

The scientific dating evidence

There is a dearth of scientifically derived evidence on the dating of souterrains. There are, in fact, only approximately half a dozen dates available for the *c.* 3500 souterrains in Ireland.

The most spectacular result came from Coolcran, Co. Fermanagh (B. Williams 1985, 75), where dendrochronology provided a date of AD 822 ± 9 for the wood-built souterrain.

The remaining scientific data have been provided by the radiocarbon dating method.

In 1981 the remains of a levelled univallate ringfort were excavated at Liscahane, Co. Cork (Ó Donnabhain 1982). It was found to contain a drystone-built souterrain. The limits of the construction trench were defined: it was 2.2m wide (on average) and lay up to 3.5m below the modern ground level (D. Power *et al.* 1997, 281). It proved possible to take charcoal samples from the trench. These yielded radiocarbon dates that centre on the sixth century AD (*loc. cit.*). Crucially, owing to the context, this would represent the construction phase of the souterrain.

During 1961 and 1962 a univallate platform ringfort at Raheennamadra, Co. Limerick, was excavated by a team of archaeologists from Sweden (Stenberger 1966). The remains of a circular house with an adjoining souterrain were discovered in the interior of the ringfort. The souterrain featured drystone-built walls. Post-holes in the floor indicated the former presence of a wooden roof (*ibid.,* 42). The two southernmost post-holes contained the butts of the original oak posts, one of which yielded a radiocarbon determination of 1260 ± 120 BP (*ibid.,* 52). This has been calibrated to cal. AD 655–975 (Stout 1997, 26). The second post yielded a radiocarbon determination of 1280 ± 120 BP (Stenberger 1966, 52), which has been calibrated to cal. AD 649–938 (Stout 1997, 26). Again, these dates would represent the construction phase of the souterrain.

In 1977 a souterrain was accidentally discovered as a result of quarrying work at Balrenny, Co. Meath (Eogan and Bradley 1977, 96). There were no indications of an enclosure in the exposed earth and thus the souterrain must have been associated with an open settlement site (*ibid.,* 103). A thin layer, no more than 5mm deep, of soggy, dark grey-flecked earth covered the bedrock floor of the souterrain. A number of fragments of wood were recovered from this stratum, including a piece of oak. This was sampled and a radiocarbon determination of 1135 ± 70 BP was obtained. The calibrated date (at two standard deviations) would be cal. AD 722–736 and cal. AD 770–1024 (Stuiver and Pearson 1993). This would represent the functional phase of the souterrain.

A large, almost circular enclosure containing over 29 acres constitutes the townland of Kill, Co. Kerry (Cahill 1989). There is an old cemetery within the enclosure and a local tradition of a church (Toal 1995, 209). In 1987 a drystone-built souterrain was discovered within the enclosure. The skeleton of a young woman was found lying on the floor of the chamber (see Fig. 22), and was dated to 1180 ± 60 BP (Mary Cahill, pers. comm.). The calibrated date (at two standard deviations) would be cal. AD 688–998 (Stuiver and Pearson 1993). Owing to the presence of the body this could be accepted as the time of termination of use of the souterrain.

In 1992 a univallate ringfort was excavated at Killanully, Co. Cork (Mount 1995). It contained a drystone-built souterrain (*ibid.*, 126). Two charcoal samples were taken from the souterrain. The first, from surface habitation material that had spilled into the open entrance feature of the souterrain, yielded a radiocarbon determination of 1155 ± 38 BP, calibrated (at two standard deviations) to cal. AD 779–977 (*ibid.*, 156). The second sample, from between the stones in the wall towards the entrance of the souterrain, yielded a radiocarbon determination of 969 ± 97 BP, calibrated (at two standard deviations) to cal. AD 880–1260 (*ibid.*, 156). There is a considerable time-span involved when both of these results are taken into consideration. However, a two-phase usage of the souterrain, as advanced by Mount (1995, 145), is unconvincing.

The lower-lying trapdoor in a souterrain at Farrandreg, Co. Louth, featured four associated wall-slots (D. Murphy 1998, 269). A carbon sample retrieved from the slots yielded a radiocarbon determination of 1061 ± 44 BP, calibrated (at two standard deviations) to cal. AD 888–1027 (*loc. cit.*). The context of the samples is of particular interest given that the material may represent vestigial remains of elements of the original covering device employed in the trapdoor. Thus the derived date would indicate the period of active use of the souterrain.

The remains of a stone hut site with a souterrain running beneath were recorded at Cool West on Valentia Island, Co. Kerry (Mitchell 1989, 41). A deposit of limpet shells and other debris was exposed on the floor of the souterrain, directly beneath the hut (A. O'Sullivan and Sheehan 1996, 398). It was suggested that these had fallen through the gaps in the lintelled roof of the souterrain (Mitchell 1989, 41). The shells yielded a radiocarbon determination of 930 ± 80 BP (*ibid.*, 10), or (at two standard deviations) cal. AD 1305–1529 (Stuiver and Braziunas 1993). This date would represent the occupation (or post-occupation?) phase of the site.

There can be problems with these methods, however, as was displayed at Darrara (Lisnagun), Co. Cork (J. O'Sullivan 1990, 227), where the proposed date of cal. AD 894–991 for the souterrain was subsequently withdrawn owing

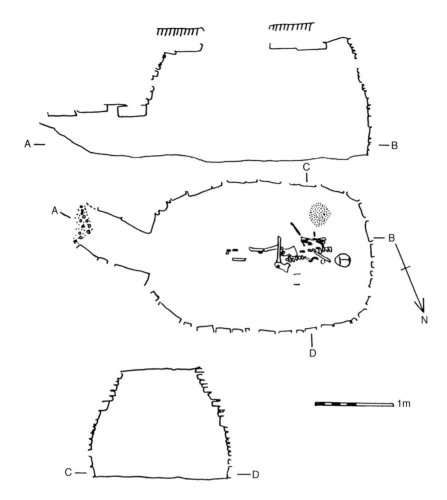

Fig. 22—Kill, Co. Kerry (after Cahill): drystone-built souterrain featuring subrectangular chamber with an extended inhumation (and charcoal spread) on chamber floor.

to doubts about the relative chronology of the stratigraphy at the site (Matthew Stout, pers. comm.).

Summary

Very few artefacts of prehistoric date have been found in souterrains. Not one of these has been proven to come from a primary position, for example from the construction trench or from the original floor stratum of the souterrain.

Ogham stones were incorporated into the structures of 44 known souterrains, mostly located in the south-west. It may be said with certainty that these souterrains were not built until after the fifth century AD. In the case of some of these souterrains, for example Tinnahally and Rockfield, both in County Kerry, and Monataggart, Co. Cork, it has been shown that they were not built until sometime after the later sixth century and the early seventh century respectively.

A substantial body of material, either discovered in souterrains or in their post-use backfilling, clearly belongs to the early historic period. Indeed, it would be difficult to prove that many, if any, of these objects pre-date the seventh century (see Fig. 23). The plain-ring/looped-head ringed pin from Dowth, Co. Meath, for example, could date from the fifth century, but it should be remembered that the same souterrain also produced a late tenth-century bramble-headed stick-pin. As the plain-ring/looped-head ringed pins survived into the tenth century there is no reason why the Dowth example could not have belonged to that period. It is also worth noting that the spiral-ring/baluster-head ringed pin from Letterkeen, Co. Mayo, came from deposits that pre-dated the construction of the souterrain. This type of pin was the earliest in the range. The long survival of such objects as Class B and Class G combs, and indeed disc quernstones, means that the examples from souterrain sites could just as easily all fall into a post-mid-eighth-century time-frame, as opposed to an earlier epoch.

The scientifically derived data, provided by dendrochronology and radiocarbon dating, are supportive, in the main, of the use of souterrains in Ireland in the period between the last quarter of the first millennium AD and the first quarter of the second millennium AD. The souterrain at Coolcran, Co. Fermanagh, was built in the early ninth century; the souterrain at Raheennamadra, Co. Limerick, was built between the seventh and tenth centuries; the souterrain at Balrenny, Co. Meath, was in use at some point between the eighth and eleventh centuries, while the souterrain at Farrandreg, Co. Louth, was active at some stage between the late ninth and early eleventh centuries. The souterrain at Killanully, Co. Cork, was in use from some time between the eighth and tenth centuries and may have remained in use until as late as the thirteenth century. The use of the souterrain at Kill, Co. Kerry, was brought to a (premature?) end at some point between the seventh and tenth centuries. The souterrain at Cool West, Co. Kerry, may still have been open in the fourteenth–sixteenth-century period.

The exception to the rule is the souterrain at Liscahane, Co. Cork. The dates obtained from the charcoal samples taken from the construction trench indicated that it was built in the sixth century. There are suggestions, discussed elsewhere (see Chapter 3), that some souterrains in the south of Ireland may have pre-dated those found in other parts of the island. It should be recalled that the tunnelled souterrrains, which are mostly located in the extreme south, have,

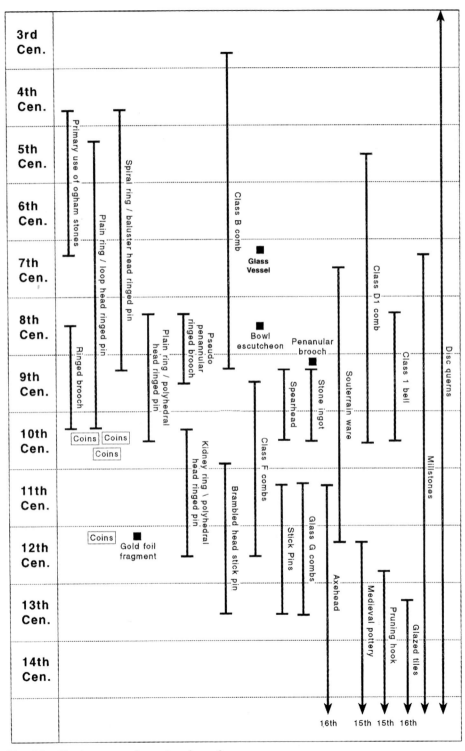

Fig. 23—Dating span of associated artefacts.

frustratingly, generally remained undated. The direct association between some souterrains and round houses in the south may also be indicative of an earlier date.

It is worth noting that at proven multiphase enclosed sites the souterrain will appear late in the sequence of development. At Deer Park Farms, Co. Antrim, a raised rath was continuously occupied for about 400 years (AD 600–1000) (Lynn 1989, 193). Two souterrains had been built in the final stage of occupation (*ibid.*, 197). Interestingly, these were both demolished and filled in before the end of the early historic period (Lynn 1985a). Again, at Rathmullan, Co. Down (Lynn 1981–2, 65), a settlement that began sometime between the mid-fifth and the early seventh century (Lynn 1985b, 131) evolved in stages into a raised rath which in the twelfth century was used as the 'base' for a motte (Lynn 1981–2, 148). The early historic period of occupation consisted of at least four main phases of activity. The souterrain belonged to Phase 3 and occurred at a 'late stage in the site's growth' (*ibid.*, 151). Excavation has also established that the souterrain-related phase at Knowth, Co. Meath (Eogan 1991, 121), was at its zenith in the ninth and tenth centuries.

The literary evidence (see Chapter 1 and Lucas 1971–3, 165, for a comprehensive appraisal) is useful in that it displays a souterrain 'awareness' on the part of the writers. The time of writing or compilation is thus very relevant in determining the period of use of the souterrains.

There are a variety of sources. The classic law-tracts, in their final written form, are not later than the beginning of the eighth century (Ó Corráin 1972, 28, 75). They would have portrayed a stylised version of life in Ireland before, and to a lesser extent during, the period of writing. Byrne (1969, 13) has argued that the annals may be accepted, with some reservations, as representative of contemporary Ireland from the second half of the sixth century. By the eleventh and twelfth centuries they had become quite detailed (Byrne 1971, 165). The *Annals of Ulster*, with their origin in Iona, became locally based (initially at Clonard?) from *c.* 740 onwards (Mac Airt and Mac Niocaill 1983, xi). The *Annals of Tigernach*, a Clonmacnoise compilation, assumed an independent character from the early tenth century (Byrne 1969, 13). The *Annals of Inisfallen* are our richest source for the history of Munster. The first part of the work was compiled in the early eleventh century (Mac Airt 1951, vii). The *Annals of the Four Masters*, a seventeenth-century compilation (Ó Muraíle 1987, 75; P. Walsh 1934, 128), ultimately derived from the Clonmacnoise annals (Byrne 1973, 237). There are many other individual works. The *Cogadh Gaedhel re Gaillaibh*, for example, was a twelfth-century text (Byrne 1969, 5; Ó Corráin 1972, 46).

The consistent thread running through the various individual entries and references is one of familiarity. Interpolation or commentary was apparently deemed unnecessary. It would appear that these writers of the latter phase of the early historic period, and by implication their readers, were fully aware of just exactly what an *uamh* was, and in some cases what their function might be.

The question of when exactly souterrains in Ireland became obsolete has never been satisfactorily resolved. Indeed, it might be argued that they never did! There is, for example, a James II coin from the souterrain at Gortacurraun, Co. Kerry (Cuppage 1986, 153). In the earlier epoch we have seen, from the pottery evidence, that the souterrain at Sheepland Mor, Co. Down, was open in the twelfth century. Similarly, the souterrains at Killegland, Co. Meath, Drumcliffe, Co. Sligo, and Dunderrow, Co. Cork, were open to receive medieval material. At least one of the souterrains at Ballycatteen, Co. Cork, may even have survived into the fifteenth century. There is, however, a strong suggestion, from the pottery evidence, that many souterrains were deliberately backfilled or sealed in the twelfth and thirteenth centuries. One of the souterrains at Ballybarrack, Co. Louth, was unroofed and used as a dump in the fourteenth century, judging by the large amount of medieval pottery in the backfill.

It is very possible that it was the impact and spread of Norman culture across the island that in effect rendered souterrains obsolete. By 1250 the Norman settlement had practically reached its peak (Martin 1967, 137; Otway-Ruthven 1968, 101). Significantly, F.X. Martin (1967, 142) has written that 'once an area was occupied by the Normans it gained peace and order, where previously there had been raids and counter-raids'. In other words, hit-and-run raiding would no longer be the norm. The new arrivals did not withdraw; they settled, and thus the *raison d'être* of the souterrain, the temporary refuge-cum-storage space, disappeared.

In conclusion, most recent writers, for example Warner (1979, 128; 1980, 84), have suggested a *c.* 500–*c.* 1200 date for souterrains in Ireland. It is proposed here that they enjoyed a *c.* 750–*c.* 1250 floruit, with some earlier examples mostly in the south and possibly some later survivals in more remote areas.

6

Structural aspects of souterrains in Ireland

outerrains are composed of a number of structural aspects or modules. The complexity of a given souterrain will thus depend on the number of modules employed by the builders.

When considered on an island-wide basis, there are only two modules which were consistently employed—an entrance feature and a chamber. It is important to stress at the outset that any description of a souterrain as consisting of 'a length of passage' is totally erroneous. A passage must lead somewhere, in this case to a chamber.

Regional variations on the theme add to the list of standard modules. For example, souterrains in the north-east will almost invariably, in their basic form, consist of an entrance feature, an access passage and a chamber. In contrast, earth-cut souterrains in the extreme south will often consist of an entrance feature and a series of short constrictions and chambers.

There are, in addition, over two dozen ancillary structural features which were at the disposal of the souterrain-builders. These were employed, or not, as circumstances and requirements dictated.

In short, the modular nature of souterrains provided the builders with an almost infinite number of variations on a theme. Thus the structures can range in form from a simple entrance feature/chamber arrangement to intricate combinations involving entrance features, several passages, chambers, air-vents and sometimes a trapdoor or two.

The ultimate tribute to the imagination, creativity and adaptability of the souterrain-builders is that no two souterrains are exactly the same.

1 Entrance features

Five types of entrance features are known to date (Fig. 24):
    ramp entrances;

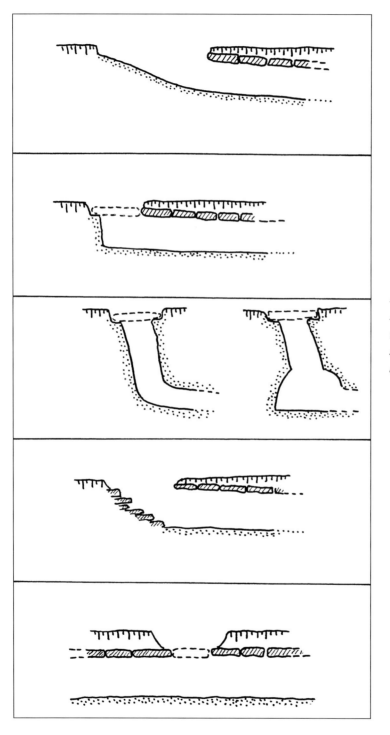

*Fig. 24—
Entrance types:
ramp, pit-drop,
shaft, stepped
and hatch.*

pit-drop entrances;
shaft entrances;
stepped entrances;
hatch entrances.

A small number of souterrains employed an amalgam of entrance types. There are also rare examples of double entrances and external exits (or 'escape passages').

Ramp entrances
Ramp entrances enjoyed a widespread distribution. Most known examples occurred in drystone-built souterrains.

At Donaghmore (Souterrain A), Co. Louth (Rynne 1965a), the entrance to the souterrain originated in a shallow depression, from which a gently sloping ramp facilitated access to the entrance passage. Its total length was less than 1.25m (Fig. 56). Similarly, at Graigue, Co. Galway (Fitzpatrick 1991; Gosling *et al.*, forthcoming, no. 5863), a gently sloping, stone-lined ramp, approximately 3m long, provided access to the entrance passage. The ramp entrance to a souterrain at Smithstown, Co. Meath (Gowen 1989, 34), had been roughly cobbled. Presumably this would have provided a surer footing for those using the souterrain.

Pit-drop entrances
Pit-drop entrances were in effect the unlintelled outer extremities of access passages. The 'drop' area could be either stone-lined or the cut-terminal of the passage trench. This type of entrance occurred more frequently in the north, north-east and south-west than in any other area.

An excavated drystone-built souterrain at Sarsfieldstown, Co. Meath (Kelly 1978), originated in an earth-cut pit. This was simply the outer 1.15m of the passage trench. It was 0.75m wide and 1.1m deep. The entrance to Souterrain 8 at Knowth, Co. Meath (Eogan 1968, 357), consisted of a pit 0.5m in depth. The side walls were stone-lined while the back wall was earth-cut (Fig. 26). A further variation on the format was recorded at Kimego West (Leacanabuaile), Co. Kerry (S.P. Ó Ríordáin and Foy 1941, 90), where the pit was completely stone-lined and was located in the floor of an associated house.

Shaft entrances
Shaft entrances are more commonly represented in tunnelled souterrains and have therefore been mostly recorded in the extreme south and extreme north. Drystone-built versions would appear to be best represented in the west.

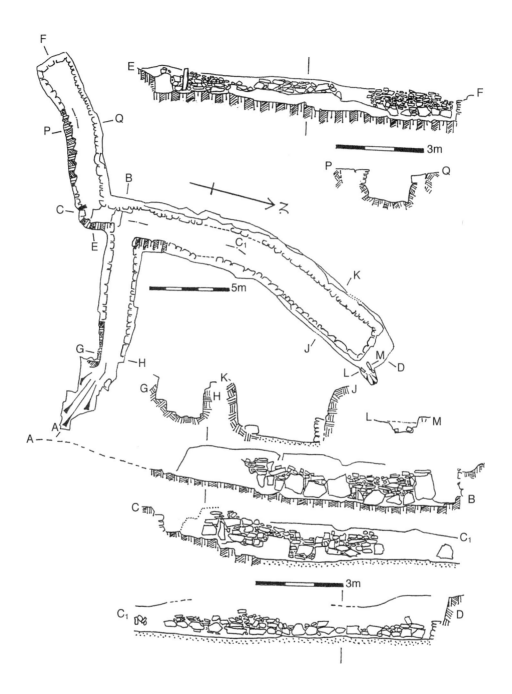

Fig. 25—Marches Upper, Co. Louth (after Gowen), Souterrain 4A: drystone-built souterrain featuring ramp entrance, internal steps, protruding jambstone and air-vent.

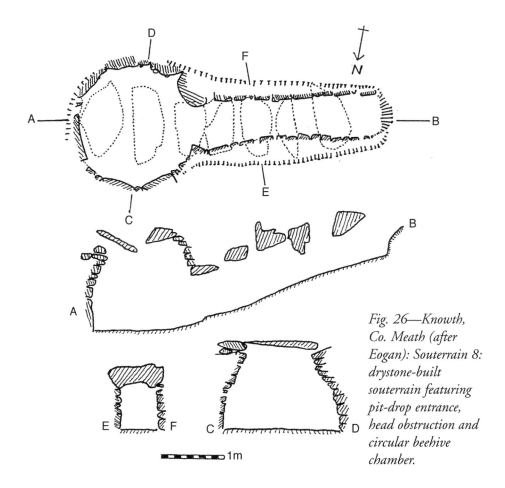

Fig. 26—Knowth, Co. Meath (after Eogan): Souterrain 8: drystone-built souterrain featuring pit-drop entrance, head obstruction and circular beehive chamber.

The tunnelled versions occur in two basic forms. The simple shaft entrance will descend directly through the roof of a chamber, at a pronounced angle, for example as at Ardahill, Co. Cork (T.F. Murphy 1964). In the more elaborate form the initial sharp drop was succeeded by a short constriction. In the earth-cut souterrain at Ballyrisode, Co. Cork (Twohig 1973, 36), the vertical shaft, 1–1.2m in depth, was succeeded by a steeply sloping constriction, 4m long (Fig. 27). The shaft in the rock-cut souterrain at Stroove, Co. Donegal (Lacy 1983, 239), was 2.5m deep. Drystone-built shafts, as apparently in evidence at Ballyvelaghan in north County Clare (T.L. Cooke 1849–51, opp. p. 295), appear to have often facilitated access to the outer extremity of an oblong chamber.

Stepped entrances

Stepped entrances appear to have enjoyed a widespread distribution. At a number of sites the stepped entrance was succeeded by an internal impediment.

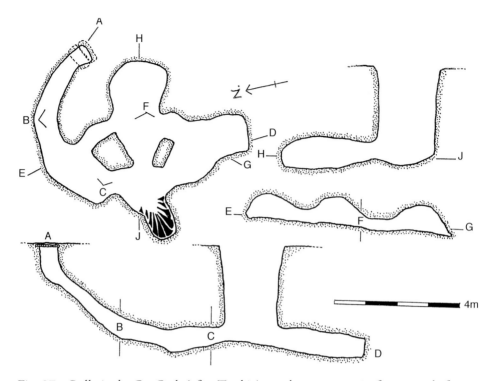

Fig. 27—Ballyrisode, Co. Cork (after Twohig): earth-cut souterrain featuring shaft entrance.

Souterrain A at Cahercommaun, Co. Clare (Hencken 1938, 20), had a flight of four drystone steps and one rock-cut step at its entrance (Fig. 28). Similarly, the side entrance to Souterrain 7 at Knowth, Co. Meath (G. Eogan, pers. comm.), featured three stone-built steps. At Tinnies Upper, Co. Kerry (O'Connell 1937; A. O'Sullivan and Sheehan 1996, 236), a flight of three steps at the entrance was immediately followed by a constriction. A variation on this scheme was recorded at Fortwilliam, Co. Longford (O'Connor 1933), where the outer chamber was entered by a flight of four or five steps. Access to the main body of the souterrain, however, was impeded by the presence of a restricted passage.

Hatch entrances
A hatch-entrance was the least elaborate of the entrance feature types. In effect one of the roofing lintels would have been removable. Their nebulous nature makes them difficult to detect and this pre-empts any attempt to project either their frequency of occurrence or their distribution.

The souterrain at Caherquin, Co. Kerry (Rynne 1966c), basically consisted of a small oval chamber with an attached cupboard. Entry can only have been

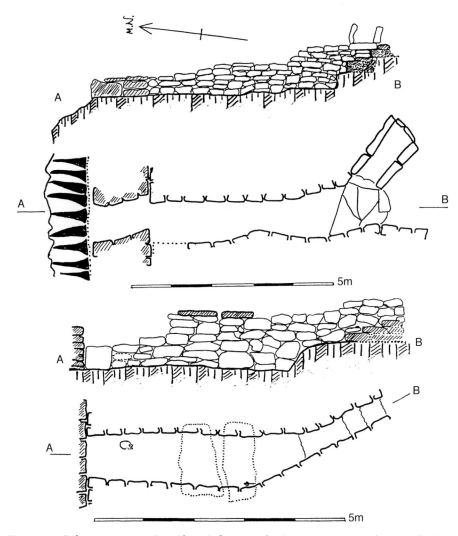

Fig. 28—Cahercommaun, Co. Clare (after Hencken), Souterrain A: drystone-built souterrain featuring stepped entrance and external exit. Souterrain B: drystone-built souterrain featuring stepped entrance and location of skull and brooch.

gained through the roof of the chamber. A more developed form was recorded at Glantane, Co. Kerry (Kelly 1982–3b, 6), where one of the lintels in a passage linking two chambers had been set at a higher level. This represented the entrance to the souterrain (Fig. 29). Negative evidence has been employed elsewhere to indicate the presence of a hatch entrance. At Killeenhugh, Co. Galway (McCaffrey 1952, 274; Gosling *et al.* forthcoming, no. 5868), for example, the surveyors could find no immediate apparent entrance into the two-chambered souterrain.

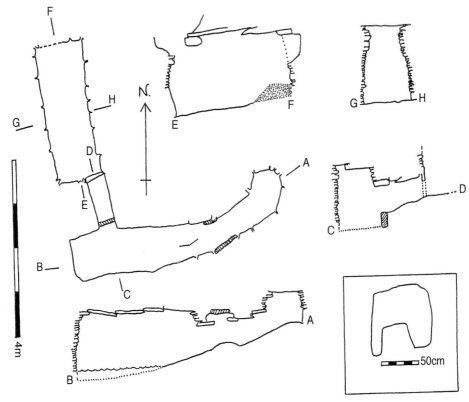

Fig. 29—Glantane, Co. Kerry (after Kelly): drystone-built souterrain featuring hatch entrance, non-obstructive sillstone and porthole-slab.

Hybrid entrance features

Hybrid entrance features only tend to come to light as a result of excavation. Whilst the creation of some examples was obviously dictated by necessity, other examples are not so easily explained.

At Ballynavenooragh, Co. Kerry (Clinton, forthcoming), the souterrain was sited directly beneath the 'back' room of the associated house. The builders were therefore obliged to employ a combination of a pit-drop, a steeply sloping ramp, a flight of two or three steps and a stepped feature in quick succession in order to achieve maximum depth (while maintaining easy accessibility) in the short space available. It is harder to explain the entrance configuration at Knockmant, Co. Westmeath (Kelly 1982–3a, 114), where a gently sloping ramp, 2.25m in length, was succeeded by a pit-drop, 1m in depth. Similarly, at Donaghmore, Co. Louth (Rynne 1957–60b, 150; 1965a), the pit-drop entrance to Souterrain B was preceded by a gently sloping ramp, 4.5m long.

The type of entrance feature employed in a given souterrain must have implications for its intended function. Ramp entrances and stepped entrances provided easy access. Their presence would have been difficult to disguise. Souterrains provided with either of these types of entrance may primarily have fulfilled a storage function. In contrast, a shaft entrance would have been awkward to negotiate, and its presence would have been very easy to disguise. Thus refuge would appear to be the intended primary function. The various types of entrance features may also provide valuable insights as to their surface associations. A ramp entrance, for example, could not easily be accommodated within the interior of a house. The reverse would be true for either a pit-drop or, especially, a shaft entrance.

Double entrances/external exits
The presence of a double entrance to a souterrain is a rare phenomenon. Indeed, practically all examples have only come to light as a result of excavation.

At Garryntemple, Co. Tipperary (Hurley 1981–2, 66), the two entrances were sited approximately 2.5m apart (Fig. 30). Modern destruction pre-empted the discovery of associated surface structures. Souterrain 1 at Darrara (Lisnagun), Co. Cork (O'Sullivan 1990, 227; O'Sullivan *et al.* 1998, 31), also had two

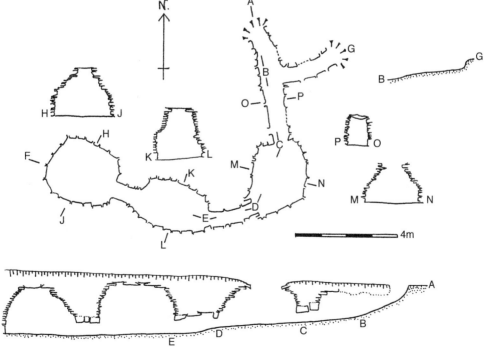

Fig. 30—Garryntemple, Co. Tipperary (after Hurley): drystone-built souterrain featuring double entrance.

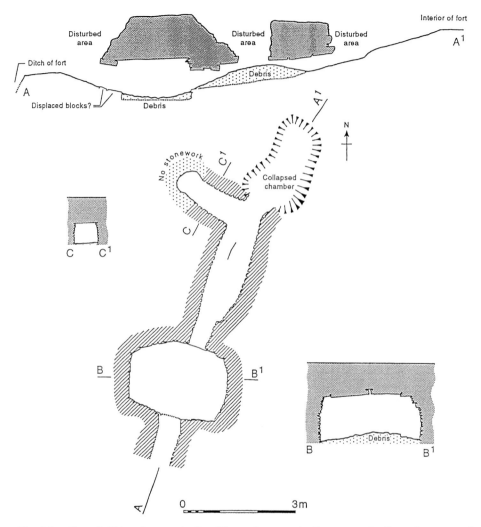

Fig. 31—Dough (Lisnaleagaun), Co. Clare: drystone-built souterrain featuring stepped features and external exit.

entrance features. It was further established that while one of these originated in an associated house, the other simply opened from the interior of the ringfort. This arrangement is paralleled in the case of Souterrain 7 at Knowth, Co. Meath (G. Eogan, pers. comm.).

External exits, or 'escape passages', are also, despite their notoriety, a rare occurrence. The known examples would seem to suggest that it was predominantly a western and south-western development. The most spectacular known example is to be found at Cahercommaun, Co. Clare (Hencken 1938, 20) (Fig. 28). An opening at the back of the short undifferentiated passage/chamber provided access to a cleft in the face of the deep ravine overlooked by the associated enclosed site. By climbing down the jagged-edged cleft the inhabitants could thus have slipped away under the cover of darkness. The more conventional escape passages would have exited in an outer bank or ditch. Examples have been recorded at such sites as Raheennamadra, Co. Limerick (Stenberger 1966, 42) (Fig. 18), and Coolcran, Co. Fermanagh (B. Williams 1985, 77) (Fig. 7).

2. Passages and constrictions

Ideally the designation 'passage' should be limited to those subterranean structures that, quite literally, provide a 'way of access' to the principal feature (i.e. a chamber). A 'passage', therefore, should not occur in isolation. It should always be succeeded by a chamber. A simple length of 'passage' with no obvious end chamber must have served some, if not all, of the functions generally served by a more self-evident end chamber. These simple features must have incorporated a chamber dimension and should therefore be termed 'undifferentiated passage/chambers'.

Passages can basically be divided into two categories, the 'unrestricted' and the 'restricted'. The former is a roomy type of passage in which the entrant's progress is relatively unhindered (Pl. 9). In the latter space is confined and movement can be difficult (Pl. 11).

To differentiate between the two types of passage an artificial set of dimensions must be adopted. The present writer is proposing a height of 0.95m as the dividing line between the unrestricted and the restricted types of passage (Warner (1979, 107) opted for 0.9m). The unrestricted passage should be more than 5m long and feature an average width of 0.7–1.1m at floor level. The restricted passage must be more than 1.5m long and should feature an average width of 0.6–0.9m at floor level.

A 'constriction' represents a simultaneous and abrupt decrease in both the height and the width of the souterrain. This may occur in a number of contexts: at the entrance to a souterrain, in the course of a passage, at the junction of a passage and chamber, or at the junction of two chambers. To differentiate between a 'simple constriction' and an 'extended constriction' a maximum length of 0.5m is proposed for the former. Owing to regional variations (see below) it has not proved possible to further compress the differentiations in width and height.

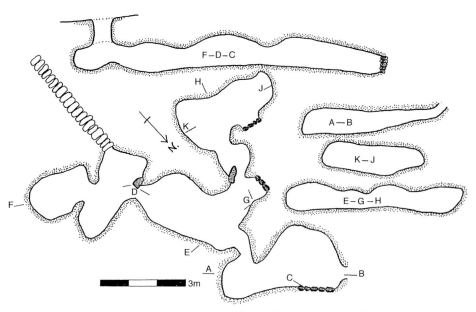

Fig. 32—Ahakeera, Co. Cork (after Twohig): earth-cut souterrain featuring simple constrictions, obstructive jambstones, construction shafts and drain.

		Length	Height	Width
1.	The unrestricted passage	>5m	>0.95m	0.7–1.1m (average)
2.	The restricted passage	>1.5m	<0.95m	0.6–0.9m (average)
3.	Simple constrictions	0–0.5m	0.4–0.6m	0.4–0.7m
4.	Extended constrictions	0.5–1.5m	0.4–1m	0.4–0.8m

As souterrains were ultimately free-form structures, not all examples will fit conveniently into the designated categories. In the event of one of the criteria (length, height, width) falling either 'short' or in excess of the suggested range, the feature in question should be classified as either 'under-realised' or 'exaggerated'. For example, the connecting artery between the two chambers at Lackanatlieve, Co. Sligo (O'Shaughnessy 1993a), was 1.8m long, 0.6m wide, and 1.05m high. Owing to its height this particular feature should be termed 'an exaggerated restricted passage'.

Unrestricted passages
Unrestricted passages are best represented in the northern parts of the island and particularly in the north-eastern group of souterrains.

Souterrain B at Donaghmore, Co. Louth (Rynne 1957–60b) (Fig. 42), contained four passages of the unrestricted type. Passage E alone was 19.7m in length. Its average width at floor level was 0.8–1m, and the average height of the

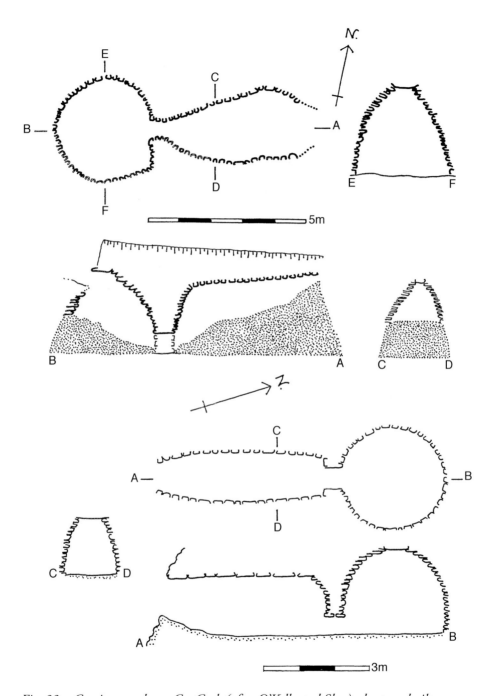

Fig. 33—Carrignagroghera, Co. Cork (after O'Kelly and Shee): drystone-built souterrain featuring circular beehive chamber, expanded-terminal-like chamber and extended construction. Manning, Co. Cork (after Coleman): drystone-built souterrain featuring circular beehive chamber, expanded-terminal-like chamber and extended constriction.

passage was 1.2m. Similarly, at Loughcrew, Co. Meath (Clinton 1993, 120) (Fig. 35), Passage III was 18.4m long. Its average width at floor level was 1.1–1.25m and its height varied from 1.3m to 1.55m. The outer passage in the recently discovered second souterrain at Newrath Big, Co. Meath (Clinton and Manning 2000, 51), attained a maximum floor width of 1.75m (Pl. 9).

Impedimental devices occur more frequently in souterrains with unrestricted passages than in those with restricted passages.

Restricted passages
Examples of the restricted type of passage may be found in most parts of the island. It does not, however, appear to be the dominant form in any given area. It is not impossible that most examples might ultimately be seen as either 'under-realised' unrestricted passages or as 'exaggerated' constrictions.

The souterrain at Herbertstown, Co. Meath, provides a perfect example of the classic meandering restricted type of passage. The passage was 34m long, with an average height of 0.85–0.95m. Average width at floor level was 0.7–0.75m. An earth-cut example at Oldcourt, Co. Cork (Ó Cuileanáin and Murphy 1961–2, 83) (Fig. 49), was 6.4m long, 0.61m wide and 0.61m in average height. A labyrinthine, mostly rock-cut, souterrain at Cloghane, Co. Kerry (Cuppage 1986, 197), featured five restricted passages (in addition to two extended constrictions). The longest of the passages was 4.5m, the shortest 2.5m. At its most restricted point the longer passage was reduced to 0.35m in width and 0.55m in height.

Simple constrictions
Simple constrictions are best represented in tunnelled souterrains. It is not surprising, therefore, that the greatest number of examples has been recorded in County Cork.

At Ahakeera, Co. Cork (Twohig 1976, 26), the constriction connecting Chambers I and III was 0.5m long, 0.4m wide and 0.4m high (Fig. 32). Similarly, at Cloonkirgeen, Co. Cork (*ibid.*, 28), the constriction connecting Chambers I and II was 0.3m long, 0.5m wide and 0.5m high. Examples are also known in the extreme north, for example in the rock-cut souterrains at Turraloskin, Co. Antrim (Brannon 1979, 86), and Norrira, Co. Donegal (Colhoun 1946, 84).

Extended constrictions
Extended constrictions are a relatively common feature in souterrains in Ireland. They enjoy a widespread distribution and can only have been intended as an obstructive device. There are more examples known from drystone-built than

from tunnelled souterrains.

The extended constriction could be employed in a number of different contexts. It could be used in tandem with a shaft entrance to make access to a souterrain extremely difficult, as for example at Castlemagner, Co. Cork (Twohig 1976, 19). It could be inserted into the main body of an unrestricted passage, as at Benagh, Co. Louth (Buckley and Sweetman 1991, 107), or at the junction of an access passage and chamber, as at Lisdornan, Co. Meath, and Millerstown, Co. Waterford (Mongey 1939, 162; M. Moore 1999, 152). It could also be used as the dominant form of inter-chamber linkage, as was the case in the north, for example at Ballymarlagh, Co. Antrim (Collins 1976, 13). In the west of Ireland the extended constriction was a crucial composite element of many of the elevated trapdoor devices, for example at Caherpeake East, Co. Galway (Knox and Redington 1915–16, 182, 184).

3. Chambers

In theory the chamber should be the most important element in the structural composition of a souterrain. Whether the intended function was one of storage or refuge it would be expected that maximum floor-space would be the primary concern. The reality, however, is not always that simple. Indeed, Macalister (1949, 271) has described the occasional disproportion between an almost epic access passage length and the size of the end chamber as being, to the 'superficial eye', almost 'ludicrous'. At Herbertstown, Co. Meath, for example, a restricted passage, 34m in length, facilitated access to a simple (beehive) chamber, 2.3m in diameter and *c.* 1.3m high. An explanation for such an arrangement is not immediately apparent.

In morphological terms, there were basically only two chamber forms available to the builders of a drystone souterrain—a corbelled chamber or a lintelled chamber. In geometrical terms, however, there was the potential for almost as many forms as there would ultimately be chambers. These were, after all, free-form creations, and even in those souterrains where the builders were apparently attempting to realise a preordained design the end result was inevitably endless variations on a theme.

The size of an individual drystone-built chamber would be ultimately determined by technical considerations. There are limits to the potential diameter of a corbelled chamber. The largest known example, to date, of a circular beehive chamber is the southern chamber at Loughcrew, Co. Meath (Clinton 1993, 124) (Fig. 35). The diameter of this corbelled chamber varied between 5.15m and 5.6m, and the height at the centre of the chamber was 2.9m. Similarly, the width of a chamber featuring a lintelled roof would be governed by the length of the lintels available. A gradual battering in the upper reaches of the chamber walls would increase the width to a limited degree. The employment of roof-supports, such as pillars, as at Roovesmore, Co. Cork (Lane-Fox 1867, 123) (Fig. 64), or of a drystone-built column, as at Demesne, Co. Louth (Tempest 1933–6, 95), could extend the width of a lintelled chamber, but these would appear to have enjoyed a very limited use (see p.162 below). The main difference between the two forms is that while the corbelled chamber had finite limits, the lintelled chamber could always compensate for a lack of width with, potentially, an almost unlimited length.

An alternative approach, and indeed the one apparently adopted almost universally, was to compensate for the technological limitations by simply increasing the number of chambers in a given souterrain as opposed to extending the overall dimensions of an individual chamber.

Earth-cut chambers, by their very nature, would have had to be kept relatively small in size. It was inevitable, then, that earth-cut souterrains, unless of the simplest form, would generally consist of a series of modestly sized chambers. These could be arranged either in a basic linear formation, as at Cloddagh on Sherkin Island, Co. Cork (Donovan 1876, 37), or, once the introduction of the construction shaft had made an impact, in a conjoined cluster of chambers, as at Knockane (McCarthy 1977, 276) or Lisheen (Fahy 1960, 142) (Fig. 2), both in County Cork.

Rock-cut chambers would have been governed by similar considerations unless the builders excavated to a considerable depth. There are, in fact, no known examples of a cavernous rock-cut chamber, which would have required an enormous amount of labour. As a consequence it should be noted that in the south many of the so-called rock-cut souterrains in fact featured an earth-cut roof, for example at Lisgoold North, Co. Cork (D. Power *et al.* 1994, 156), Dundeady, Co. Cork (McCarthy 1977, 223), or Farrandau, Co. Cork (Somerville 1931, 1). Even in County Antrim, where the rock would have been of a more impervious nature, the rock-cut chambers never achieved major proportions. Indeed, the most extensive known example of a rock-cut souterrain, approximately 130m in length, which was discovered at Rathmore, Co. Antrim (Berry 1897–8, 160; Chart 1940, 43), took the form of a long, linear, multichambered arrangement.

Any attempt to categorise chambers will be somewhat artificial as there are many hybrid and marginal forms. McCarthy (1983, 101) recognised three categories of chambers in his detailed study of the souterrains of County Cork: (i) long narrow galleries, (ii) rectangular chambers and (iii) circular cells. On a broader scale, however, there would appear to be six basic chamber types, again based on their fundamental shapes. The divarication of Types 1 and 2 was first advanced by Paul Gosling (pers. comm.) in his detailed study of the souterrains of County Louth.

The elliptical chamber
A rounded chamber, more oval than circular; in the north-east a non-angular junction of access passage and chamber (the walls of the former will curve into those of the latter); elsewhere, in the absence of substantial passages, the junction will inevitably be more angular; the profile of the roof of the chamber will not radically diverge from that of the line of the roof of the passage.

The circular chamber
A circular chamber; the classic form will feature a corbelled beehive roof; angular corners will denote the junction of access passage and chamber; the profile of the chamber roof will be pronounced.

The rectangular chamber
A four-sided chamber; the long axis should be less than three times the length of the short axis; many examples will be more rounded than squared in the corners; many might be more accurately described as subrectangular.

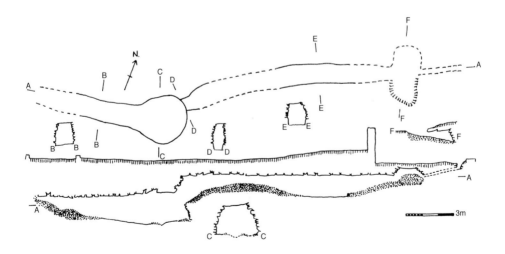

Fig. 34—Kane, Co. Louth (after Gosling and Clinton): drystone-built souterrain featuring an elliptical and a rectangular chamber, air-vent and inverted stepped feature.

113

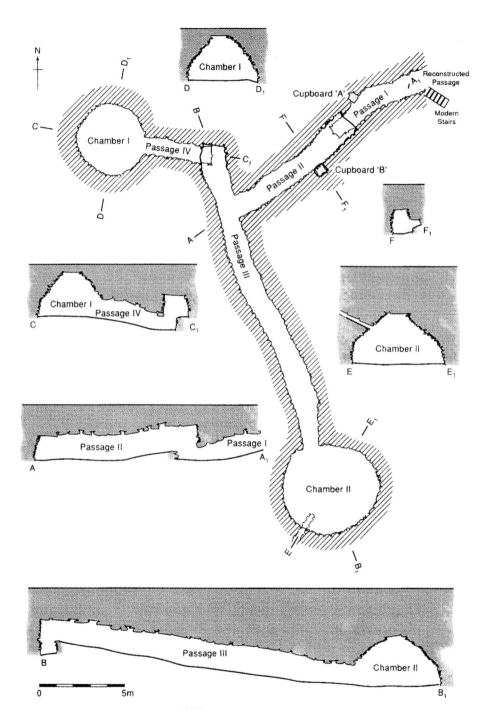

Fig. 35—Loughcrew, Co. Meath (after Clinton): drystone-built souterrain featuring unrestricted passages, cupboards, trapdoors, circular beehive chambers and air-vents.

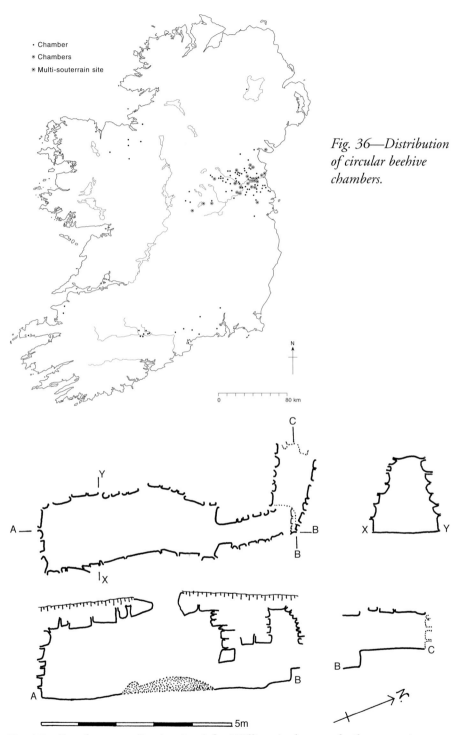

Fig. 36—Distribution
of circular beehive
chambers.

- Chamber
- Chambers
- Multi-souterrain site

N

0   80 km

Fig. 37—Loughermore, Co. Antrim (after Williams): drystone-built souterrain featuring rectangular chamber, internal steps and deliberately blocked entrance.

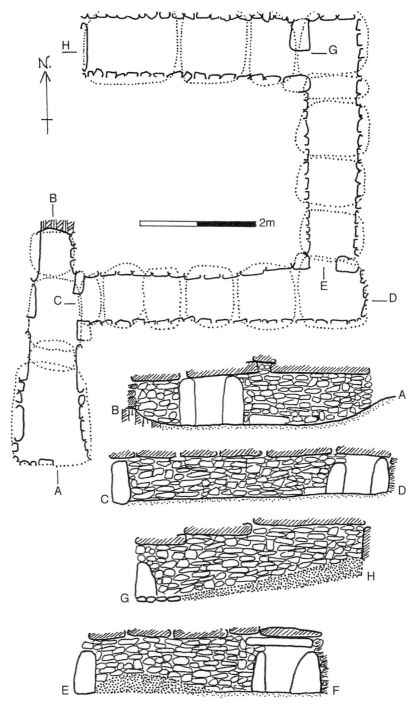

Fig. 38—Rath, Co. Cork (after McCarthy): drystone-built souterrain featuring oblong chambers, obstructive portal jambstones and partially paved floor.

The oblong chamber

A four-sided chamber; the long axis should be more than three times the length of the short axis; a formal junction of access passage (or constriction) and chamber should be evident.

The undifferentiated passage/chamber

A full length of passage which evolves into a chamber, no formalised junction of passage and chamber being evident; ideally there should be no difference between the width of the structure in its inner and outer reaches; a margin of differentiation to a limit of less than half the average width of the passage/chamber should be allowed to facilitate minor fluctuations. Therefore the inner/outer chamber/passage ratio should be <150:100.

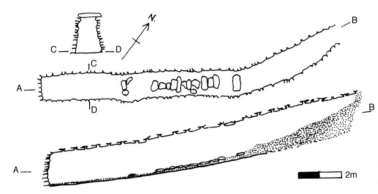

Fig. 39— Bawntaaffe, Co. Louth (after Rynne), Souterrain B: drystone-built souterrain of undifferentiated passage/chamber type featuring partially paved floor.

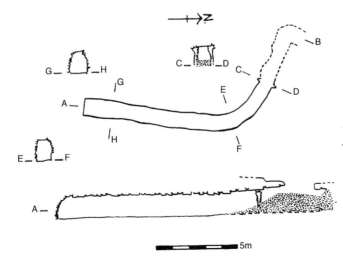

Marshes Upper 1, Co. Louth (after Gosling): drystone-built souterrain of undifferentiated passage/chamber type featuring door-jamb slots.

Expanded terminals

A basic expansion at the inner terminal of a passage, no formalised junction of passage and chamber being evident; to avoid confusion with the undifferentiated passage/chamber, the inner reaches of the expanded terminal should have increased by at least half the width of its access passage. The inner/outer chamber/passage ratio should therefore be >150:100.

The evidence available to date indicates that certain types of chambers predominated in certain areas. This is not to suggest that any given area was exclusively serviced by one particular type of chamber. Indeed, it is not unknown for different types of chamber to be employed in one souterrain. At Killala, Co. Mayo (Cochrane and McNeill 1898, 291), a circular beehive chamber was incorporated into a souterrain that also contained one rectangular and three oblong chambers. At Kane, Co. Louth (Clinton and Gosling 1979, 211), the souterrain contained two chambers, one elliptical, the other rectangular (Fig. 34). The souterrain at Ballysheen, Co. Kerry (Deady 1972, 160), contained a circular beehive chamber, a rectangular chamber and a subrectangular chamber.

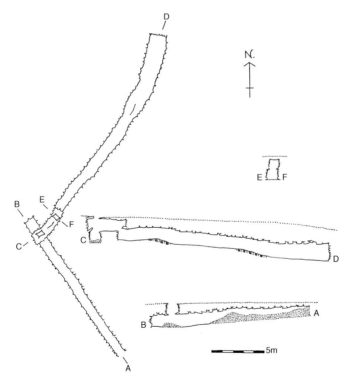

Fig. 40—Crumlin, Co. Louth (after Buckley and Sweetman): drystone-built souterrain featuring two trapdoors and expanded-terminal chamber.

It is worth reiterating at this point that there are also innumerable examples of souterrains in the drystone-built tradition that contained either hybrid or exceptional chamber forms. The souterrain at Aghnahoo, Co. Tyrone (McKenna 1930, 194), contained a polygonal chamber. The chamber at Drumena, Co. Down (Berry 1926–7, 46), could be described as adze-shaped. The western chamber at Leitrim, Co. Down (Macrory 1907, 70), was described as 'pear-shaped'. The souterrain at Ballyegan, Co. Kerry (Gorham 1914–16, 12; Byrne 1991, 5), contained a D-shaped chamber in addition to a rectangular chamber. The two chambers at Ahenny, Co. Tipperary (Sweetman and de Buitléir 1976, 73), might be described, respectively, as D-shaped and trapezoidal in form.

The earth-cut, and to a lesser degree the rock-cut, souterrains were potentially a law unto themselves. The very nature of these features would have allowed for a greater freedom as regards shape and form than was afforded to the drystone-built souterrains. It is surprising, therefore, that most of the known chambers in earth-cut souterrains have turned out to be basically either subrectangular (e.g. at Brulea, Co. Cork (Fahy 1972); Tullig, Co. Kerry (J. Cooke 1906–7, 2) (Fig. 2); Underhill, Co. Cork (O'Kelly and Shee 1968, 40), except for chamber 1, which was elliptical; and Ballyrisode (Twohig 1973, 36)), subcircular (e.g. Chamber 1 at Farranthomas, Co. Cork (Ó Drisceoil and Hurley 1978, 75); the end chamber at Coolgarrif, Co. Cork (Coleman 1945, 112); and at Garranes, Co. Cork (Gillman 1896b, 420)), or elliptical in form (e.g. at Castleventry, Co. Cork (Cleary 1981a, 40), and Deelish, Co. Cork (Gillman 1896a, 153)). There are other earth-cut chambers, however, that can only be best described as 'irregular'(e.g. both chambers at Cullenagh, Co. Cork (Twohig 1976, 33), or at Druimdaleague (McCarthy 1977, 215)).

Rock-cut souterrains also contained irregular-shaped chambers, for example Currahaly, Co. Cork (Brash 1866–9b, 72; Hartnett 1939, 114), Cloghane, Co. Kerry (Cuppage 1986, 197), and Turraloskin, Co. Antrim (Brannon 1979, 86).

Combined-media souterrains also featured irregular-shaped chambers. The two earth-cut chambers at Kilberehert, Co. Cork (Gillman 1896b, 417), fit this description. The second (earth-cut) chamber at Dromkeen East, Co. Kerry (Twohig 1974, 5), also falls into this category (its companion, interestingly, being the largest known drystone-built circular beehive chamber outside of the greater Meath group). Again, the souterrain at Grallagh Lower, Co. Waterford (McCarthy 1978b, 73; M. Moore 1999, 151), featured an irregular-shaped earth-cut chamber, an irregular-shaped rock-cut chamber, and an elliptical drystone-built chamber. The mostly rock-cut souterrain at Townparks, Co. Donegal (Lacy 1983, 227), also featured an irregular oblong-shaped rock-cut (outer) chamber.

In summary, then, while certain chamber forms are predominant in certain areas, for example the circular beehive chambers in the greater Meath area or the oblong chambers in Galway/north-west Clare/south Mayo, there are also innumerable 'erratics' and unexpected combinations and permutations of chambers that must be taken into consideration when attempting to discern the overall distribution pattern of the assorted chamber types.

Distribution of elliptical chambers
Elliptical chambers are obviously closely related morphologically to circular chambers. Some could almost be described as under-realised circular chambers. They were primarily concentrated in four areas: (a) County Louth; (b) north-east County Cork/County Waterford/south County Tipperary; (c) County Kerry; and (d) north-east Connacht.

The fundamental difference between an elliptical chamber, in its purest form, and a circular beehive chamber is that in the former the walls of the passage curve smoothly into those of the chamber. Similarly, the roof of the chamber gradually evolves from that of the passage. The end chamber at Balrobin, Co. Louth (Buckley and Sweetman 1991, 104), could be advanced as a good example. The outer chamber at Kane, Co. Louth (Clinton and Gosling 1979, 211), also conformed to this format (Fig. 34).

The elliptical chambers in the three other specified areas never achieve the symmetry of the County Louth examples. In fact it is tempting to see some of them as either under-realised circular chambers or overtly rounded subrectangular chambers. The general use of lintels rather than corbelling had a marked impact on the line of the roofs. In effect it created a more angular relationship between the roofs of the passage and the chamber. Similarly, the extensive use of extended constrictions created a more angular relationship between the access artery and the chamber. This is clearly evident at such sites as Park, Co. Waterford (A.B. Ó Ríordáin 1968b), Carhoo East, Co. Kerry (Waddell 1970a, 15), or, to a lesser extent, Lackanatlieve, Co. Sligo (O'Shaughnessy 1993a).

Distribution of circular chambers
Circular chambers are one of the most distinctive of the chamber types. The classic circular beehive chamber is remarkably consistent in its execution. The corbelled walls of the chamber either gently arc from floor level to capstone or initially rise quite vertically before adopting a curve. The junction between the walls of the passage and the chamber are sharp, angular affairs. The chambers are always 'topped' with either one (often sizeable) capstone or two smaller capstones (Pl. 14).

It has long been recognised that the greater Meath area was the primary focus for this type of chamber. Indeed, with a number of minor concentrations elsewhere, which generally parallel those of the elliptical chambers, the present research has confirmed that long-held perception (Fig. 36).

The largest known circular beehive chambers, for example the two chambers in the souterrain at Loughcrew (Clinton 1993, 120) (Fig. 35), are to be found in the western part of County Meath (to the west of Kells). There are some notable examples elsewhere, for example at Dromkeen East, Co. Kerry (Twohig 1974, 5). A small cluster of souterrains in north-east Cork also featured some fine examples of beehive chambers, for example at Manning (C. Moore 1900, 373; Coleman 1947–8, 72; Lee 1932, 27) and Carrignagroghera (O'Kelly and Shee 1968, 44) (Fig. 33).

Distribution of rectangular chambers

In many ways the rectangular chamber could be described as the most 'obvious', or indeed inevitable, of chamber forms. It is therefore not surprising to find that it enjoyed the most widespread distribution in ample numbers. It is also significant that in areas where there was a dominant chamber type, as for example the circular beehive souterrains in the greater Meath area or the oblong chambers in the west of Ireland, the occurrence of rectangular chambers decreased accordingly. It is only in Kerry, north/east Connacht, and possibly north-central Cork that the rectangular chamber would appear to have been dominant.

The geographical spread and morphological consistency of rectangular chambers may be observed in such examples as Kildalton, Co. Kilkenny (Prendergast 1958, 38) (Fig. 55), Ballyeaston, Co. Antrim (Warner 1972, 61), Graffy, Co. Mayo (O'Hara 1991, 117), and Glantane, Co. Kerry (Kelly 1982–3b, 5) (Fig. 29).

Distribution of oblong chambers

Oblong chambers could achieve the maximum amount of floor-space. To differentiate between the oblong chamber and the rectangular chamber, it is proposed that when the long axis is more than three times the length of the short axis the chamber should be classified as oblong. While there are examples of— or, to be more precise, variations on—the format elsewhere, the oblong chamber was realised in its most well-developed form in the north-west Clare/Galway/south Mayo area.

Chamber 2 at Ballinphuil, Co. Galway (Costello 1902, 115; 1903–4, 8; Alcock *et al.* 1999, 260), may be cited as a notable example of an oblong chamber (Fig. 43). It was 11.28m long, 2.13m wide and 1.83m(+) high. Less spectacular but nonetheless comparable examples were recorded at such sites as Murtyclogh, Co. Clare (T.L. Cooke 1849–51, 296) (Fig. 43), where the outer chamber was 9.75m long, and at Knock North, Co. Mayo (Wilde 1867, 108), where the outer chamber was described as being 6.71m in length.

The overall dimensions of the oblong chambers in the west of Ireland facilitated the 'housing' of the space-consuming elevated trapdoor feature. It is safe to say that no other chamber type could have contained these devices without compromising their primary function.

There are examples of oblong chambers in other parts of the island. Souterrain B at Donaghmore, Co. Louth (Rynne 1957–60b, 148) (Fig. 42), featured an end chamber that was 10.7m long, 1.7m wide and 1.7m high. The oblong chamber in the souterrain at Ballynavenooragh, Co. Kerry (Clinton, forthcoming b), was 5.5m long. It would be prudent, however, to bear in mind that as rectangular chambers were heavily represented in County Kerry, oblong chambers in the county, such as that at Ballynavenooragh, or at Duagh (Chadwick 1976), might also be considered as 'exaggerated' rectangular chambers.

The oblong chamber was also employed in County Antrim, where, however, it never achieved the overall dimensions in evidence elsewhere. The souterrain at Knockdhu (Lawlor 1915–16, 32), for example, is representative of the Antrim-style configuration of a series of oblong chambers connected by extended constrictions. This format is echoed in a series of oblong chambered souterrains in County Cork, for example at Rath (McCarthy 1977, 303) (Fig. 38).

Distribution of undifferentiated passage/chambers

Undifferentiated passage/chambers have often been misrepresented. There are many instances where a souterrain has been described as consisting of a simple 'length of passage'. These would have fulfilled all the functions of a 'normal' chamber and are thus more accurately described as undifferentiated passage/chambers. Owing to their lack of a distinctive diagnostic element their actual numbers may be considerably higher than is currently thought.

If the undifferentiated passage/chamber is the featured, i.e. the only, chamber in a souterrain, then one is dealing with a souterrain of the most basic form. These are much better represented in the west of Ireland than anywhere else on the island. S.P. Ó Ríordáin (1938–40, 179) identified the prevalent form at Cush, Co Limerick, as being of the 'gallery' (i.e. undifferentiated passage/chamber) type. Similarly, Westropp (1898, 361) defined the typical souterrain in north-west Clare as being passage-like. These could be either linear, curved, or S-shaped in plan. He advanced sites such as Poulacarran (*ibid.,* 363) and Cragballyconoal (Westropp 1899, 372) as examples. Other undifferentiated passage/chambers in the west have been recorded at Letterkeen, Co. Mayo (S.P. Ó Ríordáin and MacDermott 1951–2, 100), and in the general vicinity of Cruachain, Co. Roscommon (Herity 1987, 138).

Examples, while quite rare, are also known from elsewhere on the island, for example at Bawntaaffe (Souterrain B), Co. Louth (Rynne 1957–60a, 100) (Fig. 39), and Big Glebe, Co. Londonderry (Brannon 1982a).

It is worth noting that while the undifferentiated passage/chamber souterrains were the predominant forms in areas such as north-west Clare or County Limerick, they would appear to have been of peripheral use elsewhere. Indeed, Rynne (1957–60a, 102) has suggested that the examples in the east may have acted as simple storage facilities while their more elaborate companions fulfilled the role of refuges.

Distribution of expanded terminals
Chambers of the expanded-terminal type are more than likely a variation on the undifferentiated passage/chamber format—the only difference, or benefit, being the provision of additional floor-space. It is probably no coincidence that they enjoyed a somewhat similar distribution.

Representative examples of the expanded-terminal type of chamber may be observed at such sites as Cush (Souterrain 1), Co. Limerick (S.P. Ó Ríordáin 1938–40, 92), Crumlin, Co. Louth (Buckley and Sweetman 1991, 115) (Fig. 40), and Sheepland Mor, Co. Down (Rees-Jones 1971, 77) (Fig. 62).

The expanded terminal did not always occur at the innermost extremity of the souterrain. A number of the souterrains in north-east Cork that featured circular beehive end chambers also had outer chambers of the expanded-terminal type, for example Manning (Coleman 1947–8, 72) or Carrignagroghera (O'Kelly and Shee 1968, 45) (Fig. 33).

The siting of the north-eastern Type A trapdoor at the inner extremity of an access passage of the unrestricted type would have had the side-effect of expanding the width of the passage. Whenever the trapdoor was sealed, this area could have acted as a temporary ad hoc chamber of expanded-terminal type.

4. The trapdoor feature

One of the most noteworthy structural elements of Irish souterrains is the trapdoor feature. The existence of this device has long been recognised, as has its basic impedimental nature. T.L. Cooke (1849–51, 296) noted that their presence could cause 'a stranger … much delay', especially when allowing for the initial 'difficulty in discovering the apertures'. He further observed that the relevant openings would have been 'stopped' with flagstones. Orpen (1890–1, 153) drew close attention to the three inbuilt 'ledges' that he had uncovered at Bective 1, Co. Meath. These, he maintained, would have supported a flagstone which would in turn have concealed the existence of any further underground structure(s). It was Rotheram (1897, 428) who used the term 'trapdoor' in describing the 'purely defensive arrangement' at Crossdrum Lower, Co. Meath. Westropp (1896–1901, 669) referred to the self-same structure as an 'excellent example of an obstacle entrance' from one passage to another. Knox (1917–18, 5) recognised and advanced a description of the intrinsic characteristics of the western type of trapdoor (see below). Macalister (1949, 271) suggested that the combination of a 'trapdoor' and an inner chamber which featured a 'ventilating-shaft' would have provided a secure and suffocation-proof sanctuary. It was S.P. Ó Ríordáin (1942, 14; 1953, 29) who first alluded to a possible defined distribution pattern for the 'obstruction' or 'trap' feature when he stated that the device was characteristic of souterrains located in parts of in County Down and County Galway. He observed that the incorporation of the feature was always motivated by the objective of making it easy for the people within to ward off any unwelcome intruders. Rynne (1957–60a, 102; 1957–60b, 152) advanced both the camouflaging and the defensive potential of the feature. He further stressed that the presence of traps bore witness to the function of the souterrain as a refuge. Warner (1979, 131; 1980, 92) firmly accepted the defensive nature of the feature and touched upon the existence of different types.

The trapdoor feature has been alluded to over the years in a widely disparate range of terms. Many latter-day writers have been influenced by Warner, who has entitled this feature the 'drop-hole creep'. The present writer finds this term inappropriate. At sites such as Loughcrew, Co. Meath, or Donaghmore, Co. Louth, or indeed in the bulk of sites in the west of Ireland, where the movement of the entrant is 'up' rather than 'down' through the feature, the term 'drop-hole' is inapplicable. Furthermore, at sites such as Donaghmore, or indeed at Crumlin or Chanonrock (all in County Louth), where the interlinking arteries are of equal dimension, the term 'creep' is misleading.

The definition and identification of a trapdoor are based on two fundamental criteria:

(a) the feature was purposely constructed to obstruct, hinder or confuse an intruder's progress;

(b) the presence of inbuilt scarcements to facilitate the placing of one or more covering devices.

The proposed classification is ultimately based on two determining factors:

(1) whether the trapdoor could be sealed by those seeking refuge within the inner confines of the souterrain, or, alternatively, by willing accomplices remaining without;

(2) whether the trapdoor occurs at the junction of two passages or at the junction of a passage and a chamber.

Geographically and typologically, trapdoors occur in two distinct groups: the

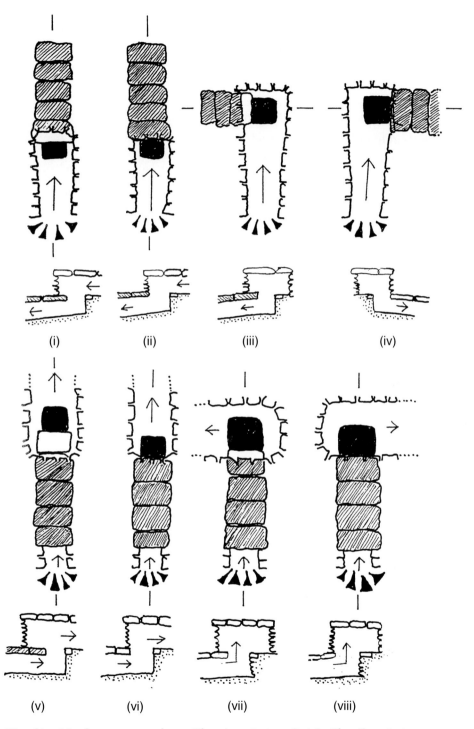

Fig. 41—North-eastern trapdoors: Class A variations (i–iv), Class B variations (v–viii).

north-eastern group and the western group. The feature is otherwise strikingly absent from the greater part of the island. Judging by both its elaborate design and its consistently skilful execution, it could be suggested that the trapdoor should be considered a later development in Irish souterrains.

The north-eastern group

Found in counties Down, Louth and Meath (with additional outliers in counties Antrim, Armagh, Londonderry and Westmeath).

The trapdoor always occurs at the junction of two passages (or in rare cases at the junction of a passage and an undifferentiated passage/chamber).

This group contains two subdivisions: the Class A and the Class B.

The Class A is the dominant form, comprising all trapdoors that had to be sealed off from without. This practice would not have been conducive to an effective internal defence. Thus the long-held view that all trapdoors were intended as a strong point of defence has been challenged. In turn, the motivation of the trapdoor-builders in the north-east must be re-evaluated.

The Class B type of trapdoor, sealed from within, would have provided the refugees in a souterrain with an almost impregnable point of defence. The relative dearth of examples must therefore be regarded as significant.

Examples of the north-eastern Class A trapdoor were recorded at such sites as Ballyhacket-Glenahorry, Co. Londonderry (Ligar 1833) (Fig. 9), Rathiddy, Co. Louth (Rynne 1962, 125) (Fig. 48), and Bective 1, Co. Meath (Orpen 1890–1, 150) (Fig. 6).

Examples of the north-eastern Class B trapdoor were recorded at such sites as Loughcrew (first trapdoor), Co. Meath (Clinton 1993, 120) (Fig. 35), and in Souterrain B (first trapdoor) at Donaghmore, Co. Louth (Rynne 1957–60b, 148) (Fig. 42).

The western group

Found in counties Clare, Galway and Mayo (with an outlying site in County Offaly).

This group contains four subdivisions: classes A, B, C and D.

While the trapdoors in the north-eastern group involved the presence of two passages lying at different levels, the interconnecting passages and chambers of the western group invariably lay on the same level. Thus it proved necessary to fabricate a structural differentiation in height—hence the term 'elevated trapdoor' (Pl. 10).

The Class A is the dominant form, comprising all trapdoors that had to be sealed from the inside. This arrangement would have offered those seeking refuge within the souterrain an almost impregnable point of defence. Thus the prime

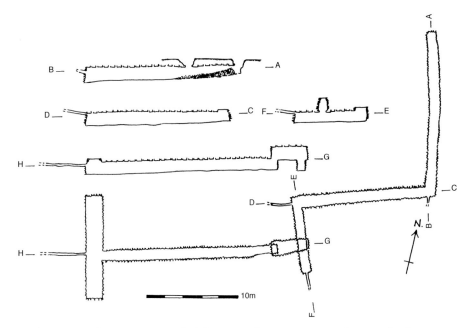

Fig. 42—Donaghmore, Co. Louth (after Rynne), Souterrain B: drystone-built souterrain featuring two trapdoors, unrestricted passages, four air-vents and oblong chamber.

motivation of the trapdoor-builders in the west would appear to have been in direct contrast to the north-east.

The other three classes occur in minimal numbers. The Class D (only one example known to date) could also be sealed from within. The Class B and the Class C could only have been sealed from the outside. Their relatively small numbers again stress the priorities of the builders in the west. The Class C and the Class D were non-elevated chamber trapdoors.

Examples of the western Class A elevated trapdoor were recorded at such sites as Murtyclogh, Co. Clare (T.L. Cooke 1849–51, 296) (Fig. 43), and Ballinphuil, Co. Galway (Costello 1902, 115; 1903–4, 8) (Fig. 43).

Examples of the western Class B elevated trapdoor were recorded at such sites as Billymore, Co. Galway (Kinahan 1883–4a, 11), and Carnmore, Co. Galway (Buckley and O'Brien 1985–6, 139) (Fig. 44).

An example of the western Class C trapdoor was recorded at Ballyvelaghan, Co. Clare (T.L. Cooke 1849–51, 295), and an example of the Class D at Lissaniska East (second trapdoor), Co. Mayo (Ronayne 1978).

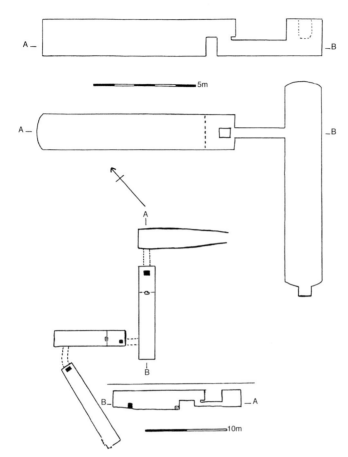

*Fig. 43—
Murtyclogh, Co.
Clare (after Cooke):
drystone-built
souterrain featuring
oblong chambers and
elevated trapdoor.
Ballinphuil, Co.
Galway (after
Costelloe): drystone-
built souterrain
featuring oblong
chambers and
elevated trapdoors.*

Discussion

There can be little doubt that the trapdoor was a specialised feature. Indeed, the more practical functional necessities, such as attaining depth or accommodating a steep incline, could have been fulfilled with considerably less effort by a simple stepped feature. Examples of the latter may be observed at such sites as Stickillin, Co. Louth (Fig. 47), Newrath Big 1, Co. Meath, or Knowth (Souterrain 2), Co. Meath (see section 5). Significantly, the north-eastern Class B traps in fact effectively 'lost' depth in the overall downward progress of the souterrain.

S.P. Ó Ríordáin (1953, 29; 1965, 29) maintained that the feature was 'always directed to the purposes of making it easy for a person in the souterrain to defend himself against an unwelcome intruder'. There is, however, a basic problem with the blanket definition of the primary objective. In fact only the north-eastern Class B, the western Class C, and the extremely rare western Class D traps could be endorsed as practical defensive structures.

In contrast, the more common north-eastern Class A traps could neither be closed nor disguised sufficiently 'from within' to confuse or mislead the average

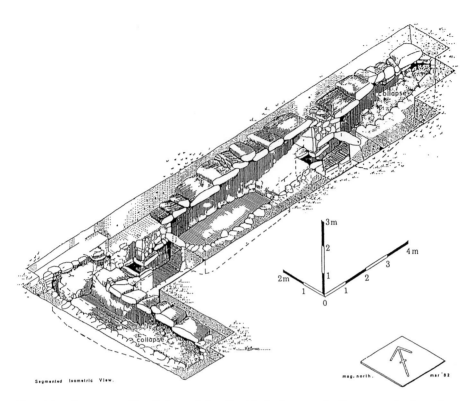

Fig. 44—Carnmore, Co. Galway (after Buckley): drystone-built souterrain featuring oblong chambers and elevated trapdoors.

intruder. Even if some willing accomplice, possibly Lucas's 'Uamchoimetaide' (1971–3, 187), sealed the trapdoor with stone lintels or split logs and subsequently covered it over with clay or gravel or organic debris in order to disguise it, a motivated intruder could undo the work without great effort. Furthermore, once the trapdoor was opened, the defenders would have been at a decided disadvantage as they would now be under attack from above.

This leaves us with an unresolved conundrum. Why construct the north-eastern Class A trapdoor at all? If depth was desired, why not utilise the stepped feature? Alternatively, if defence was the primary objective, why not employ the strategically superior north-eastern Class B or western Class A design?

It is, of course, possible that the builders of a complex souterrain had more than one function in mind. In times of relative peace, especially in hot weather, a delimited outer area might have served as a temporary storage space. Even an impromptu covering of the trapdoor at sites such as Bective 1 (Fig. 6), Stonefield or Baltrasna (in County Meath) would have activated a 'latent' chamber and thus provided adequate temporary storage space within easy access of the ground surface level. Similarly, at other sites featuring the north-eastern Class A traps there was invariably sufficient storage space even before one's encounter with the feature, for example in Chamber 1 at Dowth, Co. Meath, or in the north-western chamber at Ballinloughan, Co. Louth.

At this point it should be noted that there appears to be a regional divergence in relation to motivation. Whereas the Class A type is the dominant form in the western group, in the north-east its analogous form, the Class B type, is in the minority. Thus their respective builders may have had different priorities in mind. There can be little doubt that the north-eastern Class B and the western Class A traps were potentially highly defensive in design and execution. Indeed, they could most definitely have either obstructed, hindered or confused an intruder's progress. That, however, would not necessarily appear to have been the case in relation to the predominant form, the Class A trap, in the north-eastern group.

It is possible that some trapdoor arrangements (the elaborate double traps?) were incorporated into a souterrain in order to regulate the internal temperature. It has been suggested by de Valera (1979, 67) that the change in roof and floor levels may have conserved warm air within the inner confines of the souterrain. He further suggested (*ibid.,* 70) that these souterrains might have provided better sleeping accommodation in times of inclement weather than a surface structure. Experiments conducted in a County Galway souterrain revealed that a steady temperature of 7°C was maintained in the passage, while the end chamber averaged 10°C (*Irish Independent,* 15/3/1979; RTC Galway 1979). Whatever about sleeping conditions, the provision of a sizeable storage area enhanced by a steady, regulated temperature would have been of significant advantage to a settlement. While open, the north-eastern type of trapdoor would not in itself have proved impossibly awkward to negotiate. Therefore an argument against storage on the grounds of impassibility would not necessarily be valid. The western type of trapdoor, however, because of the integral extended constriction, or short length of restricted passage, would have made ingression/egression laborious in the extreme.

Studies conducted by the present writer seem to indicate that a significant number of souterrains in the greater Meath and south-east Ulster region were associated with open settlement sites. This appears to be particularly true in relation to souterrains containing a trapdoor feature and belonging to the north-eastern group (Appendix 2). The very nature of these open settlements would seem to preclude an extensive involvement by the occupants in a cattle-based economy. Tillage would be the natural alternative, and indeed it is clear from the written and material evidence that a well-developed and widespread tillage system had evolved by the latter half of the first millennium AD (Duignan 1944a, 141).

The historical evidence indicates that Ireland experienced a significant growth in population in the early ninth century. Demands on the food supply would therefore have risen accordingly. Cattle, which by modern standards were small in size, were chiefly kept for their dairy by-products (Mitchell 1976, 181; Lucas 1958, 4; 1989, 4), and thus beef would not have been consistently available for mass consumption. Indeed, many entries in the annals indicate that the growing of cereal crops was of prime importance. The primitive nature of crop husbandry made it very labour-intensive. Therefore, as the growth in food production developed, so too would the size of the base labour force. The threat to an open settlement-based economic unit would have risen proportionally. The loss of the extended labour force would have had very severe implications for a cereal crop farmer.

Slavery was a fact of Irish society. The evidence is available in such disparate sources as archaic linguistic forms and the Lives of the saints. The Viking raids of the ninth century undoubtedly fuelled the practice. Ó Corráin (1972, 47) has indicated that the development of Viking trade led to an increase in the slave population in ninth-century Ireland. Doherty (1980, 71) has referred to 'joint slaving raids' being conducted by the Norse and the Irish. Holm (1986, 321) has noted the gradual progression in the practice of slavery from the ninth century onwards, reaching a peak in the eleventh century. It is almost inevitable that the base labour pool constituted a significant element in the economic composition of an open settlement. In turn, the cereal crop farmer had to sustain his prime asset. He did not have the limited (potential) protection afforded by an enclosure at his disposal. In the event of a raid, if the crop was still in the field it was beyond saving. Similarly, even after the harvest had been gathered there was no completely secure method of preventing a raiding party from either looting or burning a crop-filled barn. What could hopefully be saved, and what ultimately guaranteed a reversal of fortune, was the labour force, and where better to detain them than within the relatively safe inner confines of a souterrain? Is it possible, therefore, that the relatively common north-eastern Class A and the comparatively rare western Class B traps were in effect an internal subdivision of the souterrain created in order to 'contain' as much as to simply 'repel'? In such a scenario the trapdoor at Riverstown, Co. Louth, warrants renewed attention. It was there that Twohig (1971, 131) recorded the occurrence of two slots at floor level in the opposite walls of the upper passage, immediately prior to its inner point of termination. These, he speculated, 'may have held a wooden beam which could have been used as a bolt' (*ibid.,*133) to hold down the innermost slab covering the general trapdoor area. Similarly, at Marshes Upper (Souterrain 3B) (Gowen 1992, 70), Co. Louth, two pairs of slots were recorded in the opposite walls above the trap area. While these may have contained timber

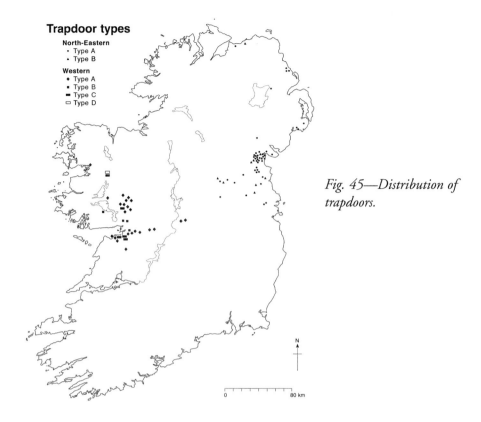

Fig. 45—Distribution of trapdoors.

beams or narrow stone slabs which held up the sealing-slabs as opposed to holding them down, they nonetheless represent further evidence of the physical sealing off of the inner section of the souterrain from without. A comparable arrangement of two pairs of opposing slots has recently been recorded in a trapdoor at Farrandreg, Co. Louth (D. Murphy 1998, 269).

The possibility must therefore be actively considered that the vast majority of known trapdoors in the north-eastern group of souterrains may have been intended to contain (and thus protect) the human assets of the tillage farmers.

The alternative scenario of the marshalling of significant numbers of indifferent labourers, in addition to family members, into an organised and speedy flight might have proved highly inefficient and ultimately very costly.

In the light of the evidence currently available it would appear that the motivation of the souterrain-builders of the western group was decidedly different. There, defence would seem to have been the governing factor. This, of course, was probably highly influenced by the fact that the vast majority of the western souterrains containing trapdoors occurred within the precincts of an enclosed site (see Appendix 2). Thus the trapdoors in the western group of souterrains probably represented the guarded entrances to the last redoubts of the non-combatants of cattle-orientated settlements. Could the disparity in suggested use also possibly be a reflection of the uneven practice of slave-taking? Holm (1986, 318) has claimed that it was much more prevalent in the east than in the west.

In conclusion, it should be noted that despite its relatively high, if somewhat ambiguous, profile the trapdoor is ultimately an extremely rare feature with a very limited distribution (Fig. 45).

5. Stepped features

The term 'stepped feature' is designed to distinguish these structures from the common or garden step which is also to be found in souterrains. Whilst the step may manifest itself in the three different media (rock-cut, earth-cut or stone-built), the 'stepped feature' designation should be applied only in reference to stone-built structures (Pl. 17). There are a number of other diagnostic elements. The feature will be stone-faced and the corresponding section of the roof of the passage will, in most cases, significantly lower its profile in tandem (Fig. 47). While the height of the stepped feature varies from souterrain to souterrain, *c.* 95% of the known examples fall in the 0.4–1m bracket (with *c.* 60% of the total number in the 0.6–1m range). It will also be observed that these features almost exclusively occur in, or are associated with, unrestricted-type passages in the east and restricted-type passages in the west (see Appendix 3).

A stepped feature could perform a number of functions. It could facilitate rapid attainment of depth in a passage. In County Meath, for example, where the end chamber would invariably be of the domed beehive variety, this would have proved highly advantageous. The alternative course would have been the more labour-intensive construction of an extended sloping passage. Representative examples have been recorded at Newrath Big 1, Co. Meath (Sweetman 1975, 54), and Stickillin (Souterrain 1), Co. Louth (Dunne *et al.* 1973–6, 274). An inverted stepped feature could alleviate the overall labour requirements by elevating the floor level of the latter (internal) segments of a souterrain. At Kane, Co. Louth (Clinton and Gosling 1979, 211) (Fig. 34), for example, Passage II extended from the upper walls (at a height of 0.9m) of Chamber I. This arrangement would have effectively reduced the depth required in the host trench for the aforementioned passage (and end chamber) by approximately 50%.

The inverted stepped feature at Kane is one of a limited number that achieved

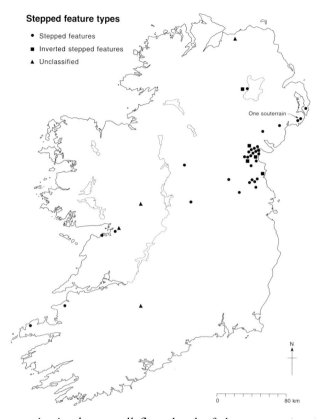

Stepped feature types

- • Stepped features
- ■ Inverted stepped features
- ▲ Unclassified

Fig. 46—Distribution of stepped features.

a rise in the overall floor level of the souterrain. A minority of these inverted stepped features may also have contributed to the defence of their respective souterrains. At Rathiddy, Co. Louth (Rynne 1962, 125), the (rising) stepped feature was preceded by a stretch of restrictive passage (Fig. 48). At Lisrenny, Co. Louth (Masser and Bradley 1957–60, 93) the (rising) stepped feature was overlooked by an elevated 'murder-hole-like' feature.

A double stepped feature is represented by a rising 'step' followed closely by a corresponding descending 'step'. To date this feature has only been recorded in a 'side' passage. The example at Termonfeckin 1, Co. Louth (Ó Floinn 1978, 128), was discovered in a disturbed condition (Fig. 53). In effect the second element (the downward 'step') was either buried beneath a deposit of compacted fill or had been disturbed at some previous date. Indeed, the floor of the adjoining main passage, at the juncture, was covered by a substantial amount of rock debris. As the writer noted, this was not the result of a roof collapse. Whilst a double stepped feature could be interpreted as a defensive arrangement, it could not, by its structural nature, have been a significantly advantageous one to the defender, and thus might be more accurately described as a minor obstructive device.

Finally, the stepped feature, in the context of a souterrain sited in either a

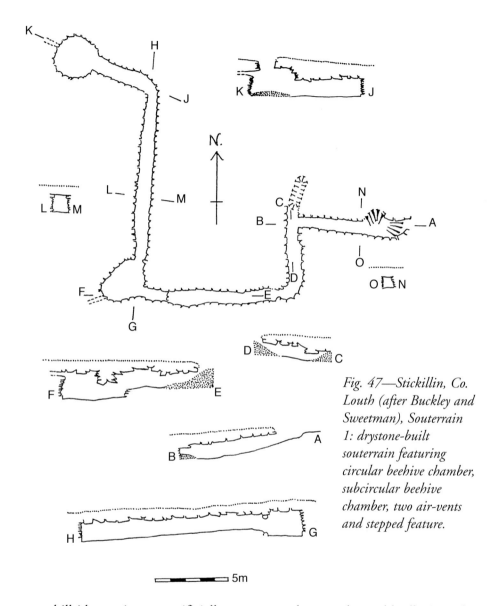

Fig. 47—Stickillin, Co. Louth (after Buckley and Sweetman), Souterrain 1: drystone-built souterrain featuring circular beehive chamber, subcircular beehive chamber, two air-vents and stepped feature.

steep hillside or in an artificially constructed mound, could alleviate the difficulties created by the resulting pronounced slope. At Knowth (Souterrain no. 2), Co. Meath (G. Eogan, pers. comm.), for example, it was only by the creation of three stages (involving two stepped features) that it proved possible for the builders to negotiate the severe angle of descent in the body of the main passage grave mound.

Structurally, unlike (in theory) the trapdoor, it would have proved impossible to disguise the presence of a stepped feature. Neither, it seems, were they generally intended as impediments as they would not have incommoded an

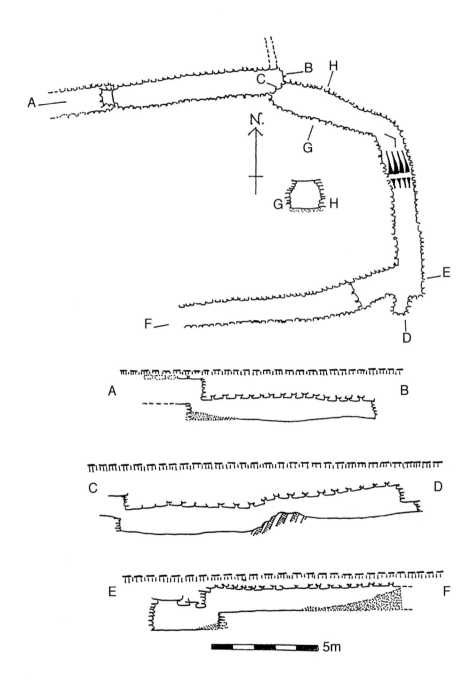

Fig. 48—Rathiddy, Co. Louth (after Rynne): drystone-built souterrain featuring trapdoor, inverted stepped feature, air-vent and cubby-hole.

unwelcome entrant's progress. Indeed, save for the rare exceptions noted above, it would appear that they could not have been intended to fulfil any other role than one of a purely technical nature.

It is interesting to note that the outer stepped feature at Spittle Quarter, Co. Down (Brannon 1990, 40), displayed some of the constituent elements of a trapdoor. Indeed, no fewer than three scarcements were in evidence. The key difference, however, was the fact that the corresponding drop in the roof of the passage was totally insufficient to accommodate the placing of a covering device. The laterally projecting lintel incorporated into the end wall of the upper passage is also worth noting as it is reminiscent of a corresponding feature in the inner 'stalac-type' obstruction at Sheepland Mor (also in County Down) (see Section 13 (5)). Thus the stepped feature (F1) at Spittle Quarter is another reminder of the close relationship between various features in a given area.

At Raheennamadra, Co. Limerick, an inverted stepped feature provided direct access from the inner chamber to an 'escape passage'/external exit. This pattern was repeated at Killosolan, Co. Galway, and again at Rinn, Co. Galway, although in this instance the exit passage extended from the penultimate chamber. An 'escape passage' was recorded at Dough (Lisnaleagaun), Co. Clare. An inverted stepped feature (Feature 2), opening from the same ovoid chamber as its companion feature, facilitated access to it (Fig. 31).

The overall distribution pattern of the stepped feature is remarkably similar to that of the trapdoor. Indeed ten, if not eleven, of the souterrains that incorporated a stepped feature also contained a trapdoor. In one instance, at Thomastown, Co. Louth (Gosling 1979, 215), the builders placed a trapdoor and a stepped feature in a combination strikingly similar to the double stepped feature arrangement employed at Termonfeckin 1 (see above).

6. Air-vents

Air-vents are narrow ducts leading from the walls of either a chamber or a passage (Pl. 21). Their surface openings were presumably disguised to avoid detection. They were mostly drystone-built. The 'average' vent has a width of 0.15–0.35m (with the majority in the 0.2–0.3m range) and a height of 0.15–0.3m (with the majority in the 0.15–0.25m range). Lengths vary; the longest air-vents in the archaeological literature were recorded at Knockdhu, Co. Antrim (Lawlor 1915–16, 32) (7.92m+), and at Palmersland, Co. Louth (Ua Cuinn 1904–7, 38) — an alleged 8.84m (see Appendix 4).

Air-vents have been recorded in all parts of the island. Their actual numbers, however, would not appear to occur in direct proportion to the number of souterrains present in any given area. The available data suggest that the overall percentage of souterrains in possession of an air-vent is low, varying from less than 2% (in County Donegal) to 12% (in the greater Meath area). These statistics should allow for the fact that the air-vent would appear to be a predominantly chamber-related feature (the chamber–passage origin ratio is currently *c.* 83% to 17%). The fact that the chamber is not always open to inspection must therefore be taken into consideration. Nevertheless, the considerable number of scientifically excavated souterrains that have failed to reveal an air-vent is significant.

It is rare for a souterrain to feature more than one or two air-vents. There are exceptions: Souterrain B at Donaghmore, Co. Louth (Rynne 1957–60b, 148) (Fig. 42), contained four vents. No individual chamber, to date, has featured more than two vents (and this is exceptional), for example Glenfahan, Co. Kerry (Deane 1893–6, 100), and Ballynahow, Co. Kerry (Clinton and Kelly, forthcoming) (Fig. 60).

Firm data on the outer extremities of air-vents are rare. Where they opened in isolation it would appear that their presence was often disguised by the placing of a field stone or thin slab across the opening, for example at Balrathboyne Glebe, Co. Meath (Hartnett 1952), and Tavnaghoney, Co. Antrim (Hobson 1909, 223). Elsewhere vents have opened into stone revetments associated with surface structures, for example at Ballynavenooragh, Co. Kerry (Clinton, forthcoming b) (Pl. 3), and Ballywee, Co. Antrim (Lynn 1975, 4). A small number of vents originated in a 'host feature', for example in a cupboard, as at Lisnagranchy 1, Co. Galway (Knox and Redington 1915–16, 179), or in a recess, as at Togherstown (Souterrain 1), Co. Westmeath (Macalister and Praeger 1929–31, 72) (Fig. 54).

Whilst the air-vent can be found in a wide variety of souterrains it would appear to occur more frequently in the more complex forms. This raises a key question. Surely it would be the smaller, more confined souterrains that would have been in need of an air supply? The occurrence of a number of peculiarly placed vents is pertinent to this debate. At Carrickananny, Co. Armagh (Chart 1940, 73; McLornan 1984b), a vent extended from a lateral chamber to the main passage. Similarly, at Mullaghfin, Co. Meath (M. Moore 1987, 53), the vent extended from the beehive roof of one chamber to that of another. It should also be remembered that the overwhelming majority of souterrains did not contain an air-vent at all. Is it possible, therefore, that these vents also performed additional tasks, for example the monitoring of surface activity during a raid?

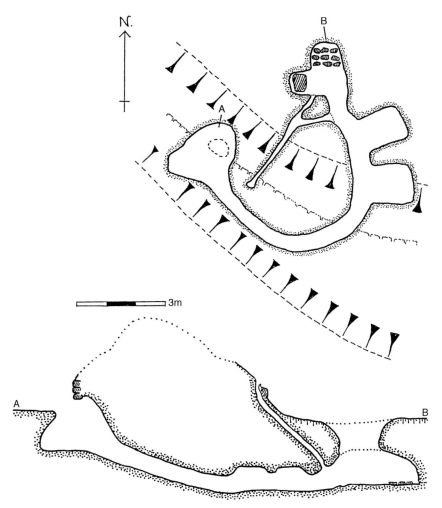

Fig. 49—Oldcourt, Co. Cork (after Ó Cuileanáin and Murphy): ringfort bank, earth-cut souterrain featuring slab-floored cubby-hole, paved recess and air-vent.

7. Drains

Drains are a rare feature in both tunnelled and drystone-built souterrains, and appear to be predominantly chamber-related (current data would suggest on a ratio of *c.* 80% to *c.* 20%). Allowing for both the low setting of the feature and the lack of information on chambers from many known souterrains, their actual number might be somewhat higher (see Appendix 5).

In drystone-built souterrains drains usually take the form of narrow stone-lined channels that extended downwards from the chamber or passage wall, for example at Ballyhacket-Glenahorry, Co. Londonderry (Ligar 1833, 23) (Fig. 9), and Rock, Co. Donegal (Dunlevy 1967, 230; Lacy 1983, 238) (Fig. 51). Indeed, even in tunnelled souterrains this was the format generally employed. Thus in tunnelled souterrains it was necessary to incorporate the drain into a 'built' element, i.e. the construction shaft, for example, as in the earth-cut souterrains at Moneygaff East (Cleary 1989) and Little Island (Fahy 1970) (Fig. 69), Co. Cork. A number of the tunnelled souterrains also contained 'feeder gullies' in the floor of the associated chamber, for example at Johnstown (McCarthy 1977, 261) (Fig. 50) and Brackcloon (S.P. Ó Ríordáin 1934–5, 78), Co. Cork. A gully in the floor of a chamber in the rock-cut souterrain at Dunisky, Co. Cork (McCarthy 1977, 237) (Fig. 70), simply emptied into a lower-lying chamber. The external ends of drains have been poorly documented. At Cush, Co. Limerick (S.P. Ó Ríordáin 1938–40, 103), the drain emptied into the fosse of the associated ringfort. At Liscahane, Co. Cork (U. Egan, pers. comm.; Ó Donnabháin 1982), the drain, 11m in length, emerged at the bottom of a steep natural slope. Ahakeera, Co. Cork (Twohig 1976, 27) (Fig. 32), provided an insight into the resolution of drains deprived of an easy or obvious outlet. There, the drain apparently emptied into a soak-pit located beneath a construction shaft.

Technical considerations would generally have dictated whether or not to incorporate a drain when constructing the souterrain. At Benagh, Co. Louth (Buckley and Sweetman 1991, 108), for example, the souterrain had been constructed in a low-lying inland promontory fort at the junction of two rivers, where flooding could be anticipated. There are indications, however, that some drains could have been secondary features. In the earth-cut souterrain at Johnstown, Co. Cork (McCarthy 1977, 261) (Fig. 50), it was observed that the hard sand wall of the chamber had not been significantly disturbed by the insertion of the drain. It was suggested that the bulk of the drain must have been constructed in an independent adjoining trench. Such a creation could have been either a primary feature or a secondary feature (i.e. as a late reaction to unexpected flooding problems).

It is extremely rare for more than one drain to be recorded in a souterrain. However, at Little Island, Co. Cork (Fahy 1970) (Fig. 69), and at Socks, Co. Leitrim (Campbell 1979), two drains were recorded. At Ballintermon, Co. Kerry (Kelly 1982–3b, 10) (Fig. 58), one chamber featured two drains — a unique occurrence, to date, in Ireland.

8. Cupboards, cubby-holes, recesses

The occurrence in souterrains of 'cupboards', 'cubby-holes', 'recesses', 'alcoves', 'annexes', 'aumbries', 'storage-recesses', etc. has been noted by many writers over

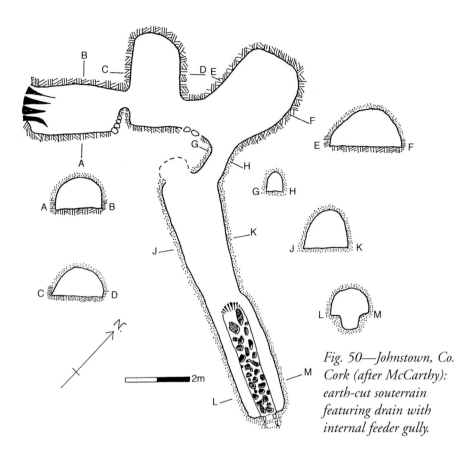

Fig. 50—Johnstown, Co. Cork (after McCarthy): earth-cut souterrain featuring drain with internal feeder gully.

the years. The descriptions, and indeed the terminology, can often prove to be interchangeable and therefore ultimately confusing.

A system of classification has been attempted by the present writer in an effort to differentiate between these hitherto amorphous features and to establish any potential patterns of recurrence in the various types.

To differentiate between the various types an artificial set of dimensions must be adopted. Other aspects, such as structural elements, context and potential function, have also been taken into consideration.

		Width	Height	Depth
1.	The cupboard	0–0.5m	0–0.5m	0–0.6m
2.	The cubby-hole	0.5–0.75m	0.5–0.7m	0.6–0.9m
3.	The recess	0.75m+	0.7m+	0.9m+

As these structures are ultimately free-form creations, a variable of ±0.25m on any one of the three qualifying dimensions may be accepted.

(1) The cupboard

The basic criterion is that this feature should only have the capacity to contain small inanimate objects. It can occur along the course of a passage or as an addendum to a chamber. Although it can occur either at floor level or as an insertion into the passage or chamber wall, to date the latter position has been predominant (see Appendix 6) Pl. 23).

(2) The cubby-hole

The basic criterion is that this feature should have the capacity to act as a functional and serviceable minor storage area. It can occur either along the course of a passage or as an addendum to a chamber. It predominantly occurs at floor level and only rarely as an insertion into a passage or chamber wall (Pl.8).

(3) The recess

This feature is of a more amorphous nature. In its most developed form it should have the capacity to serve either as a storage area or as additional occupational space. However, it should be noted that many of the known recesses were underdeveloped in depth. The feature can occur either along the course of a passage or as an addendum to a chamber. It almost exclusively occurs at floor level and only very rarely as an insertion into the wall of a passage or chamber.

There are not many indications available as to the exact purpose of these features. The small dimensions and varying positions of the cupboards, and to a lesser extent the cubby-holes, would have rendered them inadequate to fulfil any major function. They may have been employed in a number of minor roles. One possibility is that the cupboards could have been used as repositories for stone lamps. Two examples of cupboards, at Loughcrew, Co. Meath (Clinton 1993, 120) (Fig. 35), and Dunbin Little, Co. Louth (P. Corcoran 1929–32, 499), and two examples of cubby-holes, at Bawntaaffe (Souterrain 1) (Rynne 1957–60a, 99) and Millockstown (Souterrain 1) (Manning 1986, 147), Co. Louth, were located in relatively close proximity to trapdoors. The exact relationship, if any, between these features is unclear, unless the cupboards and cubby-holes in question were repositories for lamps used to aid negotiation of the impediments.

The cupboard and the cubby-hole have, to date, been discovered almost exclusively in drystone-built souterrains, or occasionally, for example at Dromkeen East, Co. Kerry (Twohig 1974, 9), or Townparks, Co. Donegal (Lacy 1983, 227), in the drystone-built sections of souterrains of mixed construction. Cubby-holes are infrequently found in tunnelled souterrains, for example at Oldcourt, Co. Cork (Ó Cuileanáin and Murphy 1961–2, 84) (Fig. 49). Recesses are most strongly represented in drystone-built souterrains, for example at

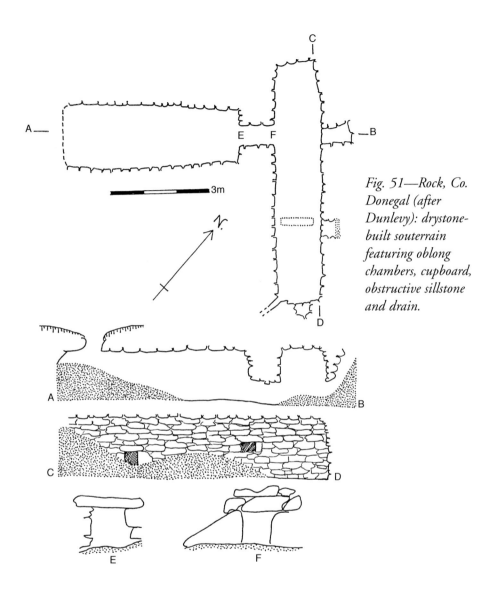

Fig. 51—Rock, Co. Donegal (after Dunlevy): drystone-built souterrain featuring oblong chambers, cupboard, obstructive sillstone and drain.

Togherstown (Souterrain 1), Co. Westmeath (Macalister and Praeger 1929–31, 71, 74) (Fig. 54). They have also been recorded in tunnelled souterrains, for example at Cavangarden, Co. Donegal (Davies 1946; Lacy 1983, 233), and Letterkeen, Co. Mayo (S.P. Ó Ríordáin and MacDermott 1951–2, 102). The relatively spacious recess, especially when occurring as an addendum to a chamber, such as the example at Termonfeckin, Co. Louth (Ó Floinn 1978, 130) (Fig. 53), may have served as a convenient storage area. In times of emergency the function may have altered, especially if the chamber became overcrowded.

A recurring theme in the drystone-built examples of all three features is the absence of formal stonework at the back. Whilst this phenomenon is least

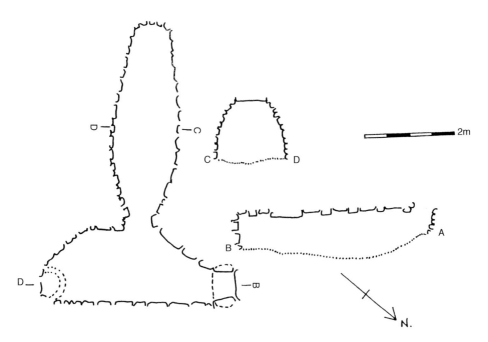

Fig. 52—Rallagh, Co. Londonderry (after Stokes): drystone-built souterrain featuring irregular-shaped chambers, simple constriction and cubby-hole.
(By permission of The Royal Irish Academy. © RIA.)

apparent in recesses, it is strongly represented in cubby-holes, for example at Craig Hill, Co. Antrim (Waterman 1956b, 90) (Fig. 17), with cupboards, like the example at Rock, Co. Donegal (Dunlevy 1967, 230; Lacy 1983, 238) (Fig. 51), statistically occupying the middle ground. The significant number of examples would seem to indicate a clearly defined rationale at work. What the exact motivation was, however, remains unknown.

A number of these receptacles acted as 'host features' to other structural devices; for example, the cupboard at Gortroe, Co. Galway (Knox and Redington 1915–16, 181), and the recess at Togherstown (Souterrain 1), Co. Westmeath (Macalister and Praeger 1929–31, 71) (Fig. 54), both had air-vents extending from their inner reaches.

9. Steps

Both earth- and rock-cut as well as drystone-built steps were employed in souterrains. To differentiate between the simple step and the stepped feature, the height of the former should not be more than 0.5m and ideally should fall between 0.25m and 0.45m. A flight of more than three steps in a souterrain

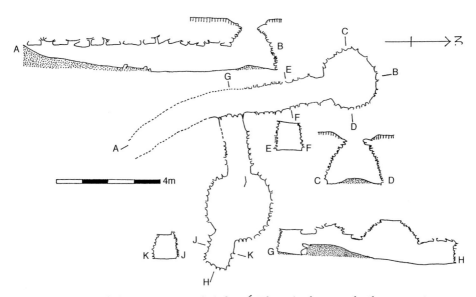

Fig. 53—Termonfeckin 1, Co. Louth (after Ó Floinn): drystone-built souterrain featuring unrestricted passage, circular beehive chambers, stepped features and recess.

would be unusual. It is inevitable that many examples of the simple step will have been either overlooked or obscured by debris, and thus it may occur more frequently than the available evidence might suggest.

Most examples of steps have been uncovered in a limited number of clearly defined locations in the souterrain (see Appendix 7).

Steps have been used to provide convenient entry into a souterrain, for example in Souterrains A and B at Cahercommaun, Co. Clare (Hencken 1938, 20, 22) (Fig. 28), and at Lisleagh 2, Co. Cork (Monk 1995, 111). Souterrain A at Cahercommaun featured a flight of four built steps and one rock-cut step, while Souterrain B featured a narrow flight of three built steps and one rock-cut step. The steps at the entrance to the souterrain at Lisleagh were earth-cut.

Steps can also be found in the context of an elevated trapdoor. They were used to aid descent or ascent from or to the platform, for example at Ballinphuil, Co. Galway (Costello 1903–4, 8) (Fig. 43), and Shanvallyhugh, Co. Mayo (Topographical Files, NMI).

A significant number of steps performed the purely perfunctory role of making minor adjustments in the internal level of the souterrain. These can occur in the course of a passage, at the junction of two passages, or at the junction of a passage and a chamber. Two souterrains made exceptional use of the simple step. In Souterrain 1 at Togherstown, Co. Westmeath (Macalister and Praeger 1929–31, 71) (Fig. 54), steps were used at four separate points in the

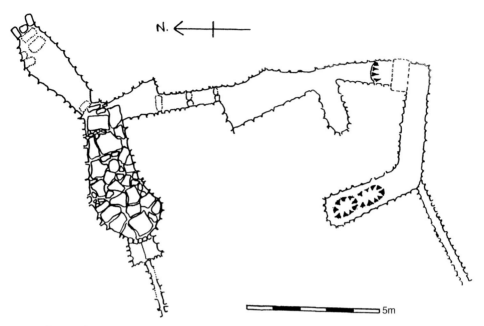

Fig. 54—Togherstown, Co. Westmeath (after Macalister and Praeger), Souterrain 1: drystone-built souterrain featuring irregular-shaped chambers, air-vents, recess, steps, paving, pits and sillstones.

structure. Similarly, in Souterrain A at Donaghmore, Co. Louth (Rynne 1965a), no fewer than five individual examples were employed.

One of the more novel uses of steps was recorded at Dowth, Co. Meath (Deane 1887, 55; Coffey 1912, 48). The northern passage grave and the souterrain had been integrated into a single complex by the builders of the latter monument. Access to the 'converted' tomb was facilitated by means of a flight of three steps.

The simple step in rare instances was used in combination with other structural elements to create a minor impediment. At Toberdoney, Co. Down (Collins 1964, 129), a large slab formed a step in the passage floor. A protruding jambstone flanked the step. The roof of the souterrain was at its lowest at this point. The passage curved immediately after the occurrence of this combination of features. Again, in Souterrain 4A at Marshes Upper, Co. Louth (Gowen 1992, 83) (Fig. 25), the western chamber was approached by two ascending (rock-cut) steps. In the light of the evidence from Toberdoney it may be significant that the steps were followed by a protruding jambstone and an immediate change of direction in the passage/chamber.

10. Cobblestones and paving

The formal paving or cobbling of a souterrain floor was an extremely rare phenomenon in Ireland. It is possible that more informal instances of partial paving or cobbling have, on occasion, been overlooked or obscured by debris.

The finest example of paving, to date, was recorded in Souterrain 1 at Togherstown, Co. Westmeath (Macalister and Praeger 1929–31, 71) (Fig. 54). The entire floor of Chamber B was covered with sandstone flags in what the excavators aptly likened to a 'crazy pavement' design. The flags varied in size and shape and yet were pieced together in a most fastidious manner.

The closest parallel to the Togherstown floor was recorded at Kildalton, Co. Kilkenny (Prendergast 1958, 38) (Fig. 55), where the featured chamber and the short (exposed) length of passage were paved with flagstones. The component slabs varied in shape and size but a closely integrated effect had been achieved.

The recorded use of cobbling in souterrains is also extremely rare. At Smithstown, Co. Meath (Gowen 1989, 34), the ramp entrance into Souterrain 1 had been covered with a layer of loosely spread small stones, undoubtedly to steady an entrant's progress down the ramp.

At Guilford, Co. Westmeath, the floor of the chamber was covered with a dense layer of tightly packed stones (Pl. 16). As this stratum of mostly small, rounded and squared stones was overlain by a layer of hard-packed gravel it is possible that it was laid as a foundation course.

It should always be remembered that as neither paving-slabs nor cobblestones are physically integrated into the actual structure of a souterrain they may be secondary features. Given the fact that many souterrains were used for various dubious purposes up to very recent times it is not impossible that some examples may turn out to be of modern date.

Other examples have all the appearances of being early secondary 'reactionary' features. In cases of ongoing problems with flooding, as, for example, at Ballynavenooragh, Co. Kerry (Clinton, forthcoming b), it was inevitable that the settlers might consider an attempt at 'damage control'. At Ballynavenooragh they laid down a dense layer of stones and rocks to raise the floor level of the chamber. In Souterrain B at Bawntaaffe, Co. Louth (Rynne 1957–60a, 101) (Fig. 39), a series of flat slabs had been laid on the steepest section of the damp, sticky mud floor of the passage/chamber, probably to facilitate steadier movement.

It is possible that some examples of paving were the result of a desire on the part of the builders to achieve a serviceable floor. At Tyrella, Co. Down, it was observed that 'the chippings' that had resulted as a by-product of the dressing of the component stones of the souterrain had been employed to form 'a perfectly

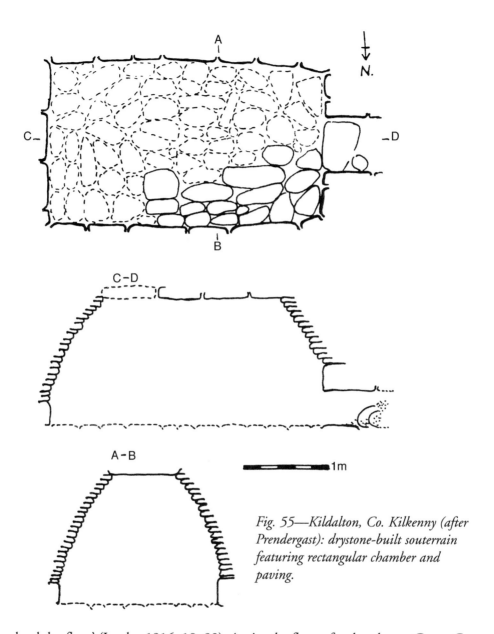

Fig. 55—Kildalton, Co. Kilkenny (after Prendergast): drystone-built souterrain featuring rectangular chamber and paving.

level dry floor' (Lawlor 1916–18, 92). Again, the floor of a chamber at Coars, Co. Kerry, had been covered with 'an even spread of stones' (A. O'Sullivan and Sheehan 1996, 210). A raised floor of (sandstone) rock chippings was recorded at Rath, Co. Cork (McCarthy 1977, 303). In Chamber IV the layer of chippings was 0.2m deep. The floor of Chamber I was also covered with rock chippings. The dense layer in Chamber IV was deposited in the lowest-lying section of the chamber. McCarthy (1977, 306) advanced the theory that the chippings may have been an original feature of the souterrain, deposited to prevent 'wet muddy floors'.

There are a number of known examples where paving or quasi-paving has been used in a limited or specific fashion — mainly as paving restricted to a defined area. The floor of the recess attached to the inner chamber at Oldcourt, Co. Cork (Ó Cuileanáin and Murphy 1961–2, 83), was paved with small slabs (Fig. 49). It occupied an area of 0.76m by 0.76m. The floor of the immediately adjacent cubby-hole (which was attached to the same chamber) featured a single sizeable flagstone, beneath which a bronze-coated iron bell was discovered in a pit. It is possible that the paving in the recess was laid down to make the flagstone on the floor of the cubby-hole appear less noticeable.

11. Door-jambs

A small number of souterrains have produced evidence for the former existence of an integral wooden door. The available evidence can manifest itself in one (or more) of three ways:
(a) by the presence of slots or niches in the opposing passage walls;
(b) by the presence in the passage floor of a pair of post-holes (flanking the opposing passage walls) or, alternatively, a single post-hole flanking one of the walls;
(c) by the presence of the remains of opposing wooden door-jambs.
   Generally speaking, the wooden doors would appear to have had two specific sitings:
(i) at the entrance to the souterrain;
(ii) as a strategically placed internal feature.
There are, to date, more known examples in the latter position (see Appendix 8).
   Souterrain A at Donaghmore, Co. Louth (Rynne 1965a) (Fig. 56), produced conclusive evidence for the former existence of a wooden door at the entrance to the souterrain. Not only were there two niches present in the opposing walls, but a series of post- and stake-holes, including two post-holes in the floors of the niches, gently arced between the latter features. There can be little doubt that this configuration represented the vestigial remains of a wooden (post-and-wattle?) door (Fig. 19).
   An example of an internally sited doorway was recorded at Marshes Upper 1, Co. Louth (P. Gosling, pers. comm.) (Fig. 39). Two opposing slots extended from floor to roof level at a point of constriction in the passage. Both the morphological aspects and the position are representative of an emerging pattern for the internally sited doorways. The fact that the souterrain was of the simple undifferentiated passage/chamber type is also indicative of the emerging trend.
   Coolcran, Co. Fermanagh (B. Williams 1985, 77) (Fig. 7), produced the

most graphic evidence for wooden doors. At a point of constriction in the subrectangular structure the remains of a pair of sturdy wooden uprights were discovered. Owing to the favourable level of the water-table not only these two timbers but the remains of 48 oak timbers were recovered *in situ*. The two uprights in question undoubtedly constituted the jambs of a wooden door separating two timber-lined chambers.

At Drumad, Co. Louth (Gosling 1979, 209), a pair of corresponding niches or 'sockets' were contained in the walls immediately outside the side chamber. The subrectangular chamber lay at right angles to the main passage, to which it was connected by a short portal. It was in the latter feature that the two niches had been inserted at floor level. The eastern niche was the better defined of the pair. It was 0.3m wide, 0.32m deep and 0.17m high. Its back wall consisted of fine sand. The western niche was more insubstantial. It was 0.4m wide, 0.13m deep and 0.13m high, and its back wall consisted of the hard natural till. Gosling suggested that the niches were connected with the former presence of a door to the chamber and had possibly contained a wooden door-sill.

A novel combination of features was recently recorded in the walls of an unrestricted passage at Killally, Co. Louth (Clinton and Stout 1997, 129) (Fig. 57). Both the western and the eastern wall of the passage had a slot or niche incorporated into its façade. While these were set directly opposite one another, they were not aligned. They occurred approximately 1m above floor level (there was a considerable amount of debris in the immediate area). The western niche was 0.13–0.17m wide, 0.14m high and 0.49m deep. Its back wall consisted of two small stacked slabs. The eastern niche was 0.1–0.12m wide, 0.08m high and 0.4–0.53m deep.

Both niches were paired with slightly protruding jambstones. These were not intrusive enough to be interpreted as obstructive features. The jambstone in the western wall was 0.67m in (exposed) height, 0.39m in 'depth' and 0.08–0.09m in width. It projected a mere 0.1m into the line of the passage. The corresponding jamb in the eastern wall was 0.88m in (exposed) height. It had all the appearances of being a deliberately unexcavated segment of bedrock. This redan-shaped rock was 0.44m wide and projected 0.28m into the line of the passage.

The elevated setting of the niches and their unaligned axes would seem to suggest that they were used to hold short wooden beams. These could have held a wooden (wattle?) door in place (pressed against the jambstones).

Discussion

A common denominator of the majority of known examples of souterrains featuring vestigial doorways is the significant amount of floor-space that was consistently closed off by their projected wooden doors. In the cases of Marshes

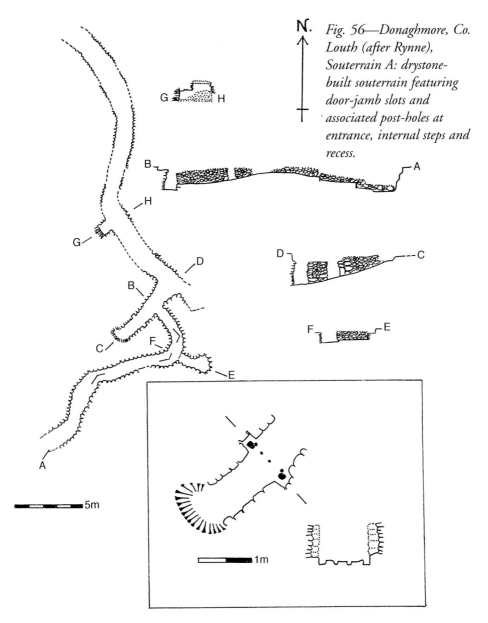

Fig. 56—Donaghmore, Co. Louth (after Rynne), Souterrain A: drystone-built souterrain featuring door-jamb slots and associated post-holes at entrance, internal steps and recess.

Upper 1 (P. Gosling, pers. comm.), Marshes Upper 3A (Gowen 1992, 64), Corderry (Buckley and Sweetman 1991, 112) and Ballybarrack 1 (E.P. Kelly, pers. comm.), all in County Louth, and (potentially) Knowth 7, Co. Meath (G. Eogan, pers. comm.), a minimum of 10m of passage/chamber had been enclosed. At Portlecka, Co. Clare (Westropp 1913, 236), complete chambers had been closed off by the wooden doors. Obviously, as in the cases of Donaghmore (Souterrain A), Co. Louth (Rynne 1965a), Ballywee 3, Co. Antrim (Lynn 1975, 6), and possibly Rathnew 3, Co. Westmeath (Macalister and Praeger 1928, 104),

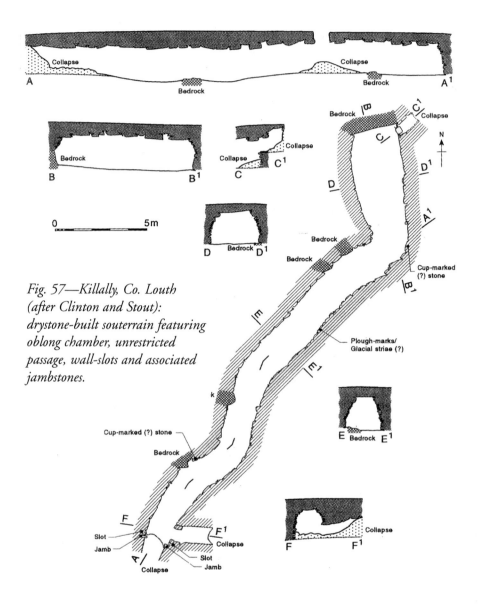

Fig. 57—Killally, Co. Louth (after Clinton and Stout): drystone-built souterrain featuring oblong chamber, unrestricted passage, wall-slots and associated jambstones.

where the doors occurred at the entrances to the souterrains, the entire floor-space had been included. At Randalstown 1, Co. Meath (K. Campbell, pers. comm.), only 4.9m of the undifferentiated passage/chamber was enclosed. However, it should be noted that the total length of the souterrain was only 13.4m (although admittedly the total length of Ballybarrack 1 was only 14m). It might be suggested that the presence of three souterrains at the latter site facilitated specific and/or separate functions. Alternatively the differences in enclosed space might have been determined by localised requirements.

A further point regarding the actual positioning of the projected doors is the fact that there does not appear to have been any conspicuous attempt to cloak their presence. Souterrains such as Marshes Upper 3A, Marshes Upper 1 (both in County Louth) and Carrickcloghan, Co. Armagh (B. Williams 1983), had a good straight run of 3–7m in the final stretch of passage leading up to the door, and although there were slight bends in the approaches at Ballybarrack 1 and Randalstown 1, and a slightly more pronounced bend at Corderry, yet there was no awkwardness or hindrance to their basic accessibility.

The construction of a door at the entrance to a souterrain is logical enough. As the outer reaches of many souterrains were probably used regularly as casual storage areas, especially for perishable goods in hot weather, a wooden door would have acted as an effective deterrent to any scavengers, even of a domestic nature. A door in this context might also suggest convenient access and therefore a sloping and gradual rather than an abrupt entrance. The only reliable data pertinent to the issue came from Donaghmore (Souterrain A) and Ballybarrack (Souterrain 1) (where the door had been constructed 3.7m from the entrance). Unfortunately the outer reaches of the lintelled roofs of both of these souterrains had not survived. Their respective floor levels, however, appear to indicate gradual entrances of a non-extreme nature.

The actual siting of the internally placed wooden doors is the most noteworthy aspect of the feature. As indicated above, they consistently enclosed a significant proportion of the total floor-space of the souterrain. The key question, however, must be why the doors were not placed at the entrance to the overall structure, thereby enclosing the entire floor area. One interpretation might be that at certain sites two classes of goods were being stored in the souterrain, possibly those marked for short-term use and those marked for long-term use. A wooden door could hardly have had much impact on temperature and thus it is difficult to speculate as to what the differentiation in goods might have been. It may, however, be relevant that the location of the two air-vents at Marshes Upper 3A lay within the inner confines as delineated by the projected wooden door.

As the doors cannot have been of a very substantial nature, it is more than likely that their role was to provide a domestic protection for the contents within, as opposed to preventing a forcible entry into either the souterrain or its inner reaches. An intruder armed with the lightest of hand-axes would have had relatively little difficulty in breaching one of these doors. Indeed, the projected nature of the doors, when taken into consideration with the fact that, with the exception of Knockballyclery, Co. Galway (Gosling *et al.*, forthcoming, no. 5881), none of the other souterrains in question possessed a significant impedimental device, tends to suggest that they were related solely to storage considerations.

12. Porthole-slabs

These are perforated slabs which are generally encountered in the course of a restricted passage or extended constriction, or at the junction of a passage/constriction and a chamber. The access hole was bored at ground level, resulting in a semicircular or angular archway (Fig. 58; Pl. 7). Only 27 examples of these porthole-slabs are known (see Appendix 9).

The apertures in the slabs do not vary greatly in size. In width they vary between 0.3m and 0.5m (with the vast majority falling in the 0.33–0.45m range). In height they vary between 0.18m and 0.6m (with the vast majority falling in the 0.3–0.45m range).

There can be little doubt that these devices were intended to be impediments. Clark (1961, 77) and Waddell (1970a, 16) have suggested that, owing to their size, the porthole-slabs may have been intended to block unwelcome adult intruders and thus afford a final refuge for children. This view may be unnecessarily restricted. Given the negligible length involved, it would be well within the physical capabilities of any average-sized adult to penetrate apertures of this size. However, it is true that an unwelcome entrant would have been placed at an enormous disadvantage. It is significant that almost 40% of the slabs were placed at the inner extremities of passage/constrictions (at the point of entry into the chamber), for example at Glantane, Co. Kerry (Kelly 1982–3b, 5) (Fig. 29). A further 23% occur midway along a restricted passage or extended constriction, for example at Carhoo East, Co. Kerry (Waddell 1970a, 15), and would thus have achieved the same objective, i.e. to confer all advantages on those taking refuge within the inner confines of the souterrain.

Of all the various structural elements of souterrains in Ireland, no other feature enjoys such a closely defined distribution area as does the porthole-slab group (Fig. 59). They are in fact confined to the Corcu Duibne-ruled areas of the Dingle and Iveragh peninsulas in west Kerry. The explanation for such a specialised device occurring in such a restricted distribution zone may lie in the existence of a regional school of souterrain-builders, or possibly in a set of (as yet) unrecognised local imperatives (see Clinton 1997, 5).

13. Additional defensive features

(1) Horizontally placed slabs
An extremely rare defensive device is the horizontally placed slab, which could be described as resembling a low-set lintel (Pl. 20), the result being the creation of both an upper and a lower aperture. This form of obstruction was first

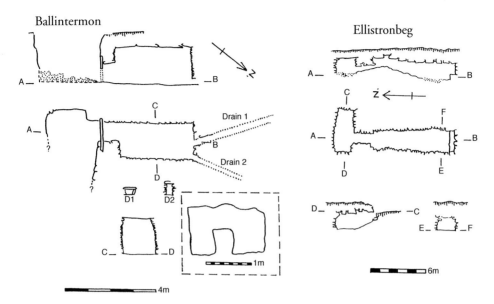

Fig. 58—Ballintermon, Co. Kerry (after Kelly): damaged drystone-built souterrain featuring (two?) rectangular chambers, an extended constriction, porthole-slab and two drains.

Ellistronbeg, Co. Mayo (after Lavelle): drystone-built souterrain featuring rectangular and oblong chambers, a restricted passage and bench.

identified by H.T. Knox, who maintained that there were not many known examples of the feature. Subsequent research has not altered that initial perception.

These features appear to have been an elaboration on a simple barrier concept. In effect the upper aperture would appear to have offered the defenders the option of a physical response.

At Rockfield, Co. Mayo (Knox 1916, 75), the horizontally placed slab subdivided an oblong chamber. It was observed that the width of the chamber contracted at the point of insertion of the horizontal slab. The entrance passage and outer chamber at Gortroe, Co. Galway (Knox and Redington 1915–16, 181), were divided by a horizontally placed slab, which rested on two outjuttings of the passage/chamber walls. Again, at Ballynahow, Co. Kerry (Clinton and Kelly, forthcoming) (Fig. 60; Pl. 20), two perpendicularly set chambers were separated by a horizontally placed slab.

The extremely limited evidence suggests that the use of a horizontally placed slab as a defensive element may have been a phenomenon with an exclusively western distribution.

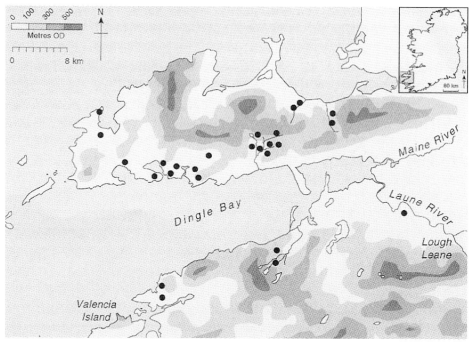

Fig. 59—Distribution of porthole-slabs.

(2) Head obstructions

Head obstructions are roofing lintels that were deliberately set at a lower level. This simple but effective ploy would have temporarily slowed the progress of an unwanted intruder. However, these 'head obstructions' are neither a homogeneous nor, at times, even an instantly recognisable feature. Indeed, it is sometimes extremely difficult to decide whether a given lintel was deliberately set low or simply badly set.

Head obstructions may be deployed at various points in a souterrain. A favoured location is the final run-in as one approaches a chamber. At Loughcrew, Co. Meath (Clinton 1993, 122) (Fig. 35), the fourth-last lintel in the lengthy Passage III constituted the head obstruction. At Bective 1, Co. Meath (Fig. 6), it was the final lintel in Passage II (prior to the junction with Chamber I). Even more graphic is the positioning of the second lintel in the steep sloping entrance passage in Souterrain 8 at Knowth, Co. Meath (Eogan 1968, 358) (Fig. 26). The deliberate nature of its intrusive setting is clearly illustrated by the succeeding lintels, which duly reverted back to the original line of the passage roof.

(3) Sills and sillstones

Sillstones, in the strictest sense, are stones placed at the foot of an aperture. The ordinary sillstone lies flush with the souterrain floor, or at least an element of it,

156

like the one used at Glantane, Co. Kerry (Kelly 1982–3b, 6) (Fig. 29). But there is a second type of sillstone, which protruded from the floor and was obviously obstructive in nature. These could be realised either with set stones or by simply leaving an unexcavated sill of bedrock in the floor. In the dark interior of a souterrain these features could have functioned as effective 'trip-stones'.

The known examples fall into three broad categories:
(i) sills or sillstones that occur in the course of a passage or undifferentiated passage/chamber;
(ii) sills or sillstones that occur in a constricted setting;
(ii) sills or sillstones that occur at the junction of a passage and chamber.

Two stones set on edge, end to end, traversed a short connecting passage in Souterrain 1 at Togherstown, Co. Westmeath (Macalister and Praeger 1929–31, 72) (Fig. 54). The excavators regarded these as being of an obstructive nature. In an undifferentiated passage/chamber at Rock, Co. Donegal (Dunlevy 1967, 230; Lacy 1983, 238) (Fig. 51), a low sillstone extended across the width of the structure.

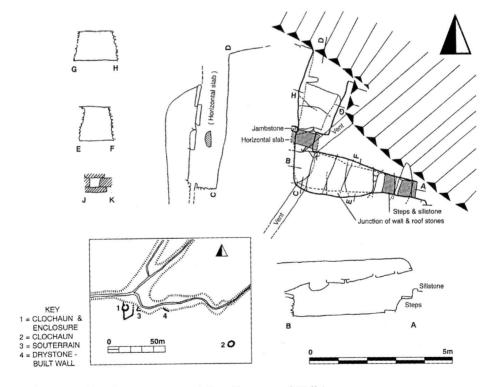

Fig. 60—Ballynahow, Co. Kerry (after Clinton and Kelly).

At Raheen, Co. Tipperary (Prendergast 1972), a constriction linking two of the chambers was impeded by a horizontally placed sillstone that rose up to half of the total height of the passageway. A natural rock version of this arrangement was recorded at Palmersland, Co. Louth (Ua Cuinn 1904–7, 38), where the sill combined with a narrowing of the passage and a slight lowering of the roof to create an effective impediment.

The souterrain at Glanfahan, Co. Kerry (Cuppage 1986, 203), and Souterrain 5 at Knowth, Co. Meath (G. Eogan, pers. comm.), both had protruding stone-built sills at the junction of the access passage and inner chamber.

(4) Jambstones/jambs-and-lintel formations

The conjunction of many chambers and passages was complemented by the presence of imposing jambstones. These were decorative effects which may have also helped to bond the walls together. A number of souterrains in the south utilised these portal jambstones as minor obstructive devices. At Rath, Co. Cork (McCarthy 1977, 303) (Fig. 38), for example, the conjunctions of the four oblong chambers were marked by three pairs of protruding jambstones. A variation on the theme was recorded at Garryntemple, Co. Tipperary (Hurley 1981–2, 65) (Fig. 30), where the entrance to the restricted passage that linked Chambers 1 and 2 was severely impeded by the insertion of two jambstones and a low-lying lintel. In effect the two jambstones began the line of the passage within the confines of the outer chamber.

There are not many examples of obstructive jambstones functioning in isolation. Even when only one jambstone is present it is generally found in combination with other features. At Ahakeera, Co. Cork (Twohig 1976, 26) (Fig. 32), for example, the two independent jambstones were combined with a pilaster-like column of hard boulder clay and a constriction respectively in order to impede the entrant's progress.

There are, however, a number of recorded examples where the siting of a single jambstone in a specific context was apparently deemed to be effective enough.

At Roovesmore, Co. Cork (Lane-Fox 1867, 123), the entrance into the chamber from the access passageway was partly closed by an elongated jambstone (Fig. 64). The entrant was thus forced either to crawl over the impediment (through an aperture approximately 0.3m high and 1.22m wide) or to squeeze past the jambstone through a gap approximately 0.45m wide and 0.66m high.

A horizontally placed slab divided the two wedge-shaped chambers in the souterrain at Ballynahow, Co. Kerry (Fig. 60). The restricted entrance to the inner chamber was further impeded by a protruding jambstone (Pl. 20).

The combination of two projecting jambstones and a low-set capstone achieves a remarkably similar end result to the porthole-slab feature. Indeed, it is not impossible that there was some relationship between the two features in the south-west (see Clinton 1997, 10). The restricted passage in the souterrain at Knockagarrane, Co. Kerry (J. Cooke 1906–7, 8) (Fig. 61), featured two protruding jambstones in the opposing walls of the passage. The addition of a low-lying capstone combined to create what the surveyor described as 'an excellent defence' (*loc. cit.*). While these features are best represented in the south-west there are parallel examples elsewhere, for example at Lurgabrack, Co. Donegal (A.B. Ó Ríordáin 1968a), where two protruding jambs-and-lintel formations were recorded.

(5) Stalac-type obstructions
Stalac-type obstructions occur in two forms. In the south-west they take the form of downward-projecting stone slabs wedged between the roofing lintels, as at Rathkieran, Co. Kerry (A. O'Sullivan and Sheehan 1996, 166), and Darrynane Beg, Co. Kerry (*ibid.,* 175). The recent discovery of a comparable example at Mill, Co. Louth (Thaddeus Breen, pers. comm.), indicates that this variant of the feature was not exclusive to the south-west.

In the north the stalac-type obstructions were generally drystone-built. They could either project from the roof or the floor of the souterrain. At Sheepland Mor, Co. Down (Rees-Jones 1971, 77) (Fig. 62), two rising projections occurred in the course of the souterrain. These took the form of drystone-built façades with earth-filled cores. At Craig Hill, Co. Antrim (Waterman 1956b, 90) (Fig. 17), the roof of the lower-lying passage/expanded-terminal chamber maintained a constant level except at one point where it suddenly (and briefly) dipped. This obstruction may have denoted the otherwise invisible juncture of passage and chamber. Other examples are not generally as well realised, for example at Ardtole, Co. Down (Bigger and Fennell 1898–9, 146) (Fig. 20), where a (probable) trapdoor was immediately prefaced by a minor (rising) stalac-type obstruction.

(6) Murder-holes
A number of ambiguous features in various parts of the island may have fulfilled a role not unlike that of a murder-hole or machicolation in a medieval castle. The common thread of these features is that they would appear to have provided the defenders within a souterrain with a potential point of ambush. The most convincing example was recently recorded at Newrath Big 2, Co. Meath (Clinton and Manning 2000, 53) (Fig. 63). The junction of a roomy, unrestricted outer passage and an inner, more confined passage was marked by the presence of a low lateral wall. Immediately overlooking the obstructive wall

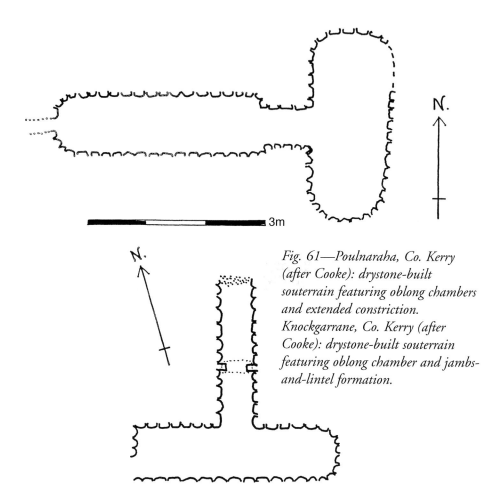

Fig. 61—Poulnaraha, Co. Kerry (after Cooke): drystone-built souterrain featuring oblong chambers and extended constriction. Knockgarrane, Co. Kerry (after Cooke): drystone-built souterrain featuring oblong chamber and jambs-and-lintel formation.

(and hidden from the entrant) was a compartment of sufficient size to contain a fully-grown defender (Pl. 12). It is difficult to advance any explanation for the siting of this feature other than one of ambush.

Similarly, at Lisrenny, Co. Louth (Masser and Bradley 1957–60, 94), an elevated compartment overlooked an inverted (i.e. rising) stepped feature. Again, it was of sufficient size to contain a (prone) defender.

At Fortwilliam, Co. Longford (O'Connor 1933), a confined passage linking Chambers 2 and 5 ran beneath an elevated compartment. An intruder negotiating the confined passage would have been at the mercy of a defender sequestered in the unsuspected compartment.

(7) Child bolt-holes
It is difficult to determine whether custom-built compartments, specifically intended for children, ever existed. The accumulation of debris or silting action

will often distort the actual dimensions of a given feature.

It has been suggested (Clark 1961, 77; Waddell 1970a, 16) that porthole-slabs were designed to permit only children to pass through. This has not, however, been conclusively established.

At Dunisky, Co. Cork (Gogan 1930; McCarthy 1977, 229) (Fig. 70), a severely restricted passageway or constriction allegedly led to a small chamber. The passageway was remarkably small in both width and height (approximately 0.25m by 0.25m). No adult could negotiate such a small passageway. At Ballintemple, Co. Londonderry (May and Cooper 1939, 85), a rock-cut opening gave access to a constriction whose overall dimensions were 0.45m by 0.3m, which in turn led to an otherwise inaccessible rock-cut chamber. At Knockanenagark, Co. Cork (Gillman 1897, 4), an unusually shaped extended constriction led to the inner chamber. It was 0.28m wide and 0.61m high, with an overall length of 0.91m. It would have been extremely awkward for an adult to negotiate.

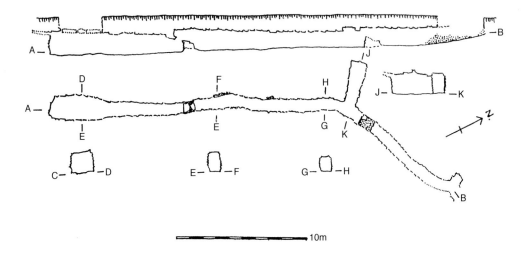

Fig. 62—Sheepland Mor, Co. Down (after Rees-Jones): drystone-built souterrain featuring an unrestricted passage, side chambers, air-vents, 'stalac-type' obstructions and expanded-terminal end chamber.

The motivation to incorporate a secure bolt-hole for children would naturally have been strong. Whether or not they existed has yet to be satisfactorily demonstrated. It can be said, however, that if the feature did exist examples were extremely rare.

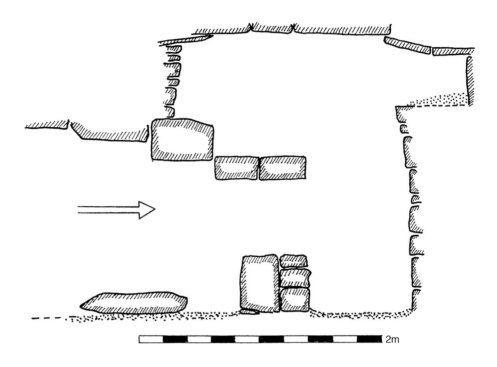

Fig. 63—Newrath Big 2, Co. Meath (after Clinton and Manning): section indicating siting of 'murder-hole', cupboard and obstructive wall (at junction of outer and inner passages).

14. Miscellaneous features

(1) Roof-supports

Roof-supports occurred in two media — stone pillars/drystone-built columns and wooden posts. The former supported lintelled roofs while the latter (invariably represented by post-holes) originally supported wooden roofs (see Appendix 10) (Fig. 65).

Pillar-supported roofs in souterrains are generally restricted to County Cork. Their existence was first recorded by Lane-Fox (1867, 123) at Roovesmore, Co. Cork (Fig. 64), where, six free-standing stone pillars were employed to support the flagstone roof of the chamber. Similarly, at Carhoovauler (O'Crowley 1906, 204; McCarthy 1977, 181) seven pillars were used to support the roof of the chamber.

Free-standing pillar supports are known from elsewhere on the island. It would appear, however, that these were secondary, and even sometimes modern insertions, as for example at Straid (Glencolmcille), Co. Donegal. There is also some doubt regarding the drystone-built columns used to support the chamber roofs at Stickillin (Souterrain 2), Co. Louth (Dunne *et al.* 1973–6, 277), and Demesne, Co. Louth (Tempest 1933–6, 95). Whilst the latter feature, which has not been open to inspection in modern times, may be genuine, and indeed its credentials have recently been greatly enhanced by the discovery of a highly comparable example at Farrandreg, Co. Louth (D. Murphy 1998, 267), it is very possible that the stone column at Stickillin is a modern repair. The chamber at Coolmagort (Dunloe), Co. Kerry (Atkinson 1866, 523), had a cracked lintel supported by a pillar bearing an ogham inscription. As six of the roofing lintels also bore ogham inscriptions, the pillar is more than likely an ancient feature. What is important, though, is that — whether ancient or modern — the stone roof-supports outside the Cork area were almost exclusively repair features. Only in County Cork can the roof-supporting pillars be definitely said to be constituent elements of the original souterrain design. Interestingly, many of the Cork examples belonged to souterrains that were otherwise largely earth-cut, and thus may represent early attempts at souterrain-building.

There is a strong possibility that many wood-built souterrains had wooden posts to assist in supporting the roof. At Ballycatteen, Co. Cork (S.P. Ó Ríordáin and Hartnett 1943–4, 16), one of the three souterrains uncovered in the excavation had six pairs of post-holes in its floor. Each of the three chambers featured two pairs. It was apparent that the posts had been suitably positioned to support a timber roof. A variation on the arrangement was recorded in an excavation at Raheennamadra, Co. Limerick (Stenberger 1966, 41) (Fig. 18). Two post-holes were positioned towards the outer extremities of the two conjoined chambers, which were divided by a stone-built cross-wall. The excavator suggested that the two posts at each end of the souterrain originally supported the outer extremities of two purlins whose inner extremities would have rested on the stone wall. The two post-holes in the southern chamber contained the butt of an oak post. The most impressive example of a timber-built souterrain was uncovered at Coolcran, Co. Fermanagh (B. Williams 1985, 75) (Fig. 7), where the remains of no fewer than 48 oak timber uprights were discovered around the edges of the two conjoined chambers. The two most substantial upright posts were located at a central point of constriction. They undoubtedly denoted a doorway and probably assisted in supporting the roof.

(2) Benches
Benches are another extremely rare feature in souterrains in Ireland. The few known examples fall into three categories: (a) rock- or earth-cut; (b) drystone-built; (c) slabs with supports. To differentiate between a bench and a ledge (or platform) the former should ideally exceed a height of approximately 0.3m.

The rock-cut souterrain at Dunisky, Co. Cork (Gogan 1930; McCarthy

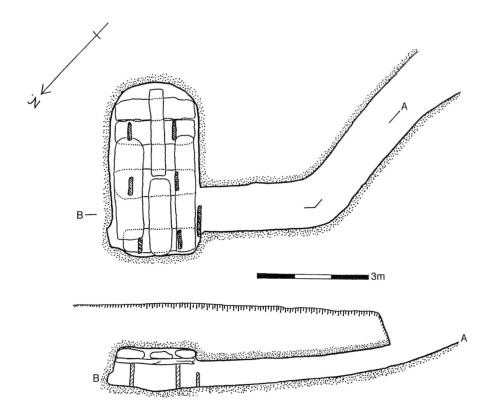

Fig. 64—Roovesmore, Co. Cork (after Lane-Fox): earth-cut souterrain featuring pillar-supported chamber roof (including reutilised ogham stones) and obstructive jambstone.

1977, 225) (Fig. 70), featured a unique chamber, Chamber III, which contained benching on three of its sides. A second chamber contained an additional bench (Pl. 18). A comparable rock-cut bench was recorded in the souterrain at Ballyegan, Co. Kerry (Byrne 1991, 12).

A drystone bench was discovered in the souterrain at Ballyeaston, Co. Antrim (Warner 1972, 61). The difficulty of determining the authenticity of a feature that is not structurally bonded into the body of a souterrain casts a slight doubt on the antiquity of features of this type. An elongated slab had been positioned close to the western end of the chamber in Souterrain 2 at Ballybarrack, Co. Louth (E.P. Kelly, pers. comm.) (Fig. 66). A bench had been created by filling in the resulting gap with redeposited boulder clay. A very similar feature was recorded at Ellistronbeg, Co. Mayo (Lavelle *et al.* 1994, 69) (Fig. 58), where an inner chamber, oblong in form, contained a stone-built bench extending along the full length of the end wall. Overall it measured 2m in length, *c.* 0.4–0.5m in width, and 0.4m in height.

Fig. 65—Distribution of
souterrains featuring stone
and wooden roof-supports.

■ Stone pillars
● Wooden posts

N

0   80 km

The third category is much more nebulous and, indeed, ultimately suspect. At Townparks, Co. Donegal (Lacy 1983, 227), a low-set bench rested on two stone supports. Similarly, at Drumman More, Co. Armagh (Rogers 1882, 67), a large smooth flag had been placed on supporting boulders. As it was surrounded by 'stone seats' (*loc. cit.*) it was advanced as a 'table and chairs' arrangement. The antiquity of these features cannot be reliably attested (see Appendix 11).

(3) Sumps and wells
A dry, naturally drained location would have been a prime prerequisite in the selection of a site by the souterrain-builders. Given the vagaries of nature, however, their choice of location may on occasion have been slightly askew. A high water-table, a closely located unsuspected spring or a slow-draining terrain would inevitably lead to flooding in the deeply set souterrain. In extreme cases this may have led to the total abandonment of the structure. However, if the problem was of manageable proportions it is more than likely that the inhabitants of the associated settlement would have taken measures to counter the water problem.

At Ballynavenooragh, Co. Kerry (Clinton, forthcoming b), the chamber was

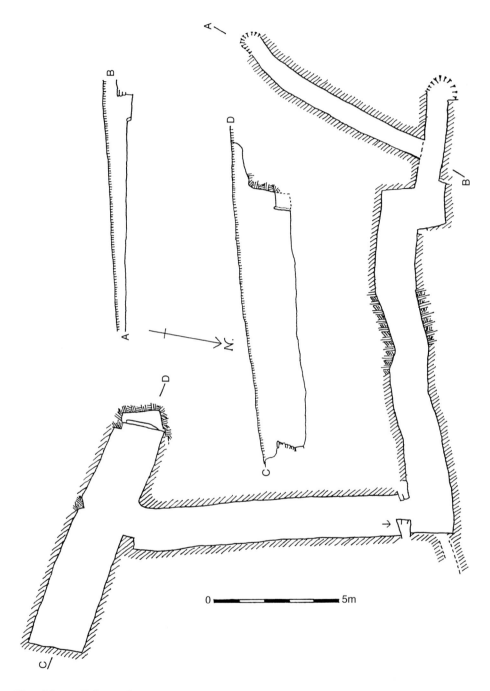

Fig. 66—Ballybarrack, Co. Louth (after Kelly), Souterrain 2: drystone-built souterrain featuring oblong chamber, jambstone displaying Bronze Age motif and bench.

apparently continuously prone to flooding, as a result of either a high water-table or the proximity of a spring. The settlers reacted to the water seepage by cutting a sump in the lowest part of the sloping souterrain floor. This was 'fed' by a shallow gully that extended along the eastern wall of the chamber. During the course of the recent excavation it proved possible to keep the souterrain dry by continually emptying the sump. Undoubtedly this repeated an ancient practice. The surveyors of the rock-cut souterrain at Ballintemple, Co. Londonderry (May and Cooper 1939, 84), had engaged in an identical operation. There too it had proved possible to keep the normally flooded souterrain water-free by draining the sump.

The souterrain at Lismenary, Co. Antrim (Fagan 1839) (Fig. 67), contained a cut well in the floor of an inner chamber. Even in the driest of summers the well was never without water. The nature of the chamber in question was in stark contrast to the other three chambers in the souterrain, being entirely rock-cut while the rest of the souterrain was completely drystone-built. It also extended at right angles to the main body of the souterrain. In overall dimensions it also failed to match the other chambers. Could it be possible, therefore, that the souterrain-builders, having become aware of the presence of a spring in the immediate vicinity of their primary structure, extended the souterrain to incorporate the source of the water?

In summary, it may be stated that in general sumps, or wells, were secondary reactionary features in the host souterrains. It might be said that these features were created out of adversity but also that they were, in at least some cases, quickly turned to advantage. An additional source of water would never go amiss in an agricultural community, especially a supply located so close at hand, indeed at the very heart of the settlement. In turn, the quality of the water would inevitably have determined its ultimate use. Finally, it might be suggested that the known examples of sump-pits are the formal manifestations of more widespread casual adaptations (see Appendix 12).

(4) Shelves

Shelves are not normally present in souterrains. There are, nonetheless, a select number of varying examples.

At Carhoovauler, Co. Cork (McCarthy 1977, 181), the western wall of the chamber did not reach the level of the chamber roof. A gap of 0.2m was thus left between the top of the wall and the roof. This aperture stretched the full width of the western end of the chamber and was 0.45m deep. The resulting shelf had a flat floor and was roofed by a single capstone.

An unusual stepped double-ledge feature was recorded at Emlagh West, Co. Kerry (Connolly 1994, 44). The shallow depth of the two 'ledges' and the relative height of the chamber would seem to indicate that the feature could only have functioned as shelving.

The most refined known example of shelving came from the souterrain at Mullagharlin, Co. Louth (Rynne 1961–4b, 319) (Fig. 68), where a stone-built shelf had been incorporated into the end wall of the lower-lying chamber. Four flat slabs set edge to edge created a continuous flat-topped shelf extending the full width of the chamber. The slabs projected about 0.25m out from the face of the chamber wall. The top of the feature was 1.4m above the floor level of the chamber. There are no known parallels for shelving of this calibre.

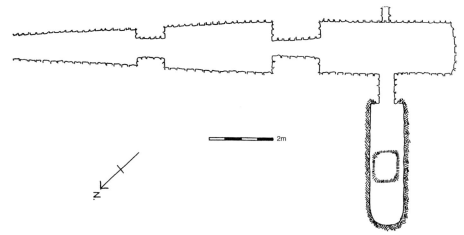

Fig. 67—Lismenary, Co. Antrim (based on Fagan): souterrain featuring three drystone-built chambers and one rock-cut chamber, three drystone-built constrictions, a cut well (and spring) and a possible air-vent. (By permission of The Royal Irish Academy. © RIA.)

(5) Construction shafts

The introduction of construction shafts would have been quite revolutionary in the preparation of tunnelled souterrains. Hitherto, these monuments would have been created by digging and removing all the resultant debris through the entrance feature. The construction shaft, or shafts, enabled the creators of the souterrain to shape the chambers and connecting passages or constrictions, and remove all the waste with relative ease, from these open-topped pits. Once the souterrain was completely excavated the openings to the shaft(s) would have been sealed with either drystone walling or flagstones, and the pits would have been backfilled to ground surface level (Pl. 5).

The number of construction shafts in a souterrain can vary from one to six, with the vast majority containing between one and three (see Appendix 13). One shaft could be used to excavate a number of surrounding chambers, as at

Brackcloon, Co. Cork (S.P. Ó Ríordáin 1934–5, 78), or alternatively a single shaft could service a single chamber, as at Castleventry, Co. Cork (Cleary 1981a, 41). The souterrain at Little Island, Co. Cork (Fahy 1970) (Fig. 69), was exceptional in that it apparently featured a total of five chambers and six construction shafts.

At a number of sites the builders availed of the presence of a construction shaft to incorporate an additional feature into the fabric of the souterrain. For example, at Curraghcrowley West, Co. Cork (Somerville 1929–30, 7), all four air-vents were constructed as integral elements of construction shafts. At Ahakeera, Co. Cork (Twohig 1976, 28) (Fig. 32), and Little Island, Co. Cork (Fahy 1970) (Fig. 69), the builders exploited the presence of the shafts by inserting drains.

The distribution pattern of souterrains featuring a construction shaft or shafts is quite striking (Fig. 3). Of the 71 souterrains known to possess the feature, and the six souterrains suspected of possessing the feature, all barring two are located in the extreme south. Remarkably, there are also two examples in the far north. An explanation for their presence there is not readily available.

(6) Pits

The discovery of a pit in the floor of a souterrain is generally the result of scientific excavation, and therefore the number of recorded examples is limited.

The excavation of the souterrain at Ballyaghagan, Co. Antrim (Evans 1950, 15), led to the discovery of four pits cut into the hard clay floor. The pits were all circular or ovoid in shape and of varying dimensions. Several sherds of Souterrain Ware, including the remains of almost complete vessels, were recovered from the pits, as were parts of two oak staves. At Ballynavenooragh, Co. Kerry (Clinton, forthcoming b), two ovoid pits were uncovered in the course of the excavation. The most fascinating use of a pit sunk in the floor of a souterrain was recorded at Oldcourt, Co. Cork (Ó Cuileanáin and Murphy 1961–2, 83) (Fig. 49). The pit was covered by a single flagstone and contained a bronze-coated iron bell, wrapped in moss.

It would be reasonable to suggest that a pit sunk into the floor of a souterrain was intended for the storage of containers of various kinds. In the north and north-east these could be either ceramic or organic. In the rest of the island they would have been made of wood or leather only. At Balrenny, Co. Meath (Eogan and Bradley 1977, 99; Edwards 1990, 30) the remains of barrel hoops were found on the floor of the souterrain. Again, at Antiville, Co. Antrim (Waterman 1971, 70), the staves and bases of at least six different wooden vessels were uncovered in the bottom fill of the souterrain.

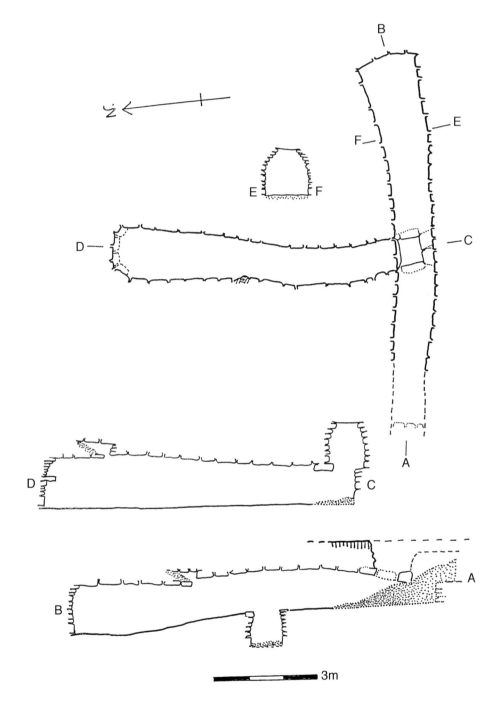

Fig. 68—Mullagharlin, Co. Louth (after Rynne): drystone-built souterrain featuring trapdoor, probable stepped feature, air-vents (in roof) and stone-built shelf.

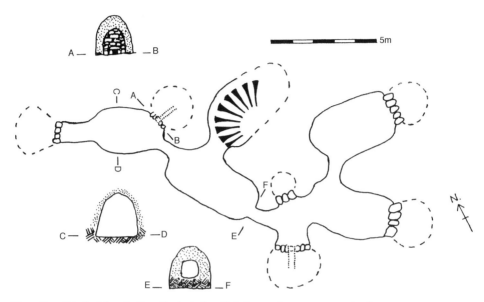

Fig. 69—Little Island, Co. Cork (after Fahy): earth-cut souterrain featuring construction shafts and drains.

(7) Platforms/ledges

To differentiate between a platform (or ledge) and a bench, the former should ideally not exceed a height of *c.* 0.3m. Localised requirements, however, would have dictated overall dimension. A low platform in a souterrain prone to severe flooding would have been of no use, and thus there are examples that rise considerably higher. The overall form, disposition and context of the feature should therefore determine its classification.

It is at Dunisky, Co. Cork (McCarthy 1977, 232) (Fig. 70), that, to date, platform/ledges are best exemplified. The rock-cut souterrain contained six examples of the feature, none of which rose above 0.2m in height. Given their position and basic form there can be little doubt that these platforms served as water-free storage areas for containers of unknown description. Two platforms, remarkably similar to the examples at Dunisky in both form and siting, were recorded in an earth-cut souterrain at Moneygaff East, Co. Cork (Cleary 1989; D. Power 1992, 254). The final 0.76m of the undifferentiated passage/chamber in Souterrain 3 at Cush, Co. Limerick (S.P. Ó Ríordáin 1938–40, 97), rose 0.15m above floor level. Interestingly, this raised area occurred in very close proximity to an air-vent. A strikingly similar configuration was recorded at Ballintemple, Co. Londonderry (May and Cooper 1939, 84).

On the limited evidence available it would appear that platforms/ledges are best represented in tunnelled souterrains.

(8) Footholds

In drystone-built souterrains, footholds are simple projections from the body of the structure, consisting of one or more jutting rocks firmly embedded in the surrounding stonework. In tunnelled souterrains the feature takes the form of minor cut indentations in the rock or earth face.

A short lateral passage extended from the main axis of Souterrain 1 at Togherstown, Co. Westmeath (Macalister and Praeger 1929–31, 73) (Fig. 54), and terminated beneath a shaft entrance. The drop from the surface to the floor of the passage was 1.52m. Three projecting stones had been inserted into the wall of the passage beneath the entrance feature. The entrance to the rock-cut souterrain at Ballintemple, Co. Londonderry (May and Cooper 1939, 86), was both narrow and steep. Two footholds had consequently been cut into the face of the rock to facilitate access.

(9) Fireplaces

The present writer would question the authenticity of this feature. None has been identified in the course of a modern excavation. The continued reuse of souterrains into recent times for various illicit purposes has undoubtedly led to the lighting of temporary 'domestic' fires. It is in this light that Farrandau (Knockdrum), Co. Cork (Somerville 1931, 1), the most superficially convincing example, should be evaluated.

Summary

The overwhelming majority of souterrains in Ireland were drystone-built structures. Tunnelled souterrains constituted a distinct minority, confined in general to the extreme north and the extreme south. Drystone-built souterrains are also well represented in both these areas. The known number of wood-built souterrains is limited in the extreme.

The only two structural aspects that are, logically, common to all souterrains are an entrance feature and a chamber. Entrance and linking passages are a feature of a significant number of souterrains, particularly in the north-east. Similarly, constrictions (both simple and extended) are well represented (particularly in the south in the case of the simple constrictions).

Examples of all the different forms of chambers have been found throughout the island. Circular beehive chambers are, however, predominantly located in the greater Meath area, and oblong chambers, in their best realised form, in the west.

Certain features are almost exclusive to specific areas. Trapdoors, for example, are basically confined to the north-east and the west. Stepped features, with some

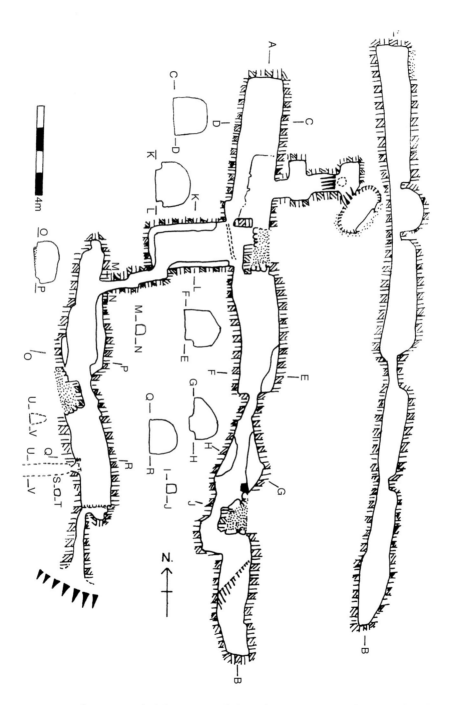

Fig. 70—Dunisky, Co. Cork (after McCarthy): rock-cut souterrain featuring benches, platforms, construction shafts and child bolt-hole?

exceptions, tend to occur in the same areas as the trapdoors. Porthole-slabs are even more localised, being confined exclusively to west Kerry. Some of the minor features also appear to be restricted in distribution. Horizontally placed slabs, for example, appear to be concentrated on the western seaboard. Similarly, pillar-supported roofs may only been have used as a primary feature in souterrains in County Cork. It should be stressed, however, that as known examples of the latter two features are very few in number, their perceived distribution might be a false one.

The better-known features, such as air-vents, drains, cupboards, cubby-holes, steps, etc., are represented in all parts of the island. It is their actual known numbers that is surprising. For example, recorded air-vents are only present in approximately 4% of souterrains in Ireland, receptacles (i.e. cupboards/cubby-holes/recesses) in approximately 3%, and drains in less than 1%. Trapdoors have only been recorded in a little over 2% of souterrains.

In the final analysis, the overwhelming majority of souterrains in Ireland were basic structures consisting of an entrance feature, a connecting artery or arteries, and a varying number of chambers.

7

Souterrains of coastal Europe

I n coastal Europe souterrains are not exclusive to Ireland. The monument is
well represented in Brittany and Scotland, and to a lesser extent in Cornwall
and Denmark. In the context of the islands, the monument is notably absent
from England and Wales (Fig. 71).

Brittany

There are approximately 200 known souterrains in Brittany, concentrated in the
three most westerly departments — Finistère, Côtes-du-Nord and Morbihan
(Fig. 72). The souterrains, with some early exceptions from the final Halstadt
phase (Giot 1973, 57), have been dated (on the basis of both ceramic and
radiocarbon evidence) to the transition between the La Tène I and La Tène II
periods, i.e. between 600 and 100 BC (Giot 1971, 213; 1973, 57).

The souterrains are, barring three poorly published examples, rock-cut. They
generally follow a format of a series of conjoined chambers connected by simple
constrictions. The most commonly recorded number of chambers has been six
(Giot 1973, 51). The constrictions are often referred to as 'a cat-hole' — *une
chatière* (Giot 1990, 55). The inner chamber at Lamphily in Finistère (Giot and
Lecerf 1971a, 125) was linked to a lateral chamber by one of these simple
constrictions. It was rounded in profile with a maximum diameter of 0.4m
(*ibid.*, 128). Interestingly, the base of the constriction, and indeed those of the
other simple constrictions in the souterrain, was raised above the floor level of
the five chambers — that is to say, the bedrock had not been excavated down to
the general floor level. If restriction of entry was the only motivation then the
original excavators of the souterrain could just as easily have lowered the roof
level of the constrictions. Indeed, the floor level of the simple constriction at
Litiez in Finistère (Giot and Lecerf 1971b, 149) was actually lowered in relation
to the two chambers. It is possible, therefore, that these 'ledges' may have been

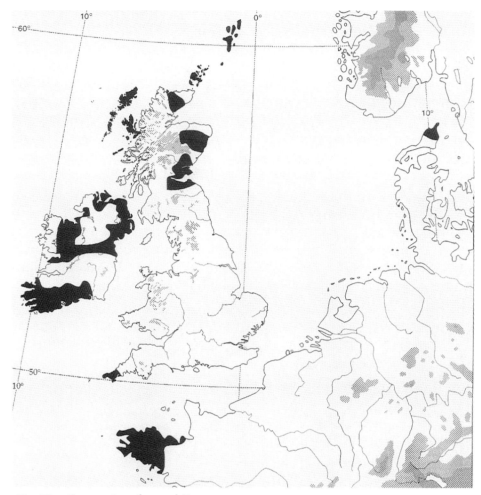

Fig. 71—Souterrains of coastal Europe.

intended to act as anti-flooding devices. Similar devices were recorded at Kermoysan in Finistère (Le Roux and Lecerf 1971, 161).

Entrances to the souterrains can take the form of either a shaft, for example at Kervéo in Finistère (Giot and Ducouret 1968, 104), or a ramp, for example in Souterrain 2 at Rocher-Martin in Côtes-du-Nord (Le Creurer and Giot 1970, 83), the former being the more common type (Giot 1990, 55).

A shaft entrance to the souterrain at Malabry in Côtes-du-Nord (Giot *et al.* 1976, 45) featured eight 'cupule-shaped' indentations in its walls. These were arranged in two corresponding sets of four and had an average diameter of 0.15m. These features were firmly advanced as footholds.

An exceptional souterrain, featuring eleven chambers, was recorded at La Motte in Finistère (Le Roux and Lecerf 1973, 79). The average length of the

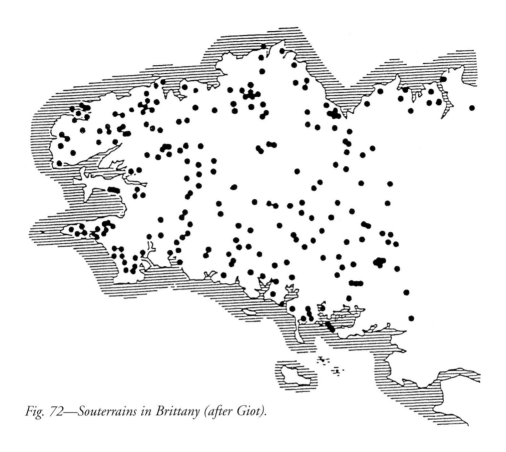

Fig. 72—Souterrains in Brittany (after Giot).

chambers was 1.2m and the height rarely exceeded 1m. The souterrain featured at least three entrances, and also incorporated a projecting section of drystone walling which would appear to have been intended as a restrictive device. A potential parallel was recorded at Keravel in Finistère (Giot and Le Roux 1971, 139), where a vertical slab of rock stood at the junction of Chambers II and IV. This upright slab was not flush with the wall of the souterrain but instead stood 0.25–0.3m out from the rock-cut wall. The writers suggested (*ibid.*, 142) that three loose blocks of stone discovered in the vicinity of the pillar may originally have filled the gap. The fact that there was a pronounced step (upwards) in the floor of the souterrain at this junction would support the interpretation of the pillar as being part of a restrictive configuration.

The souterrain at Kerglanchard in Finistère (Giot *et al.* 1976, 108) contained four chambers. The connecting constrictions between Chambers I and II and between Chambers II and III were further confined by the insertion of drystone-built partitions. The better-preserved example (joining Chambers II and III) consisted of two blocks of stone set against the opposing walls, with the drystone walling above the resultant narrowed opening extending to the roof level of the constriction. Thus the entrance into Chamber III was no more than *c.* 0.4m wide and *c.* 0.45m high. The souterrain at La Motte also contained a simple step which connected two of the chambers (Le Roux and Lecerf 1973, 83). A more pronounced step was recorded at Kermoysan in Finistère (Le Roux and Lecerf 1971, 161). This was sited at the junction of a restricted passage and Chamber II.

A souterrain at Kermeno in Morbihan (Lecornec 1970, 57) contained paving in one of the chambers (Chamber W2) but it was not conclusively proven that this was a primary feature. Indeed, a number of the souterrains were later reused and thus many 'additional' aspects must be treated with some caution.

A short section of drystone walling was recorded in Souterrain 2 at Rocher-Martin in Côtes-du-Nord (Le Creurer and Giot 1970, 73). In appearance and setting it very much resembled the 'fronting' to the construction shafts in Ireland. Interestingly, one of the chambers was capped with a large flagstone (*ibid.*, 82). Another example of drystone walling may have occurred at Keravel in Finistère (Giot and Le Roux 1971, 139). The accompanying plan appears to indicate a section of drystone walling in the south-western flank of Chamber II. Unfortunately the nature of the feature was not resolved in the text. The feature in question was fronted by a narrow platform.

The most convincing evidence for the presence of construction shafts in a number of souterrains in Brittany came from Quinrouet and La Clôture (Giot *et al.* 1976, 39, 42) in Côtes-du-Nord. In both souterrains two chambers were open to inspection. These were connected by the usual *chatière*-style constriction. At Quinrouet the north-eastern corner of the western chamber featured a section of drystone walling. In the eastern chamber a section of drystone walling occurred in the north-western corner. It was established by the surveyors that these two sections of drystone walling sealed off the openings to a shaft which extended to ground surface level. Similarly, at La Clôture short sections of drystone walling in the two adjoining chambers clearly fronted openings into a single shaft. In the case of the former site the writers suggested that the shaft was a blocked-off additional entrance feature. The present writer would suggest that the carefully sealed-off shafts in both of these souterrains, with closely positioned openings in adjoining chambers, have all the appearances of construction shafts.

A 'niche' was recorded in the wall of the inner chamber at Lamphily in Finistère (Giot and Lecerf 1971a, 125). It was interpreted as a possible storage facility (*ibid.*, 128). The exposed chamber at Maner-Soul in Finistère (Giot *et al.* 1976, 63) had four irregularly shaped 'niches' inserted halfway up the walls.

Benches have been recorded in souterrains in Brittany (Giot 1990, 55). A fine example was present in Chamber III in the souterrain at Keravel in Finistère (Giot and Le Roux 1971, 139). This souterrain also contained two additional bench-cum-platform features. The example sited in the south-western corner of Chamber II intruded into the already restricted floor-space of the simple constriction that linked the chamber to Chamber I.

The shaft entrances to a number of the souterrains in Brittany were sealed at their outer extremities by horizontally laid slabs. Examples have been recorded at such sites as Malestroit, Lanouèe and Cléguèrec, all three sites in Morbihan (Giot 1960, 54, 55).

Chamber IV, the innermost chamber in the souterrain at Le Paou in Côtes-du-Nord (Giot *et al.* 1976, 20), contained an air-vent which extended at an oblique angle from the roof of the chamber to the ground surface. It was 0.4m in diameter and 2.5m long.

There was no overall agreement on function, but refuge is the most widely held theory (Giot 1973, 53). All of the souterrains were, essentially, associated with habitation sites (*ibid.*, 49). For many years the emphasis in the study of souterrains in Brittany was on the finds rather than the structural features (Giot 1990, 55). Ironically the vast majority of these related to the infilling of the souterrains as opposed to their floruit.

Finally, it should be noted that the 1000 (plus) souterrains recorded in the central regions of France, although also rock-cut, arc of medieval (twelfth–thirteenth-century) date (Piboule 1978; Lorenz 1973, 32).

Cornwall

In Cornwall souterrains are known as 'fogous', a term derived from the Cornish word for a cave (Thomas 1966, 79fn.). One of the most surprising facts in the discussion of these monuments is that only nine known examples have survived. Both Clark (1961, xix) and Maclean (1992, 59) listed eight of these, at Boleigh, Lower Boscaswell, Carn (Chapel) Euny, Chysauster, Halligye, Pendeen, Porthmeor and Trewardreva. The existence of the ninth site, at Bodean-Veor, was confirmed in 1991 as a result of a magnetometer survey conducted by the English Heritage Ancient Monuments Laboratory (Charles Thomas, pers. comm.). Both Clark (1961, 109) and Maclean (1992, 59) had also included the Beehive Hut at Bosporthennis as a fogou. This monument, however, was built entirely above ground level with all the appearance of a house, and thus would not qualify as a fogou *per se*. It should be noted, however, that fogous can occur as above-ground structures, encased within massive stone walls. The fogou at Porthmeor (Christie 1979, 193), for example, was built entirely above ground, while the fogou at Lower Boscaswell (Clark *et al.* 1957, 213) was semi-subterranean. The fogou at Porthmeor is highly reminiscent of the mural chambers in the west of Ireland (only much larger in overall dimensions). The

179

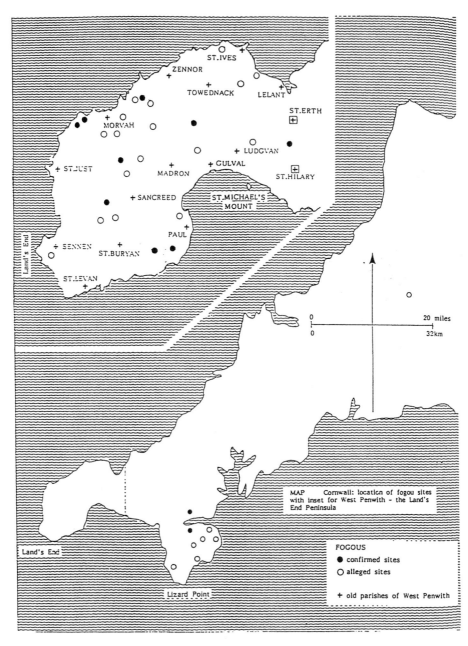

Fig. 73—Souterrains in Cornwall (after I. Cooke).

original number of known fogous is not that great either, being in the region of a maximum of 50 (Thomas 1972, 75). I. Cooke (1993, 45), in an exhaustive study of the monument, only accepted eleven sites as featuring a proven fogou, with an additional 25 being classified as 'possibles' (Fig. 73). Eight of the 'definites' listed by Cooke tallied with the Clark and Maclean inventories. His additional three sites — Higher Bodinar, Castallack and Treveneague — had been recorded as destroyed fogous by Clark. Cooke (1993, 47) noted a further 26 sites as featuring 'unlikely' examples. Amongst the latter was the intriguingly sited 'suggested' fogou at Porth Mellon on St Marys in the Isles of Scilly (Ashbee 1990). The distribution of fogous in Cornwall is in fact decidedly limited, being restricted to the extreme south-west of the region.

Recent excavations at Carn Euny (Christie 1978, 309) indicated that the fogou had been built in three stages between the fifth century BC and the second century BC, the latter date being the one suggested for the period of use of most of the fogous (*ibid.*, 331). Hencken (1932, 141) had suggested that the pottery from Carn Euny had a first-century BC–first-century AD date, with possible earlier or later adjustments. The pottery evidence from the excavations at Halligye suggested a period of use from about the fourth century BC until the second century AD (I. Cooke 1993, 60). A rim sherd of Iron Age date was uncovered in a stratified context on the floor of the entrance passage at Lower Boscaswell. This sherd indicated a date of no earlier than the second century BC for the primary period of use of the fogou (Clark *et al.* 1957, 218).

The fogou at Carn Euny featured a circular beehive chamber. The most recent account (Christie 1978, 309) argued that the chamber did not possess a complete corbelled beehive roof but rather had a wooden roof (*ibid.*, 330), if it had any roof at all (1979, 200). Earlier writers (Hencken 1932, 141; Clark 1961, 42) had argued for a standard drystone-built beehive roof. The chamber featured a recess at floor level, 0.91m wide, 0.91m high and 0.6m deep. There was inconclusive evidence regarding the back wall of the feature but it is possible that it simply consisted of the natural till (Clark 1961, 146; Christie 1978, 314). Carn Euny also contained a series of stone-lined drains (Christie 1978, 321; Hencken 1932, 141; Clark 1961, 38); at the extremity of one of these a sump was uncovered. Drains were also noted at Porthmeor (Clark 1961, 68) and at Higher Bodinar (I. Cooke 1993, 137).

The floor of the beehive chamber at Carn Euny was paved with flat slabs (Christie 1978, 314). The fogou at Pendeen had been reported as featuring a 'stone-lined floor' (Clark 1961, 24), but this has been refuted by Maclean (1992, 44).

The fogou at Pendeen (Hencken 1932, 150; Clark 1961, 21; I. Cooke 1993, 92) contained a lateral chamber which had been excavated out of the hard natural till; it was 7.72m long, 1.65m in average width, and 1.27m in average height (Clark 1961, 27). This feature was closely paralleled by a lateral chamber at Treveneague (Clark 1961, 125; I. Cooke 1993, 143) which was also earth-cut and measured 4.57m in length, 1.83m in width and 1.22m in height (Clark 1961, 127). Both chambers were entered through simple constrictions.

The impressive fogou at Halligye (Hencken 1932, 145; Clark 1961, 28; I. Cooke 1993, 53) featured two sizeable chambers in addition to two access/exit passages (one subdivided) and a small lateral chamber. The latter feature extended from the southern extremity of a long, curving, oblong chamber with an overall length in excess of 16.76m (Startin 1981, 219). The dimensions of the lateral chamber have not been explicitly stated but it would appear to have been less than 2.5m long and, according to Hencken (1932, 145), only barely high enough to crawl through. Like the earth-cut lateral chamber at Treveneague, it was ovoid in form and was entered through a simple constriction (height and width 0.41m). Interestingly, the end walls of both the curving chamber and the short lateral chamber were rock-cut.

The curving chamber also featured a rock-cut sill, consisting of a band of natural rock which had been left *in situ* across the line of the chamber. It was 0.61m high and 0.46m wide (Hencken 1932, 147). Clark (1961, 30) stated that the sill was a unique feature in the fogous of Cornwall (although I. Cooke (1993, 152) has drawn attention to a questionable parallel in the 'possible' fogou at Trevean). Restoration work at Halligye prompted a limited excavation of the fogou (Startin 1981, 219; 1982, 185). The excavator subsequently rejected the bona fides of the rock-cut 'sill'. Indeed, he concluded that the long, curving, oblong chamber originally terminated at the so-called stumbling-block. He further maintained that the band of natural rock had simply been left unquarried when the chamber was extended. The reinterpretation was primarily based on a study of the composition of the chamber walls. It should be noted, however, that in the souterrains in Ireland the structural composition of the walls was (apparently) often dictated by the relative quantities of diverse raw material available. Moreover, a change in the composition of the walls might also indicate an ancient repair operation as opposed to the building of an extension. It seems somewhat strange that an extension to such an already impressive structure should merely consist of an additional 2–2.5m of chamber and a small lateral chamber. The lateral chamber itself is somewhat reminiscent of the aforementioned lateral chambers at Pendeen and Treveneague, both apparently original features of their respective fogous.

The fogou at Halligye originally featured an exit into the ditch of an associated enclosure. Access to the exit was through a subdivided restricted passage. Startin (1981, 185) has advanced the interpretation that the southern (inner) segment of this passageway was a later addition — in effect the insertion of an inner 'sleeve' into the former northern reaches of the north/south-aligned outer oblong chamber. The junction of the northern and southern segments of the restricted passageway is denoted by the presence of a 'doorway' (a combination of two protruding jambs and a low-set lintel). The 1863 account of the fogou by Sir Richard Rawlinson Vyvyan (I. Cooke 1993, 54) noted the presence of two 'sockets' in the walls of the passage immediately to the south (i.e. internal side) of the doorway in question. These, he suggested, were intended to contain the ends of a bar to reinforce the door. Hencken (1932, 147) and Clark (1961, 30) noted the presence of the two slots but offered no further elaboration. These reported features have not been noted (nor dismissed) by later writers.

The 'sally-port' at Halligye (Hencken 1932, 145; Clark 1961, 30; Startin 1981, 219; 1982, 185) was paralleled in an analogous feature at Treveneague (Hencken 1932, 143; Clark 1961, 127; I. Cooke 1993, 143), where a linear oblong chamber, at least 10.36m long, terminated at its north-eastern end with two adjoining constrictions, represented by two sets of protruding jambs capped with lintels. The opening in the 'northern' side wall of the chamber facilitated access to an earth-cut chamber (see above). The opening in the end wall provided access to a short length (3.66m) of earth-cut, unroofed passageway, which culminated in the ditch of an associated enclosure. The existence of an earth-cut passage (of unexplored length) at Castallack prompted Ian Cooke (1993, 141) to suggest that it may have terminated in a ditch of a (theoretical) associated enclosure.

The two small niches, or cupboards, noted at Carn Euny by Hencken (1932, 140) have been explained by Christie (1978, 318) as simple gaps caused by the spacing of the uprights which supported the lintelled roof of the entrance passageway.

William Borlase, an eighteenth-century antiquarian, observed a circular depression in the middle of the main angled chamber at Pendeen (Clark 1961, 26; I. Cooke 1993, 92). His subsequent excavation of the feature revealed a pit, 0.91m in diameter and 0.61m deep. Nothing was found in the pit. The initial casual observation of the feature might cast doubt on its antiquity.

The fogou at Castallack (I. Cooke 1993, 139) was more reminiscent, in its overall dimensions, of many of the drystone-built souterrains in Ireland. Interestingly, it contained a pair of projecting jambstones at the junction of two passages (chambers?; or alternatively in the course of a continuous passageway?). The fogou was discovered in an unroofed state but undoubtedly the jambstones were originally capped by a (lower-lying?) lintel. Of further interest is the fact that a 'blocking-stone' was uncovered in the immediate vicinity of the two projecting jambstones. A severe restriction at the eastern extremity of the fogou (beyond which an earth-cut passage extended — see above) was also found to possess a 'blocking-stone'.

The only reported air-vents in a souterrain in Britain came from the fogou at Boleigh (Clark 1961, 50; Christie 1979, 191). These, unfortunately, would appear to be secondary features, late in date (possibly seventeenth-century) (Clark 1961, 58).

Regarding function, the excavation at Carn Euny has provided some key evidence. It was established that the long chamber was originally only accessible through the restricted entrance passageway (Christie 1978, 331). Hitherto it had been thought that easy access was available through entrances at both ends of the chamber (Clark 1961, 1). The original interpretation had always favoured storage as the function. The restricted access would suggest refuge. It has been argued by some writers that there was a ritual dimension to the Cornish fogous. Clark (1961, 62) first raised the issue in relation to the fogou at Boleigh. The suggested presence of a carved figure on one of the stones in the chamber wall provided the main impetus for her argument. Her tentative analysis was that the fogou might have been intended for use as a subterranean temple. Christie (1978, 332) suggested that Carn Euny, and probably other fogous as well, 'may have had more than a purely utilitarian function'. She touched upon the possibility that some may have served as 'cult centres' (Christie 1979, 210, 213). I. Cooke (1993, 327) was unequivocal in his acceptance of fogous as the 'ritual centres' of individual family units of high status. He linked the ritual dimension to the involvement of these families in the mining of tin and copper. Should there prove to be a 'ritual dimension' to the Cornish fogous it would firmly segregate them from the 'architecturally akin' (Christie 1978, 332) souterrains of Ireland and Scotland. However, not all recent writers would accept the ritual theory. Indeed, Maclean (1992, 41) in a thorough reappraisal of the evidence concerning the monuments has suggested refuge as the likeliest impetus for the building of the fogous.

Scotland

Wainwright (1953a, 219) firmly established that the souterrains in Scotland were not, morphologically, a homogeneous group. Regional variations in form are manifest in such areas as, for example, Angus, Caithness, the Orkneys and Aberdeenshire.

The distribution of souterrains in Scotland is not uniform. While areas such as Angus, Aberdeenshire and Sutherland, for example, have been found to be in possession of souterrains, other areas are almost bereft of the monument (Fig. 74). Indeed, it has been recognised that the souterrain area in Scotland lies, with exceptions, north of the River Tay (Wainwright 1963, 3). Souterrains are decidedly lacking in south-west Scotland (Thomas 1971, 45). One of the few

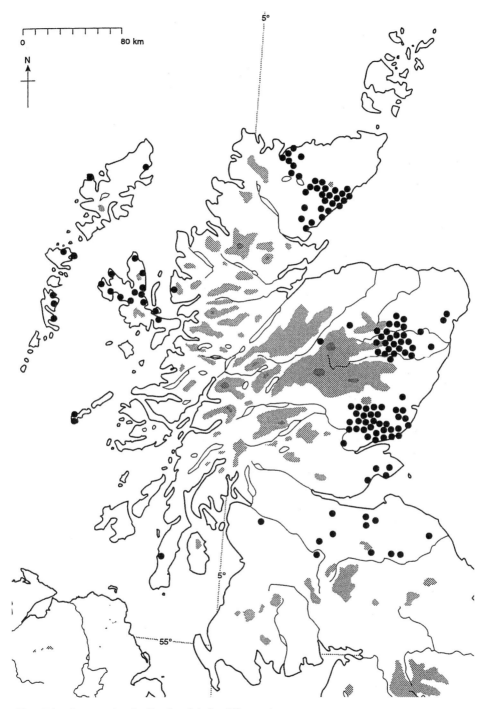

Fig. 74—Souterrains in Scotland (after Thomas).

known souterrains in the area, at Ardeer in Ayrshire (Hunter 1972–4, 296), featured a lintelled drystone passage leading to a natural cave. The most imposing examples of souterrains in Scotland come from that part of the country designated as 'Southern Pictland' (Wainwright 1955, 91; 1963, 31), comprising the shires of Angus, Perth and Fife (Wainwright 1963, 3; Barclay 1978–80, 200). The souterrains of Southern Pictland can be described as (basically) consisting of a long curving chamber, usually paved, and a narrow entrance passageway. These structures had an average width of 2.13–2.44m and an average height of 1.83m (Wainwright 1953a, 221). The complete length of these structures was only ascertained at nine sites (Barclay 1978–80, 202). They varied in length from *c.* 12.2m (Mudhall) to *c.* 39.6m (Carlungie 1). There has been an ongoing debate regarding the exact nature of the roofing of these souterrains. MacRitchie (1916–17, 186), amongst others, argued for wooden roofs. Wainwright proposed 'massive stone roofs' (1953a, 222; 1963, 156). Barclay (1978–80, 204) refuted Wainwright's reasoning and re-proposed wooden roofs. While there is considerable merit in Barclay's analysis, it should be noted that at least one souterrain in the group would appear to have featured a lintelled roof, the souterrain in question being the one discovered at Hurly Hawkin in Angus (Taylor 1982, 215).

The souterrains of Southern Pictland were not in possession of a wide range of ancillary features. Neither were they totally bereft of structural embellishments. Paving of a high standard was recorded at such sites as Carlungie 2 (Wainwright 1953b, 65), Newmill (Watkins 1979, 205; 1978–80b, 165), Hurly Hawkin (Taylor 1982, 215) and Longforgan (Wainwright 1954–6, 57). A stone-covered drain was excavated at Ardestie in Angus (Wainwright 1963, 58). Drains, however, were not a normal feature of the souterrains of Angus (*ibid.*, 7). Indeed, the drain at Ardestie was proven to be a secondary and thus a reactionary feature (*ibid.*, 59). Impediments are not a standard feature of the Southern Pictland group, although projecting jambstones have been recorded, for example at Tealing 3 (Wainwright 1953a, 220). Cup-marked stones of Bronze Age date have been used in the structural composition of souterrains in this group, for example at Ruthven (Wainwright 1963, 210), Tealing 3 (*ibid.*, 213) (Pl. 27) and Hurly Hawkin (Taylor 1982, 223). The souterrain at West Grange of Conan (Jervise 1861–2, 492) contained a circular beehive chamber. This type of chamber was atypical of the group. Indeed, the best parallel in Scotland for the circular beehive chamber at Conan was recorded at Castlelaw in Midlothian (Childe 1932–3, 362).

Souterrains in the Orkney and Shetland Islands group were notable in possessing chambers whose roofs were supported by free-standing pillars. The souterrain at Rennibister (Piggott 1982, 154) was representative of the Orcadian type. A narrow passage led down to an oval chamber, whose roof was supported

Pl. 25 —The souterrain at Ardestie in Angus.

by pillars. The presence of 'small alcoves' (*loc. cit.*) was also recorded. At Midhouse in Orkney (Craw 1930–1, 357) the roof was supported by seven upright pillars and one irregularly shaped rock. It is interesting to note that where the pillars were of insufficient height to reach the roof, smaller slabs were inserted on top to raise the support to the required height. The walls of the Midhouse chamber consisted of the natural till. Other examples of pillar-supported chamber roofs in the Orkneys were recorded at Biggings, Dale, Grain and Hatston (Wainwright 1953a, 225; Piggott 1982, 145). A souterrain at Jarlshof in the Shetlands (Curle 1935–6, 241) contained a chamber whose roof was supported by four pillars. The entrance passages to the souterrains in the Orkney and Shetland group were of the restricted type.

Souterrains in the Sutherland group basically consisted of undifferentiated passage/chambers or passages with expanded terminals. The souterrain at Salscraggie (Wainwright 1953a, 226) was entered by a flight of steps. The souterrain at Rosal (Corcoran 1967–8, 114) featured a staggered ramp entrance which facilitated entry to an undifferentiated passage/chamber almost 12.8m long. It contained what can only be described as a close approximation of a jambs-and-lintel formation. At the point of insertion the passage narrowed to a width of 0.61m. There, two opposing jambstones had been set in the walls of the passage. Their vertical projecting profiles were in contrast to the other stonework

Pl. 26—The southern Pictish souterrain at Carlungie.

in the wall. Above the two jambstones lay the lowest (surviving?) roofing lintel. The souterrain at Portnacon contained a 'hollow' (Buxton 1934–5, 433), 1.22m in diameter and about 0.61m in depth. The writer speculated that it may have been associated with drainage (the souterrain would appear to have suffered from flooding). This feature might be more accurately described as a possible sump. At Cyderhall (Pollock 1992, 149) the presence of paired post-holes suggested the former presence of a wooden roof.

The Aberdeenshire group of souterrains seem to bear some relationship to both the Sutherland and the Southern Pictland groups. They are considerably smaller than the souterrains in the latter group. Wainwright (1953a, 226) drew attention to the souterrain at Glenkindie, observing that it was more chamber- than passage-orientated. Its two (roughly) ovoid chambers linked by a constriction format is atypical of the group. The geographical siting of the Aberdeenshire group would have made them susceptible to influence from both the Sutherland and Southern Pictland groups.

Souterrains in the west of Scotland vary greatly in form (Wainwright 1953a, 223). Generally, however, they were low, narrow, and small in size (*ibid.*, 222).

Some examples were attached to wheel-houses, for example at Usinish in the Hebrides (*loc. cit.*). Research work on the souterrains in this group has not been extensive.

The function of the souterrains in Scotland has also merited extensive discussion. While most writers would credit the structures in the north and west of Scotland with a refuge role, agreement has not been as forthcoming in relation to the souterrains in Southern Pictland. Wainwright's suggestion (1953a, 231; 1963, 122) that the large, curving, paved chambers were used as byres for cattle or sheep has not been endorsed, in the main, by later writers, who would argue for a general storage function.

There are many unresolved aspects of the dating framework of the souterrains in Scotland as a whole. A broad date range has been suggested. Childe (1935, 212) and Curle (1934–5, 106) argued for a Bronze Age date for some of the examples in the extreme north. Thomas (1972, 76) has argued that it is difficult to prove that the souterrains in any of the regional groups were in use prior to the late pre-Roman Iron Age. It has been established that the souterrains at Newstead in Roxburgh and Crighton Mains in Midlothian contained dressed stones that had been purloined from abandoned Roman sites (MacRitchie 1916–17, 183; Piggott 1982, 141). The bulk of the sites in the Southern Pictland zone have been dated to between AD 50 and 250 (Wainwright 1963, 24).

At Dalladies in Kincardineshire (Watkins 1978–80a, 122) a series of subterranean features with obvious affinities to souterrains were uncovered during the course of excavation. Scientific dating suggested use from about the third century BC to the sixth century AD. A number of these souterrains, should they be accepted as such, contained wooden uprights which most likely acted as roof-supports. One of the subterranean features possessed a ramp entrance and vestigial evidence for a doorway.

The souterrain at Ardross 1 in Fife (Southern Pictland) is typical of the ongoing debate regarding dating. Wainwright (1953a, 228; 1963, 162) conceded that this souterrain, although located in Fife, had no links morphologically with the Southern Pictland structures. Basically the souterrain consisted of a passage, 18.29m in length, which led to a rounded subrectangular chamber. The entrance featured a flight of ten well-constructed steps. The passage contained a pair of projecting jambstones which effectively reduced the width of the passageway to 0.56m. The junction of passage and chamber was marked by three descending steps. The combination of features led Wainwright to suggest that the souterrain had been built by settlers from the Northern Isles. The key point is that this souterrain could not be dated. It has been established that the descendants of the builders of two typical Southern Pictland-style

Pl. 27—The southern Pictish souterrain at Tealing.

souterrains, at Carlungie and Ardestie (Wainwright 1963, 38; Henderson 1967, 29), continued to live at the sites in the post-souterrain period. Is it not possible that at a later stage their descendants were prompted by changing circumstances to construct a new and more defensively orientated style of souterrain? It is not impossible, therefore, that a later phase of souterrain construction in eastern Scotland may yet be identified.

Jutland

In Jutland, in the extreme north of Denmark, approximately twenty souterrain-like monuments have been recorded, all in the coastal area around Frederikshavn (Fig. 71); the monument is otherwise unknown in the region. All the known examples are short and simple in design. Kjaerum (1960, 62) divided them into two classes:

> Class A: a simple curving or angled passage leading to a chamber; these structures were always sited on level ground;

Class B: a short entrance passage leading to either one or two chambers, with a drain-like feature extending from the inner chamber; these structures were always sited on sloping ground.

The chambers are either rectangular or oval in form. They can be either stone-built or wood-built, and sometimes a combination of both. Corbelling is absent from the stone-built examples. All available evidence suggests that the structures featured timber roofs. It is possible that some examples were only semi-subterranean (*ibid.*, 88).

The structures are generally lacking in ancillary features. Three examples, however, at Baekmoien (*ibid.*, 88) featured a niche in the back wall of the chamber. The floor of Cellar G at Løgsten Mark was cobbled (*loc. cit.*).

The drain-like features identified in the Class B structures are the most enigmatic aspect of these monuments. They invariably lead to streams. One example, in Cellar G at Løgsten Mark, actually sloped down into the structure and ended in a stone-set 'chamber' connected to the main body of the monument by an opening 0.1m in width. The excavator suggested that this could have been sealed off (Kjaerum 1960, 88). The exact function of the Class B structures has not been resolved. The Class A subterranean structures have generally been accepted as storerooms. A wood-built example excavated at Overbygård (Lund 1978a, 3; 1978b, 10) was found to contain dozens of clay pots (containing grain), two swords, an axe, wooden tubs and barrels and a chair.

Two examples have been found to be in direct association with a longhouse. These were discovered at Baekmoien (Hatt 1937, 172) and Grønhedens Mark (Glob 1971, 242). Other examples have been proven to be unassociated with surface structures (Kjaerum 1960, 89).

The excavated sites have been dated on the basis of their pottery to the late pre-Roman and early Roman Iron Age (Hatt 1937, 172; Kjaerum 1960, 89). This would place them in or about the first century AD (B. Raftery, pers. comm.).

Parallels with or influence on Ireland

The very nature of the tunnelled souterrains of Brittany and the extreme south of Ireland makes comparison inevitable. Both groups are also well disposed geographically to allow potential contacts and/or influence (Fig. 71). The dating evidence currently available in Ireland, however, would suggest that the construction phase of the souterrains in Brittany was too early to be of direct significance.

The basic methodology involved in creating a tunnelled souterrain inevitably results in a number of superficial similarities. The elevated simple constrictions with the resulting ledges in the floor, for example at Lamphily in Finistère (Giot and Lecerf 1971a, 125), may well have been intended to act as anti-flooding devices. Rock-cut souterrains would always have been susceptible to water retention/flooding and therefore the occurrence of a similar device, the 'exaggerated step', in the rock-cut souterrains at Curraghcrowley West (Somerville 1929–30, 3) or Dunisky (McCarthy 1977, 232), Co. Cork, for example, may be simply fortuitous. Similarly, the sealing with slabs of a number of the shaft entrances in both Brittany and Ireland, for example at Malestroit in Morbihan (Giot 1960, 54) and at Currahaly, Co. Cork (Hartnett 1939, 114), might be considered as inevitable. Again, footholds in a vertical shaft would be a logical asset and thus the comparable examples at Malabry in Côtes-du-Nord (Giot *et al.* 1976, 45) and Ballintemple, Co. Londonderry (May and Cooper 1939, 82), should not be unexpected.

Ancillary features are of more potential significance. Interestingly, neither group is over-endowed with such structural elements. Air-vents, receptacles, and minor impedimental devices, for example, are present in both groups but not in any significant numbers. The air-vent at Le Paou in Côtes-du-Nord (Giot *et al.* 1976, 20) could be compared, in its form and context, to the vent at Currahaly, Co. Cork (Brash 1866–9b, 72). Similarly, the niche at Lamphily in Finistère (Giot and Lecerf 1971a, 125) is comparable to the cupboard in the souterrain at Ardahill, Co. Cork (McCarthy 1977, 139), and the vertical slab at the junction of Chambers II and IV in the souterrain at Keravel in Finistère (Giot and Le Roux 1971, 139) to the obstructive slabs at Corran South (McCarthy 1975, 59) and Moneygaff East (Cleary 1989), Co. Cork. The bench in Chamber III at Keravel is remarkably similar in form and setting to the examples recorded in the rock-cut souterrain at Dunisky, Co. Cork (McCarthy 1977, 232). Similarly, the bench in Chamber II at Keravel, in the way it intruded into the already restricted floor-space of the simple constriction linking the chamber to Chamber I, was repeating an arrangement in evidence at Moneygaff East, Co. Cork (Cleary 1989).

The possible presence of construction shafts in a number of souterrains in Brittany is potentially of great significance. Could such a technological innovation have occurred independently in two distant regions at different times? The layout and execution of the suspected examples at Quinrovet and La Clôture in Côtes-du-Nord (Giot *et al.* 1976, 39, 42) are closely paralleled by examples in the south of Ireland at such sites as Lisheen (Fahy 1960, 142) and Dundeady (McCarthy 1977, 223), Co. Cork.

As stated above, there is currently a pronounced divergence in the dating of the souterrains of Brittany and Ireland. It must be conceded, however, that the tunnelled souterrains in the extreme south of Ireland, if considered in isolation, have yet to be firmly dated. Furthermore, there was considerable secondary usage of the souterrains in Brittany, and, on a broader scale, a flourishing of the monument in medieval times in France. It is not impossible that the souterrain 'idea' travelled from Brittany to Ireland. Armorica (Brittany) has previously been advanced as the source of inspiration for the souterrains of both Cornwall and Ireland (Thomas 1972, 76). The unresolved question, however, is the period in which this theoretical movement of ideas would have taken place.

It has been suggested by previous writers (for example S.P. Ó Ríordáin 1953, 34; Clark 1961, 142) that the builders of fogous in Cornwall were influenced by the souterrains in Ireland. The dating evidence currently available would not support this view. In fact, it would appear that the fogous in Cornwall pre-dated the souterrains in Ireland.

There are a number of analogous features in the souterrains of Ireland and Cornwall. None of these, however, occur in any significant numbers in Cornwall. For example, there is only one known circular beehive chamber in Cornwall, at Carn Euny (Christie 1978, 309). Interestingly, not only did the chamber include a recess at floor level, but it is possible that the back wall of the feature simply consisted of the natural till (Clark 1961, 146; Christie 1978, 314). While acknowledging the pronounced differences in date, this aspect would still, curiously, find resonance in the cupboards and cubby-holes in Ireland. The floor of the beehive chamber at Carn Euny (Christie 1978, 314) was paved with flat stones. Otherwise paving was as poorly represented as it was in Ireland.

Drains have been recorded in three of the fogous — Carn Euny (Christie 1978, 321), Porthmeor (Clark 1961, 68) and Higher Bodinar (I. Cooke 1993, 137). These stone-covered channels, extending under the floor of the passage or chamber, have more in common with the drain at Ardestie in Scotland (Wainwright 1963, 58) (Pl. 25) than with most of the examples in Ireland. Only at Brackcloon (S.P. Ó Ríordáin 1934–5, 78), Johnstown (McCarthy 1977, 261) and Fasagh (Sweetnam and Gillman 1897, 150), all three sites in County Cork, did the drains in Ireland feature an internal feeder system. Interestingly, these three souterrains were of the tunnelled type.

The fogous of Cornwall are predominantly drystone-built structures. The fogou at Pendeen (Hencken 1932, 150; Clark 1961, 21; I. Cooke 1993, 92) and Treveneague (Clark 1961, 125; I. Cooke 1993, 143), however, contained lateral chambers which had been excavated out of the hard natural till. Both chambers were entered through simple constrictions. Both monuments were otherwise drystone-built. Souterrains of mixed construction are well represented in the extreme south of Ireland.

Treveneague also contained a 'sally-port' which opened into the ditch of the associated enclosure. An analogous feature was recorded at Halligye (Hencken 1932, 145; Clark 1961, 30; Startin 1981, 219; 1982, 185). External exits or 'escape passages', in some cases emerging in the ditches of associated enclosures, are a feature of a number of souterrains sited (predominantly) in the west and south-west of Ireland.

Impedimental features are practically unknown in Cornwall. The rock-cut sill at Halligye is one exception, although its validity has been questioned (Startin 1981, 219; 1982, 185). The rock-cut obstructive sills (or trip-stones?) recorded at such sites as Palmersland, Co. Louth (Ua Cuinn 1904–7, 38), are a comparable feature. The fogou at Castallack (I. Cooke 1993, 139) contained a pair of projecting jambstones at the junction of two passages. Obstructive 'jambs-and-lintel' formations are known in Ireland. The presence of two 'blocking-stones' in the fogou was also interesting. There is evidence to suggest that at least some of the porthole-slab devices employed in souterrains in the south-west of Ireland were originally sealed by 'blocking-stones'. There are indications that 'jambs-and-lintel' formations in the same region were related to the porthole-slabs.

Earlier writers have tended to regard fogous as either 'underground retreats' (Hencken 1932, 132) or dual storage/refuge facilities (Clark 1961, 136). Whilst some more recent writers, for example I. Cooke (1993, 327) and Christie (1979, 210), have advanced a ritual dimension, others, such as Maclean (1992, 41), have argued that the structures were intended as refuges. The majority of souterrains in Ireland would appear to have been designed as refuges, but undoubtedly also served as cold storage places.

While there are analogous features in souterrains in Scotland and Ireland, it must be stressed at the outset that it would be extremely difficult, at present, to suggest any direct links for the following reasons: (i) disparity in the apparent dating of both their construction and their usage; (ii) geographical divergence; and (iii) the comparable features in Scotland are scattered throughout the various groups as opposed to being focused in a single region.

Souterrains are decidedly lacking in south-west Scotland — the very area to which, for both geographical and historical reasons, one might look for potential precedents, no matter how tenuous. It is worth noting, however, that the souterrain at Ardeer in Ayrshire (Hunter 1972–4, 296) consisted of a lintelled drystone-built passage leading to a natural rock cave. This combination is known in Ireland at such sites as Glenballythomas, Co. Roscommon (Ferguson 1864–6, 160), and Ballyegan (Byrne 1991, 5) and Dunkerron (A. O'Sullivan and Sheehan 1996, 179), Co. Kerry.

Only those oblong chambers found in the west of Ireland could be compared at all favourably with the distinctive forms found in Southern Pictland. Lengthwise, however, the longest examples in the west of Ireland would equate with the bottom of the scale in Scotland. The distinctive curve of the Scottish examples is also absent in Ireland. The regular paving of souterrain floors, especially of the standard in evidence at such sites as Newmill (Watkins 1979, 205; 1978–80b, 165) and Hurly Hawkin (Taylor 1982, 215), was not practised in Ireland. Indeed, only the paved chambers in the souterrains at Togherstown (Souterrain 1), Co. Westmeath (Macalister and Praeger 1929–31, 71), and Kildalton, Co. Kilkenny (Prendergast 1958, 38), could be advanced as being comparable to the Scottish examples. Neither of these chambers, however, was of significant size. The circular beehive chambers at Castlelaw (Childe 1932–3, 362) and West Grange of Conan (Jervise 1861–2, 492) in Scotland could be compared to the beehive chambers of the greater Meath area in Ireland, but as the form would appear to be totally atypical of souterrains in Scotland in general this might be deemed to be of no great significance. More basic chamber forms, such as the undifferentiated passage/chambers or expanded-terminal chambers of Sutherland, can also be found in Ireland. Souterrains of such simple form are, however, so lacking in diagnostic elements that their occurrence in both lands might be regarded as coincidental.

The lintelled chamber roofs supported by free-standing pillars, so typical of souterrains in the Orkney and Shetland Islands, compare very favourably, even in the finer details, with examples in Ireland. At Midhouse in Orkney (Craw 1930–1, 357), for example, where the pillars were of insufficient height to reach the roof, smaller slabs were inserted on top to raise their height to the required level. The same technique was recorded at Carhoovauler, Co. Cork (McCarthy 1977, 181). Furthermore, in both of these souterrains the walls of the chamber consisted of the natural till. Unfortunately the pillar-supported roofs in Ireland are practically all located in County Cork, i.e. in the extreme south of the island. Such a geographical divergence would seem to preclude any potential direct association.

Ancillary structural elements would not appear to be strongly represented in souterrains in Scotland. Air-vents and trapdoors, for example, are completely absent. Similarly, the stone-covered drain at Ardestie in Angus (Wainwright 1963, 58) is exceptional. It is interesting to note that reused cup-marked stones of Bronze Age date have been recorded in souterrains in both Scotland and Ireland.

In Denmark most writers have looked abroad for precedents for the group of subterranean structures in Jutland. The perceived Bronze Age date of the souterrains in Ireland led many writers, for example Hatt (1937, 172), Glob (1971, 243) and Kjaerum (1960, 87), to suggest that the inspiration for the monuments may have originated there and ultimately arrived via Scotland. The revised dating scheme for the souterrains in Ireland would preclude such an origin. Drystone-built structures with timber roofs would, however, find precedents in Scotland. In terms of chronology and geography, a Scottish inspiration for the structures in Jutland would be feasible.

8

Souterrains in Ireland: origins, diffusion, tenure and survival—a working hypothesis

Origins

There are not an infinite number of possibilities regarding the origins of souterrains in Ireland. At a fundamental level, the concept was either home-grown or imported.

While it is possible that the tunnelled souterrains could have been inspired either by abandoned Bronze Age copper mines or simply by observation of the activities of burrowing animals such as foxes or badgers, this will always be impossible to prove. It would be fair to say that the actual creation of the simple tunnelled souterrains would have been within the average person's capabilities and did not require specialist skills.

The origins of the drystone building technique are more problematic. It could be suggested that the technique originated in the construction shafts and in those souterrains of primitive mixed construction. The sealing of the construction shafts in both earth-cut and rock-cut souterrains involved the creation of small sections of drystone walling. The roofing of earth-cut trenches, or rock clefts, involved the use of flagstones. Initially these flagstones could have been either looted ogham stones or fortuitously shaped natural slabs, the ogham stones themselves being ample proof of the ability of the indigenous population of the time to fashion rocks into the required form. On a more localised level, it is not impossible that the basic shape and corbelling technique employed in circular beehive chambers were inspired by a familiarity with passage tombs. It may not be pure coincidence that these chambers are heavily concentrated in the same area as the Boyne Valley and Loughcrew passage tomb cemeteries (Fig. 36). The integration of the tombs at Dowth and Knowth into souterrain complexes provides ample evidence of an awareness of the earlier monuments, as does the discovery of a stick-pin in Tomb T at Loughcrew (Herity 1974, 242). The pin was of the stud-headed type and can be dated to the eleventh–thirteenth-century period (O'Rahilly 1998, 33).

Souterrains featuring reused ogham stones are heavily concentrated in the extreme south (Fig. 21), as are those souterrains containing construction shafts

(Fig. 3). It may be of some significance as regards the development of souterrains that, to date, only one souterrain is known to have possessed both reused ogham stones and a construction shaft. The souterrain in question, at Underhill, Co. Cork (O'Kelly and Shee 1968, 40), was most unusual in that the ogham stones were utilised in the construction of a vestibule in a disused construction shaft — an arrangement unique among the souterrains of Ireland. It is possible, therefore, that the utilisation of looted ogham stones and the digging of construction shafts were not contemporary practices of the souterrain-builders.

The alternative suggestion in relation to the origins of souterrains in Ireland is that the idea was imported. There are only three viable possibilities as regards the actual place of origin of the idea: Scotland, Cornwall and Brittany.

There is little tangible evidence in support of Scotland as the place of origin. Nonetheless, the geographical proximity of the Western Isles to the extreme north of Ireland cannot be ignored (Fig. 71). Given the presence of the rock-cut souterrains, it is not impossible that the earliest souterrains in the north may have been an independent development (Fig. 4). As Warner (1979, 143) has observed, communities of almost identical cultural accoutrements and technology would be quite capable of developing almost identical forms of settlement. Attention has already been drawn (see Chapter 1) to a number of souterrains in the north of the island that have all the appearances of being enhanced natural caves. An additional number of either rock-cut or mostly rock-cut souterrains were entered through horizontal entrances sited in the steep sloping sides of river banks. It is not impossible that the genesis and evolution of artificial subterranean redoubts in the region lay in these adaptations and subsequent progressions. The independence of the north in the relevant period is illustrated by the distribution of the so-called Souterrain Ware (Ryan 1973, 619). The use of this native pottery was confined to the extreme north-east and, to a much lesser extent, the extreme east of the island. It is totally absent from the west and south. In relation to the north, it should also be noted that it would have had extensive communication and links with monastic communities abroad. Given the fact that souterrains of a 'late' (i.e. post-third-century AD) date may yet emerge in Scotland, an independent source of inspiration for the northern souterrains might yet prove to be a viable interpretation.

If it was accepted that either the tunnelled souterrains or the souterrains of mixed (primitive) construction were the earliest forms, then the focus of the study would be drawn primarily to the extreme south or, to be more exact, to the land south of the River Lee (Fig. 1). While there are, as noted above, a significant number of rock-cut souterrains in the extreme north, they do not occur in the same numbers as the tunnelled souterrains known in the south. The presence of at least two construction shafts in the northern group is fascinating given the overwhelming concentration of the feature in the south (Fig. 3). To suggest a direct association or derivation on the basis of two sites would, however, be extremely premature.

Thomas (1972, 76) has argued that the souterrain idea came from Armorica to Ireland, either directly or via Cornwall. The present writer (if one accepts that the idea was imported) would endorse this view. Whether the idea came directly or via Cornwall is still open to debate, but the complete absence of entirely earth- or rock-cut souterrains in Cornwall would seem to favour the former proposition. In passing it should be noted that there are only two known examples of souterrains of substantial mixed construction in Cornwall, at Pendeen and Treveneague. The disparity in dating would not necessarily preclude the idea coming from Cornwall given that many of the souterrains there, owing to their siting and imposing structural composition, would have been, in the words of Thomas, 'open to all comers' (*ibid.*, 77) from the Iron Age up to modern times. The balance of probability would, however, point to Brittany as the more likely potential external source of inspiration for the souterrain idea.

The existence of tunnelled souterrains at such unlikely locations as Duleek, Co. Meath, and Killashee, Co. Kildare, seems strange at first given the otherwise total absence of the form in the east (Clinton, forthcoming a).The fact that both souterrains were sited within the immediate environs of early church sites may ultimately transpire to be pivotal. Souterrains have been advanced as a diagnostic element of a number of enclosed ecclesiastical sites of the first millennium AD (Swan 1983, 274). McCarthy (1983, 100) has noted that the most impressive of the tunnelled souterrains in County Cork were located within the precincts of early church sites. Indeed, it might be argued that early church sites may have been in need of a souterrain since they were often relegated to low-lying riverside locations (Stout 1997, 100). The fact that they may also have been assigned the task of protecting movable assets by the laity — 'sanctuary' (Lucas 1967, 199) — might have given rise to the necessity to provide a secure 'safe'. Is it possible, especially considering their high level of mobility, that it was church personnel returning from sojourns abroad who first introduced the souterrain idea to Ireland, and that the earliest examples may thus be found in association with early church sites, particularly in the south?

Diffusion

The souterrain 'explosion' proper may not have occurred immediately. It may, however, ultimately prove to have been inspired by the increase in population, with all its attendant pressures, known to have occurred after AD 800 (Ó

Corráin 1972, 49). If the original idea had already spread across the island the 'explosion' need not necessarily have originated in the south, or indeed in any one given location.

There are a number of minor indications, however, as to the possible routes the main diffusion of the souterrain idea in Ireland may have followed. The souterrains in the south do not appear to have been structurally influenced by the souterrains of the north or north-east. There is a complete absence in the south of such features as trapdoors (with two exceptions — at Ballyegan and Kimego West, Co. Kerry, which were probably localised developments in response to very specific requirements; see Appendix 2: addendum). Neither is the predominance of unrestricted passages in the north-east paralleled in the south. Inversely, the high-rising vertical wall slabs (interspersed with drystone walling), so typical of souterrains from Rathfield, Co. Kerry (A. O'Sullivan and Sheehan 1996, 234), to Kellystown, Co. Wexford (A.B. Ó Ríordáin 1969, 49), and from Killanully, Co. Cork (Mount 1995, 119), to Ahenny, Co. Tipperary (Sweetman and de Buitléir 1976, 73), were never employed so systematically in the north-east. The limited number of beehive chambers in the south are more likely to have been inspired by earth-cut counterparts than by the souterrains of the Boyne Valley (Fig. 36).

The presence of trapdoors in both the west and the north-east would suggest a direct link (Fig. 45). It is not possible, at present, to determine where the device originated. It should be noted, however, that the trapdoors employed at Doon, Co. Offaly, east of the River Shannon, were of the western type. There are, to date, no proven examples of eastern-type trapdoors in the west. It should also be noted that the beehive chamber, so typical of the souterrains in the greater Meath zone, failed to cross the River Shannon in any significant numbers. The two principal souterrains at Rathnew (Uisneach) and the two souterrains at Togherstown, both sites in County Westmeath, and the souterrain at Fortwilliam, Co. Longford, are ultimately atypical of the greater Meath group while showing some similarities to forms known in north Connacht. A small number of air-vents in Connacht originated in 'host features': in the back walls of cupboards at both Lisnagranchy 1 and Gortroe, Co. Galway, and in the back of a cubby-hole at Rinn, Co. Galway. An air-vent similarly opened in the back wall of a recess at Togherstown (Souterrain 1), Co. Westmeath (see Chapter 6). It might therefore be tentatively suggested that there was some movement of ideas from west to east.

There are slight suggestions of similarities between souterrains in the south and souterrains in the west, the western group of stepped features, the jambs-and-lintel formations and the horizontally placed slabs being some examples. None of these features, however, has yet been discovered in sufficient numbers to argue forcibly for a direct association between the two groups. The apparent association between round houses and souterrains in these two regions may also be indicative of an early diffusion.

It is even more difficult to detect any movement, in either direction, between the extreme north and either the west and/or the east/north-east. The north-eastern-type trapdoor does extend into counties Antrim and Londonderry, but, to date, not in any great numbers. The beehive chamber is also largely absent in the north. South Down would appear to have been firmly tied into the north-eastern group. Owing to the presence of the Mountains of Mourne the relationship was probably based on sea connections. The maritime link between Lecale and north Louth was still firmly established in the twelfth/thirteenth century (J.W.H. 1853, 94). The oblong chambers at Clashygowan, Co. Donegal (Wheeler 1956), were somewhat reminiscent of some of the western-type chambers.

Tenure

Given that the vast majority of souterrains would appear to have functioned as refuges, it is quite remarkable that so few human remains have been uncovered in them. The remains of a child were recovered from a souterrain at Ballyarra, Co. Cork (Fahy 1953, 59), but these probably dated from the backfilling of the souterrain. The skeleton of a youth was allegedly discovered in primary deposits in a souterrain at Ballyboley, Co. Antrim (Lynn 1977). The skeleton of a young man was recovered from the possible entrance passage to a souterrain at Castle Balfour Demesne, Co. Fermanagh (Brannon 1981–2, 53). The most striking example, however, came from Kill, Co. Kerry (Cahill 1989), where an extended inhumation of seventh–tenth-century date was discovered on the chamber floor. These were the remains of a young woman. It is interesting to note, on a purely superficial level, that in all cases these were the remains of young people and not men of fighting age. The overall conclusion, therefore, must be that the people who took refuge in souterrains must always have been subsequently released once the danger had passed. The alternative interpretation that they were always captured would surely not have encouraged the proliferation and prolonged use of the souterrain.

A popular image has been the perceived connection between the building or use of souterrains and the arrival/activities of the Vikings. This mental association owes much to references in the annals and early literature which recorded such events as the 'foreigners' searching Knowth and Dowth in County Meath (*AU* 862) or the plundering of the Ciarraige Luachra 'under ground' (*AI*

866) (Lucas 1971–3, 171). Such a direct 'association' is not, however, evident in the overall distribution of the souterrains. The initial Viking raids of the late eighth/early ninth century. were primarily hit-and-run affairs with a pronounced coastal emphasis (Ó Corráin 1972, 82). It may now be firmly stated that — with the exception of such areas as Antrim, north Louth, south Galway, and Kerry/west Cork — there were no significant coastal concentrations of souterrains. Neither were there any heavy concentrations along the River Shannon, a major conduit of ongoing Viking activity, where, for example, a fleet was based (on Lough Ree) in 844 (*ibid.,* 9). Ó Corráin (1972, 83) has argued that, in any event, the overall impact of this initial phase of activity had a negligible effect on secular society. Thus such a reactive response as the building of souterrains should not even be expected, unless possibly in the context of early church sites. The establishment of permanent Viking/Scandinavian settlements (from the mid-ninth century onwards) does not appear to have had a marked effect either.

The settlement at Dublin did not inspire any significant construction of souterrains along the periphery of its sphere of influence (Clinton 1998, 126; 2000a, 290). Indeed, to the west and south of the city the monument is practically non-existent. To the north of the city the density of souterrains remained totally consistent with the 'even' distribution of the associated group that stretched right across counties Meath and Westmeath. The 'longphort' at Annagassan, Co. Louth, would be equally problematic in the projected equation. While those areas to the north of the settlement were heavily endowed with souterrains, the corresponding lands to the south contained considerably less. The settlement at Waterford has a few scattered souterrains in its general vicinity but again these reflect the density of the group that stretched across the county into east Cork and south Tipperary.

The evidence from the areas surrounding the Viking/Scandinavian settlement at Limerick is even more graphic. North, south, east or west, souterrains are simply not to be found. It would appear likely, therefore, that the building of souterrains was more intrinsically related to the internecine wranglings of the native Irish groupings than a direct response to the activities of extraneous hostile forces.

It has been generally accepted that the use of mortar in the building of stone churches and round towers began in the mid-tenth century (C. Manning, pers. comm.; Edwards 1990, 128). This date has recently been challenged by Berger (1995), who has advanced a seventh- to ninth-century date for the first use of mortar in churches (and round towers) in Ireland (*ibid.,* 171) based on a radiocarbon analysis of charcoal samples encased in the mortar of a number of churches and towers. No examples have yet been recorded of the use of mortar in stone-built souterrains. This fact is of particular interest regarding those souterrains discovered within the immediate environs of church sites. Whilst it has been suggested above (see Chapter 5) that the construction of souterrains in Ireland may have extended well into the twelfth century, owing to a lack of scientific excavation there are no absolute dates available for those souterrains potentially associated with church sites. Nonetheless, accepting for the moment that souterrains did continue to be built in the environs of church sites into the early centuries of the second millennium, it is worth noting that mortar was not employed in the construction of any of them. There could be a number of reasons for this: the labour and extra cost involved in the preparation of the mortar; the initial reserving of the practice for the key monuments at the site; or possibly even a (justified) reluctance to interfere with a proven formula. An alternative explanation would be that souterrains were no longer being built at church sites when the use of mortar became widespread.

A question to be resolved in the future is the precise relationship between enclosed souterrains, particularly those in the east, and the 'host' enclosure. It should be noted that at a number of sites, for example Togherstown (Souterrain 2), Co. Westmeath (Macalister and Praeger 1929–31, 54), or Kiltale, Co. Meath (Rynne 1974, 267), it was clear that the souterrains post-dated the period of active use of the ringfort fosse. Souterrain 9 at Knowth had also been built in the ditch of an earlier enclosure (Eogan 1968, 357). The point is that many souterrains, superficially located in a ringfort, may ultimately transpire to have been associated with a subsequent, and thus later, open settlement. A good location would have maintained its appeal to different settlers. This is not to say that all souterrains located in enclosures were necessarily later features. Indeed, a number of enclosed sites have been found to be in possession of more than one souterrain. At Ballybarrack, Co. Louth (E.P. Kelly, pers. comm.) (Fig. 15), three souterrains were uncovered by excavation. Again, at Killally, Co. Louth (Buckley and Sweetman 1991, 126; Clinton and Stout 1997, 129), two, if not three, souterrains have been recorded. Gosling (1991, 244) drew attention to this fact in order to illustrate that souterrains could be an integral part of sites of various social levels. Stout (1997, 24) has strongly argued that ringforts flourished between the beginning of the seventh century and the end of the ninth century. Other writers, such as Rynne (1964c, 245) and Proudfoot (1970, 44), have argued for a longer survival. Irrespective of ringforts, there is no evidence to suggest that souterrains did not continue in use until (at least?) the twelfth century. If Stout's proposal for the decline of ringforts at the end of the ninth century is accepted, then the survival of souterrains would indicate that they had already established an independent identity by that time.

Eogan (1986, 23) has described the settlement that flourished at Knowth,

Co. Meath, between the ninth and twelfth centuries as a sort of unenclosed 'village'. Nine souterrains have been identified at this site, all associated with rectangular houses (G. Eogan, pers comm.). What is of deep significance is the fact that this settlement has been identified as a royal site (Byrne 1973, 88). This is of key importance in relation to such sites as Loughcrew, Co. Meath (Clinton 1993, 120), Toberdoney, Co. Down (Collins 1964), or Knock Dhu, Co. Antrim (Lawlor 1915–16, 32). The souterrains at these sites are of massive proportions. They could not have been inexpensive to construct, and they were not associated with an enclosure. It is almost certain that they were associated with one or, in the light of Knowth, with a number of dwellings (rectangular houses?). Surely there can be little doubt that such settlements represented the abodes of personages of some importance. It might even be suggested that it was at this type of site that one would be likely to find the 'Aire Ard' (Binchy 1970, 69), if not the 'Aire Forgill' (*ibid.,* 72), or their social equivalents, who in previous centuries would have dwelt in the more complex types of ringforts (Stout 1997, 111). Could these complex souterrains, at the top of the range, have been regarded as the new status symbols?

The move from enclosed to unenclosed settlement could be linked with a decline in the primacy of cattle-rearing or an increasing diversity in settlement patterns. Localised evidence from County Meath might be regarded as supporting the latter proposition (Brady 1983, 21; Clinton 2000b, 372). The fact that the souterrain survived the apparent decline of the ringfort suggests either that it was still found to be useful or that it was adapted to a redefined role — or possibly both. The predominant trapdoor type used in the north-east (the north-eastern Class A — see Chapter 6) could not be sealed off from within, in stark contrast to the predominant type of trapdoor used in the west (the western Class A). Furthermore, while the vast majority of souterrains containing trapdoors in the west were located in enclosed sites, the souterrains containing trapdoors in the east were overwhelmingly associated with open settlements. Thus, while these western souterrains were more than likely the last redoubts of the cattle-owning inhabitants of enclosed settlements, the souterrains in the open settlements in the east, with their 'inverted' traps, must have fulfilled a slightly different function. This may ultimately suggest that many of the souterrains associated with open settlements, particularly in the east, and invariably associated with a rectangular house, were later in date than the souterrains in the west. Lynn (1978, 37) has indicated that the rectangular houses were fully established by *c.* 1000.

Tillage was never the main economic pursuit of the ringfort-dwellers (Stout 1997, 37). Corn-drying kilns were extant in Ireland from at least the fifth century AD (Gailey 1970, 68); it is interesting to note, therefore, that examples were discovered at only four out of a total of 46 excavated ringforts (Proudfoot 1961, 106). Indeed, the absence of any proven granaries in ringforts might possibly be explained by the suggestion that they were in fact primarily located at open settlement sites. Cattle-rearing, with the emphasis on cows, constituted the main economic pursuit of the ringfort-dwellers (McCormick 1995, 35). It has been suggested that the increase in tillage production was preceded, if not indeed facilitated, by the introduction of dairying towards the middle of the first millennium AD (*ibid.*, 36). The improved diet led to an increase in population, which in turn necessitated the expansion of agriculture. The finite space available within the confines of a ringfort would ultimately have dictated the size of the population of the enclosed settlement. It is possible that initial spillovers from enclosed sites eventually led to independent extramural settlements. The creation of these open settlements may finally have led to the establishment of the souterrain as the main form of protection for the agricultural community towards the end of the first millennium and into the early centuries of the second millennium AD.

The precise nature of an 'average' open settlement in the early historic period has yet to be fully determined. Their full economy has also yet to be resolved. The absence of an enclosure would suggest the non-primacy of the keeping of livestock. This is not to say that one should not expect to find animal remains at these sites. It has been stated that up to the medieval period the population of Ireland was reliant on subsistence agriculture and a barter economy (Simms 1978, 67), the assets for exchange, at a fundamental level, being animals and farm products (including cereal) (Doherty 1980, 72).

The material evidence from open settlement sites is extremely meagre. The acidic soil of County Antrim has ruined any chance of bone survival at excavated sites such as Craig Hill (Finbar McCormick, pers. comm.). Some advances have been made elsewhere. Excavations at Randalstown, Co. Meath (Campbell 1986, 32; K. Campbell, pers. comm.), revealed the presence of a souterrain of undifferentiated passage/chamber type, whose lintelled roof had been largely removed in antiquity. The floor deposit contained bird and animal bones. The remains of cattle, sheep, pig and cat were identified. Post-holes close to the entrance of the souterrain revealed the position of the associated house. A series of pits contained the fragmentary remains of additional animal bones. There was no evidence for an enclosure. The following year a second souterrain was excavated in the same townland of Randalstown (Campbell 1987, 31; K. Campbell, pers. comm.). The basal fill covering the entrance ramp was found to contain animal bones. The remains of cattle, sheep, pig and cat were again identified. A series of pits were uncovered in the immediate vicinity of the souterrain. One of these contained the articulated bones of ten horse feet, one complete horse skull and the jawbones of two others. Mechanically dug trenches confirmed that the site was unenclosed. Excavations conducted at Spiddal, Co. Meath (Eogan 1990, 41), also established the existence of an unenclosed settlement. The animal bones recovered from primary fill in the souterrain included the remains of cattle, pig, horse and cat (*ibid.*, 62), with evidence for the above, in addition to sheep/goat, dog and red deer, coming from secondary contexts (*ibid.*, 64). The practice of crop husbandry at open settlement sites has been confirmed by the finding of such objects as an unfinished (broken) quernstone at Oldbridge 1, Co. Meath, and both used quernstones and an unfinished quernstone, in addition to an unfinished millstone, at Spiddal, Co. Meath (Eogan 1990, 59). Excavations at Doonloughan, Co. Galway, in the summer of 1997 revealed the presence of early historic industrial activity and (temporary?) settlement. None of the individual sites was enclosed, or contained a souterrain. Site 11, a coastal hut site, produced very little animal bone, but considerable amounts of charred grain (mostly barley) and fish bones were recovered (Finbar McCormick and Emily Murray, pers. comm.).

Duignan (1944a, 135) has discussed the ploughing technology employed in early historic Ireland. Brady (1987, 228) subsequently eliminated some of the suggested types of ploughshares. He has also advanced the theory that the earliest examples of shares can only be dated to the eighth century AD, while coulters only made an appearance in the tenth century (Brady 1993, 37; 1994, 133). Thus it is possible that the major breakthrough may have been slightly later than initially envisaged. A slightly earlier development was the introduction of the horizontal mill. This has been dated to the seventh century AD (Lucas 1953, 3; Baillie 1975, 26; 1982, 192). These technological innovations would have increased both the efficiency and the productivity of tillage farming. A sizeable proportion of this was centred on the larger monastic foundations (Duignan 1944a, 144; Stout 1997, 129). Undoubtedly increased tillage would have contributed towards the decline in the primacy of cattle-rearing. This in turn may have prompted the decline of secular enclosed settlement. The increase in food production and the subsequent expansion in population would have made people, as opposed to cattle, the prime (movable) asset. It is probably no accident that slavery increased from the ninth century onwards and that a healthy trade was conducted between Dublin and Bristol in the eleventh and twelfth centuries (Ó Corráin 1972, 47). It is against this backdrop that the survival of the souterrain in the post-ringfort phase should be viewed.

Survival

It is, of course, impossible to say when the last souterrain was built in Ireland. It is equally impossible to say when the last souterrain fell into disuse, or was deliberately backfilled. Indeed, given the fact that they have been used for various illicit purposes down through the centuries, it could be said that their demise was relatively recent. If one was to accept that the phased Norman settlement caused the cessation of the building of souterrains, it might be reasonable to suggest that the decline was a piecemeal and gradual affair. This might help to explain the presence of finds such as the thirteenth-century (or later) gaming-piece in the souterrain at Drumcliffe, Co. Sligo (Allen-French 1883–4, 483), or the two medieval tiles in the souterrain at Dunderrow, Co. Cork (O'Mahony 1908–9, 85).

The excavation of a trivallate ringfort at Ballycatteen, Co. Cork (S.P. Ó Ríordáin and Hartnett 1943–4), revealed the presence of at least three souterrains. The 'unintelligible pattern' (*ibid.*, 42) of post-holes in the excavated quadrant of the interior of the fort led the excavators to propose the former presence of successive houses, and, indeed, successive habitation, at the site (*ibid.*, 12).

The excavators noted the intrinsic similarities in structural composition of the three souterrains and judged them to be contemporaneous features (*ibid.*, 13). The present writer would endorse this interpretation (Fig. 75). It was also suggested that only two of the structures, Souterrains A and B, had been completed, and that Souterrain C may have been left unroofed and used instead as a refuse pit (*ibid.*, 17). As there were no roofing lintels in evidence in the backfill of the three souterrains it was proposed that they originally featured timber roofs. The presence of substantial paired post-holes in the floors of the three chambers in Souterrain B supported this view. Furthermore, the discovery of a large amount of charcoal in the filling and on the floors in Souterrains A and B suggested the former presence of wooden roofs (*ibid.*, 15). Significantly, very little charcoal was uncovered in Souterrain C (*ibid.*, 17). Neither were there the stones necessary to flank and span the two connecting constrictions between the three chambers — hence the interpretation of the souterrain as unfinished.

The real crux of the matter in relation to all three souterrains, however, lies in the content of the fill, especially in Souterrains A and C.

In Souterrain A two sherds of pottery were found in the fill (*ibid.*, 38). The excavators interpreted these not only as belonging to the same vessel, but as being Irish Ware of sixteenth-century date. The significant factor was that while one of the sherds came from floor level, the other was found almost at surface level — the implication being that the souterrain was backfilled in one complete

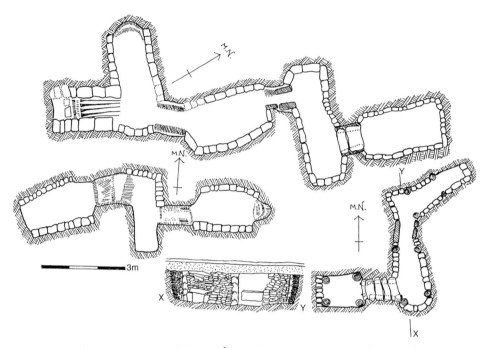

Fig. 75—Ballycatteen, Co. Cork (after Ó Ríordáin and Hartnett): drystone-built souterrains (formerly with wooden roofs); Souterrain A (top); Souterrain B (lower right); Souterrain C (lower left).

operation. The pottery has recently been reinterpreted as fifteenth/sixteenth-century North Devon Ware (Caroline Sandes, pers. comm.).

In Souterrain C an axehead was found 'almost on floor level' (*ibid.*, 41). Again, the significance of the find was in its date. The excavators advanced an eleventh–sixteenth-century date (*loc. cit.*). It has been suggested that the axehead was of the T-shaped type, and was more likely to have been a woodworker's implement than a battleaxe (Etienne Rynne, pers. comm.). The fill of the souterrain also contained large amounts of animal bones and seashells (Ó Ríordáin and Hartnett 1943–4, 17). Animal bones were not a significant element in any other context on the site. This again might be seen to strengthen the rubbish-pit suggestion for the structure.

Ó Ríordáin and Hartnett (1943–4, 31) drew attention to the several hundred perforated slates uncovered during the excavation. Many examples were found in the fill of Souterrains A and B (*ibid.*, 15). The excavators went so far as to propose that the timber roofs could have been covered with these slates. Again, the interesting aspect of the perforated slates is that they cannot be dated earlier than 'high medieval' times (P.F. Wallace, pers. comm.). It is interesting to note that none of these slates were recovered from Souterrain C, the alleged unroofed rubbish-pit. A further 'late' element was the presence of a probable wall bracket in the fill of Souterrain A. A second wall bracket was found in the immediate vicinity of Souterrain C.

It could be suggested that the three souterrains were constructed within the 'accepted' souterrain time-scale, i.e. the latter half of the first millennium/first quarter of the second millennium AD, and, having run their course, were filled in. The use of timber roofs, however, would have put a finite time-limit on the durability of the structures. It would be extremely difficult to sustain the idea of Souterrains A and B being kept in operation (by periodically providing them with new roofs) until such time as they could finally be backfilled in the fifteenth or sixteenth century. Theoretically, subsequent medieval activity within the confines of the ringfort could have led to the discovery of the filled-in 'pits'. Two of these, A and B, could then have been cleaned out and used as cellars(?), featuring timber and slate roofs, until such time as they were again backfilled, in or about the fifteenth or sixteenth century. To sustain this interpretation, however, it would have to be suggested that Souterrain C was again used as a rubbish-pit, and again not provided with a roof. Surely it would be highly unlikely that Souterrain C should be prepared and then left unfinished twice in its history? Considerable amounts of seashells (limpet shells) were uncovered in the fill of the outer chamber. These were concentrated approximately 0.75m below the surface level (the deposit was *c.* 0.3m deep), but were also to be found at floor level and even between the stones in the basal courses of the walls of the chamber. A two-phase rubbish-pit might be expected to produce a more differentiated fill, unless the chamber was cleared out in a remarkably fastidious fashion prior to its reuse.

Are we, therefore, dealing with souterrains of medieval date? It should be stressed that this was an early excavation and that many of the recorded observations are somewhat vague. For example, was Souterrain C definitely left in an unfinished state? The lack of charcoal could be explained by suggesting that the structure was de-roofed prior to its initial backfilling. The stonework absent from the constrictions could have been looted. Indeed, it is not made quite clear whether or not some of the stonework in the constrictions in Souterrains A and B had suffered just such a fate. The text seems to imply, especially in relation to Souterrain A (Ó Ríordáin and Harnett 1943–4, 15), that the lintels of the constrictions were present, if not necessarily *in situ*, but yet the accompanying plan (*ibid.*, 14) only indicates the presence of lintels covering one of the three constrictions in Souterrain A and one of the two constrictions in Souterrain B. If stone-looting took place in Souterrains A and B, then why not in Souterrain C? In any event, the absence of lintelled roofs for the overall structures meant that they could not have lasted for more than 50–100 (?) years. This key aspect of the problem was overlooked by the excavators, who suggested that partial levelling of the interior of the fort caused the filling-in of the souterrains in the medieval period (*ibid.*, 41). Therefore we are left with a limited number of difficult options. Either the souterrains, or at least two of them, were in use towards the end of the main souterrain-building period and were maintained on a periodic basis for an inordinate length of time, or else they were somehow rediscovered, emptied out, possibly reused(?) and subsequently backfilled again in medieval times. Alternatively, we are dealing with structures that were built incredibly late. As this is unprecedented and unparalleled, it would be difficult to accept at face value. Therefore it is very possible that oversights in the original excavation have distorted the evidence. Nevertheless, it should be remembered that the conclusion drawn by Ó Ríordáin and Hartnett was that the three souterrains had been backfilled 'at a time not earlier than medieval times' (*ibid.*, 13).

In conclusion, the present writer would tentatively suggest, as a working hypothesis, that souterrains may have originated in the environs of early church sites (probably in the south); spread into secular use as an integral feature of ringforts; and ultimately, after *c.* AD 1000, with the apparent general decline of the ringfort, developed into an independent feature (associated with open settlement), particularly, but not exclusively, in the north-east and north. If it is accepted that it was church personnel returning from abroad who introduced the idea of the souterrain into Ireland, and that it was the arrival and spread of Norman settlement that terminated their use, then we are dealing with a fifth- to twelfth/thirteenth-century time-span. The reality, to date, however, is that — with the exception of the scientifically dated souterrain at Liscahane, Co. Cork, which produced a sixth-century AD date (D. Power *et al.* 1997, 281) — all the indications are that the majority of souterrains in Ireland enjoyed an eighth–twelfth/thirteenth-century floruit, with many of those associated with open settlement in the east leaning towards the end of the spectrum, and possibly with later survivors elsewhere.

Appendix 1
Ogham-inscribed stones in souterrains

Table 1 – Inventory of sites

Co. Antrim

Carncome (Connor) (Carmody 1898–9, 47; Buick 1900–2; Chart 1940, 32; Macalister 1945–9, I, 297; Hamlin 1976, 429; 1982, 31)

Co. Cork

Ahalisky (Caulfield 1847–50, 387; Ferguson 1887, 100; Gogan 1929, 6; Macalister 1945–9, I, 73)

Ballyhank (Ferguson 1870–9a, 59; 1870–9b, 129; 1877–86, 51; 1887, 95; Rhys 1902, 8; Gogan 1929, 6; Macalister 1945–9, I, 92; D. Power *et al.* 1997, 272)

Ballyknock North (Barry 1890–1, 516; Macalister 1945–9, I, 84)

Barrahaurin (Macalister 1907, 38; Hartnett 1939, 176; Macalister 1945–9, I, 102)

Burnfort (Oldham 1840–4, 516; Haigh 1858–9, 182; Brash 1870–9d, 198; Ferguson 1887, 87; Gogan 1929, 6; Macalister 1945–9, I, 61)

Carhoovauler (O'Crowley 1906; Macalister 1906, 261; Gogan 1929, 6; Macalister 1945–9, I, 77; McCarthy 1977, 181)

Coolineagh (Brash 1870–9d, 199)

Cooldorragha (Ferguson 1887, 101; Gogan 1929, 6; Macalister 1945–9, I, 127)

Garranes (Ferguson 1887, 99; Henebry 1910–11, 73; Macalister 1945–9, I, 84)

Glenawillin (Ferguson 1887, 86; Macalister 1907, 37; 1916–17, 87; Gogan 1929, 5; Macalister 1945–9, I, 66)

Kilmartin Lower (Macalister 1906, 261; 1916–17, 82; Gogan 1929, 6; Hartnett 1939, 196; Coleman 1947–8, 71; Macalister 1945–9, I, 110)

Knockshanawee (Lee 1911, 59; Macalister 1914–16, 140; 1916–17, 81; Gogan 1929, 5; Macalister 1945–9, I, 112)

Lackabane (Power *et al.* 1997, 281)

Liscahane (Ó Donnabháin 1982; U. Egan, pers. comm., 1997)

Monataggart (Ferguson 1870–9c, 292; 1877–86, 53; 1887, 88; Brash 1870–9b, 172; Quarry 1870–9, 289; Gogan 1929, 6; Macalister 1945–9, I, 116)

Rathcanning (Gogan 1929, 5; Macalister 1945–9, I, 82)

Roovesmore (Lane-Fox 1867, 123; Ferguson 1870–9b, 129; 1887, 20, 98; Gogan 1929, 6; Macalister 1945–9, I, 122)

Underhill (O'Kelly and Shee 1968, 40)

Co. Kerry

Aghacarrible (Graves 1864–74, 425; Ferguson 1870–9a, 40; 1870–9b, 129; 1887, 27; Macalister 1897, 20; 1945–9, I, 135)

Ballywiheen (Hitchcock 1853–7, 439; Cuppage 1986, 194)

Ballybroman (Macalister 1945–9, II, 197; McManus 1991, 68)

Brackhill (Macalister 1902, 50; 1945–9, I, 243)

Brackloon (Graves 1847–50b, 272; Macalister 1945–9, I, 166)

Coolmagort (Dunloe) (Graves 1847–50a, 178; Haigh 1858–9, 182; Atkinson 1866, 523; Lane-Fox 1867, 129; Ferguson 1870–9b, 129; 1887, 107; Brash 1870–9d, 199; J. Graves 1883–4, 312; C. Graves 1885–6, 605; Macalister 1945–9, I, 191)

Corkaboy (Ferguson 1887, 111; Macalister 1902, 51; 1945–9, I, 244)

Emlagh West (Macalister 1945–9, I, 174; Connolly 1994, 44)

Fortwilliam (Todd 1840–4, 410; Rhys 1902, 40; Macalister 1945–9, I, 134)

Gearha South (O'Kelly and Kavanagh 1954a, 50; A. O'Sullivan and Sheehan 1996, 232)

Garrane (Lynch 1894, 291; C. Graves 1895, 1; Macalister 1945–9, I, 246)

Kilgobnet (Macalister 1945–9, I, 205; A. O'Sullivan and Sheehan 1996, 161)

'Killorglin' (C. Graves 1884, 279; Rhys 1902, 15; Macalister 1945–9, I, 247)

Rathkenny (Macalister 1945–9, II, 197; McManus 1991, 68; Toal 1995, 193)

Rathmalode (Ferguson 1877–86, 50; 1887, 20; Macalister 1945–9, I, 189)

Rockfield (Brash 1870–9a; Macalister 1945–9, I, 239)

Tinnahally (Brash 1870–9c, 186; Ferguson 1887, 109; Macalister 1907, 37; 1945–9, I, 249)

Whitefield (Macalister 1945–9, I, 208; A. O'Sullivan and Sheehan 1996, 236)

Co. Londonderry

Dunalis (Lindsay 1934–5, 61; Macalister 1945–9, I, 304; Hamlin 1982, 31)

Co. Louth

Ballybarrack (Souterrain No. 3) (E.P. Kelly, pers. comm.)

Co. Meath

Spiddal (Eogan 1990, 60)

Co. Roscommon

Glenballythomas (Rathcroghan) (Ferguson 1864–6, 160; 1870–9b, 129; 1887, 57; Rhys 1898, 232; Knox 1917–18, 7; Macalister 1945–9, I, 16; Herity 1987, 138; 1993, 131; Waddell 1998, 352)

Co. Waterford

Drumlohan (W. Williams 1868–9, 35; Brash 1866–9a, 103; Hansard 1870, 286; Ferguson 1870–9b, 129; Brash 1870–9d, 199; Ferguson 1887, 78; Macalister 1945–9, I, 267; Kirwan 1985, 6; 1987, 33)

Fox's Castle (Mongey 1934, 265; Macalister 1935, 149; 1945–9, I, 277)

Windgap or Ardmore (Du Noyer 1857–61, 251; Brash 1868, 348; Ferguson 1887, 76; Macalister 1909, 296; 1945–9, I, 295; Moore 1989a)

Addendum

The Rev. Barry (1890–1, 516), in the course of his account of the discovery of the ogham stones in the souterrain at Ballyknock North, Co. Cork, included a brief detailed inventory of sites in possession of ogham stones. The information provided therein, with the exception of Rockfield, Co. Kerry, which he credited with six as opposed to four ogham stones, has proved to be accurate. The most intriguing item in the inventory is his reference to the site of Kilgrovan, Co. Waterford. He described the five known ogham stones from the site as having been discovered in an 'uprooted Killeen-cave' (*loc. cit.*). When Brash (1879, 256) visited the site on 1 June 1869 he found the ogham stones 'huddled close together in one spot, leaning one against the other'. They had obviously been gathered together during the ongoing encroachment on the killeen. Were the ogham stones originally uncovered in a souterrain and subsequently removed by the farmer, or were they originally free-standing stones? Did Barry have specific information regarding the discovery? It should be noted that in his inventory he recorded six other killeen or graveyard sites and that only Kilgrovan was credited with an 'uprooted' cave. The original published accounts of the site do not resolve the issue. W. Williams (1856–7) simply recorded the five ogham stones as 'occurring in an unconsecrated burying-ground'. He did not specify whether they were free-standing stones or had already been 'huddled' together. It is obvious that Brash was not privy to any first-hand information regarding the circumstances of Williams's discovery. Indeed, in his first published reference to the site (1868–9c, 438) he qualified the credit for the discovery ('... discovered, I believe ...') by Williams. Macalister (1945–9, I, 280) simply repeated Williams's ambiguous report. The distinct possibility must therefore remain that the five ogham stones discovered at Kilgrovan, Co. Waterford, came from a destroyed souterrain.

The destruction of a number of ringforts in the townland of Dunbel, Co. Kilkenny (Prim 1852–3, 119), resulted in the discovery of two ogham stones (Prim 1854–5, 397; Brash 1872–3, 238), apparently standing in an almost upright position in the fosse of one of the minor ringforts (Prim 1854–5, 406).

It was further reported that the 'entrance to an artificial cave' was discovered in the general vicinity of the ogham stones (*ibid.*, 403). The belief that the ogham stones had, in fact, been discovered within a souterrain had become so prevalent that Prim thought it necessary to refute the report in a subsequent paper (1872–3, 226). While Macalister (1945–9, I, 34) made no reference to the suggestion that the ogham stones had been found in a souterrain, more recent writers, for example F. Moore (1998, 24), have again raised the issue.

It must be stressed at the outset that not only had the ogham stones been removed from their original position prior to inspection but they had been broken up into many pieces. Thus the suggested reconstruction of the various elements extant at the site was based purely on hearsay evidence. The 'entrance' to the drystone-built 'cave' was described as being *c.* 0.7m high and *c.* 0.5m wide. Its 'entire' length was given as *c.* 4.1m. A notable aspect of the report was that the drystone-built structure was said to have 'narrowed inwards' in an abrupt and pronounced fashion (Prim 1854–5, 403). A 'wall of dry stones' was uncovered in close proximity to the 'funnel'. It extended across the middle of the fosse (*loc. cit.*). The original position of the two ogham pillars was (reportedly) located between the two drystone-built features. The two pillars, both inclining outwards, stood *c.* 0.9–1.22m apart (*ibid.*, 404).

It is difficult to envisage how the various recorded elements would have constituted the remains of a souterrain. Indeed, the utilisation of two ogham pillars as 'portals' would be unprecedented. Similarly, the construction of a souterrain within the fosse of a ringfort would be decidedly rare. The abrupt and pronounced narrowing of the 'funnel' is also problematic. It may be stated that passages and constrictions tend to maintain a roughly even profile. If the three recorded elements were to be interpreted as the surviving remains of a souterrain then the 'funnel' might be seen as a possible air-vent or drain. At Rinn, Co. Galway (Knox and Redington 1915–16, 182), a cubby-hole gradually evolved into an air-vent over a distance of 1.83m. Nonetheless, it must be reiterated that Prim (1872–3, 226) stated firmly that 'no crypt was found' and that therefore the suggested direct association between the Dunbel oghams and a souterrain remains unproven.

Table 2—Statistical and contextual data

Site	No. of ogham stones	Available data
1. Carncome (Connor), Co. Antrim	2	Two roofing lintels
2. Ahalisky, Co. Cork	3	Two roofing lintels; one pillar
3. Ballyhank, Co. Cork	6	Roofing lintels?
4. Ballyknock North, Co. Cork	15	Fourteen lintels; one short pillar
5. Barrahaurin, Co. Cork	1	Roofing lintel
6. Burnfort, Co. Cork	1	
7. Carhoovauler, Co. Cork	3	One roofing lintel; two pillars
8. Coolineagh, Co. Cork	1	
9. Cooldorragha, Co. Cork	1	One pillar
10. Garranes, Co. Cork	1	
11. Glenawillin, Co. Cork	2	Two roofing lintels (one souterrain?)
12. Kilmartin Lower, Co. Cork	1	One roofing lintel
13. Knockshanawee, Co. Cork	6	Five roofing lintels; one pillar
14. Lackabane, Co. Cork	1	Roofing level
15. Liscahane, Co. Cork	2	Two roofing lintels
16. Monataggart, Co. Cork	4	
17. Rathcanning, Co. Cork	1	Roofing lintel?
18. Roovesmore, Co. Cork	3	Three roofing lintels
19. Underhill, Co. Cork	3	Two roofing lintels; one pillar/jamb
20. Aghacarrible, Co. Kerry	3	One roofing lintel; two pillars
21. Ballywiheen, Co. Kerry	1	Roofing lintel
22. Ballybroman, Co. Kerry	1	
23. Brackhill, Co. Kerry	1	Roofing lintel
24. Brackloon, Co. Kerry	1	
25. Coolmagort (Dunloe), Co. Kerry	7	Six roofing lintels; one pillar

26. Corkaboy, Co. Kerry	1	Roofing lintel
27. Emlagh West, Co. Kerry	1	Either a roofing lintel or a jamb
28. Fortwilliam, Co. Kerry	1+	
29. Gearha South, Co. Kerry	1	One pillar
30. Garrane, Co. Kerry	1	
31. Kilgobnet, Co. Kerry	1	
32. 'Killorglin', Co. Kerry	1	
33. Rathkenny, Co. Kerry	3	Three roofing lintels
34. Rathmalode, Co. Kerry	2	Two roofing lintels
35. Rockfield, Co. Kerry	4	
36. Tinnahally, Co. Kerry	2	
37. Whitefield, Co. Kerry	2–4	
38. Dunalis, Co. Londonderry	1	Roofing lintel
39. Ballybarrack (No. 3), Co. Louth	1	Roofing lintel
40. Spiddal, Co. Meath	3	Three roofing lintels
41. Glenballythomas, Co. Roscommon	2	Two roofing lintels
42. Drumlohan, Co. Waterford	10	Five roofing lintels; five 'lining' stones
43. Fox's Castle, Co. Waterford	1–2?	One a (displaced) roofing lintel?
44. Windgap or Ardmore, Co. Waterford	1–2	One (probably two) roofing lintels
Total (approx.)	**113**	

Appendix 2

Trapdoor features

Table 1 — Inventory of sites

Part 1 — The north-eastern group

Site	Association	Reference
Co. Antrim		
1. Killyglen	Ringfort	Waterman 1968, 67
2. Knockdhu	Open settlement?	Lawlor 1915–16, 32
3. Tirgracey	Open settlement?	Fennell 1896, 272
Co. Armagh		
1. Carrickananny	Open settlement	McLornan 1984b
Co. Down		
1. Ardtole	Church site?	Bigger and Fennell 1898–9, 146
2. Ballygrainey	Open settlement?	Lawlor 1915–16, 37
3. Ballyholland Lower	Cashel?	Nic Shean 1986
4. Ballytrustan	Open settlement	Lynn and Warner 1977
5. Carrickrovaddy	Open settlement	Collins and Harper 1974
6. Glovet	Open settlement	Gray 1894, 45; Lawlor 1916–18, 91
7. Rathmullan	Ringfort	Lynn 1981–2, 65
Co. Londonderry		
1. Ballyhacket-Glenahorry	Open settlement?	Ligar 1833
2. Island Vardin	Open settlement	J. Williams 1835
Co. Louth		
1. Allardstown	Open settlement	Cahill and Ryan 1976
2. Ballinloughan	Open settlement	Ua Cuinn 1904–7, 38
3. Balregan	Open settlement	Wright 1758, 16
4. Balrobin	Open settlement	Buckley and Sweetman 1991, 104

5. Bawntaaffe   Open settlement   Rynne 1957–60a, 96
    (Sou. A)
6. Bellurgan   Open settlement   Tipping 1864–6, 183
7. Benagh   Inland prom. fort   Buckley and Sweetman 1991, 107
8. Carrickacreagh Open settlement   Gosling 1979, 206
9. Carrickleagh   Open settlement   Buckley and Sweetman 1991, 110
10. Carrickrobin   Open settlement   Buckley and Sweetman 1991, 111
11. Chanonrock   Enclosure   A.B. Ó Ríordáin 1953–6, 441
12. Crumlin   Open settlement   Buckley and Sweetman 1991, 115
13. Donaghmore   Open settlement   Rynne 1957–60b, 148
    (Sou. B)
14. Dunbin Little   Open settlement   P. Corcoran 1929–32
15. Farrandreg 2   Open settlement   D. Murphy 1998, 269;
                                         M. Seaver, pers. comm.
16. Haggardstown   Open settlement   M. Stout, pers. comm.
17. Marshes Upper 3B Enclosure?   Gowen 1992, 66
18. Marshes Upper 6 Open settlement   Buckley and Sweetman 1991, 129
19. Millockstown   Enclosure?   Manning 1986, 147
    (Sou. 1)
20. Millockstown   Enclosure?   Manning 1986, 149
    (Sou. 2)
21. Millpark   Open settlement   Rynne 1966b
22. Mullagharlin   Open settlement   Rynne 1961–4b, 317
23. Mullameelan   Open settlement   Leask 1941–4, 70
24. Palmersland   Open settlement   Ua Cuinn 1904–7, 38
25. Rathiddy   Enclosure?   Rynne 1962, 125
26. Riverstown   Open settlement   Twohig 1971, 131
27. Thomastown   Open settlement   Gosling 1979, 213
*   Donaghmore 3   Open settlement   Clarke 1963

Co. Meath
1. Baltrasna   Open settlement   M. Moore 1987, 184
2. Bective 1   Open settlement   Orpen 1890–1, 150
3. Crossdrum Lower Open settlement   Rotheram 1897, 427
4. Donaghmore   Open settlement   A.B. Ó Ríordáin 1956
5. Dowth   Open settlement   Coffey 1912, 49; O'Kelly and
                                         O'Kelly 1983, 154
6. Fennor 2   Open settlement   Rynne 1965c, 229
7. Loughcrew   Open settlement   Clinton 1993, 120
8. Monktown 3   Open settlement   Ronayne 1991a

9. Newrath Big 1	Ringfort?	Sweetman 1975
10. Spiddal (Sou. 2)	Open settlement	Eogan 1990, 41
11. Stonefield	Open settlement	Rotheram 1893–6, 308
* Alexander Reid	Open settlement	Ronayne 1991b
* Kilbrew	Open settlement	Clinton 1996, 30

Co. Westmeath

1. Reynella	Open settlement	R. Murray 1932, 224
2. Banagher	Open settlement	Rynne 1966a

Part 2 — The western group

Site	Association	Reference

Co. Clare

1. Ballyvelaghan	Ringfort	T. Cooke 1849–51, 295
2. Finvarra Demesne	Open settlement	T. Cooke 1849–51, 297
3. Murtyclogh	Ringfort	T. Cooke 1849–51, 296

Co. Galway

1. Aghlisk	Rath	Costello 1902, 112; 1903–4, 1
2. Ardacong	Rath	Costello 1902, 111; 1903–4, 3
3. Ballinphuil	Ringfort	Costello 1902, 115; 1903–4, 8
4. Billymore	Ringfort	Kinahan 1883–4a, 11
5. Caheravoley	Ringfort	Alcock *et al.* 1999, 262
6. Caherfurvaus	Open settlement	E. Rynne, pers. comm.
7. Caherpeake E.	Ringfort	Knox and Redington 1915–16, 184
8. Caltragh	Ringfort	Costello 1902, 116; 1903–4, 9
9. Carnmore	Open settlement	Buckley and O'Brien 1985–6, 139
10. Derryfrench	Ringfort	Gosling *et al.,* forthcoming, no. 5846
11. Gardenfield	Rath	Costello 1902, 111; 1903–4, 4
12. Gortroe	Ringfort	Knox and Redington 1915–16, 180
13. Killeenhugh	Ringfort	Gosling *et al.,* forthcoming, no. 5868
14. Knockballyclery	Ringfort	Gosling *et al.,* forthcoming, no. 5881

15. Lecarrow-nagoppoge	Ringfort	Knox and Redington 1915–16, 187
16. Lissananny	Rath	Costello 1903–4, 5
17. Oranhill	Ringfort	Gosling *et al.*, forthcoming, no. 5907
18. Rinn	Ringfort	Knox and Redington 1915–16, 182
19. Seefin	Ringfort	McCaffrey 1952, 67
20. Termon	Open settlement?	McCarron 1940
21. Toberroe	Ringfort	O. Alcock, pers. comm.
* Drummina-cloghaun	Rath	Gosling *et al.*, forthcoming, no. 5848
* Garraun Lower	Ringfort	Westropp 1919, 172; Gosling *et al.*, forthcoming, no. 5855

Co. Mayo

1. Cooslughoga	Ringfort	Wilde 1867, 110
2. Knock N.	Ringfort	Wilde 1867, 108; Lavelle *et al.* 1994, 71
3. Shanvallyhugh	Ringfort	O'Kelly 1942
4. Killala	Church enclosure	Cochrane and McNeill 1898, 291
5. Lissaniska E.	Ringfort	OPW File
6. Caherduff	Enclosure?	Hayward 1968, 99

Co. Offaly

1. Doon	Ringfort	Foot 1860–1, 222

Table 2 — Trapdoor types

North-eastern Class A:

Co. Antrim: Killyglen (two examples); Knockdhu; Tirgracey
Co. Armagh: Carrickananny
Co. Down: Ardtole; Ballyholland Lower; Ballytrustan; Glovet; Rathmullan
Co. Londonderry: Ballyhacket-Glenahorry
Co. Louth: Allardstown; Ballinloughan; Balregan; Balrobin; Bawntaaffe (Souterrain A); Bellurgan; Benagh; Carrickacreagh; Carrickrobin; Chanonrock; Crumlin; Donaghmore (Souterrain B); Dunbin Little (two examples); Farrandreg 2 (two examples); Haggardstown; Marshes Upper 3B; Marshes Upper 6; Millockstown (Souterrain 1); Millockstown (Souterrain 2); Millpark; Mullagharlin; Mullameelan; Palmersland; Rathiddy; Riverstown

Co. Meath: Baltrasna; Bective 1; Donaghmore; Dowth; Loughcrew; Newrath
   Big 1; Spiddal (Souterrain 2); Stonefield
Co. Westmeath: Reynella

North-eastern Class B:
Co. Down: Carrickrovaddy
Co. Londonderry: Island Vardin
Co. Louth: Balregan; Bawntaaffe (Souterrain A); Chanonrock; Crumlin;
   Donaghmore (Souterrain B); Thomastown
Co. Meath: Crossdrum Lower; Fennor 2; Loughcrew; Monktown 3

Western Class A:
Co. Clare: Ballyvelaghan; Finvarra Demesne; Murtyclogh
Co. Galway: Aghlisk; Ardacong; Ballinphuil (two examples); Caheravoley;
   Caherpeake East; Caltragh (two examples); Gardenfield; Gortroe;
   Lecarrownagoppoge (two examples); Lissananny; Seefin (two examples);
   Termon
Co. Mayo: Knock North; Shanvallyhugh
Co. Offaly: Doon

Western Class B:
Co. Galway: Billymore; Carnmore (two examples); Rinn

Western Class C:
Co. Clare: Ballyvelaghan
Co. Galway: Caltragh; Knockballyclery (two examples)
Co. Mayo: Lissaniska East

Western Class D:
Co. Mayo: Lissaniska East

Addenda
Alexander Reid (Co. Meath): Suspected trap feature
Ballygrainey (Co. Down): Suspected trap feature
Banagher (Co. Westmeath): Suspected trap feature
Caherduff (Co. Mayo): A potential Western Class B
Caherfurvaus (Co. Galway): Two elevated trapdoors, both either Western Class
   A or Western Class B
Carrickleagh (Co. Louth): Probably a North-eastern Class A

Cosslughoga (Co. Mayo): Unclassified

Derryfrench (Co. Galway): A possible Western Class C

Donaghmore 3 (Co. Louth): Suspected trap feature

Drumminacloghaun (Co. Galway): A potential Western Class A

Garaun Lower (Co. Galway): A potential Western Class B

Glovet (Co. Down): The second and third traps are possibly variations on a North-eastern Class A

Kilbrew (Co. Meath): Suspected trap feature

Killala (Co. Mayo): Suspected trap feature

Killeenhugh (Co. Galway): A Western Class A or a Western Class B

Oranhill (Co. Galway): The first trap is a potential Western Class A; the second trap is either a Western Class A or a Western Class D

Toberroe (Co. Galway): Variation on a Western Class C

Table 3 — Elevated trapdoors

Co. Clare
Ballyvelaghan — platform type
Finvarra Demesne — platform type
Murtyclogh — platform type

Co. Galway
Aghlisk — stepped type
Ardacong — platform type
Billymore — stepped type
Caheravoley — platform type?
Caherpeake East — platform type
Caltragh — (a) platform type?; (b) stepped type?
Carnmore — platform type
Gardenfield — stepped type
Gortroe — stepped type
Killeenhugh — platform type
Lecarrownagoppoge — stepped type
Lissananny — platform type
Ballinphuil — (a) platform type; (b) platform type
Rinn — platform type
Seefin — (a) platform type?; (b) platform type?
Termon — platform type

Co. Mayo
Cooslughoga — stepped type?
Knock North — platform type
Shanvallyhugh — stepped type

Co. Offaly
Doon — platform type

Addendum

A souterrain located in a cashel at Ballyegan, Co. Kerry, was discovered to contain a trapdoor device (Gorham 1914–16, 12; Byrne 1991, 5). A short (2m) length of sloping passage extended from the western flank of the main access passage/undifferentiated chamber. The trapdoor was sited in the floor of the short passage at its inner terminal. The device facilitated access to a lower-lying linear arrangement of two drystone-built chambers and a natural cave.

The presence of a trapdoor in a souterrain in County Kerry is quite remarkable. It would be difficult to advance any suggested connections with the examples of the feature located in either the western or especially the north-eastern groups. Except for an unclarified reference to 'a manhole' in the inner chamber of a souterrain at Coolnaharrigle, Co. Kerry (Topographical Files 1944, NMI), there are no other reports of the feature occurring as an element of the souterrains of Munster (north-west Clare being morphologically aligned with the souterrains of Connacht). It is possible that the presence of the natural cave tempted the souterrain-builders to aspire to a greater depth than would have been the norm for the region. The earlier account (Gorham 1914–16, 16) recorded the former existence of an opening to the cave in the steep bank of an adjacent stream. It is more than likely, therefore, that the builders were aware of the presence of the cave prior to their excavation. It is possible that the trapdoor was their inspired solution to a novel situation.

There was a reported 'obstruction' in the souterrain at Killala, Co. Mayo (Cochrane and McNeill 1898, 291). The feature in question appeared to be sited at the junction of an upper-lying passage and a lower-lying passage. Superficially, therefore, this 'obstruction' may represent an intriguingly sited approximation of the north-eastern type of trapdoor.

The cashel at Kimego West (Leacanabuaile), Co. Kerry (S.P. Ó Ríordáin and Foy 1941, 85; A. O'Sullivan and Sheehan 1996, 184), contained the remains of a number of houses. A souterrain extended from an entrance in the floor of the western house and terminated beneath the cashel wall. An opening had, however, been left in its inner roof and through this aperture access was gained to a chamber built in the cashel wall. Whilst the aperture, strictly speaking, was not necessarily a trapdoor, it had the potential to be used as one. It is more likely that the genesis of this feature was prompted by the self-determining conjunction of a subterranean passage and an over-ground mural chamber rather than being the end result of a pre-chosen formal design.

Appendix 3
Stepped features

Table 1 — Inventory of sites

Co. Antrim
* Bushmills ('The Crags') (possible) (Hobson 1909, 223)

Co. Clare
Finvarra Demesne (T. Cooke 1849–51, 297)
Dough (Lisnaleagaun) (two examples) (Westropp 1909, 116; 1914, 162)

Co. Donegal
Straid (Glencolmcille) (Lacy 1983, 289)

Co. Down
Drumena (Berry 1926–7, 50; Chart 1940, 125; Jope 1966, 176; Hamlin 1982, 93)
Slanes (four possible examples) (Harris and Smith 1744, 195; Hobson 1909, 224)
Spittle Quarter (two examples) (Brannon 1990, 39)
Turmore (Buckley 1978, 28)

Co. Galway
Caherpeake East (Knox and Redington 1915–16, 184)
Killosolan (Alcock *et al.* 1999, 271)
Rinn (Knox and Redington 1915–16, 182)

Co. Kerry
Ballynavenooragh (Clinton, forthcoming b)
Dromkeen East (Twohig 1974, 9)

Co. Limerick
Raheennamadra (Stenberger 1966, 42)

Co. Londonderry
Dunalis (Lindsay 1934–5, 63)

Co. Louth
Castletown (two examples) (Tempest 1912–15, 25)
Donaghmore (Sou. A) (Rynne 1965a)
Dromiskin 1 (Tempest 1921–4)
Dunbin Little (P. Corcoran 1929–32)
Fairhill (Tempest 1912–15, 24)
Faughart Upper (Rynne 1965b)
Kane (Clinton and Gosling 1979, 211)
Kilcurry (Tempest 1957–60)
Lisrenny (Masser and Bradley 1957–60, 93)
Millpark (Rynne 1966b)
Mullagharlin (Rynne 1961–4b, 317)
Rathiddy (two examples) (Rynne 1962, 125)
Stickillin 1 (Dunne *et al.* 1973–6, 274)
Termonfeckin 1 (Ó Floinn 1978, 128)
Thomastown (two examples) (Gosling 1979, 213)
* Carrickmullan (two possible examples) (NMI Card Index)
* Drumiskin 2 (possible) (Halpin 1989, no. 45)

Co. Mayo
Killala (Cochrane and McNeill 1898, 291)
Money (Rynne 1964a)

Co. Meath
Bective II (Orpen 1890–1, 153)
Boolies Little (Sweetman 1982–3, 42)
Dowth
Knowth (Souterrain 2) (two examples) (G. Eogan, pers. comm.)
Newrath Big 1 (Sweetman 1975)
Oldbridge 1
* Ardbraccan (possible) (Duignan 1944b)
* Cabragh (possible) (Hickey and Rynne 1953, 220)

Co. Sligo
* Rinroe (possible) (O'Donovan 1836b, 215)

Co. Tyrone
Mullanahoe (two examples) (Bigger and Fennell 1897–8, 65)

Co. Westmeath
Togherstown 1 (Macalister and Praeger 1929–31, 73)

Table 2 — Stepped features: structural and contextual data

	Site	Passage type	Stone facing	Roof profile	Height (of 'step') (m)
1.	Dough, Co. Clare (F1)	C assoc.	X	X	Approx. 0.6+?
2.	Finvarra, Co. Clare	R assoc.	X	–	c. 1.22
3.	Drumena, Co. Down	U	X?	?-	0.46
4.	Slanes, Co. Down (F1)	?	X?	?-	0.81–0.91
5.	Spittle Quarter, Co. Down (F1)	U	X	X	c. 0.40
	(F2)	U	X	X	c. 0.75
6.	Turmore, Co. Down	U?	X	X	c. 0.55–0.60
7.	Caherpeake E., Co. Galway	R assoc.	X	–	0.94
8.	Ballynavenooragh, Co. Kerry	R assoc.	X	(X)	0.80
9.	Drumkeen E., Co. Kerry	R assoc.	X	(X)	0.40
10.	Castletown, Co. Louth (F1)	?	X	X	?
	(F2)	?	X	X	c. 0.30
11.	Donaghmore A., Co. Louth	?	X	?	c. 0.50
12	Dromiskin 1, Co. Louth	U	X	X	c. 0.46
13.	Dunbin Little, Co. Louth	U	X	X	?
14.	Fairhill, Co. Louth	U	X	X	0.30
15.	Faughart Upper, Co. Louth	U	X	X	0.60
16.	Millpark, Co. Louth	U	X	X	0.60
17.	Mullagharlin, Co. Louth	R?	X?	X	c. 0.61
18.	Rathiddy, Co. Louth (F1)	U assoc.	X	X	0.65
19.	Stickillin 1, Co. Louth	U	X	X	0.55–0.60
20.	Termonfeckin 1, Co. Louth (F2)	U assoc.	X	X	?
21.	Thomastown, Co. Louth (F1)	U	X	X	0.42
	(F2)	U	X	X?	c. 0.60

22.	Killala, Co. Mayo	R assoc.	X	X?	0.61
23.	Money, Co. Mayo	U?	X	–	0.80–0.85
24.	Bective II, Co. Meath	U?	X?	X?	0.62
25.	Boolies Little, Co. Meath	U	X	?.	0.50
26.	Dowth, Co. Meath	U	X?	X	?
27.	Knowth (Sou. 2), Co. Meath (F1)	U	X	X	0.80
	(F2)	U	X	(X)	0.85
28.	Newrath Big 1, Co. Meath	U	X	X	0.60
29.	Oldbridge 1, Co. Meath (F1)	R	X	–	0.75
30.	Mullanahoe, Co. Tyrone (F1)	U assoc.	X	X	0.46
31.	Togherstown (Sou. 1), Co. Westmeath	U	X	X	0.91

Inverted stepped features

1.	Dough, Co. Clare (F2)	R assoc.	X	X	?
2.	Killosolan, Co. Galway	R assoc.	X	–	0.80
3.	Rinn, Co. Galway	R assoc.	X	?.	0.76
4.	Raheenamadra, Co. Limerick	R assoc.	X	X	0.80
5.	Kane, Co. Louth	U	X	X	0.90
6.	Kilcurry, Co. Louth	U	X?	?.	c. 0.45
7.	Lisrenny, Co. Louth	U	X	X	0.40–0.60
8.	Rathiddy, Co. Louth (F2)	U assoc.	X	X	0.70
9.	Termonfeckin 1, Co. Louth (F1)	U assoc.	X	X	0.40
10.	Mullanahoe, Co. Tyrone (F2)	U assoc.	X	X	?

Key: X = present; U = unrestricted-type passage; R = restricted-type passage; C = constriction; assoc. = associated.

Appendix 4

Air-vents

Table 1 — Inventory of sites

Co. Antrim
Aird (two air-vents) (Wright 1964, 123)
Ballyhemlin (Fogg 1989)
Ballyhome (O'Laverty 1887, 271)
Ballyligpatrick (O'Laverty 1884, 436, 438)
Ballymartin (Lawlor 1916–18, 83)
Ballywee (Lynn 1975, 5)
Cloughorr (Harper 1972, 60)
Drumourne (Brannon 1982c)
Holestone (Warner 1994)
Kilmandil (two air-vents) (O'Laverty 1887, 57)
Knockdhu (Lawlor 1915–16, 36)
Rathmore ('The Hill') (V. Buckley, pers. comm.)
Tavnaghoney (Hobson 1909, 223)
Tawnybrack (O'Laverty 1884, 438)
* Lismanery (possible) (Fagan 1839, 27)
* Stranocum (two possible air-vents) (Bigger and Fennell 1896–7, 203)

Co. Armagh
Aghmakane (McLornan 1984a)
Carrickananny (two air-vents) (Chart 1940, 73; McLornan 1984b)
Corliss (two air-vents) (Davies 1937–40, 340; McLornan 1984c)
* Tannyoky (possible) (Neill 1985)

Co. Clare
Portlecka (two air-vents) (Westropp 1913, 237)
* Mortyclogh II (possible) (Westropp 1911, 353)

Co. Cork
Ballyanly 1 (McCarthy 1977, 146)
Ballyhindon (Gillman 1896b, 422)
Barnagore (D. Power *et al.* 1997, 273)
Cappeen West (McCarthy 1977, 202)

Carrigbaun (D. Power 1992, 231)
Castlemagner (Twohig 1976, 19)
Cloddagh (Sherkin Is.) (possible) (Donovan 1876, 37)
Curraghcrowley West (four air-vents) (Somerville 1929–30, 7)
Currahaly (Brash 1866–9b, 73)
Darrara (two air-vents) (J. O'Sullivan *et al.* 1998, 41)
Darrara (one air-vent, two branches) (J. O'Sullivan *et al.* 1998, 43)
Dunisky (Gogan 1930)
Fasagh (two air-vents) (Sweetnam and Gillman 1897, 150)
Kilmore (D. Power *et al.* 1997, 280)
Liscahane (two air-vents) (U. Egan, pers. comm.)
Lisgoold North (D. Power *et al.* 1994, 156)
Lissardagh (D. Power *et al.* 1997, 282)
Mallowgaton (Ó Drisceoil and Hurley 1978, 76)
Monataggart II (McCarthy 1977, 299)
Oldcourt (one air-vent, two branches) (Ó Cuileanáin and Murphy 1961–2, 83)
Rossnakilla (two air-vents) (D. Power *et al.* 1997, 283)
Tullig More (D. Power *et al.* 1997, 284)
* Ballynora (possible) (Coleman 1947–8, 69)
* Darrara (possible) (D. Power 1992, 233)
* Keelnameela (possible) (Twohig 1971, 128)
* Loughmarsh (possible) (Cleary 1981a, 38)
* Moneygaff West (possible) (Cleary 1981a, 40)
* Sheepwalk (possible) (Twohig 1973, 45)

Co. Donegal
* Killydesert (two possible air-vents) (Lacy 1983, 236)

Co. Down
Ardglass (Gaffikin 1938, 95)
Ballylenagh (Mayne 1993)
Drumena (Berry 1926–7, 51; Jope 1966, 176)
Finnis (Buckley 1978, 91)
Sheepland Mor (two air-vents) (Rees-Jones 1971, 78)
Spittle Quarter (Brannon 1990, 41)
Toberdoney (four air-vents) (Lawlor 1916–18, 91)
Tyrella (Lawlor 1916–18, 92)
* Audleystown (possible) (Lawlor 1915–16, 45)
* Ballyginny (possible) (Brannon 1983)
* Castleskreen (possible) (Jope 1966, 170)

Co. Dublin
Hampton Demesne (Hamilton 1845–7, 250; Clinton 1998, 118)

Co. Galway
Aghlisk (Costello 1903–4, 2; Alcock *et al.* 1999, 259)
Ballygarraun N. (Cody 1989, 101, 307)
Ballymanagh (Rynne 1978; Gosling *et al.,* forthcoming, no. 5774)
Ballynamannin (Gosling *et al.,* forthcoming, no. 5781)
Ballynastaig (Gosling *et al.,* forthcoming, no. 5785)
Caherpeake East (two air-vents) (Knox and Redington 1915–16, 185)
Cartoonfrench (Rynne 1968a)
Cloghnakeava (two air-vents) (Gosling *et al.,* forthcoming, no. 5830)
Garraun L. (Gosling *et al.,* forthcoming, no. 5855)
Gortroe (Knox and Redington 1915–16, 180)
Kilbeacanty (Gosling *et al.,* forthcoming, no. 5866)
Lack (Alcock *et al.* 1999, 272)
Lackan (RTC Galway 1979)
Lisnagranshy 1 (Knox and Redington 1915–16, 180)
Lissycgan (Alcock *et al.* 1999, 274)
Loughcurra S. (Gosling *et al.,* forthcoming, no. 5897)
Rinn (Knox and Redington 1915–16, 182)
* Furzypark (possible) (Gosling *et al.,* forthcoming, no. 5853)
* Lavally 1 (possible) (Gosling *et al.,* forthcoming, no. 5886)
* Lavally 2 (possible) (Gosling *et al.,* forthcoming, no. 5887)
* Lissard (possible) (Topographical Files, OPW)
* Rathanlon (possible) (McCaffrey 1952, 286; Gosling *et al.,* forthcoming, no.
    5912)

Co. Kerry
Ballybrack (Cuppage 1986, 392)
Ballyegan (Byrne 1991, 12)
Ballynahow (two air-vents) (Clinton and Kelly, forthcoming)
Ballynavenooragh (Clinton, forthcoming b)
Ballyrishteen (Cuppage 1986, 122)
Coars (A. O'Sullivan and Sheehan 1996, 227)
Gearha North (A. O'Sullivan and Sheehan 1996, 403)
Glanfahan (three air-vents) (Deane 1893–6, 100)
Gortmore (Cuppage 1986, 240)
Kilteenbane (Cuppage 1986, 162)
Rathcrihane (NMI File, 1938; Waddell 1970a, 18)

Rathkenny (Toal 1995, 195)
Rathkieran (A. O'Sullivan and Sheehan 1996, 166)
Scrallaghbeg (Cuppage 1986, 182)
* Camp (possible) (Cuppage 1986, 127)
* Dromavally (possible) (Clark 1961, 77)
* Ducalla (possible) (A. O'Sullivan and Sheehan 1996, 230)
* Dunbeg (possible) (Barry 1981, 309)
* Dunkerron (possible) (A. O'Sullivan and Sheehan 1996, 179)
* Glanfahan (possible) (Cuppage 1986, 407)
* Kilteenbane (possible) (Cuppage 1986, 162)

Co. Kildare
* Killashee (possible) (V. Buckley, pers. comm.)

Co. Kilkenny
* Dunbel (possible) (Prim 1854–5, 403)

Co. Leitrim
Conray (Casey, n.d.)
Socks (Campbell 1979)
* Lurgan (possible) (M. Moore 1994)

Co. Limerick
Cush (Souterrain 2) (S.P. Ó Ríordáin 1938–40, 96)
Cush (Souterrain 3) (S.P. Ó Ríordáin 1938–40, 97)
Cush (Souterrain 4) (S.P. Ó Ríordáin 1938–40, 103)
Cush (Souterrain 8) (S.P. Ó Ríordáin 1938–40, 128)

Co. Londonderry
Ballintemple (two probable air-vents) (May and Cooper 1939, 84, 85)
Coshquin (McCourt 1959)
* Big Glebe (possible) (Brannon 1982a)
* Culhame (possible) (O'Keeffe 1996)
* Lettermire (possible) (Day and McWilliams 1995, 43)

Co. Longford
Fortwilliam (two air-vents) (O'Connor 1933)

Co. Louth
Ballybarrack (Souterrain 2) (Kelly 1977)

Ballybarrack (Souterrain 3) (two air-vents) (Kelly 1977)
Bellurgan (Gillman 1897, 6)
Demesne (A.B. Ó Ríordáin 1953–6, 445)
Donaghmore (four air-vents) (Rynne 1957–60b, 148)
Donaghmore (two air-vents) (Tempest 1912–15)
Dromiskin (Tempest 1921–4)
Dunbin Little (two air-vents) (Corcoran 1929–32)
Farrandreg (Buckley and Sweetman 1991, 123)
Farrandreg 2 (D. Murphy 1998, 269; M. Seaver, pers. comm.)
Glaspistol (Gosling 1977, 17)
Glebe (P. Gosling, pers. comm.)
Haggardstown (M. Stout, pers. comm.)
Kane (Clinton and Gosling 1979, 211)
Littlemill (Rynne 1961–4c, 320)
Mapastown (Buckley and Sweetman 1991, 128)
Marshes Upper (3A) (two air-vents) (Gowen 1992, 66)
Marshes Upper (3B) (Gowen 1992, 70)
Marshes Upper (4A) (Gowen 1992, 82)
Millpark (Rynne 1966b)
Mullagharlin (Rynne 1961–4b, 317)
Newtownbabe (Gosling 1979, 213)
Palmersland (Ua Cuinn 1904–7, 38)
Rathiddy (Rynne 1962, 128)
Stickillin 2 (two air-vents) (Dunne *et al.* 1973–6, 274)
Termonfeckin 2 (Carroll and Murphy 1987, 289)
Thomastown (two air-vents) (Gosling 1979, 214)
* Newtownbalregan (possible?) (Ryan 1973–6, 195)

Co. Mayo
Ballyhenry (two air-vents) (Lavelle *et al.* 1994, 67)
Ballyhenry or Caraun (Raftery 1968)
Cooslughoga (two air-vents) (Lavelle *et al.* 1994, 69)
Kilquire Upper (two air-vents) (Lavelle *et al.* 1994, 71)
Knock North (Wilde 1867, 109; Lavelle *et al.* 1994, 71)
Lissaniska East (Ronayne 1978)
Rockfield (Lawless 1987)
Shanvallyhugh (two air-vents) (O'Kelly 1942)
Shanvallyhugh (Souterrain 2) (NMI File)
'Shrule' (Morgan 1890–1)

Co. Meath
Athlumney (Souterrain 1) (C. Jones, pers. comm.)
Balrathboyne Glebe (Hartnett 1952)
Crossdrum Lower (two air-vents) (Rotheram 1897, 427)
Drakestown (NMI File, 1935)
Grangegeeth 1 (MacWhite 1946)
Kilbrew (Clinton 1996, 33)
Killegland (Clinton, forthcoming a)
Loughcrew (Clinton 1993, 124)
Monktown 3 (Ronayne 1991a)
Mullaghfin (M. Moore 1987, 53)
Newrath Big 1
Newrath Big 2 (Clinton and Manning 2000, 54)
Rathbran More
* Monktown 2 (possible) (Sweetman 1987)

Co. Monaghan
Lemgare (Brindley 1986, 18)
Shancoduff (Coffey and Jamison 1897, 276)
Trostan (Prendergast 1963)

Co. Roscommon
Cross South (one definite and one possible air-vent) (M. Moore 1995d)
Killiaghan and Gort (two air-vents) (F. Moore 1986)
Sheegeeragh (M. Moore 1995b)
Steill (M. Moore 1995e)
Tonroe (M. Moore 1995c)

Co. Sligo
Bunduff (two air-vents) (Wheeler 1955)
Cloghboley (Milligan 1890–1, 576)
Rathdoony (MacSitric 1934)
* Carrowntemple (possible) (Wallace and Timoney 1987, 46)
* Leaffony (possible) (O'Shaughnessy 1993b)
* Rathlee (possible) (O'Shaughnessy 1993c)

Co. Tipperary
Cloharden (six air-vents) (J. Graves 1870–1, 207)

Co. Tyrone
Aghnahoo (two air-vents) (McKenna 1930, 196; Chart 1940, 228)
Co. Waterford
* Ballykilmurry (possible) (Mongey 1933, 250)

Co. Westmeath
Gorteen (Prendergast 1959, 48)
Reynella (R. Murray 1932, 224)
Togherstown 1 (two air-vents) (Macalister and Praeger 1929–31, 72)

Table 2 — Air-vents: structural and contextual data

	Site	Dimensions (m) (width; height; length)	Context	Structural composition
1.	Aird, Co. Antrim	(1) ?; ?; 1.83+	C	SB
		(2) 0.23; 0.23; c. 1.22	C	SB
2.	Cloughorr, Co. Antrim	c. 0.20; ?; ?	C	SB
3.	Drumourne, Co. Antrim	0.20 x 0.16; ?	C	SB
4.	Knockdhu, Co. Antrim	0.30 x 0.36; 7.92+	C	SB
5.	Rathmore (The Hill), Co. Antrim	0.25–0.12; 0.10–0.15; 0.63+	C	SB
6.	Aghmakane, Co. Armagh	0.30; 0.30; 1+	C	SB
7.	Ballyanly 1, Co. Cork	0.20; 0.15; 1.20	C	EC/SR
8.	Castlemagner, Co. Cork	0.30; 0.20; 1.90	C	SB
9.	Curraghcrowley W., Co. Cork	(Aver.) 0.10 x 0.15; (aver.) 0.61–0.91;	C (4)	RC/SB
10.	Currahaly, Co. Cork	0.23; 0.23; ?	C	RC
11.	Fasagh, Co. Cork	c. 0.46; c. 0.46; ?	C	EC
12.	Liscahane, Co. Cork	(1) 0.30; 0.25; 7–10?	C	SB
		(2) c. 0.30; c. 0.25; ?	C	SB
13.	Mallowgaton, Co. Cork	0.35/0.22; 0.20/0.15; 1+	C	SB
14.	Oldcourt, Co. Cork	0.23; 0.23; 3.96	C & P	EC
15.	Ballynora, Co. Cork	?; ?; 0.75	C	EC
16.	Moneygaff W., Co. Cork	0.45; ?; ?	C	EC
17.	Ballylenagh, Co. Down	0.28; 0.20; 1.22–1.83+	P/C	SB

No.	Location		P/C	SB
18.	Sheepland Mor, Co. Down	(1) ?; ?; 0.61+	C	SB
		(2) ?; ?; 1.22+		SB
19.	Drumena, Co. Down	0.30; 0.15; ?	C	SB
20.	Hampton Demesne, Co. Dublin	0.30; 0.30; ?	C	SB
21.	Aghlisk, Co. Galway	0.30; 0.20; 1.85+	C	SB
22.	Ballymanagh, Co. Galway	0.45–0.45+; 0.23; 1.35	C	SB
23.	Ballynamannin, Co. Galway	0.40 x 0.28; ?	C	SB
24.	Caherpeake E., Co. Galway	(1) 0.30; 0.20; ?	C	SB
		(2) 0.30; 0.20; ?	C	SB
25.	Cloghnakeava, Co. Galway	(1) 0.60; 0.15; ?	P/C	SB
		(2) 0.50; 0.15; ?	P/C	SB?
26.	Kilbeacanty, Co. Galway	?; ?; 0.35+	P?	SB?
27.	Lack, Co. Galway	0.15; 0.15?; ?	?.	?.
28.	Loughcurra S., Co. Galway	0.86?; 0.23; 1	C	SB
29.	Ballybrack, Co. Kerry	?; ?; 2+	C	SB?
30.	Ballynahow, Co. Kerry	(1) 0.40–0.24; 0.10–0.13; 1.80+	C	SB
		(2) 0.30–0.40; 0.20–0.30; 1.84+	C	SB
31.	Ballynavenooragh, Co. Kerry	0.17–0.35; 0.16; 1.30	C	SB
32.	Glanfahan, Co. Kerry	(1) 0.20–0.40; 0.18–0.20; 1.15+	C	SB
		(2) 0.27–0.34; 0.18; 1.20+	C	SB
		(3) 0.23–0.25; 0.17–0.20; 2m+	P	SB
33.	Gortmore, Co. Kerry	0.20 x 0.25; ?	C	SB
34.	Rathcrihane, Co. Kerry	c. 0.10 x 0.15; c. 0.61	C	SB
35.	Dunbeg, Co. Kerry	0.10 x 0.40; ?	P/C	?.
36.	Socks, Co. Leitrim	0.32; 0.16; 1.40+	C	SB

Site	Dimensions (m) (width; height; length)	Context	Structural composition
37. Lurgan, Co. Leitrim	0.50; 0.25; 0.70+	P/C	SB
38. Cush (No. 3), Co. Limerick	?; ?; 5.79	C	SB
39. Cush (No. 8), Co. Limerick	0.25; 0.30; 4.88	C	SB
40. Coshquin, Co. Londonderry	0.23; 0.30; ?	C	SB
41. Fortwilliam, Co. Longford	(1) 0.30; 0.30; ?	C	SB
	(2) 0.30; 0.30; ?		
42. Ballybarrack (Sou. 2), Co. Louth	0.30–0.35?; ?; 1.70+	P	SB/RC
43. Ballybarrack (Sou. 3), Co. Louth	(1) 0.40; 0.35; 1+	P	SB
	(2) 0.30; 0.20; 0.90+	C	SB
44. Bellurgan, Co. Louth	0.23; 0.23; ?	P	SB
45. Demesne, Co. Louth	0.15; 0.20; 0.30+	C	SB
46. Donaghmore, Co. Louth	(1) 0.20; 0.15; 0.70+	P	EC
	(2) 0.15 x 0.20; c. 2.50	P	EC
	(3) 0.15; 0.15; c. 1.50	P	?
	(4) 0.15; 0.22; 5–6	C	EC
47. Donaghmore, Co. Louth	c. 0.15; c. 0.15; ?	C	SB
48. Dromiskin, Co. Louth	?; ?; 0.91–1.22	P/C	SB
49. Farrandreg, Co. Louth	0.20; 0.20; 0.70	C	SB
50. Farrandreg 2, Co. Louth	0.50; 0.26; 6.50	C	SB
51. Glaspistol, Co. Louth	0.25; 0.20; 1.50+	P	SB
52. Kane, Co. Louth	0.27; 0.15; 2.35+	C	SB
53. Marshes Upper (3A), Co. Louth	(1) 0.20–0.22; 0.15–0.20; 3+	P	SB
	(2) 0.25; 0.25–0.30; 2.70+	C	SB

54.	Marshes Upper (3B), Co. Louth	0.20; 0.10–0.40; 0.80+	C	SB
55.	Millpark, Co. Louth	0.28; 0.23; 6+	C	SB
56.	Newtownbabe, Co. Louth	0.25; 0.30; 1+	P	SB
57.	Palmersland, Co. Louth	?; ?; c. 8.84	P	SB
58.	Rathiddy, Co. Louth	0.25; 0.15; 1.80+	P	EC
59.	Termonfeckin 2, Co. Louth	0.35; 0.30; 2+	C	SB
60.	Thomastown, Co. Louth	(1) 0.18; 0.15; 0.29+ (2) 0.20; 0.17; 0.35+	C	SB
61.	Lissaniska East, Co. Mayo	0.20; c. 0.18; 1.50+?	C	SB
62.	Balrathboyne Glebe, Co. Meath	0.25; 0.25; 4	C	SB
63.	Crossdrum Lower, Co. Meath	(1) 0.30; 0.15–0.30; 3.20+ (2) 0.30; 0.20–0.25; c. 2.25+	C	SB
64.	Drakestown, Co. Meath	?; c. 0.46; c. 2.13	C	SB
65.	Grangegeeth 1, Co. Meath	0.20 x 0.15; 1.40+	C	SB
66.	Kilbrew, Co. Meath	0.32; 0.30; 1.20+	C	SB
67.	Killegland, Co. Meath	0.22; 0.20; 0.50+	C	SB
68.	Loughcrew, Co. Meath	0.20–0.25; 0.20–0.25; 1.65+	C	SB
69.	Monktown 3, Co. Meath	c. 0.20; c. 0.18; 1.05+	C	SB
70.	Mullaghfin, Co. Meath	0.20–0.35; 0.22–0.25; 1.25	C	SB
71.	Newrath Big 1, Co. Meath	0.28; c. 0.17; ?	P	SB
72.	Newrath Big 2, Co. Meath	0.32; 0.15–0.20; 1.30+	C	SB
73.	Rathbran Mor, Co. Meath	0.37; 0.23; 1+	C	SB
74.	Monktown 2, Co. Meath	c. 0.16; ?; 0.18+	C	SB?
75.	Shancoduff, Co. Monaghan	0.15; 0.20; 0.61+	P	SB
76.	Trostan, Co. Monaghan	0.20; 0.15; 1	C	SB

Site	Dimensions (m) (width; height; length)	Context	Structural composition
77. Sheegeeragh, Co. Roscommon	0.24; 0.39; 2	C	SB
78. Steill, Co. Roscommon	0.20; 0.40; 0.80+	P/C	SB
79. Tonroe, Co. Roscommon	0.36; 0.26; 1.05	P/C	SB
80. Bunduff, Co. Sligo	c. 0.30; c. 0.30; ?	C	SB
81. Leaffony, Co. Sligo	0.25; 0.25; ?	C	SB
82. Aghnahoo, Co. Tyrone	0.51; 0.36; 2.44	P	SB
83. Gorreen, Co. Westmeath	0.20; 0.15; ?	C	SB
84. Togherstown 1, Co. Westmeath	(1) ?; ?; 2.29+	C	SB
	(2) 0.38; 0.23; 3.96	P	SB

Key: C = chamber; P = passageway; SB = stone-built; EC = earth-cut; RC = rock-cut; SR = slab roof

Appendix 5
Drains

Table 1 — Inventory of sites

Co. Antrim
Ballyaghagan (Evans 1950, 14)
Ballyaghagan ('Cave Hill') (Reynolds and Turner 1902, 78)
Coggrey (Lawlor 1916–18, 86)
Stiles (Collins 1976, 14)
* Stranocum (possible) (Bigger and Fennell 1896-7, 202)
* Tirgracey (possible) (Fennell 1896, 272; Lawlor 1915–16, 39)

Co. Armagh
Carrickcloghan (B. Williams 1983)
Corliss (Davies 1937–40, 341)

Co. Cork
Ahakeera (Twohig 1976, 27)
Brackcloon (S.P. Ó Ríordáin 1934–5, 78)
Dunisky 1 (McCarthy 1977, 233)
Fasagh (Sweetnam and Gillman 1897, 150)
Johnstown (McCarthy 1977, 261)
Liscahane (U. Egan, pers. comm.; Ó Donnabháin 1982)
Little Island (two drains) (Fahy 1970; McCarthy 1977, 290; Kelly 1982–3b, 13)
Manning 1 (McCarthy 1977, 298)
Moneygaff East (Cleary 1989; D. Power 1992, 254)
Rossnakilla (D. Power *et al.* 1997, 283)
Tooreen More W. (McCarthy 1977, 317)

Co. Donegal
Rock (Dunlevy 1967, 230; Lacy 1983, 238)

Co. Galway
* Aghlisk (possible) (Costello 1903–4, 2)

Co. Kerry
Ballintermon (two drains) (Kelly 1982–3b, 7)
* Castlegregory (possible) (Cuppage 1986, 236)
* Glanfahan (possible) (Cuppage 1986, 407)
* Kilteenbane (possible) (Cuppage 1986, 162)

Co. Leitrim
Socks (two drains) (Campbell 1979)

Co. Limerick
Cush (Souterrain 4) (S.P. Ó Ríordáin 1938–40, 103)

Co. Londonderry
Ballyhacket-Glenahorry (Ligar 1833, 23)

Co. Louth
Benagh (Buckley and Sweetman 1991, 108)
Thomastown (Gosling 1979, 213)

Co. Mayo
Carrowjames (NMI File, 1987)

Co. Meath
* Patrickstown (possible)

Co. Monaghan
Shancoduff (Coffey and Jamison 1897, 276)

Table 2 — Drains: structural and contextual data

Site	Dimensions (m) (width; depth/height; length)	Context	Structural composition
1. Ballyaghagan, Co. Antrim	0.28–0.23; 0.38–0.30; 0.38+	C	SB
2. Ballyaghagan ('Cave Hill'), Co. Antrim	?; 0.15; ?	EP	RC
3. Coggrey, Co. Antrim	(No data available)	C	SB
4. Stranocum, Co. Antrim	0.46; 0.61; 1.83	C	SB
5. Stiles, Co. Antrim	?; 0.10; ?	RE	RC
6. Tirgracey, Co. Antrim	(No data available)	C	SB
7. Carrickcloghan, Co. Armagh	(No data available)	P/C	SB
8. Corliss, Co. Armagh	–0.10; ?–0.10; ?	C?	SB
9. Ahakeera, Co. Cork	0.40; 0.20; 4m	C	EC/SR
10. Brackcloon, Co. Cork	0.15–0.20; 0.24; 11.60+	C	RC/SR
11. Dunisky 1, Co. Cork	0.10; 0.05; 1.20–1.70	C	RC
12. Fasagh, Co. Cork	(No data available)	C	RC/SR
13. Johnstown, Co. Cork	0.25; 0.20; 0.80+	C	SB
14. Liscahane, Co. Cork	0.25; 0.15; 11	C	SB
15. Little Island, Co. Cork	(1) 0.25; 0.23; 1.22+ (2) ?; ?; ?	C	SB
16. Manning 1, Co. Cork	(No data available)	P	?
17. Moneygaff E., Co. Cork	0.25; 0.15; ?	C	SB?
18. Toureen More W., Co. Cork	?; ?; 1.36+	C	EC/SR
19. Rock, Co. Donegal	0.25 x 0.17; ?	P/C	SB

Site	Dimensions (m) (width; depth/height; length)	Context	Structural composition
20. Aghlisk, Co. Galway	(No data available)	C	SB
21. Ballintermon, Co. Kerry	(1) 0.38 (top)–0.26; 0.22; 3+	C	SB
	(2) 0.22; 0.43; 2.08+	C	SB
22. Castlegregory, Co. Kerry	(No data available)	C	?.
23. Glanfahan, Co. Kerry	0.30; 0.25; ?	C	SB?
24. Kilteenbane, Co. Kerry	0.46; 0.20; ?	P	SB
25. Socks, Co. Leitrim	(1) 0.20; ?; 2+	C	SB
	(2) 0.40; 0.14+?; 2+	C	SB
26. Cush (No. 4), Co. Limerick	?; ?; 3.05+	R	SB
		P/C	SB/SR/WR
27. Ballyhacket-Glenahorry, Co. Londonderry	c. 0.25; c. 0.30–0.35; 1.22+	C	SB
28. Benagh, Co. Louth	?; ?; 3.50+	C	SB
29. Thomastown, Co. Louth	0.30; 0.30; 5+	C	SB
30. Carrowjames, Co. Mayo	(No data available)	C	SB
31. Patrickstown, Co. Meath	0.27; 0.27; ?	P	SB
32. Shancoduff, Co. Monaghan	0.30; 0.30; 0.61+	P	SB

Key: C = chamber; P = passageway; SB = stone-built; EC = earth-cut; RC = rock-cut; SR = slab roof; WR = wooden roof; RE = ramp entrance; EP = entrance passage; R = recess.

Appendix 6

Cupboards, cubby-holes and recesses

Table 1—Cupboards: inventory of sites

Co. Armagh
Carrickcloghan (Feature 3) (B. Williams 1983)

Co. Cork
Ardahill (McCarthy 1977, 139)
Dunisky (McCarthy 1977, 225)

Co. Donegal
Ballymacool (Lacy 1983, 232)
Killinangel More (Features 1 and 2) (Diver 1956)
Rock (Lacy 1983, 238; Topographical Files, NMI)
Tonregee (Lacy 1983, 239)
Townparks (Lacy 1983, 227)

Co. Down
Ballytrustan (Feature 1) (Lynn and Warner 1977)

Co. Galway
Ballynamannin (McCaffrey 1952, 215; Gosling *et al.,* forthcoming, no. 5781)
Cloonbeg (Gosling *et al.,* forthcoming, no. 5832)
Drumminacloghaun (Gosling *et al.,* forthcoming, no. 5848)
Furzypark (Features 1 and 2) (Gosling *et al.,* forthcoming, no. 5853)
Gortroe (Knox and Redington 1915–16, 181)
Lavally 1 (Features 1, 2 and 4) (Gosling *et al.,* forthcoming, no. 5886)
Lisnagranshy 1 (Knox and Redington 1915–16, 180)
Roo (Features 1 and 2) (McCaffrey 1952, 249; Gosling *et al.,* forthcoming, no. 5920)

Co. Kerry
Ballynavenooragh II (Cuppage 1986, 396)
Caherquin (Rynne 1966c; Cuppage 1986, 234)

Cullenagh Upper (A. O'Sullivan and Sheehan 1996, 230)
Dromkeen East (Twohig 1974, 9)
Emlagh West (Connolly 1994)

Co. Meath
Loughcrew (Feature 1) (Clinton 1993, 122)
Loughcrew (Feature 2) (Clinton 1993, 122)
Newrath Big 2 (Clinton and Manning 2000, 53)

Co. Roscommon
Cuillawinnia (Corlett 1995)
Sheegeeragh (M. Moore 1995b)

Co. Sligo
Eskragh (O'Conor 1994a)

Co. Tipperary
Ahenny (Sweetman and de Buitléir 1976, 73)

Co. Tyrone
Aghnahoo (McKenna 1930, 196)

Co. Westmeath
Banagher (Rynne 1966a)
Rathnew 1 (Feature 1) (Macalister and Praeger 1928, 113)
Rathnew 1 (Feature 2) (Macalister and Praeger 1928, 114)

Probable examples
Moneygaff E. (Feature 2), Co. Cork (Cleary 1989); Cloyfin S. (Feature 1), Co. Londonderry (Brannon and Warner 1978); Lohercannan, Co. Kerry (McDonnell 1957); Dunbin Little, Co. Louth (P. Corcoran 1929–32); Farrandreg 2, Co. Louth (D. Murphy 1998, 271; M. Seaver, pers. comm.); Knock North, Co. Mayo (Wilde 1867, 109); Oghambaun (Features 1, 2 and 3), Co. Sligo (O'Conor 1994c); Graigue, Co. Tipperary (Callanan 1932); Togherstown 1 (Feature 2), Co. Westmeath (Macalister and Praeger 1929–31, 74).

Table 2 — Cupboards: structural and contextual data

	Site	Dimensions (m) (width; height; depth)	Placement	Context	Structural composition
1.	Carrickcloghan (F3), Co. Armagh	0.47; ?; 0.60	Floor level	C	D/E back
2.	Ardahill, Co. Cork	0.44; 0.25; 0.25	Wall	(Inner) C	EC
3.	Dunisky (F2), Co. Cork	0.40; ?; 0.40	Floor level	(An inner) C	RC
4.	Ballymacool, Co. Donegal	0.50?; 0.40?; ?	Wall	P	D?
5.	Killinangel (F1), Co. Donegal	0.46; ?; 0.46	Floor level	(Inner) C	D
6.	Rock, Co. Donegal	0.45; 0.33; 0.74	Wall	(Outer) C	D/E back
7.	Tonregee, Co. Donegal	0.42?; 0.39?; 0.58?	Wall	C?	D?
8.	Townparks, Co. Donegal	0.30; 0.40; 0.54	Floor level	C	D
9.	Ballynamannin, Co. Galway	0.45; 0.40; 0.25	Wall	P?	D?
10.	Ballytrustan (F1), Co. Down	0.25–45; 0.30; 0.60–80	Wall	C	D/E & R back
11.	Cloonbeg, Co. Galway	?; 0.20; 0.40	Floor level?	C?	D/E roof?
12.	Drumminacloghaun, Co. Galway	0.30; 0.25; 0.60	Wall?	(Outer?) C	D
13.	Furzypark (F1), Co. Galway	c. 0.70; c. 0.34–40; c. 0.60	Wall	(Inner) C	D
14.	Gortroe, Co. Galway	0.41; 0.43; 0.69	Wall	(Outer) P	D
15.	Lavally (F1), Co. Galway	0.44; 0.25; 0.57	Wall	(Outer) C	D/E back?
16.	Lavally (F2), Co. Galway	0.42; 0.33; c. 0.56	Wall	(Outer) C	D/E back
17.	Lavally (F4), Co. Galway	0.42; 0.33; 0.36	Wall	(Inner) C	D
18.	Lisnagranshy 1, Co. Galway	0.46; 0.46; 0.46	Wall	(Inner) C	D
19.	Roo (F1), Co. Galway	0.33; 0.24; 0.70	Wall	C	D?

Site	Dimensions (m) (width; height; depth)	Placement	Context	Structural composition
20. Roo (F2), Co. Galway	0.43; 0.31; 0.67	Wall	P?	D?
21. Ballynavenooragh II, Co. Kerry	c. 0.25; <0.45; c. 0.65	Wall	(Outer) P	D
22. Caherquin, Co. Kerry	0.45–50; 0.45; 0.70	Wall	C	D/partly E
23. Cullenagh Upper, Co. Kerry	0.45; 0.35; 0.25	Wall	C	D
24. Dromkeen East, Co. Kerry	0.40; 0.50; 0.50	Floor level	(Inner) P	D/E back
25. Emlagh West, Co. Kerry	0.40; 0.73; 0.40	Wall	C	D
26. Loughcrew (F1), Co. Meath	0.35; 0.38; 0.55	Floor level	(Outer) P	D
27. Loughcrew (F2), Co. Meath	0.45; 0.45; 0.45	Wall	(Inner) P	D
28. Newrath Big 2, Co. Meath	0.38; 0.40; 0.63	Wall	(Inner) P	D
29. Cuillawinnia, Co. Roscommon	0.58; 0.42; 0.60	Wall	P/C	D/E back?
30. Sheegeeragh, Co. Roscommon	0.35; 0.30+; 0.50	Wall	C	D
31. Eskragh, Co. Sligo	0.40; ?; c. 0.50–60	Floor level?	C	D
32. Ahenny, Co. Tipperary	0.50; 0.45; ?	Wall	(Inner) C	D
33. Aghnahoo, Co. Tipperary	0.36; ?; 0.25	Floor level	(Outer) C	D
34. Banagher, Co. Westmeath	0.40–45; 0.42–45; 0.65–70	Floor level	(Inner) P	D/E back
35. Rathnew 1 (F1), Co. Westmeath	0.41; 0.38; 0.71	Wall	(Inner) C	D/E back
36. Rathnew 1 (F2), Co. Westmeath	0.53; 0.41; c. 0.40	Floor level	(Inner) C	D/E back
* Moneygaff E. (F2), Co. Cork	0.55; ?; 0.50	Floor level	C	EC
* Lohercannan, Co. Kerry	(No specific details)	Floor level	(Outer) C	D?
* Cloyfin S. (F1), Co. Londonderry	?; 0.35?; c. 0.20–25?	Wall	P/C	D
* Dunbin Little, Co. Louth	(No specific details)	Wall	(Inner) P	D/E back
* Farrandreg 2, Co. Louth	?; ?; 0.62	Wall	(Inner) C	D/E back
* Knock North, Co. Mayo	(No specific details)	Floor level?	(Inner) C	D?

*	Oghambaun (F1), Co. Sligo	(No specific details)	Wall	C	D
*	Oghambaun (F2), Co. Sligo	(No specific details)	Wall	C	D
*	Oghambaun (F3), Co. Sligo	(No specific details)	Wall	C	D
*	Graigue, Co. Tipperary	Depth 0.76m	Wall	P/C	R/C
*	Togherstown 1 (F2), Co. Westmeath	(No specific details)	Wall	(Inner) P	D

Key: P = passageway; C = chamber; D = drystone; E = earthen; R = rock; EC = earth-cut; RC = rock-cut.

Table 3—Cubby-holes: inventory of sites

Co. Antrim
1. Ballyaghagan (Evans 1950, 14)
2. Bushmills (Hobson 1909, 223)
3. Coggrey (Feature 1) (Lawlor 1916–18, 87)
4. Coggrey (Feature 2) (Lawlor 1916–18, 87)
5. Craig Hill (Waterman 1956b, 90)
6. Moneynick (Stokes 1838)

Co. Cork
1. Oldcourt (Feature 2) (Ó Cuileanáin and Murphy 1961–2, 84)

Co. Down
1. Ballylenagh (Mayne 1993)

Co. Galway
1. Corbally South (Rynne 1968b)
2. Rinn (Knox and Redington 1915–16, 182)

Co. Londonderry
1. Ballintemple (May and Cooper 1939, 84)
2. Magheramenagh (May 1955)
3. Rallagh (Stokes 1835)

Co. Louth
1. Bawntaaffe 1 (Rynne 1957–60a, 99)
2. Faughart Upper (Rynne 1965b)
3. Millockstown 1 (Manning 1986, 147)
4. Mullameelan (Leask 1941–4, 71)
5. Rathiddy (Rynne 1962, 129)

Co. Mayo
1. Cross South (Feature 2) (Sweeney 1981)
2. Tullyduff (Lavelle *et al.* 1994, 72)

Co. Meath
1. Dowth

Co. Sligo
1. Lackanatlieve (Feature 1) (O'Shaughnessy 1993a)

Co. Westmeath
1. Guilford
2. Rathnew I (Feature 3) (Macalister and Praeger 1928, 114)
3. Togherstown II (Feature 2) (Macalister and Praeger 1929–31, 76)

Probable examples
Carrickcloghan (Features 1 and 2), Co. Armagh (B. Williams 1983); Cloyfin S.
(Feature 2), Co. Londonderry (Brannon and Warner 1978); Lavally (Feature 3),
Co. Galway (Gosling *et al.*, forthcoming, no. 5886).

Table 4 — Cubby-holes: structural and contextual data

	Site	Dimensions (m) (width; height; depth)	Placement	Context	Structural composition
1.	Ballyaghagan, Co. Antrim	0.41; 0.61; 0.76	Floor level	(Inner) C	D/E back
2.	Bushmills, Co. Antrim	0.38; 0.51; 0.84	Floor level	P/C	D
3.	Coggrey (F1), Co. Antrim	0.61; 0.56; 0.41	Floor level	C	D/E back
4.	Coggrey (F2), Co. Antrim	0.61; 0.61; 0.48	Floor level	C	D/E back
5.	Craig Hill, Co. Antrim	c. 0.56; 0.56; c. 0.61	Floor level	C	D/R back
6.	Moneynick, Co. Antrim	0.61; 0.61? 0.61?	Floor level	C	D
7.	Oldcourt (F2), Co. Cork	0.76; 0.61; 0.76	Floor level	(Inner) C	EC
8.	Ballylenagh, Co. Down	c. 0.50; c. 0.53/c. 0.71; c. 1	Floor level	P/C	D & RC
9.	Corbally South, Co. Galway	0.70; 0.60; 0.40	Floor level	C	D/E back
10.	Rinn, Co. Galway	0.53; 0.58; <1.83	Wall	(Inner) C	D
11.	Ballintemple, Co. Londonderry	0.91; 0.61; c. 0.46–0.61	Wall	(Inner) C	RC
12.	Magheramenagh, Co. Londonderry	0.61?; ?; c. 0.71	Floor level	P/C	D
13.	Rallagh, Co. Londonderry	0.56; 0.56?; 0.56	Floor level	C	D
14.	Bawntaaffe 1, Co. Louth	0.65; 0.70; 0.60	Floor level	(Inner) P	D/E & R back
15.	Faughart Upper, Co. Louth	0.50; ?; 0.80	Floor level	P	D/E back
16.	Millockstown 1, Co. Louth	0.45/0.60; 0.70; 0.40	Floor level	(Inner) P	D/R back
17.	Mullameelan, Co. Louth	0.61; 0.76; c. 0.90	Floor level	C	D/E back
18.	Rathiddy, Co. Louth	0.50; 0.42; 0.85	Floor level	(Inner) P	D
19.	Cross South (F2), Co. Mayo	0.63; ?; 0.65	Wall	C	D
20.	Tullyduff, Co. Mayo	0.50; ?; 1.10	Floor level	P/C	D

21.	Dowth, Co. Meath	0.65; 0.30–0.35; 0.90	Wall	('Inner') P	D
22.	Lackanatlieve (F1), Co. Sligo	0.61; 0.57; c. 0.80	Floor level	(Outer) C	D/E back
23.	Guilford, Co. Westmeath	0.63; 0.30–0.35; 0.75	Floor level	C	D/D & E back
24.	Rathnew 1 (F3), Co. Westmeath	0.46; 0.61; 0.90	Floor level	P	D/E back
25.	Togherstown 2 (F2), Co. Westmeath	0.51; 0.51; 0.61	Floor level?	(Inner) C	D/E back
*	Carrickcloghan (F1), Co. Armagh	0.70; ?; 0.50	Floor level	P	D/R back
*	Carrickcloghan (F2), Co. Armagh	0.60; ?; 0.50	Floor level	P	D/R back
*	Cloyfin S. (F2), Co. Londonderry	c. 0.45; ?; 0.90	Wall	C	D
*	Lavally (F3), Co. Galway	0.90; ?; 0.59	Wall	P	D

Key: P = passageway; C = chamber; D = drystone; EC = earth-cut; RC = rock-cut; E = earthen; R = rock.

Table 5—Recesses: inventory of sites

Co. Clare
1. Ballyvelaghan (T. Cooke 1849–51, 296)

Co. Cork
1. Carrigbaun (D. Power 1992, 231; U. Egan, pers. comm.)
2. Coolbane (D. Power 1992, 232; U. Egan, pers. comm.)
3. Curraghcrowley (Feature 1) (Somerville 1929–30, 3)
4. Curraghcrowley (Feature 2) (Somerville 1929–30, 3)
5. Dunisky (Feature 2) (McCarthy 1977, 225)
6. Foildarrig (McCarthy 1977, 245)
7. Lough Marsh (Cleary 1981a, 38)
8. Moneygaff E. (Feature 1) (Cleary 1989)
9. Oldcourt (Feature 1) (Ó Cuileanáin and Murphy 1961–2, 84)

Co. Donegal
1. Cavangarden (Davies 1946; Lacy 1983, 233)

Co. Down
1. Drumena (Berry 1926–7, 51)

Co. Dublin
1. Lucan and Pettycannon (Rotheram 1893–6, 310; Clinton 1998, 119)
2. Stephenstown (Clinton 1998, 120)

Co. Galway
1. Cloghalahard (Gosling *et al.*, forthcoming, no. 5826)

Co. Kerry
1. Ballyegan (Byrne 1991, 5)
2. Derrymore East (Cuppage 1986, 136)

Co. Leitrim
1. Socks (Campbell 1979)

Co. Louth
1. Ballybarrack (Sou. 3) (Kelly 1977)
2. Donaghmore (Sou. A) (Rynne 1965a)

3. Glaspistol (Gosling 1977, 19)
4. Marshes Upper (Site 3B) (Gowen 1992, 70)
5. Marshes Upper (Site 4B) (Gowen 1992, 85)
6. Marshes Upper (Site 4C) (Gowen 1992, 91)
7. Stickillin II (Dunne *et al.* 1973–6, 273)
8. Termonfeckin I (Ó Floinn 1978, 130)

Co. Mayo
1. Cross South (Feature 1) (Sweeney 1981)

Co. Meath
1. Crossdrum Lower
2. Knowth (Souterrain 4) (G. Eogan, pers. comm.)

Co. Monaghan
1. Bocks Upper (McCabe 1967; Danaher 1967)

Co. Sligo
1. Farranaharpy (Forbes, n.d.)
2. Lackanatlieve (Features 2 and 3) (O'Shaughnessy 1993a)

Co. Westmeath
1. Togherstown I (Feature 1) (Macalister and Praeger 1929–31, 71, 74)
2. Togherstown II (Feature 1) (Macalister and Praeger 1929–31, 76)

Probable examples
Mortyclogh 2, Co. Clare (Westropp 1911, 353); Farrandreg (Features 1 and 2), Co. Louth (Buckley and Sweetman 1991, 123); Letterkeen, Co. Mayo (S.P. Ó Ríordáin and MacDermott 1951–2, 102); Athlumney (Features 1 and 2), Co. Meath (Wakeman 1858, 39); Ballykilmurry, Co. Waterford (Mongey 1933, 248).

Table 6 — Recesses: structural and contextual data

	Site	Dimensions (m) (width; height; depth)	Placement	Context	Structural composition
1.	Ballyvelaghan, Co. Clare	0.61; 1.37; 1.52	Floor level	(Inner) C	D
2.	Carrigbaun, Co. Cork	1.25; 0.72; 1.80	Floor level	C	EC
3.	Coolbane, Co. Cork	c. 0.50; 0.75; c. 1	Floor level	C	EC/RC
4.	Curraghcrowley (F1), Co. Cork	0.91–1.22; 1.12; 0.38	0.08 above floor	C	RC/CS back
5.	Curraghcrowley (F2), Co. Cork	0.61–0.91; 1.09; ?	0.28 above floor	C	RC/CS back
6.	Dunisky (F1), Co. Cork	0.80; 0.95; 0.80	Floor level	P	RC
7.	Foildarrig, Co. Cork	1.40; 0.60; 1.40	0.20+ above floor	(Outer) C	EC
8.	Lough Marsh, Co. Cork	1; 0.70; 0.80	Floor level	C	EC/CS back
9.	Moneygaff E. (F1), Co. Cork	0.70–90; 0.90; 0.85	Floor level	C	EC
10.	Oldcourt (F1), Co. Cork	0.91; 0.91; 0.91	Floor level	(Inner) C	EC
11.	Cavangarden, Co. Donegal	0.80; 0.75; 1	Floor level	P/C	RC
12.	Drumena, Co. Down	0.69/1.22; 1.07+; 1.37	Floor level	P	D
13.	Lucan and Petrycannon, Co. Dublin	0.99; c. 1; 0.61	Floor level	P	D
14.	Stephenstown, Co. Dublin	0.90; 1.05; 0.65	Floor level	P	D
15.	Cloghalahard, Co. Galway	0.70; 0.70; 1.50	Floor level	C	D
16.	Ballyegan, Co. Kerry	0.68; 0.75; 1.75	Floor level?	(Inner) C	D/RC
17.	Derrymore East, Co. Kerry	0.45; 1; 1	Floor level	C	D
18.	Socks, Co. Leitrim	1–0.75; 0.75–85; 1.10	Floor level	C	D
19.	Ballybarrack (Sou. 3), Co. Louth	0.80; 0.80; ?	Floor level	P	D?
20.	Donaghmore (Sou. A.), Co. Louth	0.65–0.75; c. 0.80; 0.80	Floor level	(Inner) P	EC/R back

	Site	Measurements	Location	Type	Notes
21.	Glaspistol, Co. Louth	0.80; c. 1.10+; c. 0.30	Floor level	P	D
22.	Marshes Upper, Site 3B, Co. Louth	0.80/1.20; 1.10; 0.50–0.60	Floor level	P	RC/F roof
23.	Marshes Upper, Site 4B, Co. Louth	1.20; ?; 0.90	Floor level	P	(Damaged)
24.	Marshes Upper, Site 4C, Co. Louth	c. 1.40; 1+; c. 1	Floor level	P	D
25.	Stickillin 2, Co. Louth	c. 1.80; c. 1.20; 0.40–0.60	Floor level	C	D
26.	Termonfeckin 1, Co. Louth	0.85; 0.90; 1.30	Floor level	C	D
27.	Cross South (F1), Co. Mayo	0.82; 0.93; 0.75	Wall	C	D
28.	Crossdrum Lower, Co. Meath	0.35/0.95; 0.65–0.70; 1.35	Floor level	C	D/R back
29.	Knowth (Sou. 4), Co. Meath	0.90; 0.70; 1.10	Floor level	P	D
30.	Bocks Upper, Co. Monaghan	0.58; 0.74; 0.97	0.50 above floor	C	D
31.	Farranaharpy, Co. Sligo	0.76; 0.76; 1.07	Wall	(Inner) C	D/R back
32.	Lackanatlieve (F2), Co. Sligo	0.88; 0.70; 0.85	Wall	(Outer) C	D
33.	Lackanatlieve (F3), Co. Sligo	1; 0.80; ?	?	(Inner) C	D
34.	Togherstown 1 (F1), Co. Westmeath	0.91; 0.76; 0.81–0.91	1.14 above floor	C	D
35.	Togherstown 2 (F1), Co. Westmeath	c. 1; ?; c. 0.90	Floor level	P	D
*	Mortyclogh 2, Co. Clare	1.37; ?; 0.41	?	C?	D?
*	Farrandreg (F1), Co. Louth	c. 0.90; 1.30??; 0.20–30	Floor level	P	D
*	Farrandreg (F2), Co. Louth	c. 0.70; 1.30??; 0.35–0.40	Floor level	P	D
*	Letterkeen, Co. Mayo	?; ?; ?	Wall	C	EC
*	Athlumney (F1), Co. Meath	c. 1; ?; c. 0.75	Floor level	P	D
*	Athlumney (F2), Co. Meath	c. 1; ?; c. 0.75	Floor level	P	D
*	Ballykilmurry, Co. Waterford	1.30; ?; 0.53	Floor level	C	D?

Key: P = passageway; C = chamber; D = drystone; EC = earth-cut; RC = rock-cut; CS = construction shaft (with drystone facing); F = flagstone (lintels); R = rock; E = earthen.

Table 7—Unclassifiable examples of cupboard, cubby-hole or recess features

1. Ballytweedy, Co. Antrim (Brannon 1985). A 'small niche' in the back wall of the chamber. Width 0.5m; height 0.5m; depth 1.5m. Floor level. Drystone-built with exposed natural rock (basalt) at back. A cubby-hole classification would be valid except for the excessive depth.
2. Ballywee (Souterrain 2), Co. Antrim (Buckley 1978, 29). A 'cupboard' in souterrain wall. Floor level. Drystone. No further details.
3. Bushmills, Co. Antrim (Buckley 1978, fig. 54). Two features indicated on plan: one at floor level (a possible recess?); the other apparently above floor level. No further details.
4. Holestone, Co. Antrim (Warner 1994). A 'creep' at end of passage leading to 'airhole'. A second report (apparently of the same souterrain) described the feature as a 'creep' leading to an 'alcove in bedrock'. No further details.
5. Dough (Lisnaleagaun), Co. Clare (Westropp 1909, 118). A 'recess' extending from an extended constriction. Width 0.75m; height 0.5m+; depth 1.7m. It was partly obscured. It was suggested that it might have represented an additional extended constriction. Its siting might not support such an interpretation.
6. Drum South, Co. Cork (D. Power 1992, 233; U. Egan, pers. comm.). Single earth-cut chamber featuring 'annexes' on southern and western flanks. No further details available.
7. Ballyholland Lower, Co. Down (Nic Shean 1986). A 'hollow' in the wall (a shallow curving indentation according to the sketch-plan) of the passage. Floor level. Drystone. No further details.
8. Ballytrustan (Feature 2), Co. Down (Lynn and Warner 1977). Inserted into the wall of chamber. Width 0.6m; height 0.65m; depth 1.25m. Drystone-built with natural rock/hard clay forming the back of the feature. A cubby-hole classification would be valid except for the depth.
9. Cargagh, Co. Down (Harris and Smith 1744, 195). A 'semicircular nich' and a 'quadrangle nich' (both occurring in the course of the passage). Drystone? No further details.
10. Finnis, Co. Down (Buckley 1978, 91). A small 'recess' (cupboard?) in souterrain wall. Floor level. Drystone. No further details.
11. Moneylane, Co. Down (Brannon 1982b). A 'small niche' in the end wall of an undifferentiated chamber. Width 0.4m; height ?; depth *c.* 1m. Drystone? Described as being 'unusually high up in the wall'.
12. Billymore, Co. Galway (Kinahan 1883–4a, 13). Described as a 'blind passage' but possibly an earth-backed wall feature (judging by the accompanying plan). No specific details.

13. Killosolan, Co. Galway (Alcock *et al.* 1999, 271). A 'small recess or cupboard' in chamber. Floor level. It extended for *c.* 1m. No further details.
14. Lavally 2, Co. Galway (Gosling *et al.*, forthcoming, no. 5887). A 'recess' in chamber wall. Width 0.88m; height 0.48m; depth 0.77m. It was described as connecting with the looping passage.
15. Oranhill, Co. Galway (Gosling *et al.*, forthcoming, no. 5907). A 'recess' in chamber wall. Modern 'excavation' had distorted its original dimensions. Probably a cupboard, if not a cubby-hole. It appeared to have originally featured an earth-cut back.
16. Renville East, Co. Galway (Athy 1913–14, 133). 'A nook with a projecting stone slab over it' in chamber. Drystone? No further details.
17. Fahan, Co. Kerry (Cuppage 1986, 223). A 'cupboard recess' in chamber wall. Drystone? No further details.
18. Borrismore, Co. Kilkenny (Healy 1890–1). Described as a 'doorway' to an unbuilt chamber. Located in the innermost chamber. Possibly a drystone-built cupboard or cubby-hole. Floor level? Earth-backed? No further details.
19. Ballybarrack, Co. Louth (Coffey and Jamison 1897, 275). A 'recess' in passage. Floor level. The reported dimensions (width 0.3m; height at opening 0.3m; internal height 0.61m; depth 0.91m) and its siting might suggest a cubby-hole.
20. Lisnawully, Co. Louth (Tempest 1912–15, 22). Feature 1: a 'peculiar built recess' in chamber. No further details. Feature 2: a 'recess' that 'seems complete in itself'. No further details.
21. Aghamore, Co. Mayo (Raftery 1956). A 'small side recess' (cupboard?) sited at floor level in the corner of the inner chamber. Drystone. No further details.
22. Ballynacarragh, Co. Mayo (Lavelle *et al.* 1994, 67). An 'alcove', 'in' the eastern wall of the chamber. Drystone? No further details.
23. Candlefort, Co. Monaghan (Reade 1874–5, 326). 'A recess or small chamber' in passage. Drystone? No further details.
24. Cross South, Co. Roscommon (M. Moore 1995d). A triangular 'alcove' sited in the northern wall of the chamber. Width 0.6m; depth 0.5m; height obscured by debris accumulation but potentially in excess of 1.4m. Drystone.
25. Church Hill, Co. Sligo (O'Conor 1993e). A cupboard-like feature in the wall of the inner chamber. Drystone. No further details.
26. Carrignadoura, Co. Cork (D. Power *et al.* 1997, 274). A 'small annexe' in south-west wall of Chamber 1. Earth-cut. No further details.
27. Kilmore, Co. Cork (D. Power *et al.* 1997, 280). Small 'annexe' at south end of chamber. Width 0.9m. No further details.

Appendix 7

Steps

Table 1—Inventory of sites

Co. Antrim
1. Aird (Wright 1964, 123)
2. Ballaghmore (Fagan 1838b)
3. Donegore (Lawlor 1915–16, 41, 42)
4. Loughermore (B. Williams 1977)
5. Stiles (Collins 1976, 14)
6. Stranocum (Bigger and Fennell 1896–7, 203)
7. Tobergill (Collins 1960, 80)
* Liminary (possible) (Skillen 1904, 120)
* Tawnybrack (possible) (O'Laverty 1884, 422 fn.)

Co. Armagh
1. Corliss (Davies 1937–40, 341)

Co. Clare
1. Cahercommaun (Hencken 1938, 20, 22)
* 'Cahir Hill' (possible) (Lillis 1935)

Co. Cork
1. Ballycatteen (S.P. Ó Ríordáin and Hartnett 1943–4, 14)
2. Brackcloon (S.P. Ó Ríordáin 1934–5, 80)
3. Brulea (Fahy 1972)
4. Cappeen West (McCarthy 1977, 202)
5. Coolanarney (D. Power *et al.* 1997, 275)
6. Curraghcrowley W. (Somerville 1929–30, 3)
7. Deelish (Gillman 1896a, 153)
8. Dunisky (McCarthy 1977, 232)
9. Farrandau (Knockdrum) (Somerville 1931, 7)
10. Inchydoney Is. (Cleary 1989)
11. Lisleagh II (Monk 1995, 111)
12. Raheens (No. 2) (Lennon 1994, 55)
* Kilmartin Lower (possible) (Coleman 1947–8, 70; McCarthy 1977, 273)

Co. Donegal
1. Ballymacool (Lacy 1983, 232)
2. Norrira (Colhoun 1946, 86)
3. Stroove (Lacy 1983, 239)
* Ballymagrorty Irish (possible) (Davies 1940)

Co. Down
1. Carrickrovaddy (Collins and Harper 1974)
2. Toberdoney (Collins 1964)

Co. Galway
1. Billymore (Kinahan 1883–4a, 13)
2. Caherbulligin (Gosling *et al.*, forthcoming, no. 5799)
3. Cluidrevagh (Alcock *et al.* 1999, 437)
4. Fiddaun (Gosling *et al.*, forthcoming, no. 5852)
5. Garraun Lower (Westropp 1919, 172; Gosling *et al.*, forthcoming, no. 5855)
6. Gortroe (Knox and Redington 1915–16, 180)
7. Greenville (Broderick 1879–82, 637)
8. Killosolan (Alcock *et al.* 1999, 271)
9. Lecarrownagoppoge (Knox and Redington 1915–16, 189)
10. Ballinphuil (Costello 1902, 115; 1903–4, 8)
11. Rinn (Knox and Redington 1915–16, 184)
12. Termon (McCarron 1940)

Co. Kerry
1. Ballinknockane
2. Ballybrack (Cuppage 1986, 392)
3. Ballyledder (A. O'Sullivan and Sheehan 1996, 141)
4. Ballynahow (Clinton and Kelly, forthcoming)
5. Ballynavenooragh (Clinton, forthcoming b)
6. Boulerdah (A. O'Sullivan and Sheehan 1996, 225)
7. Cloghane (Cuppage 1986, 199)
8. Darrynane More (A. O'Sullivan and Sheehan 1996, 177)
9. Dromavally (Clark 1961, 77; Cuppage 1986, 239)
10. Glanballyma (O'Connell 1938)
11. Glantane (Kelly 1982–3b, 6)
12. Gowlin (Cuppage 1986, 241)
13. Illauntannig (Cuppage 1986, 293)
14. Keeas (A. O'Sullivan and Sheehan 1996, 233)

15. Rathea (Toal 1995, 173)
16. Lohercannan (McDonnell 1957)
17. Tinnies Upper (O'Connell 1937; A. O'Sullivan and Sheehan 1996, 236)
* Ballywiheen (possible) (Cuppage 1986, 276)

Co. Kilkenny
* Graigue (possible) (Tighe 1802, 628)

Co. Limerick
1. Cush (Souterrain 4) (S.P. Ó Ríordáin 1938–40, 103)

Co. Londonderry
1. Ballintemple (May and Cooper 1939, 85)
2. Cloyfin South (Brannon and Warner 1978)
3. Dunalis (Lindsay 1934–5, 64)

Co. Longford
1. Fortwilliam (O'Connor 1933)

Co. Louth
1. Ballybarrack (Souterrain 2) (Kelly 1977)
2. Baltray (Raftery 1942)
3. Donaghmore (Souterrain A) (Rynne 1965a)
4. Farrandreg 2 (D. Murphy 1998, 267; M. Seaver, pers. comm.)
5. Marshes Upper (Souterrain 4A) (Gowen 1992, 83)
6. Millockstown (Souterrain 2) (Manning 1986, 149)
* Balregan (possible) (Buckley and Sweetman 1991, 104)

Co. Mayo
1. Aghamore (Raftery 1956)
2. Letterkeen (S.P. Ó Ríordáin and MacDermott 1951–2, 100)
3. Shanvallyhugh (Topographical Files, NMI)
* 'Doagh' (possible) (Moran 1933)
* Kiltarnaght (possible) (Topographical Files, NMI)

Co. Meath
1. Cabragh (Hickey and Rynne 1953, 220)
2. Dowth (Deane 1887, 55; Coffey 1912, 48)
3. Knowth (Souterrain 5) (George Eogan, pers. comm.)
4. Knowth (Souterrain 7) (George Eogan, pers. comm.)

5. Knowth (Souterrain 9) (Eogan 1968, 357)
6. Nevinstown (Mary Cahill, pers. comm.)

Co. Monaghan
* Bocks Upper (possible) (Danaher 1967)

Co. Offaly
1. Doon (Foot 1860–1, 224)

Co. Roscommon
1. Ballymacurly South (OPW File, 1979)
* Correal (possible) (Moran 1986)

Co. Sligo
1. Clogher (Mount 1994)
2. Gortersluin (O'Conor, 1994e)
3. Rathdoony (Mac Sitric 1934)
* Carroward (possible) (OPW)

Co. Tipperary
1. Cloharden (J. Graves 1870–1, 207)

Co. Waterford
1. Ballykilmurry (Mongey 1933, 250)

Co. Westmeath
1. Gorteen (Falkiner 1898–1900, 213)
2. Rathnew (Souterrain 1) (Macalister and Praeger 1928, 114)
3. Rathnew (Souterrain 3) (Macalister and Praeger 1928, 104)
4. Togherstown (Souterrain 1) (Macalister and Praeger 1929–31, 71)

Table 2 — Steps: structural and contextual data

	Site	No. of steps	A/D	Siting	Form	H (m)	Perceived function
1.	Aird, Co. Antrim	3	A	C to C	RC	(1) 0.43 (2) 0.41 (3) 0.20	Accommodating ascent
2.	Ballyvaghmore, Co. Antrim	'Steps'	A?	C to C?	?	?	Internal adjustment in level
3.	Donegore, Co. Antrim	3–4	D	E	RC	?	Aiding access to souterrain
4.	Loughermore, Co. Antrim	2	D	P to P	(1) EC (2) EC/SB	c. 0.45/50 c. 0.30/35	Accommodating descent Accommodating descent
5.	Stiles, Co. Antrim	1	A	C to P	RC	0.10	Internal adjustment in level
6.	Stranocum, Co. Antrim	5	D	E	SB	?	Aiding access to souterrain
7.	Tobergill, Co. Antrim	1	D	P to C	?	0.30	Aiding descent to chamber
*	Liminary, Co. Antrim	1	?	C to P	?	?	Countering sloping floor?
8.	Corliss, Co. Armagh	1	D	E	EC?	?	Aiding access to souterrain
9.	Cahercommaun, Co. Clare	5	D	E	4SB/1RC	?	Aiding access to souterrain
10.	Cahercommaun, Co. Clare	4	D	E	3SB/1RC	?	Aiding access to souterrain
*	'Caher Hill', Co. Clare	'Steps'	D	E?	?	?	Aiding access to souterrain
11.	Ballycatteen, Co. Cork	2	D	E	1SB/1RC	?	Aiding access to souterrain
12.	Brackcloon, Co. Cork	4	D	E?	RC	?	Aiding access to souterrain
13.	Cappeen West, Co. Cork	'Steps'	D	P to C	EC	?	Aiding access to souterrain
14.	Coolanarney, Co. Cork	2–3	D	P to C	?	?	Aiding descent to souterrain
15.	Curraghcrowley W., Co. Cork	2	D	E	RC	?	Aiding access to souterrain
	Curraghcrowley W., Co. Cork	1	A	C to C	RC	0.64	Anti-flooding device?
16.	Deelish, Co. Cork	3	D	E	SB?	?	Aiding access to souterrain

No.	Site						
17.	Dunisky, Co. Cork	1	A	C to P	RC	0.45	Anti-flooding device?
18.	Farandau, Co. Cork	1	D	C to C	RC	0.61	Internal adjustment in level
19.	Lisleagh 2, Co. Cork	'Steps'	D	E	EC	?	Aiding access to souterrain
20.	Inchydoney Is., Co. Cork	1	D	C to C	EC	c. 0.70	Defensive adjustment
21.	Raheens (No. 2), Co. Cork	'Stepped'	D	E	EC?	?	Aiding access to souterrain
*	Kilmartin Lower, Co. Cork	2	D	E?	SB	?	Aiding access to souterrain?
22.	Ballymacool, Co. Donegal	1	?	P to P	?	0.28	Internal adjustment in level
23.	Norrira, Co. Donegal	1	D	E	RC	0.30	Aiding access to souterrain
24.	Stroove, Co. Donegal	1	D	P to C	RC	?	Aiding access to souterrain
*	Ballymagrorty Irish, Co. Donegal	15?	D	E	?	?	Aiding access to souterrain?
25.	Carrickrovaddy, Co. Down	1	A	TD	?	0.30	Defensive adjustment in level
26.	Toberdoney, Co. Down	1	D	P	SB	0.38	Internal adjustment in level
27.	Ballinphuil, Co. Down	'Steps'	D	ETD	SB	?	Aiding descent from platform
28.	Billymore, Co. Galway	2–3	D	ETD	SB	?	Aiding descent from platform
29.	Caherbulligin, Co. Galway	'Stepped'	D	E	?	?	Aiding access to souterrain
30.	Fiddaun, Co. Galway	2	D	E	SB	?	Aiding access to souterrain
31.	Garraun L., Co. Galway	2–3	D	E	?	?	Aiding access to souterrain
	Garraun L., Co. Galway	4	A	Const.	SB?	?	Component of impedimental device
32.	Gortroe, Co. Galway	3	D	ETD	SB	(1)? (2) 0.25 (3) 0.56	Aiding descent from platform
33.	Greenville, Co. Galway	3–4	D	E	?	?	Aiding access to souterrain
34.	Killosolan, Co. Galway	3	A	Const.	SB?	?	Components of impedimental device
	Killosolan, Co. Galway	3	D	Const.	SB?	?	Components of impedimental device

Site		No. of steps	A/D	Siting	Form	H (m)	Perceived function
35.	Lecarrownagoppoge, Co. Galway	2	D	ETD	SB	(1) 0.30 (2) 0.61	Aiding descent from platform
	Lecarrownagoppoge, Co. Galway	2	D	ETD	SB	?	Aiding descent from platform
36.	Rinn, Co. Galway	1	D	P to C	SB	0.51	Part of obstructive configuration
37.	Termon, Co. Galway	1	D	ETD	SB	0.61	Aiding descent from platform
38.	Ballinknockane, Co. Kerry	'Steps'	D	E	SB?		Aiding access to souterrain?
39.	Ballybrack, Co. Kerry	1	D	P to C	SB	?	Aiding descent to chamber
40.	Ballyledder 1, Co. Kerry	2	A/D	C to E	EC	?	Aiding access/exit from souterrain
41.	Ballynahow, Co. Kerry	2	D	E?	SB	(1) 0.10 (2) 0.12	Aiding descent to chamber
42.	Ballynavenooragh, Co. Kerry	2–3	D	P to C	SB	(1) 0.30 (2) 0.18	Aiding descent to chamber
43.	Boulerdah, Co. Kerry	'Steps'	D	E	?	?	Aiding access to souterrain
44.	Cloghane, Co. Kerry	2	D	C to P	SB?	?	Internal adjustment in level
45.	Derrynane More, Co. Kerry	1	D	P	?	0.40	Internal adjustment in level
46.	Dromavally, Co. Kerry	1	A	P to 'C'	SB	0.45	Defensive adjustment in level?
47.	Glanballyma, Co. Kerry	'Steps'	D	E	?	?	Aiding access to souterrain
48.	Glantane, Co. Kerry	1	A	C to P	SB	c. 0.30	Internal adjustment in level
49.	Gowlin, Co. Kerry	2	D	E	SB/EC	?	Aiding access to souterrain
50.	Illauntannig, Co. Kerry	1	–	P to 'C'	?	0.50	Aiding access from passage to wall chamber
51.	Keeas, Co. Kerry	'Steps'	D	E	?	?	Aiding access to souterrain
52.	Rathea, Co. Kerry	1	A?	C to P	SB?	0.20	Internal adjustment in level

No.	Site						Description
53.	Lohercannan, Co. Kerry	1	D	P	?	0.46	Internal adjustment in level
54.	Tinnies Upper, Co. Kerry	3	D	E	SB	(1) ? (2) 0.40 (3) 0.40	Aiding access to souterrain
*	Tinnies Upper, Co. Kerry	'Steps'	D	P	?	?	Accommodating descent?
*	Ballywiheen	14–20?	D	E	?	?	Aiding access to souterrain?
55.	Cush (Sou. 4), Co. Limerick	1	D	P to P	SB	?	Internal adjustment in level
56.	Ballintemple, Co. Londonderry	1	A?	C to C	RC	0.84	Anti-flooding device?
57.	Dunalis, Co. Londonderry	1	D	C to C	SB	?	Aiding descent to chamber
58.	Cloyfin S., Co. Londonderry	1	A	C to C	SB	c. 0.15/20	Defensive adjustment in level
59.	Fortwilliam, Co. Longford	4–5?	D	E	?	?	Aiding access to souterrain
60.	Ballybarrack 2, Co. Louth	1	D	P to P	SB	c. 0.15	Internal adjustment in level
61.	Baltray, Co. Louth	1	?	P	?	?	Internal adjustment in level
62.	Donaghmore (A), Co. Louth	1?	A	P to C?	RC	0.25–30	Internal adjustment in level?
	Donaghmore (A), Co. Louth	1	A	P to P	SB	0.40	Internal adjustment in level
	Donaghmore (A), Co. Louth	1	A	P to P	SB	0.20	Internal adjustment in level
	Donaghmore (A), Co. Louth	1	D	P	RC	0.12	Accommodating descent
	Donaghmore (A), Co. Louth	1	D	P	RC	0.12	Accommodating descent
63.	Farrandreg 2, Co. Louth	1	D	P	EC	0.22	Accommodating descent
	Farrandreg 2, Co. Louth	1	D	P	EC	0.20	Accommodating descent
64.	Marshes Upper (4A), Co. Louth	2	A	P to C	RC	?	Internal adjustment in level
65.	Millockstown (No. 2), Co. Louth	1? 2?	D	E	SB	0.15?	Aiding access to souterrain
*	Millockstown (No. 2), Co. Louth	1	A	P to P	SB	?	Badly damaged/undefined feature

Site	No. of steps	A/D	Siting	Form	H (m)	Perceived function
* Balregan, Co. Louth	2–3?	D	P	?	?	Internal adjustment in level
66. Aghamore, Co. Mayo	1	A	P to C	?	?	Defensive adjustment in level
67. Letterkeen, Co. Mayo	1	D	E	EC	?	Aiding access to souterrain
Letterkeen, Co. Mayo	1	D	C	EC	0.40	Internal adjustment in level
68. Shanvallyhugh, Co. Mayo	4	D	ETD	SB	?	Aiding descent from platform
* 'Doagh', Co. Mayo	'Steps'	D	E?	?	?	Aiding access to souterrain?
* Kiltarnaght, Co. Mayo	4	D	E	SB	?	Aiding access to souterrain?
69. Cabragh, Co. Meath	3?	D	P	RC	?	Accommodating descent
70. Dowth, Co. Meath	3?	A	P to PG	SB	?	Aiding incorporation of passage grave into souterrain
71. Knowth (Sou. 5), Co. Meath	1	D	P	SB	0.30	Accommodating descent
Knowth (Sou. 5), Co. Meath	1	D	P	SB	0.30	Accommodating descent
72. Knowth (Sou. 7), Co. Meath	3	D	E (side)	SB	?	Aiding access to souterrain
Knowth (Sou. 7), Co. Meath	1	?	P	EC	?	Internal adjustment to level
73. Knowth (Sou. 9), Co. Meath	1	D	E	EC	0.12–15	Aiding access to souterrain
74. Nevinstown, Co. Meath	1	D	P	SB	0.13–16	Internal adjustment in level
* Bocks Upper, Co. Monaghan	'Steps'	D	E	?	?	Aiding access to souterrain
75. Doon, Co. Offaly	3–4	D	ETD	SB	?	Aiding descent from platform
Doon, Co. Offaly	3	D	ETD	SB	?	Aiding descent from platform
76. Ballymacurly S., Co. Roscommon	2	D	E	SB	?	Aiding access to souterrain
* Correal, Co. Roscommon	1	D?	P to C?	EC	0.15	Internal adjustment in level
77. Clogher, Co. Sligo	8	D	E	SB	?	Aiding access to souterrain
78. Gortersluin, Co. Sligo	1	A	C to P	SB	?	Defensive adjustment in level?
* Carroward, Co. Sligo	'Stairway'	D?	E	SB?	?	Aiding access to souterrain

No.	Site	'Steps'				Height	Description
79.	Rathdoony, Co. Sligo	'Steps'	D	E	?	?	Aiding access to souterrain
	Rathdoony, Co. Sligo	1?	A	P to C	?	?	Internal adjustment to level
80.	Cloharden, Co. Tipperary	'Flight'	D	E	?	?	Aiding access to souterrain
81.	Ballykilmurry, Co. Waterford	1	D	P to C	RC?	0.25	Aiding descent to chamber
82.	Gorteen, Co. Westmeath	1	D	P to P	SB	0.25	Internal adjustment in level
*	Rathnew (Sou. 1), Co. Westmeath	1	D	P	EC	c. 0.30	Internal adjustment in level
83.	Rathnew (Sou. 3), Co. Westmeath	1	–	C to C	SB	?	Internal adjustment in level
84.	Togherstown (Sou. 1), Co. Westmeath	2	D	E	SB	(1) ? (2) 0.36	Aiding access to souterrain
	Togherstown (Sou. 1), Co. Westmeath	1	D	C to C	SB	0.23	Internal adjustment in level
	Togherstown (Sou. 1), Co. Westmeath	1	D?	C to P	SB	0.25	Internal adjustment in level
	Togherstown (Sou. 1), Co. Westmeath	1	D	P to C	SB	0.30	Internal adjustment in level

Key: A = ascending; D = descending; H = height; E = entrance; C = chamber; P = passageway; EC = earth-cut; RC = rock-cut; SB = drystone-built; PG = passage grave; Const. = constriction; TD = trapdoor; ETD = elevated trapdoor

Appendix 8

Door-jambs

Table 1—Wall-slots/niches

Site	Siting
1. Ballybarrack (Sou. 1), Co. Louth (E.P. Kelly, pers. comm.)	Internal
2. Carrickcloghan, Co. Armagh (B. Williams 1983)	Internal
3. Corderry, Co. Louth (Buckley and Sweetman 1991, 112)	Internal
4. Drumad, Co. Louth (Gosling 1979, 209)	Internal
5. Donaghmore (Sou. A), Co. Louth (Rynne 1965a)	Entrance
6. Haggardstown, Co. Louth (McLoughlin 2000, 214)	Entrance
7. Killally (Sou. 1), Co. Louth (Clinton and Stout 1997, 129)	Internal
8. Knockballyclery, Co. Galway (Gosling *et al.*, forthcoming)	Internal
9. Lissard, Co. Galway (P. Gosling, pers. comm.)	Internal
10. Marshes Upper 1, Co. Louth (P. Gosling, pers. comm.)	Internal
11. Marshes Upper 3A, Co. Louth (Gowen 1992, 64)	Internal
12. Portlecka, Co. Clare (Westropp 1913, 236)	Internal

Table 2—Post-holes

Site	Siting
1. Ballywee (Sou. 3), Co. Antrim (Lynn 1975, 6)	Entrance
2. Donaghmore (Sou. A), Co. Louth (Rynne 1965a)	Entrance
3. Knowth (Sou. 7), Co. Meath (G. Eogan, pers. comm.)	Entrance
4. Haggardstown, Co. Louth (McLoughlin 2000, 214)	Internal
5. Knowth (Sou. 7), Co. Meath (G. Eogan, pers. comm.)	Internal
6. Randalstown 1, Co. Meath (K. Campbell, pers. comm.)	Internal
7. Rathnew (Sou. 3), Co. Westmeath (Macalister and Praeger 1928, 104)	Entrance
8. Rathnew (Sou. 3), Co. Westmeath (Macalister and Praeger 1928, 104)	Internal

Table 3—Wooden door-jambs

Site	Siting
1. Coolcran, Co. Fermanagh (B. Williams 1985, 77)	Internal

Appendix 9
Porthole-slabs

Table 1—Inventory of sites and associated monument types

	Site	Site type	Location
1.	Ardraw	Ringfort	Iveragh Peninsula
2.	Ballintaggart	Ringfort (destroyed)	Dingle Peninsula
3.	Ballintermon	Ringfort	Dingle Peninsula
4.	Beenbane	Open settlement	Dingle Peninsula
5.	Carhoo East	Open settlement	Dingle Peninsula
6.	Cloghane	Cashel	Dingle Peninsula
7.	Coolnaharragle Lower	Ringfort	Iveragh Peninsula
8.	Coumduff	Ringfort	Dingle Peninsula
9.	Derrygorman	Open settlement	Dingle Peninsula
10.	Doonsheane	Ringfort (destroyed)	Dingle Peninsula
11.	Dromavally	Open settlement	Dingle Peninsula
12.	Duagh 1	Ringfort	Dingle Peninsula
13.	Duagh 2	Early ecclesiastical site	Dingle Peninsula
14.	Emlagh West	Ringfort?	Dingle Peninsula
15.	Glandine	Ringfort	Dingle Peninsula
16.	Glantane	Ringfort	Dingle Peninsula
17.	Gortmore	Open settlement	Dingle Peninsula
18.	Gowlin	Open settlement	Dingle Peninsula
19.	Kealduff Upper	Open settlement	Iveragh Peninsula
20.	Kilduff	Ringfort	Dingle Peninsula
21.	Kilteenbane	Ringfort	Dingle Peninsula
22.	Kimego West 1	Ringfort	Iveragh Peninsula
23.	Kimego West 2	Open settlement	Iveragh Peninsula
24.	Kinard East	Open settlement	Dingle Peninsula
25.	Smerwick	Cashel	Dingle Peninsula
26.	Tobernamoodane	Open settlement	Dingle Peninsula

Note added in press

27.	Bray (Valencia Island)	Open settlement (circular house)	Off Iveragh Peninsula

Table 2—Porthole-slabs: statistical data and context of slabs

	Site	Dimensions of aperture (width; height) (m)	Internal position
1.	Ardraw	No specific data	
2.	Ballintaggart	No specific data	
3.	Ballintermon	0.45; 0.55	Access to EC
4.	Beenbane	0.40; 0.30	Midway along EC
5.	Carhoo East	0.33; 0.33	Midway along EC
6.	Cloghane	(1) *c.* 0.45; *c.* 0.35	Midway along EC
		(2) 0.35; 0.41	Midway along RP
7.	Coolnaharragle Lower	No specific data	Constriction joining chambers
8.	Coumduff	No specific data	Access from RP to chamber
9.	Derrygorman	No specific data	Junction of C and chamber
10.	Doonsheane	No specific data	Entrance to chamber from P
11.	Dromavally	0.33; 0.43	Entrance to chamber from 'alcove'
12.	Duagh 1	0.36; 0.38	Access to chamber from UP
13.	Duagh 2	0.33; 0.18	
14.	Emlagh West	0.40; 0.41	Access to chamber from EC
15.	Glandine	No specific data	Junction of two P
16.	Glantane	0.44; 0.30	Access from EC to chamber
17.	Gortmore	0.50; 0.50	Access from C to chamber
18.	Gowlin	0.32; 0.60	Access from UP to chamber
19.	Kealduff Upper	0.36; 0.30	Access to C from chamber
20	Kilduff	?; 0.45	Entrance to chamber
21.	Kilteenbane	No specific data	Towards end of P
22.	Kimego West 1	0.46; 0.23	
23.	Kimego West 2	No specific data	Mid-passageway

24. Kinard East	No specific data	Midway along EC
25. Smerwick	0.48; 0.33	Access from RP to chamber
26. Tobernamoodane	0.40; 0.26	Junction of two chambers
27. Bray (Valencia)	0.40; 0.25	Junction of two chambers

Key: P = passageway; C = constriction; EC = extended constriction; RP = restricted passage; UP = unrestricted passage.

Appendix 10

Roof-supports in souterrains

Table 1 — Stone pillar supports

Aghmanister and Spital, Co. Cork (Shee 1969)
Ahaliskey, Co. Cork (McCarthy 1977, 137)
Ballyknock N., Co. Cork (Barry 1890–1, 517)
Carhoovauler, Co. Cork (O'Crowley 1906)
Cooldorragha, Co. Cork (McCarthy 1977, 196)
Coolmagort (Dunloe), Co. Kerry (Atkinson 1866, 523)
Darrara (Sou. 2), Co. Cork (J. O'Sullivan *et al.* 1998, 43)
Gearha South, Co. Kerry (O'Kelly and Kavanagh 1954a, 50)
Dunbeacon, Co. Cork (Rynne 1963)
Killeens, Co. Cork (D. Power *et al.* 1994, 156)
Knockshanawee, Co. Cork (Lee 1911, 61)
Roovesmore, Co. Cork (Lane-Fox 1867, 123)
Underhill, Co. Cork (O'Kelly and Shee 1968, 40)
* Kilcrea, Co. Cork (McCarthy 1977, 269)

Table 2 — Wooden post supports

Ballycatteen, Co. Cork (S.P. Ó Ríordáin and Hartnett 1943–4, 16)
Coolcran, Co. Fermanagh (B. Williams 1985, 75)
Cush (Sou. 3), Co. Limerick (S.P. Ó Ríordáin 1938–40, 97)
Cush (Sou. 4), Co. Limerick (S.P. Ó Ríordáin 1938–40, 103)
Cush (Sou. 8), Co. Limerick (S.P. Ó Ríordáin 1938–40, 129)
Letterkeen, Co. Mayo (S.P. Ó Ríordáin and MacDermott 1952, 100)
Raheennamadra, Co. Limerick (Stenberger 1966, 41)

Table 3 — Miscellanea

Demesne, Co. Louth (Tempest 1933–6, 95)
Farrandreg 2, Co. Louth (D. Murphy 1998, 267)
Killarney, Co. Kilkenny (Prendergast 1961)
Stickillin (Sou. 2), Co. Louth (Dunne *et al.* 1973–6, 277)
Straid (Glencolmcille), Co. Donegal (Lacy 1983, 292)

Appendix 11

Benches

Table 1 — Inventory of sites

Co. Antrim
Ballyeaston (Warner 1972, 61)

Co. Cork
Dunisky (three benches) (Gogan 1930; McCarthy 1977, 225; 1983, 101)
Ummera (D. Power *et al.* 1997, 284)

Co. Kerry
Ballyegan (Byrne 1991, 12)
* Cloghane (possible) (Creedon 1977; Cuppage 1986, 199)

Co. Kildare
Killashee (R. Moore 1918–21)

Co. Louth
Ballybarrack (Sou. 2) (E.P. Kelly, pers. comm.)
* Paughanstown (possible) (Rowland 1847–50, 404; Bigger 1921–4, 63;
        MacIvor   1949–52, 273)

Co. Mayo
Ellistronbeg (Lavelle *et al.* 1994, 69)

Table 2 – Bench?/table?/seat?

Co. Armagh
Dromman More (Rogers 1882, 67)

Co. Antrim
* Croghfern (possible) (O'Laverty 1884, 12)
* Duncarbit (possible) (O'Laverty 1887, 459)

Co. Clare
Finvarra Demesne (T. Cooke 1849–51, 297)

Co. Donegal
Townparks (Lacy 1983, 227)

Co. Louth
Millpark (Rynne 1966b)

Co. Wexford
* Motabower (possible) (Kinahan 1883–4a, 14)

Appendix 12

Sumps and wells

Table 1 — Cut wells/sumps

Ballintemple, Co. Londonderry (May and Cooper 1939, 84)
Ballynavenooragh, Co. Kerry (Clinton, forthcoming b)
Dunisky, Co. Cork (Gogan 1930; McCarthy 1977, 234)
Lismenary, Co. Antrim (Fagan 1839)
Stiles, Co. Antrim (Collins 1976, 14)

Table 2 — Unsubstantiated reports

Ballinafoy, Co. Down (Day and McWilliams 1992a, 15): 'A fine spring well in the interior [of the souterrain]'.

Ballynag Upper, Co. Londonderry (O'Laverty 1887, 232): '… and spring-wells were found in [the souterrain]'.

Ballywee, Co. Antrim (O'Laverty 1884, 188): 'There are five [souterrains in the townland], in one of which there is a spring well'.

Barnmeen, Co. Down (Day and McWilliams 1990, 20): 'There is a well at the far end [of the cave] about two feet in depth. The water was considered beneficial in healing sores'.

Bushmills or Ballaghmore, Co. Antrim (O'Laverty 1887, 287; Day and McWilliams 1992b, 116): 'There was formerly a well in the [souterrain, now dry]'.

Cahermaclanchy, Co. Clare (Westropp 1896–1901, 669): '… one passage in the stone fort of Cahermaclanchy, near Lisdoonvarna, ended in a very deep pit leading down to water at an unknown depth'.

Candlefort, Co. Monaghan (Reade 1874–5, 326; Orpen 1910, 219): '… [in] a recess or small chamber … a well of water, so very cold …'.

Carnmoon, Co. Antrim (O'Laverty 1887, 399): 'A [souterrain] in which there is a spring of water'.

Doobeg, Co. Sligo (Mulligan 1942–4; O'Conor 1994d): 'There is a well in the centre of one of the [chambers of the souterrain]'. Souterrain now flooded.

Fawney, Co. Londonderry (Day and McWilliams 1995, 43): 'In the cave … there was a well nicely built round with stones and containing a spring of clear water, very cold'.

Moyargat Upper, Co. Antrim (O'Laverty 1887, 404): 'A well within the entrance of this cave supplies the neighbouring village with water'.

Mullaghgaun, Co. Antrim (Bleakly 1837, 41): 'A spring well [in the souterrain]'.

Outhill, Co. Antrim (O'Laverty 1887, 265): 'A [souterrain] where there was found a spring well'.

Rinroe, Co. Sligo (O'Donovan 1836a, 141): '... in the next [chamber] ... there is a good spring well'.

'St John's Point', Co. Down (Harris and Smith 1744, 195): '... a circular chamber ... in which is a fine cool limpid well'.

Toberbride, Co. Sligo (O'Rorke 1878, 241): 'A [souterrain] containing, at or near the middle, a well'.

Appendix 13

Construction shafts

Table 1 — Inventory of sites and morphological data

Site	Type	No. of shafts	No. of chambers	Reference
1. Ahakeera, Co. Cork	EC	2–3	5	Twohig 1976, 26
2. Ardgroom Outward, Co. Cork	EC/SB	2–3	5	McCarthy 1977, 141
3. Ardahill, Co. Cork	EC	3	4	T. Murphy 1964
4. Ballythomas W., Co. Cork	EC	1	2	D. Power et al. 1994, 155
5. Ballyva, Co. Cork	RC/EC/SB	1	1	D. Power 1992, 230
6. Bengour W., Co. Cork	EC	1–2?	5	Cleary 1989
7. Bigmarsh, Co. Cork	EC	1?3?	3	D. Power 1992, 230
8. Brackcloon, Co. Cork	RC	1	3?	S.P. Ó Ríordáin 1934–5
9. Caherbarnagh, Co. Cork	EC	1	2	D. Power et al. 1997, 274
10. Cappeen E., Co. Cork	EC	2	4	McCarthy 1977, 201
11. Carrigbaun, Co. Cork	EC	1?3?	3	D. Power 1992, 231
12. Carrigdangan, Co. Cork	EC	1	3+	D. Power et al. 1997, 274
13. Carrigdarrery, Co. Cork	RC	2	2	D. Power et al. 1997, 274
14. Carrignadoura, Co. Cork	EC/SB	2	3	D. Power et al. 1997, 274
15. Carrigroe, Co. Cork	EC/SB	1–2?	3	Cleary 1989

Site	Type	No. of shafts	No. of chambers	Reference
16. Castleventry, Co. Cork	EC	1	1	Cleary 1981a, 41
17. Cloonkirgeen, Co. Cork	EC	2–3	4	Twohig 1976, 28
18. Coolabaun, Co. Cork	EC	3?	3	D. Power 1992, 245
19. Coolbane, Co. Cork	EC	4?	4	D. Power 1992, 232
20. Corran S., Co. Cork	RC/SB	1–2	4	McCarthy 1975, 59
21. Cullenagh, Co. Cork	RC/EC	1	2	Twohig 1976, 33
22. Curraghcrowley W., Co. Cork	RC	3	5	Somerville 1929–30, 6
23. Curraghely, Co. Cork	RC	2	4	Brash 1866–9b, 73
24. Darrara (Sou. 1), Co. Cork	EC	2	4	J. O'Sullivan et al. 1998, 39
25. Darrara (Sou. 2), Co. Cork	EC/SB	3	4	J. O'Sullivan et al. 1998, 43
26. Darrara (Sou. 3), Co. Cork	EC	1+?	2+?	J. O'Sullivan et al. 1998, 43
27. Driminidy S., Co. Cork	EC	1	4	D. Power 1992, 233
28. Drom S., Co. Cork	EC	1	1	D. Power 1992, 233
29. Dundeady, Co. Cork	EC/RC	1	3	McCarthy 1977, 223
30. Dunisky, Co. Cork	RC	3	7	McCarthy 1977, 225
31. Farran, Co. Cork	EC	1	1+	D. Power 1992, 233
32. Farrandau (Knockdrum), Co. Cork	EC/SB	1?	3	Somerville 1931, 6
33. Farranthomas, Co. Cork	EC	1	2	Ó Drisceoil and Hurley 1978, 75
34. Ferm, Co. Cork	EC	1	1	McCarthy 1977, 244
35. Foildarrig, Co. Cork	EC	1	4?	McCarthy 1977, 245
36. Froe Upper, Co. Cork	EC/SB	1?3?	5	Cleary 1981b, 102
37. Garryantaggart, Co. Cork	EC/RC	2	2	Cleary 1986, 146
38. Gortgarriff, Co. Cork	EC	1	3	D. Power 1992, 404

39. Gortnaclohy, Co. Cork	EC	2	3	McCarthy 1977, 254
40. Inchydoney Is., Co. Cork	SB/EC	2	6	Cleary 1989
41. Inchincurka, Co. Cork	EC	3	3	McCarthy 1977, 258
42. Johnstown, Co. Cork	EC	1?	4	McCarthy 1977, 260
43. Keelaraheen, Co. Cork	EC	1	3+	D. Power 1992, 236
44. Keelnameela, Co. Cork	EC	2	4	Twohig 1971, 130
45. Kilberehert, Co. Cork	SB/EC	1	2	Gillman 1896b, 417
46. Kilcondy, Co. Cork	EC	3	3	McCarthy 1977, 267
47. Kilcrohane, Co. Cork	RC/EC	1	3	D. Power 1992, 404
48. Knockane, Co. Cork	EC	1	4	McCarthy 1977, 277
49. Knocknagoul, Co. Cork	EC	1?	2	Cleary 1989
50. Lisgoold N., Co. Cork	EC/RC	3	3	D. Power et al. 1994, 156
51. Lisheen, Co. Cork	EC	3	7	Fahy 1960, 143
52. Lissaclarig E., Co. Cork	EC	1	3	D. Power 1992, 237
53. Lissardagh, Co. Cork	RC/EC	3?	3	D. Power et al. 1997, 282
54. Little Island, Co. Cork	RC/EC	6	5	Fahy 1970
55. Lough Marsh, Co. Cork	EC	4–5	6	Cleary 1981a, 38
56. Lyroe, Co. Cork	EC	1	2+	D. Power et al. 1997, 282
57. Madame, Co. Cork	RC/EC	1	2+	D. Power 1992, 237
58. Mallowgaton, Co. Cork	RC/EC	1	2	Ó Drisceoil and Hurley 1978, 76
59. Moneygaff W., Co. Cork	EC	1	2	Cleary 1981a, 40
60. Moneygaff E., Co. Cork	EC	6	6	Cleary 1989
61. Rathonoane, Co. Cork	EC	1	1	D. Power et al. 1997, 283
62. Rossnakilla, Co. Cork	EC	5	5	D. Power et al. 1997, 283
63. Shanaway Middle, Co. Cork	EC	1?	3	T. Murphy 1962

Site	Type	No. of shafts	No. of chambers	Reference
64. Templebryan N., Co. Cork	EC	2	3	Twohig 1976, 31
65. Tooms East, Co. Cork	EC	3	3	D. Power et al. 1997, 284
66. Townlands, Co. Cork	EC	1	1+	D. Power 1992, 238
67. Tullyneasky, Co. Cork	EC	2	2	D. Power 1992, 239
68. Ummera, Co. Cork	EC	2	4	D. Power et al. 1997, 284
69. Underhill, Co. Cork	EC/SB	3	5	O'Kelly and Shee 1968, 40
70. Norrira, Co. Donegal	RC	1	5	Colhoun 1946, 84
71. Ardsheelhane W., Co. Kerry	SB/EC	1	2	A. O'Sullivan and Sheehan 1996, 225
72. Ballyledder, Co. Kerry	SB/EC	2	6	A. O'Sullivan and Sheehan 1996, 140
73. Cloghane, Co. Kerry	SB/RC/EC	2	8	Cuppage 1986, 197
74. Ballintemple, Co. Londonderry	RC	3?	9	May and Cooper 1939, 82

Possible sites

Site	Type	No. of shafts	No. of chambers	Reference
* Ballyrisode, Co. Cork	EC	1?	4?	Twohig 1973, 36
* Cloddagh (Sherkin Is.), Co. Cork	EC	1?	6	Donovan 1876, 37
* Glanturkin, Co. Cork	EC	1?	1+	D. Power et al. 1994, 156
* Kilmalooda, Co. Cork	EC	1?	3	D. Power 1992, 236
* Ardraw (Sou. 2), Co. Kerry	EC	1?	?	Proceedings 1906, 340
* Gearha N., Co. Kerry	SB/EC	1?	3	A. O'Sullivan and Sheehan 1996, 403

Key: EC = earth-cut; RC = rock-cut; SB = drystone-built.

Bibliography

Abbreviations

Arch. J.	*Archaeological Journal*
BAR	British Archaeological Reports
CBA	Council for British Archaeology
CLAJ	*County Louth Archaeological Journal*
DOE	Department of the Environment (Northern Ireland): Monuments and Buildings Record Section
ITA	Irish Tourist Association
JCHAS	*Journal of the Cork Historical and Archaeological Society*
JGAHS	*Journal of the Galway Archaeological and Historical Society*
JKAHS	*Journal of the Kerry Archaeological and Historical Society*
JKAS	*Journal of the Kildare Archaeological Society*
J. Wat. S.E. Ire. Arch. Soc.	*Journal of the Waterford and Southeast of Ireland Archaeological Society*
JRSAI	*Journal of the Royal Society of Antiquaries of Ireland*
NLI	National Library of Ireland
NMAJ	*North Munster Antiquarian Journal*
NMI	National Museum of Ireland
OPW	Office of Public Works (National Monuments Branch)
OSM	Ordnance Survey Memoirs
Proc. Belfast Nat. Hist. Phil. Soc.	*Proceedings and Reports of the Belfast Natural History and Philosophical Society*
PPS	*Proceedings of the Prehistoric Society*
PRIA	*Proceedings of the Royal Irish Academy*
PSAS	*Proceedings of the Society of Antiquaries of Scotland*
QUB	Queen's University, Belfast
RIA	Royal Irish Academy
TRIA	*Transactions of the Royal Irish Academy*
UCC	University College, Cork
UCG	University College, Galway
UJA	*Ulster Journal of Archaeology*

Aalen, F.H.A., Whelan, K. and Stout, M. (eds) 1997 *Atlas of the Irish rural landscape.* Cork.

Alcock, O., de hÓra, K. and Gosling, P. 1999 *Archaeological inventory of County Galway. Vol. 2: North Galway.* Dublin.

Allen-French, J. 1883–4 Note on a souterraine at Drumcliffe, Co. Sligo. *JRSAI* **16**, 483.

Armstrong, E.C.R. 1921–2 Irish bronze pins of the Christian period. *Archaeologia* **72**, 71–86.

Ashbee, P. 1990 A souterrain on Scilly? *Cornish Archaeology* **29**, 49–51.

Athy, M.L. 1913–14 Notes on the Ordnance Survey Letters (relating to the Barony of Dunkellin, Co. Galway. *JGAHS* **8**, 129–98.

Atkinson, G.M. 1866 Ogham cave at Dunloe, County of Kerry. *JRSAI* **8**, 523–4, pls 1 and 2.

Atkinson, R. 1901 *Ancient laws of Ireland,* vol. 5. Dublin.

Baillie, M.G.L. 1975 A horizontal mill of the eighth century A.D. at Drumard, Co. Derry. *UJA* (3rd series) **38**, 25–32.

Baillie, M.G.L. 1982 *Tree-ring dating and archaeology.* London.

Barclay, G. 1978–80 Newmill and the 'souterrains of Southern Pictland'. In T. Watkins, 'Excavation of a settlement and souterrain at Newmill, near Bankfoot, Perthshire'. *PSAS* **110**, 200–8.

Barry, E. 1890–1 On fifteen ogham inscriptions recently discovered at Ballyknock, in the Barony of Kinnatalloon, County of Cork. *JRSAI* **21**, 514–35.

Barry, T.B. 1981 Archaeological excavation at Dunbeg promontory fort, Co. Kerry, 1977. *PRIA* **81**C, 295–329.

Barry, T.B. 1988 Medieval moated sites in Ireland: some new conclusions on their chronology and function. In G. Mac Niocaill and P.F. Wallace (eds), *Keimelia — Studies in medieval archaeology and history in memory of Tom Delaney,* 525–35. Dublin.

Beauford, W. 1789 A memoir respecting the antiquities of the church of Killossy, in the County of Kildare; with some conjectures on the origin of the ancient Irish churches. *TRIA* **3**, 84–5.

Bennett, I. 1989 The settlement pattern of ringforts in County Wexford. *JRSAI* **119**, 50–61.

Berger, R. 1995 Radiocarbon dating of early medieval Irish monuments. *PRIA* **95**C, 159–74.

Berry, R.G. 1897–8 The royal residence of Rathmore of Moylinne. *UJA* (2nd series) **4**, 160–70, 241–55.

Berry, R.G. 1926–7 Report on the work carried out at Drumena. *Proc. Belfast Nat. Hist. Phil. Soc.,* 46–55.

Bigger, F.J. 1921–4 Souterrains: tumuli in County Louth opened and destroyed. *CLAJ* **5**, 63–4.

Bigger, F.J. and Fennell, W.J. 1896–7 Souterrain at Stranocum, Co. Antrim. *UJA* (2nd series) **3**, 202–3.

Bigger, F.J. and Fennell, W.J. 1897–8 Souterrain in the parish of Ardboe, Co. Tyrone. *UJA* (2nd series) **4**, 65–6.

Bigger, F.J. and Fennell, W.J. 1898–9 Ardtole souterrain, County Down. *UJA* (2nd series) **5**, 146–7.

Binchy, D.A. 1970 *Críth Gablach.* Medieval and Modern Irish Series XI. Dublin Institute for Advanced Studies.

Blanchet, A. 1923 *Les souterrains — refuges de la France.* Paris.

Bleakly, J. 1835 Ordnance Survey Memoirs. Box 39 [Co. Londonderry]; **I** (Dunboe Parish); Section **1**, **2**, **3**. Royal Irish Academy, Dublin.

Bleakly, J. 1837 Ordnance Survey Memoirs. Box 10 [Co. Antrim]; **IV** (Duneane Parish); Section **3**. Royal Irish Academy, Dublin.

BNFC 1874 *Guide to Belfast and the adjacent counties.* Belfast Naturalists' Field Club.

Bourke, C. 1980 Early Irish hand-bells. *JRSAI* **110**, 52–89.

Bourke, E. 1994 Glass vessels of the first nine centuries AD in Ireland. *JRSAI* **124**, 163–209.

Brady, N.D.K. 1987 A late ploughshare type from Ireland. *Tools and Tillage* **5**, 228–42.

Brady, N. 1983 An analysis of the spatial distribution of early historic settlement sites in the barony of Morgallion, County Meath. Unpublished dissertation, University College Dublin.

Brady, N. 1993 Reconstructing a medieval Irish plough. In *I Jornadas Internacionales sobre Technologia Agraria Tradicional,* 31–44. Museo Nacional del Pueblo Español, Madrid.

Brady, N. 1994 Labor and agriculture in early medieval Ireland: evidence from the sources. In A.J. Frantzen and D. Moffat (eds), *The work of work: servitude, slavery, and labor in medieval England,* 125–45. Glasgow.

Brannon, N.F. 1979 A small excavation in Turraloskin townland, County Antrim. *UJA* (3rd series) **42**, 86–7.

Brannon, N.F. 1981–2 A rescue excavation at Lisdoo Fort, Lisnaskea, Co. Fermanagh. *UJA* (3rd series) **44–5**, 53–9.

Brannon, N.F. 1982a Souterrain at Big Glebe, Co. Londonderry. Topographical Files, DOE.

Brannon, N.F. 1982b Souterrain at Moneylane, Co. Down. Topographical Files, DOE.

Brannon, N.F. 1982c Souterrain at Drumourne, Co. Antrim. Topographical Files, DOE.

Brannon, N.F. 1983 Souterrain at Ballyginny, Co. Down. Topographical Files, DOE.

Brannon, N.F. 1985 Souterrain at Ballytweedy, Co. Antrim. Topographical Files, DOE.

Brannon, N.F. 1988a Downpatrick. In S.M. Youngs, J. Clark, D.R.M. Gaimster and T. Barry (eds), 'Medieval Britain and Ireland in 1987'. *Medieval Archaeology* **32**, 295.

Brannon, N.F. 1988b Archaeological excavations at Cathedral Hill, Downpatrick, 1987. *Lecale Miscellany* **6**, 3–9.

Brannon, N.F. 1990 A souterrain in Spittle Quarter Townland, Co. Down. *Lecale Miscellany* **8**, 39–41.

Brannon, N.F. and Warner, R.B. 1978 Souterrain at Cloyfin South, Co. Londonderry. Topographical Files, DOE.

Brash, R.R. 1868 Proceedings: visit to Ballyquin and Windgap in the county of Waterford. *JRSAI* **10**, 348–9.

Brash, R.R. 1866–9a An account of the ogham chamber at Drumloghan, County of Waterford. *PRIA* **10**, 103–19.

Brash, R.R. 1866–9b An account of a souterrain discovered at Curraghely, near Kilcrea, Co. Cork. *PRIA* **10**, 72–4.

Brash, R.R. 1868–9c Proceedings: half erased cilleen, at Kilgravane, near Dungarvan. *JRSAI* **10**, 438–9.

Brash, R.R. 1870–9a On an ogham inscribed stone, at Kiltera, Co. Waterford. *PRIA* **15**, 5.

Brash, R.R. 1870–9b On an ogham-inscribed pillar-stone at Monataggart, County Cork. *PRIA* **15**, 172–5.

Brash, R.R. 1870–9c On two ogham-inscribed stones from Tinnahally, Co. Kerry. *PRIA* **15**, 186–9.

Brash, R.R. 1870–9d On an ogham-inscribed pillar-stone at Ballycrovane, Co. Cork. *PRIA* **15**, 198, 199.

Brash, R.R. 1872–3 The Dunbel ogham inscriptions. *JRSAI* **12**, 238–46.

Brash, R.R. 1879 *The ogham inscribed monuments of the Gaedhil in the British Islands.* London.

Bremer, W. 1926 A founder's hoard of the Copper Age at Carrickshedoge, Nash, Co. Wexford. *JRSAI* **56**, 88–91.

Brindley, A.L. 1986 *Archaeological inventory of County Monaghan.* Dublin.

Brindley, A. and Kilfeather, A. 1993 *Archaeological inventory of County Carlow.* Dublin.

Broderick, T. 1879–82 Cave in the townland of Greenville. *JRSAI* **15**, 637–8.

Browne, F.M. 1922 Footsteps of St Patrick: near the River Liffey. *Irish Messenger Series* **10**, 10–15.

Buckley, V.M. 1978 Uaimha na Ulaid: some research on the souterrains of Cos Antrim and Down. Unpublished BA thesis, QUB.

Buckley, V.M. 1986 Ulster and Oriel souterrains — an indicator of tribal areas? *UJA* (3rd series) **49**, 108–10.

Buckley, V.M. 1987 Souterrain at Borrismore, Co. Kilkenny. Topographical Files, OPW.

Buckley, V.M. 1988–9 Meath souterrains: some thoughts on Early Christian distribution patterns. *Ríocht na Midhe* **8** (2), 64–7.

Buckley, V.M. and O'Brien, K. 1985–6 A recently discovered souterrain at Carnmore townland, Co. Galway. *JGAHS* **40**, 139–42.

Buckley, V.M. and Sweetman, P.D. 1991 *Archaeological survey of County Louth.* Dublin.

Buckley, V.M., O'Brien, K. and Woodman, R. 1984 A recently discovered souterrain at Carnmore Td, Co. Galway. *Subterranea Britannica*, Bulletin No. 19, 18–19.

Buick, G.R. 1900–2 Report on the oghams recently discovered near Connor, Co. Antrim. *PRIA* **22**, 265.

Buxton, R.J. 1934–5 Earth-house at Portnacon, Sutherland. *PSAS* **69**, 431–3.

Byrne, F.J. 1968 Historical note on Cnogba (Knowth). In G. Eogan, 'Excavations at Knowth, Co. Meath, 1962–1965'. *PRIA* **66**C, 383–400.

Byrne, F.J. 1969 *The rise of Uí Néill and the high-kingship of Ireland.* Dublin.

Byrne, F.J. 1971 Tribes and tribalism in early Ireland. *Ériu* **22**, 128–66.

Byrne, F.J. 1973 *Irish kings and high-kings.* London.

Byrne, M.E. 1991 A report on the excavation of a cashel at Ballyegan, near Castleisland, Co. Kerry. *JKAHS* **24**, 5–31.

Cahill, M. 1977 Excavation of souterrain at Nevinstown, Co. Meath. Topographical Files, NMI.

Cahill, M. 1989 Skeleton in souterrain chamber: Kill, Co. Kerry. In I. Bennett (ed.), *Excavations 1988*, 21. Dublin.

Cahill, M. and Ryan, M. 1976 Souterrain at Allardstown, Co. Louth. Topographical Files, NMI.

Callanan, M. 1932 Report on excavation of souterrain at Graigue, Co. Tipperary. Topographical Files, NMI.

Campbell, K. 1979 Souterrain at Socks, Co. Leitrim. Topographical Files, NMI.

Campbell, K. 1986 Early Christian souterrain. In I. Bennett (ed.), *Excavations 1985*, Dublin.

Campbell, K. 1987 Souterrain (at Randalstown, Co. Meath). In I. Bennett (ed.), *Excavations 1986*, 31–2. Dublin.

Carmody, W.P. 1898–9 Notes on the discovery of two ogham stones in the parish of Connor, Co. Antrim. *UJA* (2nd series) **5**, 47–50.

Carroll, F. and Murphy, D. 1987 A second souterrain at Termonfeckin. *CLAJ* **21** (3), 287–9.

Casey, D. 1987 Souterrain at Carrigeencullia, Co. Kerry. Topographical Files, OPW.

Casey, M. 1993 Report on the archaeological excavation of Doonagappul promontory fort, Strake townland, Clare Island, Co. Mayo. In P. Gosling (ed.), *Royal Irish Academy New Survey of Clare Island 1991–1995*, Archaeological Section (1st Report), 53–66.

Casey, M. (n.d.) Souterrain at Conray, Co. Leitrim. Topographical Files, OPW.

Caulfield, R. 1847–50 On an inscription on a gravestone found in the ancient church of Keel, East Carbery, County Cork. *PRIA* 4, 387–8.

Caulfield, S. 1969 Some quernstones in private possession in Co. Kerry. *JKAHS* 2, 59–73.

Caulfield, S. 1977 The beehive quern in Ireland. *JRSAI* 107, 104–38.

Chadwick, B. 1976 Note on a Kerry souterrain. Topographical Files, NMI.

Chart, D.A. (ed.) 1940 *A preliminary survey of the ancient monuments of Northern Ireland.* Belfast.

Childe, V.G. 1932–3 Excavations at Castlelaw Fort, Midlothian. *PSAS* 67, 362–88.

Childe, V.G. 1935 *The prehistory of Scotland.* London.

Christie, P.M.L. 1978 The excavation of an Iron Age souterrain and settlement at Carn Euny, Sancreed, Cornwall. *PPS* 44, 309–433.

Christie, P.M. 1979 Cornish souterrains in the light of recent research. *Bulletin of the Institute of Archaeology* (University of London) 16, 187–213.

Clark, E. 1961 *Cornish fogous.* London.

Clark, E.V., Ford, E.B. and Thomas, C. 1957 The fogou of Lower Boscaswell, Cornwall. *PPS* 23, 213–19.

Clarke, J.P. 1961–4 Souterrain at Crossabeagh, Co. Louth. *CLAJ* 15, 255–61.

Clarke, J.P. 1963 Souterrains at Donaghmore, Co. Louth. Topographical Files, NMI.

Cleary, R.M. 1981a Three recently discovered souterrains in Co. Cork. *JCHAS* 86, 38–42.

Cleary, R.M. 1981b A souterrain at Froe Upper, Co. Cork. *JCHAS* 86, 100–2.

Cleary, R.M. 1986 Souterrains in the North Cork area. *Mallow Field Club Journal* 4, 144–8.

Cleary, R.M. 1987 Souterrains at Carrigeen and Boherascrub East, Co. Cork. *Mallow Field Club Journal* 5, 155–8.

Cleary, R.M. 1989 Souterrains in County Cork. Topographical Files, OPW.

Cleere, H. 1990 *Archaeology in Britain: report of the CBA.* Council for British Archaeology. London.

Clinton, M. 1993 Souterrain at Loughcrew, near Oldcastle, County Meath. *JRSAI* 123, 120–6.

Clinton, M. 1996 Two recently discovered souterrains in County Meath. *Ríocht na Midhe* 9 (2), 30–6.

Clinton, M. 1997 Porthole-slabs in souterrains in Ireland. *JRSAI* 127, 5–17.

Clinton, M. 1998 The souterrains of County Dublin. In C. Manning (ed.), *Dublin and beyond the Pale — studies in honour of Patrick Healy,* 117–28. Dublin.

Clinton, M. 2000a Settlement patterns in the early historic kingdom of Leinster (seventh to mid-twelfth century). In A.P. Smyth (ed.), *Seanchas: Studies in early and medieval Irish archaeology, history and literature in honour of Francis J. Byrne,* 275–98. Dublin.

Clinton, M. 2000b Settlement dynamics in Co. Meath: the kingdom of Lóegaire. *Peritia* 14, 372–405.

Clinton, M. (forthcoming a) Souterrains in potential association with church sites in County Meath. In T. Condit, C. Corlett and P.F. Wallace (eds), *Above and beyond: essays in memory of Leo Swan.* Bray.

Clinton, M. (forthcoming b) Souterrain report. In E. Gibbons, 'Excavation of a cashel at Ballynavenooragh, Co. Kerry'.

Clinton, M. and Gosling, P. 1979 [Souterrain at] Kane. In P. Gosling, 'Five Louth souterrains'. *CLAJ* **19** (3), 211–12.

Clinton, M. and Kelly, E.P. (forthcoming) A souterrain and clochauns, Ballynahow, Co. Kerry. *NMAJ*.

Clinton, M. and Manning, C. 2000 A second souterrain in the townland of Newrath Big, Co. Meath. *Ríocht na Midhe* **11**, 51–7.

Clinton, M. and Stout, M. 1997 Two souterrains and an enclosure at Killally, Co. Louth. *CLAJ* **24** (1), 129–34.

Cochrane, R. and McNeill, Mr 1898 The souterrain at Killala. *JRSAI* **28**, 291–3.

Cody, E. 1989 An archaeological survey of the Barony of Athenry, Co Galway. Unpublished MA thesis, UCG.

Cody, P. 1849–51 Primaeval remains in the Mullinavat district. *JRSAI* **1**, 385–8.

Coffey, G. 1912 *New Grange (Brugh na Boinne) and other incised tumuli in Ireland.* Dublin.

Coffey, G. and Jamison, H.L. 1897 Fort and souterrain at Shancoduff, Co. Monaghan. *UJA* (2nd series) **3**, 275–6.

Coleman, J.C. 1945 Souterrain near Bealnamorrive, Co. Cork. *JRSAI* **75**, 112–14.

Coleman, J.C. 1947–8 Some souterrains in County Cork. *JCHAS* **52–3**, 69–73.

Colhoun, M.R. 1946 Ballylin, Malin, Co. Donegal. *UJA* (3rd series) **9**, 84–6.

Collins, A.E.P. 1960 A souterrain at Tobergill, Co. Antrim. *UJA* (3rd series) **23**, 80–1.

Collins, A.E.P. 1964 Toberdoney souterrain, Co. Down. *UJA* (3rd series) **27**, 129.

Collins, A.E.P. 1968 Settlement in Ulster, 0–1100 A.D. *UJA* (3rd series) **31**, 53–8.

Collins, A.E.P. 1976 Three souterrains in County Antrim. *UJA* (3rd Series) **39**, 13–14.

Collins, A.E.P. and Harper, A.E.T. 1974 Souterrain at Carrickrovaddy, Co. Down. Topographical Files, DOE.

Connolly, M. 1992 An iron sickle from a previously unrecorded souterrain at Beaufort, Co. Kerry. *JKAHS* **25**, 20–36.

Connolly, M. 1994 Emlagh West: souterrains. In I. Bennett (ed.), *Excavations 1993,* Site 122. Bray.

Connor, J. 1987 Souterrain at Carrowjames, Co. Mayo. Topographical Files, NMI.

Conroy, G. 1995a Souterrain at Ishlaun, Co. Roscommon. Topographical Files, OPW.

Conroy, G. 1995b Souterrain at Kiltybranks, Co. Roscommon. Topographical Files, OPW.

Conroy, G. 1995c Souterrain at Lisduff, Co. Roscommon. Topographical Files, OPW.

Cooke, I. McN. 1993 *Mother and sun: the Cornish fogou.* Penzance.

Cooke, J. 1906–7 Antiquarian remains in the Beaufort district, County Kerry. *PRIA* **26**, 1–14.

Cooke, T.L. 1849–51 On some subterraneous chambers in the County of Clare. *JRSAI* **1**, 294–8.

Corcoran, J.X.W.P. 1967–8 The souterrain at Rosal, Strath Naver, Sutherland. *PSAS* **100**, 114–18.

Corcoran, P. 1929–32 Townland survey of Co. Louth: Dunbin. *CLAJ* **7**, 499.

Corlett, C. 1995 Souterrain at Cuillawinnia, Co. Roscommon. Topographical Files, OPW.

Costello, T.B. 1902 Tuam raths and souterrains. *JGAHS* **2** (2), 109–15.

Costello, T.B. 1903–4 Tuam raths and souterrains. *JGAHS* **3** (1), 1–9.

Craw, J.H. 1930–1 An underground building at Midhouse, Orkney. *PSAS* **65**, 357–9.

Crawford, H.S. 1922 The sepulchral slab and round tower at Meelick, Co. Mayo. *JRSAI* **52**, 179–81.

Creedon, T. 1977 Souterrain at Cloghane, Co. Kerry. Topographical Files, NMI.

Cuppage, J. 1986 *Corca Dhuibhne: Dingle Peninsula archaeological survey.* Ballyferriter.

Curle, A.O. 1934–5 An account of the excavation, on behalf of H.M. Office of Works, of another prehistoric dwelling (No. V) at Jarlshof, Sumburgh, Shetland, in the summer of 1934. *PSAS* **69**, 85–107.

Curle, A.O. 1935–6 Account of the excavation of a hut-circle with an associated earth-house at Jarlshof, Sumburgh, Shetland. *PSAS* **70**, 238, 241.

Danaher, P. 1964 Souterrain at Duneel, Co. Westmeath. Topographical Files, NMI.

Danaher, P. 1967 Souterrain at Bocks Upper, Co. Monaghan. Topographical Files, OPW.

Darby, M. 1899–1902 The Core-ally. *JKAS* **3**, 191–2.

Davies, O. 1937–40 Excavations at Corliss Fort. *CLAJ* **9**, 338–43.

Davies, O. 1939 A. Mahr; new aspects and problems in Irish prehistory — a review. *UJA* (3rd series) **2**, 126.

Davies, O. 1940 Ballymagrorty Irish, Co. Donegal. Topographical Files, NMI.

Davies, O. 1946 Souterrain at Cavangarden, Co. Donegal. Topographical Files, NMI.

Davison, B.K. 1964 Recent investigations of souterrains: three souterrains at Downview Park West, Belfast. *UJA* (3rd series) **27**, 124–8.

Day, A. and McWilliams, P. 1990 *Ordnance Survey Memoirs of Ireland. Vol. 3: Parishes of County Down I: 1834–6.* Belfast.

Day, A. and McWilliams, P. 1992a *Ordnance Survey Memoirs of Ireland. Vol. 12: Parishes of County Down III: 1833–8.* Belfast.

Day, A. and McWilliams, P. 1992b *Ordnance Survey Memoirs of Ireland. Vol. 16: Parishes of County Antrim V: 1830–8.* Belfast.

Day, A. and McWilliams, P. 1995 *Ordnance Survey Memoirs of Ireland. Vol. 28: Parishes of County Londonderry IX: 1832–8. W. Londonderry.* Belfast.

Deady, J. 1972 A souterrain at Ballysheen, Abbeydorney. *JKAHS* **5**, 160–1.

Deane, T. 1887 *Appendix to the 55th report of the Commissioners of Public Works in Ireland, 1886–87.* Dublin.

Deane, T.N. 1887–91 On some ancient monuments, scheduled under Sir John Lubbock's Act 1882. *PRIA* **17**, 161–2.

Deane, T.N. 1893–6 A report on ancient monuments in Co. Kerry. *PRIA* **19**, 100–7.

de Paor, L. 1955 A survey of Sceilg Mhichíl. *JRSAI* **85**, 174–87.

de Paor, M. and de Paor, L. 1958 *Early Christian Ireland.* London.

de Valera, R. (ed.) 1979 *Antiquities of the Irish countryside,* by S.P. Ó Ríordáin (5th edn). London.

Diver, J. 1956 Souterrain at Killinangel More, Co. Donegal. Topographical Files, NMI.

Doherty, C. 1980 Exchange and trade in early medieval Ireland. *JRSAI* **110**, 67–89.

Dolley, M. 1969 The Anglo-Saxon pennies from the 'Upper Souterrain' at Knowth. *British Numismatic Journal* **38**, 16–21.

Donovan, D. 1876 *Sketches in Carbery County Cork, its antiquities, history, legends and topography.* Dublin.

Duignan, M. 1944a Irish agriculture in early historic times. *JRSAI* **74**, 124–45.

Duignan, M. 1944b Souterrain at Ardbraccan, Co. Meath. *JRSAI* **74**, 224.

Dunlevy, M. 1967 A souterrain at the rock of Doorin, Co. Donegal. *Donegal Annual* **7** (2), 229–32. [Plan in *Donegal Annual* **7** (3) (1968), opp. p.322.]

Dunlevy, M. 1988 A classification of early Irish combs. *PRIA* **88**C, 341–422.

Dunne, N. 1995 Souterrain at Castlesampson, Co. Roscommon. Topographical Files, OPW.

Dunne, N., Gosling, P. and Ronayne, B. 1973–6 The Stickillin souterrain(s). *CLAJ* **18**, 272–8.

Du Noyer, G.V. 1857–61 Description of drawings of Irish antiquities presented by him. *PRIA* 7, 249–62.

Du Noyer, G.V. 1858 On the remains of ancient stone-built fortresses and habitations occurring to the west of Dingle, County Kerry. *Arch. J.* 15, 1–24.

Durnford, E.W. 1835 Ordnance Survey Memoirs. Box 27 [Co. Fermanagh]: IV (Killesher Parish); Section 1, 27, 28. Royal Irish Academy, Dublin.

Eames, E.S. and Fanning, T. 1988 *Irish medieval tiles.* Dublin.

Edwards, N. 1990 *The archaeology of early medieval Ireland.* London.

English, N.W. 1971 Cave dwelling at the Doon in King's County. Topographical Files, NMI.

Eogan, G. 1965 *Catalogue of Irish bronze swords.* Dublin.

Eogan, G. 1968 Excavations at Knowth, Co. Meath, 1962–65. *PRIA* 66C, 299–382.

Eogan, G. 1974 Report on the excavation of some passage graves, unprotected inhumation burials and a settlement site at Knowth, Co. Meath. *PRIA* 74C, 11–112.

Eogan, G. 1977 The Iron Age–Early Christian settlement at Knowth, Co. Meath, Ireland. In Vladimir Markotic (ed.), *Ancient Europe and the Mediterranean. Studies presented in honour of Hugh Hencken,* 68–76. Warminster.

Eogan, G. 1986 *Knowth and the passage-tombs of Ireland.* London.

Eogan, G. 1990 Ballynee souterrains, County Meath. *JRSAI* 120, 41–64.

Eogan, G. 1991 Prehistoric and early historic culture change at Brugh na Bóinne. *PRIA* 91C, 105–32.

Eogan, G. and Bradley, J. 1977 A souterrain at Balrenny, near Slane, County Meath. *JRSAI* 107, 96–103.

Evans, E.E. 1944 Excavations at Ballyhornan, Co. Down. *UJA* (3rd series) 7, 102–4.

Evans, E.E. 1946 Newly discovered souterrains. *UJA* (3rd series) 9, 80–2.

Evans, E.E. 1950 Rath and souterrain at Shaneen Park, Belfast, townland of Ballyaghagan, Co. Antrim. *UJA* (3rd series) 13, 6–27.

Evans, E.E. 1958 *Irish heritage: the landscape, the people and their work.* London.

Evans, E.E. 1966 *Prehistoric and Early Christian Ireland: a guide.* London.

Fagan, T. 1838a Ordnance Survey Memoirs. Box 5: [Co. Antrim]: I (Parish of Billy); Section 5; 35. Royal Irish Academy, Dublin.

Fagan, T. 1838b Ordnance Survey Memoirs. Box 10: [Co. Antrim]: V (Parish of Dunluce); Section 4, 15 and Section 3, 11. Royal Irish Academy, Dublin.

Fagan, T. 1839 Ordnance Survey Memoirs. Box 4: [Co. Antrim]: II (Parish of Ballynure); Section 3; 26–28; 32. Royal Irish Academy, Dublin.

Fahy, E.M. 1953 A souterrain at Ballyarra, Co. Cork. *JCHAS* 58, 55–9.

Fahy, E.M. 1954 Ringfort and souterrain at Ballysallagh, Co. Waterford. Topographical Files, NMI.

Fahy, E.M. 1960 A souterrain at Lisheen, Co. Cork. *JCHAS* 65, 142–3.

Fahy, E.M. 1970 Souterrains on lands of Mr F. Hayes: Little Island: Co Cork. Topographical Files, NMI.

Fahy, E.M. 1972 A souterrain at Brulea near Glandore. Topographical Files, NMI.

Falkiner, W. 1898–1900 Notes upon a rath souterrain at Gurteen, Gainstown, County Westmeath. *PRIA* 21, 211–15.

Fanning, T. 1969 The bronze ringed pins in the Limerick City Museum. *NMAJ* 12, 6–11.

Fanning, T. 1976 Excavations at Clontuskert Priory, Co. Galway. *PRIA* 76C, 97–169.

Fanning, T. 1983 Some aspects of the bronze ringed pin in Scotland. In A. O'Connor and D.V. Clarke (eds), *From the Stone Age to the 'Forty-five — studies presented to R.B.K.*

Stevenson, 324–42. Edinburgh.

Fanning, T. 1988 Three ringed pins from Viking Dublin and their significance. In J. Bradley (ed.), *Settlement and society in medieval Ireland — studies presented to F.X. Martin OSA*, 161–75. Kilkenny.

Fanning, T. 1994 *Viking Age ringed pins from Dublin*. Dublin.

Feehan, J. 1979 *The landscape of Slieve Bloom*. Dublin.

Feeley, E. 1990–1 Early Christian and Anglo-Norman settlement in the townland of Baltrasna, Ashbourne, Co. Meath. *Ríocht na Midhe* **8** (3), 151–3.

Fennell, W.J. 1896 Souterrain in the grange of Muckamore. *UJA* (2nd series) **2** (4), 272–3.

Ferguson, S. 1864–6 Account of ogham inscriptions, in the cave at Rathcroghan, County of Roscommon. *PRIA* **9**, 160–70.

Ferguson, S. 1870–9a On the difficulties attendant on the transcription of ogham legends and the means of removing them. *PRIA* **15**, 30–64.

Ferguson, S. 1870–9b On some evidence touching the age of rath-caves. *PRIA* **15**, 129–36.

Ferguson, S. 1870–9c On further ogham inscriptions discovered at Monataggart, Co. Cork. *PRIA* **15**, 292–4.

Ferguson, S. 1877–86 Fasciculus of prints from photographs of casts of ogham inscriptions. *TRIA* **27**, 47–56.

Ferguson, S. 1887 *Ogham inscriptions in Ireland, Wales and Scotland*. Edinburgh.

Fitzgerald, E. 1858 *Vestiges and relics of remarkable Irishmen in the vicinity of Youghal, of the primeval or pagan period*. Cork.

Fitzgerald, W. 1899–1902 Three disused townland names in the south of the County Kildare. *JKAS* **3**, 132–3.

Fitzgerald, W. 1903–5 Timolin. *JKAS* **4**, 166–7.

Fitzgerald, W. 1930 Souterrain at Ballygarrane, Co. Tipperary. Topographical Files, OPW.

Fitzpatrick, M. 1990 Excavation report from Graigue, Co. Galway. Topographical Files, OPW.

Fitzpatrick, M. 1991 Graigue, Loughrea. In B.S. Nenk, S. Margeson and M. Hurley (eds), 'Medieval Britain and Ireland in 1990'. *Medieval Archaeology* **35**, 209.

Fogg, T. 1989 Souterrain at Ballyhemlin, Co. Antrim. Topographical Files, DOE.

Foot, C.H. 1860–1 An account of the exploration of a remarkable series of subterranean chambers situated on the estate of Robert J.E. Mooney, Esq., J.P., The Doon, Townland of Doon, Parish of Lis, Barony of Garrycastle, King's County. *JRSAI* **6**, 222–9.

Forbes, W. (n.d.) Souterrain at Farranaharpy, Co. Sligo. Topographical Files, OPW.

Forsayeth, G.W. 1911 Souterrain at Cragg. *J. Wat. S.E. Ire. Arch. Soc.* **14**, 140–1.

Forsayeth, G.W. 1913 Souterrain at Craggs. *JRSAI* **43**, 176–7.

Frith, R.H. 1974 Memoranda of recent operations at Dowth. In M. Herity, *Irish passage graves*, 247–50. Dublin.

Gaffikin, M. 1938 Souterrain at Ardglass, County Down. *UJA* (3rd series) **1**, 94–5.

Gailey, A. 1970 Irish corn-drying kilns. In D. McCourt and A. Gailey (eds), *Studies in folklife presented to Emyr Estyn Evans*, 52–71. Belfast.

Gerriets, M. 1985 Money among the Irish: coin hoards in Viking Age Ireland. *JRSAI* **115**, 121–39.

Gibbons, E. (forthcoming) Excavation of a cashel at Ballynavenooragh, Co. Kerry.

Gillman, H.F.W. 1896a Souterrain at Deelish, County Cork. *JCHAS* (2nd series) **2**, 153–7.

Gillman, H.F.W. 1896b The problem of the souterrains: 1. Some in County Cork described. *JCHAS* (2nd series) **2**, 417–22.

Gillman, H.F.W. 1897 The problem of the souterrains. *JCHAS* (2nd series) **3**, 1–7.

Giot, P.R. 1960 Les souterrains Armoricains de l'âge du fer. *Annales de Bretagne* **67**, 45–65.

Giot, P.R. and Ducouret, J.P. 1968 Le souterrain de l'âge du fer de Kervéo en Plomelin (Finistère). *Annales de Bretagne* **75**, 101–16

Giot, P.R. 1971 The impact of radiocarbon dating on the establishment of the prehistoric chronology of Brittany. *PPS* (new series) **37**, Part 2, 208–17.

Giot, P.R. 1973 Les souterrains Armoricains de l'âge du fer. *Les Dossiers de l'archéologie, Document Archéologia* no. 2, 48–58.

Giot, P.R. 1990 Souterrains en habitats à l'âge du fer en Armorique. *Revue Archéologie Ouest.* Supplément **3**, 53–61.

Giot, P.R. and Lecerf, Y. 1971a Fouille d'un souterrain de l'âge du fer près de Lamphily en Concarneau (Finistère). *Annales de Bretagne* **78**, 125–37.

Giot, P.R. and Lecerf, Y. 1971b Fouille d'un souterrain de l'âge du fer près de Litiez a la Feuillée (Finistère). *Annales de Bretagne* **78**, 149–60.

Giot, P.R. and Le Roux, C.T. 1971 Le souterrain de l'âge du fer de Keravel en Plouguerneau (Finistère). *Annales de Bretagne* **78**, 139–47.

Giot, P.R., Le Roux, C.T., Lecerf, Y. and Lecornec, J. 1976 *Souterrains Armoricains de L'Age du Fer.* Rennes.

Glasscock, R.E. 1969–75 Two raths in Coyne townland, Co. Westmeath. *Journal of the Old Athlone Society* **1**, 230–1.

Gleeson, C. 1991 The promontory forts of Co. Clare. *The Other Clare* **15**, 57–60.

Glob, P.V. 1971 *Danish prehistoric monuments.* London.

Gogan, L.S. 1929 Currycrowley souterrain, Ballineen. *JCHAS* **34**, 1–7.

Gogan, L.S. 1930 Large souterrain explored in Co. Cork. Topographical Files, NMI.

Gorham, A. 1914–16 An interesting 'fort'. *Kerry Archaeological Magazine* **3**, 12–19.

Gosling, P. 1977 Souterrain, Glaspistol townland, Co. Louth. *CLAJ* **19** (1), 17–19.

Gosling, P. 1979 Five Louth souterrains. *CLAJ* **19** (3), 206–17.

Gosling, P. 1981 Topographical notes. In H. Roe, *Monasterboice and its monuments,* 74–8. Longford.

Gosling, P. 1991 From Dún Delca to Dundalk: the topography and archaeology of a medieval frontier town, A.D. *c.* 1187–1700. *CLAJ* **22** (3), 227–353.

Gosling, P. *et al.* (forthcoming) *Archaeological inventory of County Galway: Vol. 3 — South Galway.* Dublin.

Gowen, M. 1989 Early Christian settlement (?) with souterrains. In I. Bennett (ed.), *Excavations 1988,* 34–5. Dublin.

Gowen, M. 1992 Excavation of two souterrain complexes at Marshes Upper, Dundalk, Co. Louth. *PRIA* **92**C, 55–121.

Graham, B. 1980 The mottes of the Norman Liberty of Meath. In H. Murtagh (ed.), *Irish midland studies — essays in commemoration of N.W. English,* 39–56. Athlone.

Graham-Campbell, J. 1987 From Scandinavia to the Irish Sea: Viking art reviewed. In M. Ryan (ed.), *Ireland and Insular art AD 500–1200,* 144–52. Dublin.

Graves, C. 1847–50a On the ogham character. *PRIA* **4**, 173–80.

Graves, C. 1847–50b An account of the discovery of ogham stones presented by Mr Richard Hitchcock. *PRIA* **4**, 271–2.

Graves, C. 1864–74 On a previously undescribed class of monuments. *TRIA* **24**, 421–31.

Graves, C. 1884 Remarks on an ogam monument, with some introductory remarks thereon by Sir S. Ferguson. *PRIA* **16**, 279–82.

Graves, C. 1885–6 Note on the ogam cave at Dunloe. *JRSAI* 17, 605–7.

Graves, C. 1895 On an ogam inscription lately discovered near Gortatlea, Co. Kerry. *JRSAI* 25, 1–4.

Graves, J. 1870–1 Rath souterrain near Ardfinnan, County of Tipperary. *JRSAI* 11, 207–8.

Graves, J. 1883–4 Note of excursions to Muckross Abbey and Inisfallen; Ardfert and Barrown-Eanach; Aghadoe and Dunloe. *JRSAI* 16, 312–13.

Gray, W. 1894 Notes on some County Down souterrains. *JRSAI* 24, 45–6.

Grogan, E. and Kilfeather, A. 1997 *Archaeological inventory of County Wicklow.* Dublin.

Grose, F. 1791 *The antiquities of Ireland,* vol. 1. London.

Haigh, D.H. 1858–9 Cryptic inscriptions on the cross at Hackness, in Yorkshire. *JRSAI* 5, 170–94.

Halpin, E. 1989 Dromiskin: souterrains, later features. In I. Bennett (ed.), *Excavations 1988,* 27–8. Dublin.

Hamilton, G.A. 1845–7 On a north house, in the demesne of Hampton, and the opening of a tumulus near Knockingen. *PRIA* 3, 249–51.

Hamlin, A.E. 1976 The archaeology of early Christianity in the north of Ireland. Unpublished Ph.D thesis, QUB.

Hamlin, A. 1982 *Historical monuments of Northern Ireland.* Belfast.

Hamlin, A. 1985 The archaeology of the Irish church in the eighth century. *Peritia* 4, 279–99.

Hansard, J. 1870 *The history, topography and antiquities of the County and City of Waterford.* Dungarvan.

Harbison, P. 1970 *Guide to the national monuments in the Republic of Ireland.* Dublin.

Harden, D.B. 1956 Glass vessels in Britain and Ireland, A.D. 400–1000. In D.B. Harden (ed.), *Dark Age Britain: studies presented to E.T. Leeds,* 132–67. London.

Harper, A.E.T. 1972 A souterrain at Cloughorr, Co. Antrim. *UJA* (3rd series) 35, 59–61.

Harris, W. and Smith, C. 1744 *The antient and present state of the County of Down.* Dublin.

Hartnett, P. 1939 A survey of the antiquities in the barony of East Muskerry. Unpublished MA thesis, UCC.

Hartnett, P.J. 1952 Souterrain at Balrathboyne Glebe, Co. Meath. Topographical files, NMI.

Hatt, G. 1937 Dwelling-houses in Jutland in the Iron Age. *Antiquity* 11, 162–73.

Hayward, R. 1968 *The Corrib country.* Dundalk.

Healy, W. 1890–1 The rath at Borrismore. *JRSAI* 21, 490.

Hencken, H. O'N. 1932 *The archaeology of Cornwall and Scilly.* London.

Hencken, H. O'N. 1938 Cahercommaun: a stone fort in County Clare. *JRSAI*, extra volume.

Henderson, I. 1967 *The Picts.* London.

Henebry, R. 1910–11 An ogham inscribed stone in University College Cork. *Journal of the Ivernian Society* 3, 73–81.

Hennessy, W.M. (ed.) 1871 *The Annals of Loch Cé,* vol. 1. London.

Henry, F. 1957 Early monasteries, beehive huts, and dry-stone houses in the neighbourhood of Caherciveen and Waterville, Co. Kerry. *PRIA* 58C, 45–166.

Herity, M. 1971 *Glencolumbkille: a guide to 5,000 years of history in stone.* Togra Ghleanncholmcille Teoranta.

Herity, M. 1974 *Irish passage graves.* Dublin.

Herity, M. 1987 A survey of the royal site of Cruachain in Connacht: III. Ringforts and ecclesiastical sites. *JRSAI* 117, 125–41.

Herity, M. 1993 Motes and mounds at royal sites in Ireland. *JRSAI* **123**, 127–51.

Herity, M. and Eogan, G. 1977 *Ireland in prehistory*. London.

Herity, M., Kelly, D. and Mattenberger, U. 1997 List of Early Christian cross slabs in seven north-western counties. *JRSAI* **127**, 80–124.

Hickey, E. and Rynne, E. 1953 Two souterrains on the lower slopes of Tara. *JKAS* **13** (4), 220–2.

Hitchcock, R. 1853–7 On an inscription in the ogham character. *PRIA* **6**, 439–41.

Hobson, M. 1909 Some Ulster souterrains. *Journal of the Anthropological Institute* **39**, 220–7.

Hogan, E. 1910 *Onomasticon Goedelicum*. Dublin/London.

Holm, P. 1986 The slave trade of Dublin, ninth to twelfth centuries. *Peritia* **5**, 317–45.

Hunter, J. 1972–4 Excavation at Ardeer, Ayrshire. *PSAS* **105**, 296–301.

Hurley, M.F. 1981–2 Garryntemple, Grange, Co. Tipperary. In R.M. Cleary, M.F. Hurley and E.A. Twohig (eds), *Archaeological excavations on the Cork–Dublin gas pipeline*, 65–70. Cork.

Hurley, V. 1984 Cashel, houses and souterrain at Kilcashel, Co. Mayo. Topographical Files, OPW.

Jackson, J.S. 1968 Bronze Age copper mines on Mount Gabriel, west County Cork, Ireland. *Archaeologia Austriaca* **43**, 92–114.

Jackson, K.H. 1950 Notes on the ogham inscriptions of southern Britain. In C. Fox and B. Dickens (eds), *The early cultures of north-west Europe*, 197–213. London.

Jackson, K.H. 1955 The Pictish language. In F.T. Wainwright (ed.), *The problem of the Picts*, 129–60. Edinburgh.

Jervise, A. 1861–2 An account of the excavation of the round or 'bee-hive' shaped house, and other underground chambers, at West Grange of Conan, Forfarshire. *PSAS* **4**, 492–8.

Jope, E.M. 1950 A souterrain at Harryville, Ballymena, Co. Antrim. *UJA* (3rd series) **13**, 53.

Jope, E.M. 1966 *An archaeological survey of County Down*. Belfast.

J.W.H. 1853 The Anglo-Norman families of Lecale (in the County of Down). *UJA* (1st series) **1**, 92–100.

Kavanagh, R. 1976 Collared and Cordoned Cinerary Urns in Ireland. *PRIA* **76C**, 293–403.

Kealy, P. and Ryan, J. 1973 Souterrain at Garryvonne, Co. Waterford. *Old Kilkenny Review* **25**, 65–7.

Keenan, T.M. 1945–8 Townland survey of County Louth: twld of Monasterboice. *CLAJ* **11**, 52–7.

Kelly, E.P. 1977 Enclosure with three souterrains at Ballybarrack, Co. Louth. Topographical Files, NMI.

Kelly, E.P. 1978 Souterrain at Sarsfieldstown, Co. Meath. Topographical Files, NMI.

Kelly, E.P. 1982–3a A souterrain at Knockmant, Co. Westmeath. *Ríocht na Midhe* **7** (2), 114–18.

Kelly, E.P. 1982–3b Three Kerry souterrains. *JKAHS* **15–16**, 5–14.

Kelly, E.P. 1986 Ringed pins of County Louth. *CLAJ* **21** (2), 179–99.

Kenny, M. 1987 The geographical distribution of Irish Viking-Age coin hoards. *PRIA* **87C**, 507–27.

Killanin, Lord and Duignan, M.V. 1967 *The Shell guide to Ireland* (2nd edn). London.

Kinahan, G.H. 1883–4a Luscas in raths. *JRSAI* **16**, 11–14.

Kinahan, G.H. 1883–4b Report on some megalithic structures, Co. Donegal. *JRSAI* **16**, 434–6.

Kirker, S.K. 1905a Souterrain at Slidderyford, near Dundrum, Co. Down. *JRSAI* **35**, 266–8.

Kirker, S.K. 1905b Souterrain at Markstown, County Antrim. *JRSAI* **35**, 269–71.

Kirwan, E.M. 1985 The ogham stones at Drumlohan, reconsidered. *Decies: Journal of the Old Waterford Society* **28**, 6–12.

Kirwan, E.M. 1987 Drumlohan: a survey of its antiquities. *Decies: Journal of the Old Waterford Society* **35**, 33–40.

Kjaerum, P. 1960 Stensatte Jernalder-Kaeldre 1 Vendsyssel. *KUML* (1960), 62–89.

Knox, H.T. 1916 Carnfree and Carnabreckna, Co. Roscommon. *JGAHS* **9** (2), 74–7.

Knox, H.T. 1917–18 Caher and rath caves of Galway and Meath. *JGAHS* **10**, 1–45.

Knox, H.T. and Redington, M. 1915–16 Some rath-caves in and near the Barony of Dunkellin. *JGAHS* **9** (Parts iii and iv), 178–90.

Lacy, B. 1983 *Archaeological survey of County Donegal.* Lifford.

Lane-Fox, A. 1867 Roovesmore Fort and stones inscribed with oghams, in the parish of Aglish, County Cork. *Arch. J.* **24**, 123–39.

Langtry, G. 1870–1 The following notice of the Church of Killeena and the 'Goban Saer's Cave' in Co. Antrim. *JRSAI* **11**, 571–4.

Lanyon, J. 1858 Subterranean chambers at Connor, County of Antrim. *UJA* (1st series) **6**, 97–100.

Lavelle, D., Crumlish, R., Gallagher, B., Jones, J. and Moran, B. 1994 *An archaeological survey of Ballinrobe and district (including Lough Mask and Lough Carra).* Castlebar.

Lawless, C. 1987 Souterrain at Rockfield, Co. Mayo. Topographical Files, OPW.

Lawlor, H.C. 1915–16 Some notes on the investigation of dwelling places of prehistoric man in N.E. Ireland. *Proc. Belfast Nat. Hist. Phil. Soc.,* 31–61.

Lawlor, H.C. 1916–18 Prehistoric dwelling-places. *Proc. Belfast Nat. Hist. Phil. Soc.,* 77–103.

Lawlor, H.C. 1918–19 Ballymartin church ruins, and the rath of Dreen. *Proc. Belfast Nat. Hist. Phil. Soc.,* 1–9.

Lawlor, H.C. 1918–20 Some investigations on the souterrain. *PRIA* **35**, 214–17.

Leask, H.G. 1941–4 Souterrain at Mullameelan, Ardee. *CLAJ* **10**, 70–1.

Leask, H.G. 1955 *Irish churches and monastic buildings.* Dundalk.

Lecornec, J. 1970 Le souterrain de l'âge du fer de Kermeno à Grandchamp (Morbihan). *Annales de Bretagne* **77**, 57–71.

Le Creurer, R.P.R. and Giot, P.R. 1970 Les souterrains de l'âge du fer du Rocher-Martin en St. Brieuc (Côtes du Nord). *Annales de Bretagne* **77**, 73–94.

Lee, P.G. 1911 Notes on the ogham chamber at Knock-shan-a-wee. *JCHAS* **17**, 59–62.

Lee, P.G. 1932 Some notes on the districts of Killavullen, Ballyhooly and Glanworth. *JCHAS* **37**, 24–5.

Lefroy, J.H. 1870–1 On a bronze object bearing a runic inscription, found at Greenmount, Castle-Bellingham, Co. Louth. *JRSAI* **11**, 471–502.

Lennon, A.-M. 1994 Summary report on excavation of ringfort, Raheens, No. 2, near Carrigaline, Co. Cork. *JCHAS* **99**, 47–65.

Le Roux, C.T. and Lecerf, Y. 1971 Fouille d'un souterrain de l'âge du fer à Kermoysan en Plabennec (Finistère). *Annales de Bretagne* **78**, 161–7.

Le Roux, C.T. and Lecerf, Y. 1973 Le souterrain de lâge du fer de la Motte en Sizun (Finistère). *Annales de Bretagne* **80**, 79–87.

Lewis, S. 1837 *Topographical dictionary of Ireland* (2 vols). London.

Ligar, C.W. 1833 Ordnance Survey Memoirs. Box 39: [Londonderry XI]: 1 (parish of Dunboe); Section 2. Royal Irish Academy, Dublin.

Lillis, J.K. 1935 Antiquities in Clongulane, Co. Clare. Topographical Files, NMI.

Lindsay, A.W. 1934–5 The Dunalis souterrain and ogham stone. *Proc. Belfast Nat. Hist. Phil. Soc.*, 61–70.

Lionard, P. 1960–1 Early Irish grave slabs. *PRIA* **61**C, 95–169.

Lorenz, C. 1973 Les souterrains: études récentes et essai de classification. In *Les Dossiers de l'Archéologie, Document Archéologia*, no. 2, 14–35.

Lucas, A.T. 1953 The horizontal mill in Ireland. *JRSAI* **83**, 1–36.

Lucas, A.T. 1958 Cattle in ancient and medieval Irish society. *O'Connell School Union Record 1937–1958,* 1–11. Dublin.

Lucas, A.T. 1967 The plundering and burning of churches in Ireland, seventh to sixteenth centuries. In E. Rynne (ed.), *North Munster studies: essays in commemoration of Monsignor Michael Moloney,* 172–229. Limerick.

Lucas, A.T. 1971–3 Souterrains: the literary evidence. *Béaloideas* **39–41**, 165–91.

Lucas, A.T. 1989 *Cattle in ancient Ireland.* Kilkenny.

Lund, J. 1978a I en Kaelder. *SKALK* **1**, 3–10.

Lund, J. 1978b Allerdybest Nede. *SKALK* **6**, 10–13.

Lynch, P.J. 1894 Discovery of an ogham-stone in County Kerry. *JRSAI* **24**, 291–2.

Lynch, P.J. 1902 Some of the antiquities around Ballinskelligs Bay, County Kerry. *JRSAI* **32**, 321–52.

Lynn, C.J. 1975 Ballywee: ringfort. In T.G. Delaney (ed.), *Excavations 1974,* 4–6. Belfast.

Lynn, C.J. 1977 Souterrain at Ballyboley, Co. Antrim. Topographical Files, DOE.

Lynn, C.J. 1978 Early Christian period domestic structures: a change from round to rectangular plans? *Irish Archaeological Research Forum* **5**, 29–45.

Lynn, C.J. 1979 A destroyed souterrain on Bonfire Hill, Ballyhornan, Co. Down. *UJA* (3rd series) **42**, 88–90.

Lynn, C.J. 1981–2 The excavation of Rathmullan, a raised rath and motte in County Down. *UJA* (3rd series) **44 & 45**, 65–171.

Lynn, C.J. 1985a Deer Park Farms, Co. Antrim: preliminary excavation report. Topographical Files, DOE.

Lynn, C.J. 1985b The excavation of Rathmullan, County Down: Addenda'. *UJA* (3rd series) **48**, 130–1.

Lynn, C.J. 1989 Deer Park Farms; a visit to an Early Christian settlement. *Current Archaeology* **113**, 193–8.

Lynn, C.J. and Warner, R. 1977 Souterrain at Ballytrustan, Co. Down. Topographical Files, DOE.

Mac Airt, S. (ed.) 1951 *The Annals of Inisfallen.* Dublin.

Mac Airt, S. and Mac Niocaill, G. (eds) 1983 *The Annals of Ulster.* Dublin.

Macalister, R.A.S. 1896–1901 On an ancient settlement in the south-west of the barony of Corkaguiney, Co. Kerry. *TRIA* **31**, 209–344.

Macalister, R.A.S. 1897 *Studies in Irish epigraphy: part 1.* London.

Macalister, R.A.S. 1902 *Studies in Irish epigraphy: part 2.* London.

Macalister, R.A.S. 1906 Eight newly-discovered ogham inscriptions in Co. Cork. *JRSAI* **36**, 259–61.

Macalister, R.A.S. 1907 The ogham inscriptions preserved in the Queen's College Cork. *JCHAS* **13**, 36–42.

Macalister, R.A.S. 1909 The ogham stones near Clonmel and Carrick-on-Suir. *JRSAI* **39**, 294–6.

Macalister, R.A.S. 1911 Souterrain at Cams, Co. Sligo. Topographical Files, OPW.

Macalister, R.A.S. 1914–16 On some recently discovered ogham inscriptions. *PRIA* **32**C, 138–46.

Macalister, R.A.S. 1916-17 Notes on certain Irish inscriptions. *PRIA* **33**C, 81–92.

Macalister, R.A.S. 1935 The ogham inscription from Fox's Castle, Co. Waterford. *JRSAI* **65**, 149–50.

Macalister, R.A.S. 1943–4 A preliminary report on the excavations of Knowth. *PRIA* **49**C, 131–66.

Macalister, R.A.S. 1945–9 *Corpus inscriptionum insularum Celticarum* (2 vols). Dublin.

Macalister, R.A.S. 1949 *The archaeology of Ireland* (2nd revised edn). London.

Macalister, R.A.S. and Praeger, R.L. 1928 Report on the excavation of Uisneach. *PRIA* **38**C, 69–127.

Macalister, R.A.S. and Praeger, R.L. 1929–31 The excavation of an ancient structure on the townland of Togherstown, Co. Westmeath. *PRIA* **39**C, 54–83.

McAuley, M. 1991 Souterrain at Pollee, Co. Antrim. Topographical Files, DOE.

McAuley, M. 1992 Souterrain at Drumnakeel, Co. Antrim. Topographical Files, DOE.

McAuley, M. 1994 Souterrain at Donegore ('Nettle Bush'), Co. Antrim. Topographical Files, DOE.

McCabe, J. 1967 Souterrain at Bocks Upper, Co. Monaghan. Topographical Files, OPW.

McCabe, J. 1975 Rath/cashel and souterrain at Lisduff, Co. Longford. Topographical Files, OPW.

McCaffrey, P. 1952 A contribution to the archaeology of the barony of Dunkellin, Co. Galway. Unpublished MA thesis, UCG.

McCarron, J. 1940 Cave at Tarmon, Co. Galway. Topographical Files, NMI.

MacCarthy, B. (ed.) 1895 *The Annals of Ulster. Vol. 3. AD 1379–1541*. Dublin.

McCarthy, J.P. 1975 A souterrain at Corran, Co. Cork. *JCHAS* **80**, 59–60.

McCarthy, J.P. 1977 The souterrains of County Cork. Unpublished MA thesis, UCC.

McCarthy, J.P. 1978a The Aghadown bronze axes, Paddock Td, Co. Cork. *JCHAS* **83**, 71–2.

McCarthy, J.P. 1978b Souterrain in Grallagh Lower Td, Co. Waterford. *JCHAS* **83**, 73–4.

McCarthy, J.P. 1983 Summary of a study of County Cork souterrains. *JCHAS* **88**, 100–5.

McConkey, R. 1993 Souterrain at Ballyness, Co. Antrim. Topographical Files, DOE.

McCormick, F. 1978 Two souterrains in County Monaghan. *Clogher Record* **9** (3), 326–9.

McCormick, F. 1995 Cows, ringforts, and the origins of Early Christian Ireland. *Emania* **13**, 33–7.

McCourt, D. 1959 Souterrain at Cushquin, Co. Londonderry. Topographical files, DOE.

McDonnell, J. 1957 Souterrain at Lohercannan, Co. Kerry. Topographical Files, NMI.

McGuinness, E. 1991 Souterrain at Cloghboley, Co. Sligo. Topographical Files, OPW.

Mac Iomhair, D. 1961–4 The boundaries of Fir Rois. *CLAJ* **15**, 144–79.

MacIvor, D. 1949–52 Supplement to townland survey of Paughanstown and Hacklim. *CLAJ* **12**, 272–75 .

MacIvor, D. 1955 In search of Saint Diomic. *CLAJ* **13** (3), 225–51.

McKenna, J.E. 1930 Souterrain in Aghnahoo, parish of Termonamongan, Co. Tyrone. *JRSAI* **60**, 194–6.

Maclean, R. 1992 The fogou: an investigation of function. *Cornish Archaeology* **31**, 41–64.

McLornan, M. 1984a Souterrain at Aghmakane, Co. Armagh. Topographical Files, DOE.

McLornan, M. 1984b Souterrain at Carrickananny, Co. Armagh. Topographical Files, DOE.

McLornan, M. 1984c Souterrain at Corliss, Co. Armagh. Topographical Files, DOE.

Murphy, T.F. 1962 Souterrain at Shanaway Middle, Co. Cork. Topographical Files, NMI.

Murphy, T.F. 1964 Souterrain at Ardhill, Co. Cork. Topographical Files, NMI.

Murray, L.P. 1940 The Pictish kingdom of Conaille Muirthemhne. In J. Ryan (ed.), *Féil-sgríbhinn Eóin Mhic Néill: Essays and studies presented to Professor Eoin MacNeill*, 445–53. Dublin.

Murray, R. 1932 A souterrain near Reynella, Co. Westmeath. *JRSAI* 62, 224–5.

Neill, K. 1985 Inventory of sites in Co. Armagh: souterrains. Topographical Files, DOE.

Newman, C. 1989–90 Notes on some Irish hanging bowl escutcheons. *Journal of Irish Archaeology* 5, 45–8.

Newman, C. 1990 A composite bronze escutcheon. In G. Eogan, 'Ballynee souterrains', County Meath, *JRSAI* 120, 41–64.

Nic Shean, N. 1986 Souterrain at Ballyholland Lower, Co. Down. Topographical Files, DOE.

O'Brien, C. and Sweetman, P.D. 1997 *Archaeological inventory of County Offaly*. Dublin.

Ó Ciobháin, P. 1944 Coolnaharragle, Co. Kerry. Topographical Files, NMI.

O'Connell, D.B. 1937 Souterrain at Tinnies Upper, Co. Kerry. Topographical Files, NMI.

O'Connell, D.B. 1938 Fort with souterrain at Glanballyma, Co. Kerry. *JRSAI* 68, 145.

O'Connell, D.B. 1939 *Kerry Archaeological Survey. Publication No. 1: Letters to 'The Kerryman' (Sept. 1936–Dec. 1938)*. Tralee.

O'Connor, M. 1933 Irish cave discovery at Fortwilliam, Co. Longford. Topographical Files, NMI.

O'Conor, K. 1993a Souterrain at Cloonbaniff, Co. Sligo. Topographical Files, OPW.

O'Conor, K. 1993b Souterrain at Mullaghanarry, Co. Sligo. Topographical Files, OPW.

O'Conor, K. 1993c Souterrain at Gortersluin, Co. Sligo. Topographical Files, OPW.

O'Conor, K. 1993d Souterrain at Carrowreagh, Co. Sligo. Topographical Files, OPW.

O'Conor, K. 1993e Souterrain at Church Hill, Co. Sligo. Topographical Files, OPW.

O'Conor, K. 1993f Souterrain at Rinbaun, Co. Sligo. Topographical Files, OPW.

O'Conor, K. 1993g Souterrain at Killoran South, Co. Sligo. Topographical Files, OPW.

O'Conor, K. 1994a Souterrain at Eskragh, Co. Sligo. Topographical Files, OPW.

O'Conor, K. 1994b Souterrain at Quarryfield, Co. Sligo. Topographical Files, OPW.

O'Conor, K. 1994c Souterrain at Oghambaun, Co. Sligo. Topographical Files, OPW.

O'Conor, K. 1994d Souterrain at Doobeg, Co. Sligo. Topographical Files, OPW.

O'Conor, K. 1994e Rath and souterrain at Gortersluin, Co. Sligo. Topographical Files, OPW.

Ó Corráin, D. 1972 *Ireland before the Normans*. Dublin.

O'Crowley, J. 1906 Newly-discovered ogham stones, County Cork. *JRSAI* 36, 204.

Ó Cuileanáin, C. and Murphy, T.F. 1961–2 A ringfort at Oldcourt, Co. Cork. *JCHAS* 66–7, 79–92.

Ó Donnabháin, B. 1982 Interim excavation report on Liscahane, Co. Cork. Topographical Files, OPW.

O'Donovan, J. 1836a Ordnance Survey Letters: Co. Sligo, Entry 341. Typed copies. RIA, Dublin.

O'Donovan, J. 1836b Ordnance Survey Name Books. Co. Sligo — Parish of Castleconnor. Typed copies. NLI, Dublin.

O'Donovan, P.F. 1995 *Archaeological inventory of County Cavan*. Dublin.

O'Dowd, P. 1982 The archaeology of Mayo. In B. O'Hara (ed.), *Mayo — aspects of its heritage*, 36–54. Galway.

Ó Drisceoil, D.A. and Hurley, V. 1978 A souterrain at Farranathomas, near Newcestown, Co. Cork. *JCHAS* **83**, 75–7.

O'Flaherty, B. 1986 Cashel; Loher, Co. Kerry. In C. Cotter (ed.), *Excavations 1985,* 26–7. Dublin.

Ó Floinn, R. 1978 A souterrain at Termonfeckin. *CLAJ* **19** (2), 128–30.

Ó Floinn, R. 1992 Catalogue. In E. Roesdahl and D.M. Wilson (eds), *From Viking to Crusader: Scandinavians and Europe 800–1200,* 333. Copenhagen.

O'Hara, B. 1991 *The archaeological heritage of Killasser, Co. Mayo.* Galway.

O'Keeffe, J. 1996 Souterrain at Culhame, Co. Londonderry. Topographical Files, DOE.

O'Kelly, M.J. 1942 Souterrain at Shanvallyhugh, Co. Mayo. Topographical Files, NMI.

O'Kelly, M.J. 1952 Three promontory forts in Co. Cork. *PRIA* **55C**, 25–59.

O'Kelly, M.J. 1957–9 Church Island near Valentia, Co. Kerry. *PRIA* **59C**, 57–136.

O'Kelly, M.J. and Kavanagh, S. 1954a A new ogham stone from County Kerry. *JCHAS* **59**, 50–3.

O'Kelly, M.J. and Kavanagh, S. 1954b An ogham inscribed cross-slab from Co. Kerry. *JCHAS* **59**, 101–10.

O'Kelly, M.J. and O'Kelly, C. 1983 The tumulus of Dowth, Co. Meath. *PRIA* **83C**, 135–90.

O'Kelly, M.J. and Shee, E. 1968 Three souterrains in Co. Cork. *JCHAS* **73**, 40–7.

O'Laverty, J. 1878 *An historical account of the diocese of Down and Connor, ancient and modern,* vol. I. Dublin.

O'Laverty, J. 1879–82 Notes on pagan monuments in the immediate vicinity of ancient churches in the dioceses of Down, and on peculiar forms of Christian interments observed in some of the ancient graveyards. *JRSAI* **15**, 108.

O'Laverty, J. 1884 *An historical account of the diocese of Down and Connor, ancient and modern,* vol. III. Dublin.

O'Laverty, J. 1887 *An historical account of the diocese of Down and Connor, ancient and modern,* vol. IV. Dublin.

Oldham, T. 1840–4 On some stones with ogham characters. *PRIA* **2**, 513–17.

O'Mahony, Canon 1908–9 Windele's papers on three prehistoric monuments in the County Cork. *Journal of the Ivernian Society* **1**, 77–88.

Ó Muráile, N. 1987 The autograph manuscripts of the Annals of the Four Masters. *Celtica* **19**, 75–95.

O'Rahilly, C. 1998 A classification of bronze stick-pins from the Dublin excavations 1962–72. In C. Manning (ed.), *Dublin and beyond the Pale: studies in honour of Patrick Healy,* 23–33. Bray.

Ó Ríordáin, A.B. 1953–6 Three souterrains in County Louth. *CLAJ* **13**, 441–50.

Ó Ríordáin, A.B. 1956 Souterrain at Donaghmore, Co. Meath. Topographical Files, NMI.

Ó Ríordáin, A.B. 1968a Souterrain at Lurgabrack, Co. Donegal. Topographical Files, NMI.

Ó Ríordáin, A.B. 1968b Souterrain at Park in County Waterford. Topographical Files, NMI.

Ó Ríordáin, A.B. 1969 Notes on a souterrain at Kellystown, Co. Wexford. *Journal of the Old Wexford Society* **2**, 49–50.

Ó Ríordáin, S.P. 1934–5 Rock-cut souterrain at Brackcloon, Castletown Bere, Co. Cork. *Irish Naturalist's Journal* **5**, 78–80.

Ó Ríordáin, S.P. 1938–40 Excavations at Cush, Co. Limerick. *PRIA* **45C**, 83–181.

Ó Ríordáin, S.P. 1942 *Antiquities of the Irish countryside.* London.

Ó Ríordáin, S.P. 1953 *Antiquities of the Irish countryside* (3rd edn). London.

Ó Ríordáin, S.P. 1965 *Antiquities of the Irish countryside* (4th edn). London.

Ó Ríordáin, S.P. and Foy, J.B. 1941 The excavation of Leacanabuaile stone fort, near Caherciveen, Co. Kerry. *JCHAS* **46**, 85–99.

Ó Ríordáin, S.P. and Hartnett, P.J. 1943–4 The excavation at Ballycatteen Fort, Co. Cork. *PRIA* **49**C, 1–43.

Ó Ríordáin, S.P. and MacDermott, M. 1951–2 The excavation of a ringfort at Letterkeen, Co. Mayo. *PRIA* **54**C, 89–119.

O'Rorke, T. 1878 *History, antiquities, and present state of the parishes of Ballysadare and Kilvarnet, in the County of Sligo.* Dublin.

O'Rorke, T. 1890 *The history of Sligo: town and county*, vol. 1. Dublin.

Orpen, G.H. 1890–1 Subterranean chambers at Clady, Co. Meath. *JRSAI* **21**, 150–4.

Orpen, G.H. 1907 Motes and Norman castles in Ireland. *English Historical Review* **22**, 228–54, 440–67.

Orpen, G.H. 1910 The mote of Street, County Westmeath. *JRSAI* **40**, 214–22.

Orpen, R. d'A. 1908–12 Antiquities near Lispole, Co. Kerry. *Kerry Archaeological Magazine* **1**, 9–15.

O'Shaughnessy, J. 1993a Souterrain at Lackanatlieve, Co. Sligo. Topographical Files, OPW.

O'Shaughnessy, J. 1993b Souterrain at Leaffony, Co. Sligo. Topographical Files, OPW.

O'Shaughnessy, J. 1993c Souterrain at Rathlee, Co. Sligo. Topographical Files, OPW.

O'Shea, K. 1952 Souterrain at Keelties, Co. Kerry. Topographical Files, NMI.

O'Sullivan, A. and Sheehan, J. 1996 *The Iveragh Peninsula: an archaeological survey of south Kerry.* Cork.

O'Sullivan, D.F. 1955 Notes on Clongill. *Ríocht na Midhe* **1** (1), 19.

O'Sullivan, J. 1990 Excavation of Lisnagun Ringfort. In D.R.M. Gaimster, S. Margeson and M. Hurley (eds), 'Medieval Britain and Ireland in 1989'. *Medieval Archaeology* **34**, 225–7.

O'Sullivan, J., Hannon, M. and Tierney, J. 1998 Excavation of Lisnagun Ringfort, Darrara, Co. Cork (1987-89). *JCHAS* **103**, 31–66.

Otway-Ruthven, A.J. 1968 *A history of medieval Ireland.* London.

Pagan, H.E. 1974 An Anglo-Saxon coin hoard from the west of County Cork. *JCHAS* **79**, 62–3.

Parke, A.M. 1967 Souterrain at Lackagh, Co. Donegal. Topographical Files, NMI.

Pentland, G.H. 1898 The Great Cross at Monasterboice. *JRSAI* **28**, 264–5.

Piboule, P. 1978 Les souterrain aménages de la France au Moyen Age. *Archéologie Médievale* **8**.

Piggott, S. 1982 *Scotland before history.* Edinburgh.

Plummer, C. 1910 *Vitae sanctorum Hiberniae*, vol. 2. Oxford.

Pollock, R.W. 1992 The excavation of a souterrain and roundhouse at Cyderhall, Sutherland. *PSAS* **122**, 149–60.

Power, C. 1987 Three souterrains in the Cork/Waterford region of Ireland. *Subterranea Britannica* **23**, 16–20.

Power, C., Ó Donnabháin, B. and O'Donnell, M.G. 1984 A souterrain at Rhinecrew, Co. Waterford. *Decies: Journal of the Old Waterford Society* **26**, 38–40.

Power, D. 1984 A souterrain at Kilburn, near Doneraile, Co. Cork. *Mallow Field Club Journal* **2**, 40–2.

Power, D., Byrne, E., Lane, S. and Sleeman, M. 1992 *Archaeological inventory of County Cork. Vol. 1: West Cork.* Dublin.

Power, D., Byrne, E., Lane, S. and Sleeman, M. 1994 *Archaeological inventory of County Cork. Vol. 2: East and South Cork.* Dublin.

Power, D., Byrne, E., Lane, S. and Sleeman, M. 1997 *Archaeological inventory of County Cork. Vol. 3: Mid-Cork.* Dublin.

Power, D., Lane, S. Byrne, E., and Sleeman, M. 2000 *Archaeological inventory of County Cork. Vol. 4: North Cork (Part 2).* Dublin.

Power, P. 1887–8 Casey's Lios, Ballygunnermore, Co. Waterford. *JRSAI* **18**, 407.

Power, P. 1894–5 Interesting discovery of bee-hive chambers. *J. Wat. S.E. Ire. Arch. Soc.* **1**, 230–2.

Power, P. 1906 Place names of the Decies. *J. Wat. S.E. Ire. Arch. Soc.* **9**, 12–39.

Power, P. 1926 Find of bronze celts at Aghadown, Co. Cork. *JRSAI* **56**, 57–8.

Prendergast, E. 1956a Souterrain at Flemingtown, Co. Meath. Topographical Files, NMI.

Prendergast, E. 1956b Souterrain at Kildalton, Co. Kilkenny. Topographical Files, NMI.

Prendergast, E. 1958 An ancient monument recently discovered in Co. Kilkenny. *Old Kilkenny Review* **10**, 38–41.

Prendergast, E.M. 1959 Ring-fort with souterrain, at Gorteen, Co. Westmeath. *Ríocht na Midhe* **2** (1), 45–8.

Prendergast, E.M. 1961 Report on ringfort with souterrain at Killarney, Co. Kilkenny. Topographical Files, NMI.

Prendergast, E. 1963 Souterrain at Trostan, Co. Monaghan. Topographical Files, NMI.

Prendergast, E. 1970a Souterrain at Carrigcastle, Co. Waterford. Topographical Files, NMI.

Prendergast, E.M. 1970b Souterrain at Ballyquin, Co. Waterford. Topographical Files, NMI.

Prendergast, E. 1971 A souterrain at Scurlockstown. *Ríocht na Midhe* **5** (1), 60–1.

Prendergast, E. 1972 Souterrain at Raheen, County Tipperary. Topographical Files, NMI.

Price, L. 1941 Glencolumcille, Co. Donegal, and its Early Christian cross-slabs. *JRSAI* **71**, 71–88.

Prim, J.G.A. 1852–3 Notes on the excavation of a rath at Dunbel, County of Kilkenny. *JRSAI* **2**, 119–27.

Prim, J.G.A. 1854–5 On the discovery of ogham monuments and other antiquities in the raths of Dunbel, County of Kilkenny. *JRSAI* **3**, 397–408.

Prim, J.G.A. 1872–3 Some introductory observations. In S. Ferguson, 'The ogham monuments of Kilkenny'. *JRSAI* **12**, 222–38.

Proceedings 1897 Cruise in connexion with the Munster meeting. *JRSAI* **27**, 271.

Proceedings 1906 Notes descriptive of the places visited (Munster outing). *JRSAI* **36**, 327–46.

Proudfoot, V.B. 1961 The economy of the Irish rath. *Medieval Archaeology* **5**, 94–122.

Proudfoot, V.B. 1970 Irish raths and cashels: some notes on chronology, origins and survivals. *UJA* (3rd series) **33**, 37–48.

Quarry, J. 1870–9 On stones bearing ogham inscriptions discovered at Monataggart, Co. Cork. *PRIA* **15**, 289–91.

Raftery, B. 1994 *Pagan Celtic Ireland: the enigma of the Irish Iron Age.* London.

Raftery, J. 1942 Souterrain at Baltray, Co. Louth. Topographical Files, NMI.

Raftery, J. 1951 *Prehistoric Ireland.* London.

Raftery, J. 1956a Souterrain at Clashygowan, Co. Donegal. Topographical Files, NMI.

Raftery, J. 1956b Souterrain at Aghamore, Co. Mayo. Topographical Files, OPW.

Raftery, J. 1967 Souterrain at Meelick, Co. Mayo. Topographical Files, NMI.

Raftery, J. 1968 Souterrain at Ballyhenry or Caraun, Co. Mayo. Topographical Files, OPW.

Raftery, J. 1974 Preliminary report on sites of archaeological interest in Co. Sligo. Unpublished report, An Foras Forbartha.

Reade, G.H. 1874–5 On a prick-spur of bronze gilt, found in the mound of Ash, Co. Louth. *JRSAI* **13**, 322–6.

Rees-Jones, S.G. 1971 A souterrain at Sheepland Mor, near Chapeltown, Co. Down. *UJA* (3rd series) **34**, 77–8.

Reynolds, P. and Turner, S. 1902 The caves in Ben Madighan. *UJA* (2nd series) **8**, 73–82.

Rhys, P. 1898 Some ogam-stones in Connaught. *JRSAI* **28**, 230–6.

Rhys, J. 1902 The ogham-inscribed stones of the Royal Irish Academy, and of Trinity College, Dublin. *JRSAI* **32**, 1–41.

Richards, M. 1960 The Irish settlements in south-west Wales. *JRSAI* **90**, 133–62.

Richardson, P. 1938 The cashels of Moneygashel, County Cavan. *UJA* (3rd series) **1**, 19–21, pl. IId.

Robinson, T.D. 1977 *The Burren: a map of the uplands of north-west Clare.* Cill Ronain.

Rogers, E. 1882 *Memoir of the Armagh Cathedral, with an account of the ancient city.* Belfast.

Ronayne, B. 1978 Survey of souterrain at Lissaniska East, Co. Mayo. Topographical Files, OPW.

Ronayne, B. 1991a Survey of souterrain at Monktown, Co. Meath. Topographical Files, OPW.

Ronayne, B. 1991b Souterrain at Alexander Reid, Co. Meath. Topographical Files, OPW.

Rotheram, E.C. 1893–6 On some caves in the Slieve na Cailliagh district, County Meath. *PRIA* **19**, 305–10.

Rotheram, E.C. 1897 On a cave recently discovered near Oldcastle. *JRSAI* **27**, 427–9.

Rotheram, E.C. 1915 Bronze pin from Crossdrum Quarry souterrain. *JRSAI* **45**, 171–2.

Rowland, J.T. 1847–50 On a rudely cut stone found at Ardee. *PRIA* **4**, 404–6.

RTC Galway 1979 Sleeping in a souterrain/monitoring temperatures. Unpublished class project; Mechanical Engineering **1** (1978–9).

Ryan, J. 1949 Pre-Norman Dublin. *JRSAI* **79**, 64–83.

Ryan, M.F. 1972 Souterrain in Creggan townland, Ballybofey, Co. Donegal. Topographical Files, NMI.

Ryan, M. 1973 Native pottery in early historic Ireland. *PRIA* **73C**, 619–45.

Ryan, M. 1973–6 Two new souterrains near Dundalk. *CLAJ* **18**, 195–7.

Ryan, M. 1975 A souterrain at Painestown, Co. Meath. *Ríocht na Midhe* **6** (1), 35–7.

Ryan, M. 1976 A souterrain in Kealduff Upper townland, Glenbeigh. *JKHAS* **9**, 5–10.

Rynne, E. 1957-60a Two souterrains at Bawntaaffe, near Monasterboice, County Louth. *CLAJ* **14**, 96–102.

Rynne, E. 1957–60b Souterrain at Donaghmore, Co. Louth. *CLAJ* **14**, 148–53.

Rynne, E. 1961–2 Souterrain at Lissarow, near Ardmore, Co. Waterford. *JCHAS* **66–7**, 28–32.

Rynne, E. 1961–4a Souterrain at 'Killylagan', Cortial, County Louth. *CLAJ* **15**, 5–10.

Rynne, E. 1961–4b Souterrain at Mullagharlin, near Dundalk. *CLAJ* **15**, 317–20.

Rynne, E. 1961–4c Souterrain near Ballybarrack: a correction. *CLAJ* **15** (4), 320.

Rynne, E. 1962 Souterrain at Rathiddy, County Louth. *CLAJ* **15** (2), 125–30.

Rynne, E. 1962–5 Souterrain at Boolareagh, Co. Tipperary. *NMAJ* **9**, 188–90.

Rynne, E. 1963 Investigation of souterrain at Dunbeacon, Co. Cork. Topographical Files, NMI.

Rynne, E. 1964a Investigation of souterrain at Money, near Westport, Co. Mayo. Topographical Files, NMI.

Rynne, E. 1964b Souterrain at Fore, Co. Westmeath. *Ríocht na Midhe* 3 (2), 118–23.

Rynne, E. 1964c Some destroyed sites at Shannon Airport, Co. Clare. *PRIA* 63C, 245–77.

Rynne, E. 1965a Report on excavation of souterrains at Donaghmore, Co. Louth. Topographical Files, NMI.

Rynne, E. 1965b Souterrain at Faughart Upper, Co. Louth. Topographical Files, NMI.

Rynne, E. 1965c Souterrain at Fennor, near Slane, Co. Meath. *Ríocht na Midhe* 3 (3), 229–33.

Rynne, E. 1966a Souterrain at Banagher, Co. Westmeath. Topographical Files, NMI.

Rynne, E. 1966b Investigation of souterrain at Millpark, near Dundalk, Co. Louth. Topographical Files, NMI.

Rynne, E. 1966c Souterrain at Caherquin, Co. Kerry. Topographical Files, NMI.

Rynne, E. 1967a Souterrain at Athboy, Co. Meath. Topographical Files, NMI.

Rynne, E. 1967b Souterrain at Kilmacanoge South, Co. Wicklow. Topographical Files, NMI.

Rynne, E. 1968a Souterrain at Cartoonfrench, Co. Galway. Topographical Files, NMI.

Rynne, E. 1968b Souterrain at Corbally South, Co. Galway. Topographical Files, NMI.

Rynne, E. 1972 Souterrain in (?) ringfort at Cartron, Co. Galway. Topographical Files, NMI.

Rynne, E. 1974 Excavations at 'Madden's Hill', Kiltale, Co. Meath. *PRIA* 74C, 267–75.

Rynne, E. 1978 Souterrain at Ballymana, Co. Galway. Topographical Files, NMI.

Rynne, E. 1981 A classification of pre-Viking Irish iron swords. In B.G. Scott (ed.), *Studies on early Ireland: essays in honour of M.V. Duignan*, 93–7. Belfast.

Rynne, E. 1989–90 Ringfort at Ballybane, Galway. *JGAHS* 42, 136–8.

Rynne, E. 1992 Dún Aengus (and some similar Celtic ceremonial centres). In A. Bernelle (ed.), *Decantations: a tribute to Maurice Craig*, 196–207. Dublin.

Rynne, E. and Prendergast, E. 1962 Two souterrains in Co. Meath. *Ríocht Na Midhe* 2 (4), 37–43.

Scully, O.M.B. 1997 Metal artefacts. In M.F. Hurley, O.M.B. Scully and S.W.J. McCutcheon, *Late Viking Age and medieval Waterford. Excavations 1986–1992*, 438–48. Waterford.

Shaw Mason, W. 1819 *A statistical account or parochial survey of Ireland*, vol. 3. Dublin.

Shee, E. 1969 Souterrain at Aghmanister & Spital, Co. Cork. Topographical Files, NMI.

Simms, K. 1978 Guesting and feasting in Gaelic Ireland. *JRSAI* 108, 67–100.

Skillen, J. 1904 Discovery of a souterrain near Ballymena. *UJA* (2nd series) 10, 119–20.

Smith, W.S. 1897 The souterrain at Holywell, near Antrim. *UJA* (2nd series) 3, 137–9.

Smyth, A.P. 1982 *Celtic Leinster: towards an historical geography of early Irish civilization AD 500–1600*. Dublin.

Somerville, B.T. 1929–30 Descriptive account of the Curraghcrowly souterrain, Ballineen. *JCHAS* 34–5, 1–16.

Somerville, B.T. 1931 The fort on Knock Drum, West Carbery, County Cork. *JRSAI* 61, 1–14.

Startin, B. 1981 Halligye fogou, Trelowarren. *Cornish Archaeology* 20, 219–20.

Startin, B. 1982 Halligye fogou; excavations in 1981. *Cornish Archaeology* 21, 185–6.

Stenberger, M. 1966 A ring-fort at Raheennamadra, Knocklong, Co. Limerick. *PRIA* 65C, 37–54.

Stokes, J. 1835 Ordnance Survey Memoirs. Box 32: [Co. Londonderry IV]: 1 (Parish of Banagher); Section 4, 11, 39–40. Royal Irish Academy, Dublin.

Stokes, J. 1838 Ordnance Survey Memoirs. Box 10: [Co. Antrim X]: IV (Parish of

Duneane); Section 3, 20. Royal Irish Academy, Dublin.

Stokes, W. 1887 *The Tripartite Life of Patrick (with other documents relating to that saint)*. London.

Stokes, W. 1894 The prose tales in the Rennes Dindsenchas. *Revue Celtique* **15**, 272–336, 418–84.

Stout, M. 1997 *The Irish ringfort*. Dublin.

Stuiver, M. and Braziunas, T.F. 1993 Radiocarbon Calibration Program Rev 3.0.3. *Radiocarbon* **35**, 137–89. University of Washington Quaternary Isotope Lab.

Stuiver, M. and Pearson, G.W. 1993a Radiocarbon Calibration Program Rev 3.0.3. *Radiocarbon* **35**, 1–23. University of Washington Quaternary Isotope Lab.

Stuiver, M. and Pearson, G.W. 1993b Radiocarbon Calibration Program Rev 3.0.3. *Radiocarbon* **35**, 25–33. University of Washington Quaternary Isotope Lab.

Swan, L. 1983 Enclosed ecclesiastical sites and their relevance to settlement patterns of the first millennium A.D. In T. Reeves-Smyth and F. Hamond (eds), *Landscape archaeology in Ireland*, 269–94. BAR British Series, 116. Oxford.

Sweeney, J. 1981 Souterrain at Cross South, Co. Mayo. Topographical Files, NMI.

Sweetman, P.D. 1975 Souterrain in the townland of Newrath Big, Co. Meath. *Ríocht na Midhe* **6** (1), 54.

Sweetman, P.D. 1981 Excavation of a medieval moated site at Rigsdale, Co. Cork, 1977–8. *PRIA* **81**C, 193–205.

Sweetman, P.D. 1982–3 Souterrain and burials at Boolies Little, Co. Meath. *Ríocht na Midhe* **7** (2), 42–57.

Sweetman, P.D. 1987 Souterrain at Monktown, Co. Meath. Topographical Files, OPW.

Sweetman, P.D. and de Buitléir, M. 1976 Souterrain in the townland of Ahenny, Co. Tipperary. *NMAJ* **18**, 73–4.

Sweetman, P.D., Alcock, O. and Moran, B. 1995 *Archaeological inventory of County Laois*. Dublin.

Sweetnam, G.B. and Gillman, H.W. 1897 The problem of the souterrains. *JCHAS* (2nd series) **3**, 149–52.

Taylor, D.B. 1982 Excavation of a promontory fort, broch and souterrain at Hurly Hawkin, Angus. *PSAS* **112**, 215–53.

Tempest, H.G. 1912–15 Some further Louth souterrains. *CLAJ* **3**, 21–6.

Tempest, H.G. 1921–4 A souterrain at Dromiskin. *CLAJ* **5** (1), 65.

Tempest, H.G. 1933–6 Three souterrains. *CLAJ* **8** (1), 95–7.

Tempest, H.G. 1957–60 Souterrain in Kilcurry townland. *CLAJ* **14** (1), 37.

Thomas, C. 1966 The character and origins of Roman Dumnonia. In C. Thomas (ed.), *Rural settlement in Roman Britain*, 74–98. CBA Research Report 7. Oxford.

Thomas, C. 1971 *Britain and Ireland (in Early Christian times AD 400–800)*. London.

Thomas, C. 1972 Souterrains in the Sea Province: a note. In C. Thomas (ed.), *The Iron Age in the Irish Sea Province*, 75–8. CBA Research Report 9. Oxford.

Thomas, C. 1994 *And shall these mute stones speak? Post-Roman inscriptions in western Britain*. Cardiff.

Tighe, W. 1802 *Statistical observations relative to the County of Kilkenny made in the years 1800 and 1801*. Dublin.

Tipping, E. 1864–6 A description of an artificial cave. *JRSAI* **8**, 183–4.

Toal, C. 1995 *North Kerry archaeological survey*. Dingle.

Todd, J.H. 1840–4 On an ogham inscription. *PRIA* **2**, 410–11.

Todd, J.H. 1867 *War of the Gaedhil with the Gaill (Cogadh Gaedhel re Gallaibh)*. London.

Twohig, D.C. 1971 Souterrains in Cos Cork and Louth. *JCHAS* 76, 128–33.

Twohig, D.C. 1973 Souterrains at Sheepwalk and Ballyrisode, Co. Cork. *JCHAS* 78, 35–9.

Twohig, D.C. 1974 Excavation at Dromkeen East, Causeway. *JKAHS* 7, 5–10.

Twohig, D.C. 1976 Recent souterrain research in Co. Cork. *JCHAS* 81, 19–38.

Ua Cuinn, S. 1904–7 Some souterrains of Co. Louth. *CLAJ* 1, 37–9.

Vandeleur, R.S. 1964 Souterrain at Tullaghansleek, Co. Westmeath. Topographical Files, NMI.

Waddell, J. 1970a Notes on some Kerry souterrains. *JKAHS* 3, 15–18.

Waddell, J. 1970b Irish Bronze Age cists: a survey. *JRSAI* 100, 91–139.

Waddell, J. 1998 *The prehistoric archaeology of Ireland*. Galway.

Waddell, J. and Clyne, M. 1995 M.V. Duignan's excavations at Kiltiernan, Co. Galway, 1950–53. *JGAHS* 47, 149–203.

Wainwright, F.T. 1953a Souterrains in Scotland. *Antiquity* 27, 219–32.

Wainwright, F.T. 1953b A souterrain identified in Angus. *Antiquaries Journal* 33, 65–71.

Wainwright, F.T. 1954–6 A souterrain at Longforgan in Perthshire. *PSAS* 88, 57–64.

Wainwright, F.T. 1955 Houses and graves. In F.T. Wainwright (ed.), *The problem of the Picts*, 90–5. Edinburgh.

Wainwright, F.T. 1963 *The souterrains of Southern Pictland*. London.

Wakeman, W.F. 1858 *Archaeologia Hibernica. A handbook of Irish antiquities*. Dublin.

Wallace, P.F. and Timoney, M.A. 1987 Carrowntemple, Co. Sligo, and its inscribed slabs. In E. Rynne (ed.), *Figures from the past: studies on figurative art in Christian Ireland in honour of Helen M. Roe*, 43–61. Dublin.

Walsh, M. 1964 A souterrain at Annagloor, Co. Cork. *JCHAS* 69, 60–1.

Walsh, P. 1934 The Four Masters. *The Irish Book Lover* 22, 128–31.

Walsh, P. 1940 Meath in the Book of Rights. In J. Ryan (ed.), *Féil-sgríbhinn Eóin Mhic Néill: essays and studies presented to Professor Eoin Mac Neill*, 508–21. Dublin.

Wardman, A.M. 1976 Souterrain at Aghafatten, Co. Antrim. Topographical Files, DOE.

Warhurst, C. 1971 Excavation of a rath at Shane's Castle, Co. Antrim. *UJA* (3rd series) 34, 58–64.

Warner, R.B. 1972 A souterrain at Ballyeaston, Co. Antrim. *UJA* (3rd series) 35, 61–3.

Warner, R.B. 1974 Ballymacpeake Upper, Co. Londonderry; souterrain. In T.G. Delaney (ed.), *Excavations 1973*, 8. Belfast.

Warner, R.B. 1979 The Irish souterrains and their background. In H. Crawford (ed.), *Subterranean Britain: aspects of underground archaeology*, 100–44. London.

Warner, R.B. 1980 Irish souterrains: later Iron Age refuges. *Archaeologia Atlantica* 3, 81–99.

Warner, R.B. 1986 Comments on 'Ulster and Oriel souterrains'. *UJA* (3rd series) 49, 111–12.

Warner, R.B. 1994 Souterrain at Holestone, Co. Antrim. Topographical Files, DOE.

Waterman, D.M. 1956a The excavation of a house and souterrain at White Fort, Drumaroad, Co. Down. *UJA* (3rd series) 19, 73–86.

Waterman, D.M. 1956b The excavation of a house and souterrain at Craig Hill, Co. Antrim. *UJA* (3rd series) 19, 87–91.

Waterman, D.M. 1968 Note on a destroyed rath and souterrain at Killyglen, Co. Antrim. *UJA* (3rd series) 31, 67–70.

Waterman, D.M. 1971 A marshland habitation site near Larne, Co. Antrim. *UJA* (3rd series) 34, 65–76.

Waterman, D.M. and Collins, A.E.P. 1952 The excavation of two raths at Ballywillwill, Co. Down. *UJA* (3rd series) **15**, 71–83.

Watkins, T. 1978–80a Excavation of an Iron Age open settlement at Dalladies, Kincardineshire. *PSAS* **110**, 122–64.

Watkins, T. 1978–80b Excavation of a settlement and souterrain at Newmill, near Bankfoot, Perthshire. *PSAS* **110**, 165–208.

Watkins, T. 1979 The Newmill souterrain. *Current Archaeology* **66**, 205–9.

Weir, H. 1938 Fort at Emper, Co. Westmeath. *JRSAI* **68**, 146–7.

Westropp, T.J. 1896–1901 The ancient forts of Ireland: being a contribution towards our knowledge of their types, affinities, and structural features. *TRIA* **3**, 666–71.

Westropp, T.J. 1898 Prehistoric remains in the Burren, Co. Clare. *JRSAI* **28**, 352–66.

Westropp, T.J. 1899 Prehistoric remains in the Burren, Co. Clare (Part 2). *JRSAI* **29**, 367–84.

Westropp, T.J. 1900–2 The churches of County Clare, and the origin of the ecclesiastical divisions in that county. *PRIA* **22**, 100–80.

Westropp, T.J. 1909 Ringforts in the barony of Moyarta, County Clare, and their legends: (part 2). *JRSAI* **39**, 113–26.

Westropp, T.J. 1911 Prehistoric remains (forts and dolmens) in the Burren, Co. Clare. *JRSAI* **41**, 343–67.

Westropp, T.J. 1913 Prehistoric remains (forts and dolmens) in the Corofin District, Co. Clare. *JRSAI* **43**, 232–60.

Westropp, T.J. 1914 Kilkee (Co. Clare) and its neighbourhood (Part 4). *NMAJ* **3** (3), 153–69.

Westropp, T.J. 1917 Notes on the primitive remains (forts and dolmens) in central County Clare (Addenda), part XVI. *JRSAI* **47**, 1–20.

Westropp, T.J. 1919 Notes on several forts in Dunkellin and other parts of southern Galway. *JRSAI* **49**, 167–86.

Westropp, T.J. 1920 The promontory forts of the three southern provinces of Ireland. *JGAHS* **11**, 112–131.

Wheeler, H.A. 1955 Souterrains at Clogherrevagh and Banduff, Co. Sligo. Topographical Files, NMI.

Wheeler, H. 1956 Souterrain at Clashygowan, Co. Donegal. Topographical Files, NMI.

Wilde, W.R. 1849 *The Boyne and the Blackwater*. Dublin.

Wilde, W.R. 1867 *Loch Coirib*. Dublin.

Williams, B.B. 1977 A souterrain in Loughermore townland, County Antrim. *UJA* (3rd series) **40**, 91.

Williams, B.B. 1983 Souterrain at Carrickcloghan, Co. Armagh. Topographical Files, DOE.

Williams, B.B. 1985 Excavation of a rath at Coolcran, County Fermanagh. *UJA* (3rd series) **48**, 69–80.

Williams, B.B. 1986 Souterrain at Ballyhill Lower, Co. Antrim, In C. Cotter (ed.), *Excavations 1985*, 8–9. Dublin.

Williams, J.B. 1835 Ordnance Survey Memoirs. Box 30: (Co. Londonderry II): II (Parish of Ballyaghran); Section 1, Appendix 10. Royal Irish Academy, Dublin.

Williams, W. 1856–7 Proceedings: five ogham monuments at Kilgrovane, County of Waterford. *JRSAI* **4**, 391.

Williams, W. 1868–9 On an ogham chamber at Drumloghan, in the County of Waterford. *JRSAI* **10**, 35–9.

Wood, T. 1821 *An inquiry concerning the primitive inhabitants of Ireland.* Cork.

Wood-Martin, W.G. 1887–8 The rude stone monuments of Ireland. *JRSAI* **18**, 118–59.

Wood-Martin, W.G. 1895 *Pagan Ireland.* London.

Wright, T. 1758 *Louthiana.* Dublin.

Wright, W.S. 1964 Recent investigations of souterrains: a souterrain at Aird, Co. Antrim. *UJA* (3rd series) **27**, 121–3.